a
*F*eminist *C*ompanion

——— to ———

Esther,
Judith and
Susanna

edited by Athalya Brenner

The Feminist Companion to the Bible

7

Editor
Athalya Brenner

Sheffield Academic Press

Sheffield Academic Press Ltd
Mansion House
19 Kingfield Road
Sheffield S11 9AS
England

Typeset by Sheffield Academic Press
and
Printed on acid-free paper in Great Britain
by The Cromwell Press
Melksham, Wiltshire

British Library Cataloguing in Publication Data

A catalogue record for this book is available
from the British Library

ISBN 1-85075-527-2

To the memory of

_____

Fokkelien van Dijk-Hemmes

ת·נ·צ·ב·ה·

CONTENTS

ABBREVIATIONS

AB	Anchor Bible
ABD	D.N. Freedman (ed.), *Anchor Bible Dictionary*
BARev	*Biblical Archaeology Review*
BHS	*Biblia hebraica stuttgartensia*
Bib	*Biblica*
BKAT	Biblischer Kommentar: Altes Testament
BR	*Biblical Research*
BZ	*Biblische Zeitschrift*
CBQ	*Catholic Biblical Quarterly*
ConBNT	Coniectanea biblica, New Testament
CRINT	Compendia rerum iudaicarum ad Novum Testamentum
EJL	Early Judaism and its Literature
EncJud	*Encyclopaedia Judaica*
HBC	Harper's Bible Commentary
IB	*Interpreter's Bible*
ICC	International Critical Commentary
IEJ	*Israel Exploration Journal*
JBL	*Journal of Biblical Literature*
JQR	*Jewish Quarterly Review*
JSOTSup	*Journal for the Study of the Old Testament*, Supplement Series
KAT	Kommentar zum Alten Testament
KB	L. Koehler and W. Baumgartner (eds.), *Lexicon in Veteris Testamenti libros*
OTG	Old Testament Guides
SBLDS	SBL Dissertation Series
SBLMS	SBL Monograph Series
SNTSMS	Society for New Testament Studies Monograph Series
SPB	Studia postbiblica
SR	*Studies in Religion/Sciences religieuses*
SVTP	Studia in Veteris Testamenti pseudepigrapha
VT	*Vetus Testamentum*
ZAW	*Zeitschrift für die alttestamentliche Wissenschaft*

INTRODUCTION

Athalya Brenner

Esther, Judith and Susanna have many things in common.
Although only the book of Esther is included in the Hebrew
Bible, all three texts present figurations of Jewish (as distinct
from 'Israelite' or 'Judahite') female protagonists in an environment of dependency on foreign powers. These common
settings—and the religious, cultural, gender and other socio-
political concerns reflected in the three texts—indicate a relatively late date (the Hellenistic or Greco-Roman period) and
location (outside the territorial boundaries of ancient 'Israel') for
their composition. Differences between the three stories are of
course to be found on various levels, for example in plot-line,
religiosity, community ideology. Nevertheless, these differences
do not obscure the structural similarities. And, perhaps the most
important of all, the three texts make female characters *visible*.
This focused vision, into which we the readers are drawn as
accomplices, is an opportunity for contemplation. What does this
vision imply? Do 'Esther', 'Judith' and 'Susanna' play the role of
subject more than that of object, or vice versa, and to what
extent? Among other things, these three stories furnish a context for reflecting, once again, on the (in)visibility of women in
history and historiographical constructs.

'Esther', 'Judith' and 'Susanna' are ostensibly the subjects of
'their' stories. All three are defined by the text as physically
beautiful, although they are revealed as much more than just
pretty dames as the stories unfold. All three exhibit or display
this beauty, one way or another. Beauty, although not described in detail, is the common index. All three are socially
legitimized by entering a marriage. However, they differ in the
details of their male-relational state: Esther is a young virgin to

begin with, married to a royal spouse later; Judith is a widow; Susanna is married. Presumably, they also differ in age. But since all three are beautiful, all three are desired by males. Consequently, all three are involved in or implicated by unconventional sexual circumstances: Esther and Judith with a foreign leader (Ahasuerus and Holofernes respectively); Susanna is accused of illicit sex by the lecherous elders of her own community, whose advances she rebuffs. All three are members of threatened (Jewish) communities: the first two become involved with a *foreign* male. In all three cases, the authority of the males is questioned by the female subjects and their sexuality. The encounter between Jewish females and foreign or Jewish males entails mortal danger for the females, a recurrent biblical motif when a female figure allegedly steps outside the strictures of appropriate female behaviour. The encounter between (Jewish) female and male (doubly-other: socially superior; foreign or elder) sexuality results in the subversion of male power.

If success is a measure of moral superiority, the three female protagonists must be considered morally superior to the subverted male figures. All three manage to save themselves. Esther succeeds in destroying Haman and saving her source community besides saving her own life. Judith murders Holofernes and saves her town and people, the elders of which have been too ineffectual to find a solution. Susanna is saved by her piety and divine intervention in the guise of the young Daniel, and rids the community of its corrupt leaders. Consequently, the male leaders (Haman and Ahasuerus; Holofernes and the local leaders; the elders) are either killed or, at the very least, censured, hence symbolically castrated by or because of the female agent.[1] Thus, the three female figures manage to avert disaster for their people and their own selves by a combination of two means: judicious use of their natural resources, and loyalty or faith. The admixture in each case differs; the result is an ostensible happy ending.

Viewed as a series, the three texts display a line of development from the worldly to the piously devout. What is implied in

1. Cf. A. Bach, '"So the Witch Won't Eat Me..."', a paper delivered at the AAR/SBL Annual Meeting in Washington, DC, November 1993; forthcoming in *Semeia*.

Esther becomes overt in the other two texts. Esther is an assimilated Jew who conceals her origins until they cannot be ignored any longer. Her sexuality is compromised: she has sex with Ahasuerus; is it a saving grace that she does so in the matrimonial bed? She acts out of loyalty to her cousin Mordecai and the other Jews. God is neither explicitly mentioned nor appealed to. Judith and Susanna do not have to undergo the indignity of being sexually tainted: is this the reward for proper Jewish pride, or does the text stop short of having Jewish women commit adultery or engage in extramarital activities? At any rate, they do not have sex with the male aggressor(s). Their piety is pronounced: both pray and call on God.[1] God helps them, of course—indirectly in Judith's case, more directly in Susanna's. It therefore seems that the differences between the three stories are not differences of literary *topos* or social/ethnic ideology but of *religious* ideology.

In biblical literature figurations of women often serve as metaphors or symbols for territories, towns and communities. Esther, Judith and Susanna are individual protagonists. But, on another level, they seem to be imaged[2] as three separate albeit similar signifiers, representations, projections or metaphors for the Jewish community in exile, or as surrounded by actual and potential enemies. In such imagined situations of danger to the community's welfare or existence, the communal fabric is threatened from without and, consequently, also from within. The basic situation is identical: the environment is experienced as dangerous. The basic premise is: the danger can be averted (repeatedly) by mixing attractiveness, sense and faith. A pretty and resourceful woman, although she is enclosed by predominantly androcentric norms, can survive and even prosper (according to those same norms). It would appear by analogy that the (Jewish) community can survive among the nations and overcome the hostility it experiences. Nevertheless, and this is the obverse side of the coin, a price-tag is attached in the case of the imaged female protagonists and in the case of the (signified) Jewish community.

1. As does Esther in the Greek additions to the MT Esther; see K. De Troyer's article in this volume.
2. Or, may be read as though they are imaged.

The 'price-tag' is subtexted, perhaps overlaid by the apparent success of each female protagonist's story. But gaps and ambiguities remain. They repose in the basic incongruity of Esther's apparently non-problematic assimilation in the foreign court, for example; in the unconventional sexual behaviour ascribed to the female figures (although it does not amount to actual fornication); in the more fundamental issue of associating unconventional female sexuality (and murder, in Judith's case) with Jewish piety;[1] in the manifest incompetence of traditional (male) leadership; in the narrative gaps.[2] How do the ambiguities and gaps reflect on the female protagonists thus depicted? In what way are the textual women—and the community they embody by representation—subverted or deconstructed, in spite of their conspicuous accomplishments? Do the happy endings carry a sting—for women, for communities, Jewish and otherwise? Interpreters of the texts, of the female figures per se and of their symbolic community value, have used some of the ambiguous features as loci for departure from early antiquity onwards; and such is the case in the present volume too. The ambiguities, it seems, are at least as indispensable for the tracing of plots and world-views as the overt properties of the narratives.

1.   For instance, is 'Esther' or 'Judith' a 'role model'? Cf. S.A. White, 'Esther: A Feminine Model for Jewish Diaspora?', in P.L. Day (ed.), *Gender and Difference in Ancient Israel* (Minneapolis: Fortress Press, 1989), pp. 161-77. On the problematics of Judith in this respect see also the brief discussion in E.M. Schuller, 'The Apocrypha', in C.A. Newsom and S.H. Ringe (eds.), *The Women's Bible Commentary* (Louisville, KY: Westminster Press/John Knox, 1992), p. 243. On the 'gap' concept see 'Gaps, Ambiguity and the Reading Process', in M. Sternberg, *The Poetics of Biblical Narrative* (Bloomington: Indiana University Press, 1985), pp. 186-229.

2.   For instance, while all three figures are labelled 'beautiful' or 'good looking', and their attractiveness is assumed by the reader, no physical description is forthcoming. Although this is in keeping with the rest of biblical literature (excluding the Song of Songs, perhaps; and a short elaboration of maturing female beauty, from a divine or male perspective, in Ezek. 16.3-14—although here, as in Esther, the emphasis is on the packaging, clothing and accessories, rather than the physique), the absence of some kind of description in such contexts constitutes a narrative gap which readers, including artists, rush to fill in their various fashions. And see below.

Part I: Esther: When Gender Politics Represent Power Politics

The first two articles on Esther are general discussions of form, language, style and broader issues. In both, links are established between Esther and other Hebrew Bible texts on the one hand, and extrabiblical intertexts on the other hand. The third is a response to the second. Subsequent articles are of a more specific nature: they highlight a certain section of the book, or textual figure, or individual motif(s).

The narrative form of the MT Esther has been discussed by many scholars. It has been variously described as a short story, simply a 'story', even a novella.[1] Although some feminist analyses tend to focus on gender issues and their implications, wider matters of form and contexts cannot and should not be disregarded. The similarities of the Esther story and the Joseph cycle/story/novella, in matters of ideology as well as setting and contents, have been widely noticed: the correspondences between the two highlight the differences, some of which stem from the different gender attributed to each story's chief protagonist.[2] This indeed is the starting point for the first

1.   See, for instance, W.L. Humphreys, 'The Story of Esther and Mordecai: An Early Jewish Novella', in G.W. Coats (ed.), *Saga, Legend, Tale, Novella, Fable: Narrative Forms in Old Testament Literature* (JSOTSup, 35; Sheffield: JSOT Press, 1985), pp. 97-113, 149-50. It is worth noting that Humphreys modifies the name of the story, as his title indicates. His arguments for so doing relate to the history of the text and his apparent wish to 'cleanse' it of the vindictiveness against the Gentiles it is often accused of (pp. 97-99). However, by choosing this (ideological) critical move, Humphreys unproblematically reduces the predominance accorded to the figure of Esther by the book's title. Since the female figure Esther is symbolic of her community I wonder whether, by so doing, Humphreys does not in fact (unwittingly) reduce the community that he attempts to defend through critical-historical methods.

2.   Thus Joseph is so often compared to Mordecai and to Daniel (who, as we remember, is Susanna's saviour in court). Indeed, these three men are rewarded for their 'wisdom'. However, the true parallel of Joseph is Esther: both come to a foreign court, undergo sexual tribulations, and manage to save their people. This cross-gender correspondence, however, is seldom taken up. Interestingly, whereas Joseph remains the protagonist of 'his' narrative until his death and beyond it, Esther disappears from hers

contribution, Susan Niditch's 'Esther: Folklore, Wisdom, Feminism and Authority'.[1] Niditch draws our attention to the Joseph story and, through this intertext, to the wider framework of biblical 'wisdom' traditions. Another, still broader framework in which to set the Esther narrative is that of folk tales, old and new. The moral problematics of the female figures are presented as trickster/underdog behaviour, permissible and even requisite within the situation and the ironic justice folk-theme. Finally, Niditch discusses the issues of authority, in and of the text, authorship and date of composition.

Niditch writes about Esther's distinctive style, replete with duplications and multiplications. The linguistic repetitions reflect and refract, and are reflected and refracted, in the structure (symmetry and chiasm) and plot (the reversal-of-fortune theme). This is the point of departure for my article, 'Looking at Esther through the Looking Glass'. After classifying the multiplications/repetitions, I too go on to read Esther with an inter-text, Lewis Carroll's *Alice through the Looking Glass*. When read with *Alice*, Esther is highlighted as a hall of mirrors—for textual characters of both genders and for the presumed author(s), the source and foreign communities, and the readers. In the mirror/symmetry *topos*, everybody (including the threatened community, females and males) is satirized; and this has implications for the understanding of the book's female figures and also its ideology.

Alice Bach responds to my article in 'Mirror, Mirror, in the Text: Reflections on Reading and Rereading'. Unlike Esther, Alice is not a treat for a king. She is a pre-sexual girl who duels with a ('married' but) asexual chess queen. Theirs is a power, not a beauty, contest. But how would such a queen play in the

in ch. 9 and leaves Mordecai to reap the benefits (ch. 10). Or Joseph gets narrative descendants whereas Esther does not. A small gender-motivated difference, perhaps. On the correspondences between the Joseph and Susanna stories see Levin, 'Susanna', in this volume.

1.   This is ch. 5 of Niditch's book, *Underdogs and Tricksters: A Prelude to Folklore* (San Francisco: Harper & Row, 1987). For a fuller view about the value of folklore studies for biblical studies in general, and the correspon-dences between the Joseph and Esther narratives in particular, the reader is referred to the first four chapters of the book.

Persian court? Vashti is the clue: she does not have an either/or choice. In Esther, the prettiest wins. The battle of wits that follows is a battle for escaping the looking glass, the gazed-at female position. Alice slips past the looking glass, the fixed male gaze. Esther is caught in the gaze (and then uses whatever power the game has given her to checkmate Haman). Vashti reflects Alice better. She goes through the looking glass, is no longer visible, is no longer a vision to be ogled by men.

The two Greek translations of Esther (the LXX and the AT or Alpha Text) are in fact textual versions that differ from the MT (Hebrew) Esther. The next two articles read segments of these translations as intertexts for the Hebrew version, with an emphasis on the modification in gender roles introduced by the Greek versions. Beal's 'Tracing Esther's Beginnings' is a reading of ch. 1; De Troyer's 'An Oriental Beauty Parlour: An Analysis of Esther 2.8-18 in the Hebrew, the Septuagint and the Second Greek Text' is a discussion of the process Esther undergoes until she meets the king and becomes his queen. Beal begins by analysing how the reader of the MT is co-opted into an alignment with the non-Jewish Vashti, then proceeds to examine how the first chapter leaves 'traces' which problematize the gender codes in the rest of the story. Finally, he compares the beginning of MT Esther with the two Greek versions: those introduce a male solidarity from the beginning, so that an intra-textual critique of gender codes is undermined. De Troyer retranslates and discusses the three texts in detail, verse by verse, in order to show how minute components of the MT text were altered in each Greek text, sometimes almost imperceptibly. The Greek story introduces God into the narrative and invests the figure of Esther with religious dimensions, thus sidestepping some moral difficulties outlined above. Her conclusions are that the Hebrew text delivers a male perspective, the LXX softens this male bias, and the AT reconfirms it. We notice that Beal's conclusions concerning the three versions of ch. 1 are dissimilar to those De Troyer reaches for the same versions of ch. 2.

In 'Esther: The Incomplete Emancipation of a Queen', Wyler focuses on two, largely analogous, issues: the book's pronounced Jewishness, and Esther's 'queenship'. She begins by establishing the Jewishness of the book although, as she points out, this remains a covert problem until ch. 3. She then proceeds to analyse the Esther character and the treatment of 'authority' that she embodies. Her conclusion is that whereas the book is satisfactory for contemporary Jewish readers from a contemporary Jewish perspective, it is hardly so from a feminist perspective. To illustrate this, Wyler outlines an alternative (midrashic) ending which would have suggested Esther's 'emancipation'.

The question of Esther's authority is the subject of Gitay's article too. The symbol of queenship in the Esther text is the crown.[1] Gitay's article uses visual art as interpretive examples. In artistic depictions of Esther, the royal throne is perhaps more important than the crown, hence Gitay's title, 'Esther and the Queen's Throne'. Is the crowned Esther as narrated a queen by title and her husband's fondness only, or a regnal authority by personal wisdom? The text does not answer this question explicitly: when Esther is crowned, the outcome seems open-ended. Gitay traces the treatment of this issue in the visual interpretations of artists from varied reading locations, such as the wall painter of the Dura Europos synagogue (third century CE), Rembrandt, and Baskin (a contemporary Jewish painter). Gitay concludes that the Esther character undergoes a development, from beauty queen to a fully fledged political authority, through acting for her people.

In 'Honor and Shame in Esther', Klein examines the honour/shame paradigm of living a Jewish existence in the diaspora. She proceeds from modern anthropological definitions of the honour/shame matrix. The matrix is usually gendered; in most cultures distinctions are drawn between females and males in that respect, and the accepted norms, although complementary, are heavily loaded in favour of androcentrism. By applying the matrix to the book of Esther, Klein shows how important such cultural boundaries are for the Jewish group's identity. Within the text, male 'honour' and female 'shame' interchange, and 'in threatening situations, social paradigms may be

---

1. See De Troyer's article. For the conjectured physical appearance of the crown cf. S.M. Paul, 'Jerusalem of Gold—A Song and an Ancient Crown', *BARev* 3 (1977), pp. 38-41; and also 'Jerusalem—A City of Gold', *IEJ* 17.4 (1967), pp. 259-63.

creatively interpreted as long as the prescribed gender role is publicly observed. Powerless women—and Jews—can invoke power as long as they maintain required appearances'.

Esther embodies a Jewish community in foreign surroundings. Her Jewish identity is strong. However, the representation is problematic because her textual Jewishness is vague and her cultural position is of assimilation to the other, predominant, enveloping culture. From their reading locations, the Jewish rabbis obviously felt that gap-filling was called for, as was done in the LXX. In 'Esther Revisited: An Aggadic Approach', Bronner lists the rabbinic sources briefly and then supplies classified examples of the themes introduced by this gap-filling process. One cluster of midrashic interpretations pertains to the figure of Esther herself: her name, attractiveness, sexuality and intermarriage with Ahasuerus. Another deals directly with constitutives of Jewishness, endowing the Esther character with piety, kosher food, prayer and even prophetic and leadership traits. Yet another sets her up as a positive foil to Vashti.[1] Rabbinic midrash, in short, supplements the text according to the rabbis' interest: to emphasize the god-fearing and spirituality of its plot and especially the chief protagonist. In the process, Esther's problematic aspects are glossed over and explained away so that she can be approved of as a community emblem.

The rabbis' concerns are communal and androcentric. They relativize Esther to fit in with their world. Their midrashic readings may be fanciful for our taste but, since they are time-, place- and ideology-bound, they have immense value for reconstructing the rabbis' culture. In her contemporary midrash, 'Esther's Story', Wolkstein constructs a picture that is both similar and dissimilar to the rabbinic midrashic constructs. While she shares the rabbis' interest in Jewish identity as evident (or lacking) in the text, her focus is gynocentric. The resultant interpretation, while a relativistic gap-filler as much as theirs, allows Esther to function as the focalizer: Esther tells her story in the first person narrative mode. By making Esther the narrator, and the reporter whose words envelop even dialogues, her position is made much stronger. She is given a *voice*. This

---

1. Cf. Beal's article on the functions of ch. 1, and his tracing of Vashti's figure in the MT as against the Greek versions.

narrating voice fills the worrying textual lacunae that have long troubled translators, rabbis, Christian commentators, believers of both religions and scholars, feminist and otherwise: The list of fillers—or, let us say, admittedly fictitious solutions—includes, for instance, the matters of food, prayer, God's presence and loyalty to the source group (cf. the Greek texts and ancient midrash, as in Bronner); the reasons for the initial concealment of Esther's ancestry (cf. Bronner); the nature of the twelve-month education course at the palace (cf. De Troyer, Gitay); various details concerning Esther's appearance, attractiveness and sterling qualities (cf. Bronner); the initial meeting with the king and the reason for his love (cf. Gitay, Niditch, Brenner);[1] the missing link between Vashti's story (ch. 1) and the main story line, beginning with Bigtan and Teresh's conspiracy (2.21, cf. Beal); the need for indirectness, hence a duplicated feast (chs. 5 and 7) before Esther makes her appeal to the king (cf. Klein); the reasons for the two-day defence and celebration in Susa (ch. 9); and many more. Esther is presented as much more active than she is in the biblical text: she often takes the initiative instead of Mordecai.[2] Without forgetting her gender and cultural location (cf. Klein), she develops into a competent politician (cf. Gitay): she can even write. Indeed, her story is in the form of a diary or journal. And she has a history before and after the events she narrates (cf. Wyler).

Wolkstein's midrash is primarily a *story*, a *yarn*. As such, it does not pretend to scholarly status, although it contains many scholarly allusions.[3] It is printed here as an interpretation, as

1.   In Wolkstein's story, Esther mimes every movement of Ahasuerus when she first meets him, thus making him break into a therapeutic laughter and endearing herself to him. The mirror-miming is a folkloristic element which links this modern midrash with Niditch's concerns. The mirror-imaging is explored from another angle in my article on Esther and *Alice*.

2.   And so is Ahasuerus; his depiction—and marital bliss with Esther—in Wolkstein's midrash is similar to the story's recounting by Josephus Flavius (*Ant.* 11.6).

3.   How does Esther come to know what goes on in the Palace? In Wolkstein's story, through her favourite maid Zuleika. The name Zuleika is imported from Islamic poetic traditions, where it is the name of Potiphar's wife (anonymous in the biblical text, Gen. 39) who tried to seduce Joseph.

legitimate and relativistic as rabbinic midrash, of the Esther text and, especially, its narrative gaps; and because, like the agendas of rabbis and feminists (especially Jewish feminists), its far from hidden agenda involves a reconstructing of the Esther figure as a true, sensible role model for the diaspora. Or, in other words, it negotiates ways for empowering the biblical Esther and, through her, the community she emblematizes. By so doing, in her own special way, Wolkstein addresses many issues raised by academic Bible critics and commits Esther/herself/the community to certain solutions.

Part II: Judith: On Power, Leadership and Knowledge

This section contains three essays. The first two concern the Judith figure as represented in the text (gender and leadership roles), and as an embodiment of the Jewish community. The third is a study of visual representations of an interpreted Judith in painting and sculpture.

Levine explores the motifs of otherness and foreignness and their opposites on the dual matrix of community and gender in 'Sacrifice and Salvation: Otherness and Domestication in the Book of Judith'. Judith inverts gender roles: she enters the public sphere and salvages her people, which the elders of her community were unable to do. She murders Holofernes, a foreign (male) general. By so doing, she transforms the community's traditional power bases and the social role of marginalized groups. She, a woman, becomes an *ad hoc* leader; ethnic (Achior the Gentile), gender (women) and class (her maidservant) distinctions are blurred. But not for long: after the celebrations, the widow Judith returns to her house. In spite of her piety and success, she does not remain in the public arena. Her actions, while redemptive, subvert her own representation of the community, a representation strongly suggested by her name. She remains enclosed in her domestic female sphere, without remarrying, until she dies. In Levine's words, 'Only by remaining unique and apart can Judith be tolerated, domesticated, and even treasured by Israelite society'. Gender

The intertextuality of the Joseph and Esther stories is well-established; the imported name constitutes a gentle hint in this direction.

conventions are perceived as a safeguard to group identity, their transgression in time of danger notwithstanding. The community is represented by a woman for a purpose; then, the only remains are fame and a certain ambiguous reputation. Thus, for Levine, the problem of the woman-as-Jewish-community is subtly resolved in and by the text itself.

Van Henten views the issue of Judith's representation and leadership differently. In his article, 'Judith as Alternative Leader: A Reading of Judith 7–13', he begins by discussing the cohesion of the section. He then forgoes reading the Judith story with the obvious biblical intertext about Jael's killing of Sisera (Judg. 4–5). Instead, he moves to the cluster (Exod. 17; Num. 20; Deut. 33.8-11) in which Moses and the Israelites face troubles similar to those of Judith's community. The shared motifs are: lack of water; the people suffer and complain; leaders are tested; a leader calls upon God; God is apparently supportive; the leader acts; salvation is effected. Van Henten therefore concludes that Judith's leadership and performance are constructed along the Moses paradigm. The representation of the community by a woman, he contends, may be explained by Hasmonaean political ideology. Judith's 'all-Israelite' fictitious genealogy contributes to her legitimation as leader. Van Henten concludes by reflecting upon the question 'is Judith an F (Female/Feminine) or an M (Male/Masculine) composition?' He finally speculates that, because of the analogy with Moses and Judith's representational value, it seems possible that at least some sections of the book express F voices within a dominant male framework, inclusive of adapted androcentric patterns.

Judith severs Holofernes' head. Levine observes that the decapitation makes Judith a threatening phallic woman whose power should be stayed. In 'Head Hunting: "Judith" on the Cutting Edge of Knowledge', Bal reads the biblical Judith through visual images and their interpretation by artists and viewers. She defines the narrative as an ideo-story, unstable and ambiguous. Judith is in this reading not just a phallic woman, man-killing woman, but the castrator: the beheading is symbolic of 'the event that underlies Freud's theory of fetishism: castration'. Proceeding from Carravagio's *Medusa* (a female head), Bal demonstrates through a series of images (and references to psychoanalysis) how 'the viewer is implicated in the gendered myth by assigning lethal power' to the gazed-at female figure. Bal calls for allowing more complexity in viewing gender and other relations in the art works discussed. There is anxiety in the text about cognitive issues, knowledge and representation and ambiguities that are carried over into the different visual representations of the beheading scene. This anxiety affects the gazing and reading modes. Judith is a *topos*, Bal concludes, and 'Instead of, or in addition to I should say, trying to reconstruct the irretrievably lost origin of this ideo-story's M or F subjectivity, I suggest we give it at least its epistemological due, acknowledge its status as theory, and look around to see what we can still learn from it'.

Part III: Susanna: The Reader's Power/Knowledge—
On Viewing a Jewish Woman/Community

The narrative figure of Susanna is gazed at: by the elders who desire her, by the community, by the reader. This gazed at/gazing at mutuality and its implications for understanding the narrative are explored in the two articles of this section.

Glancy's 'The Accused: Susanna and her Readers' examines the 'looking' or 'gazing' code 'Susanna' is subject to. Taking her cue from feminist film theory, Glancy argues that the gazing code is gendered. Women are looked at. Men look. Therefore, scholars describe the garden scene as seduction rather than coercion or attempted rape. In other words, critics adopt the elders' voyeuristic tendencies to the point of complicity. Susanna, pious and interpreted as virtuous because of her wish to compromise her life rather than sin, might be interpreted as an unwilling object of the gaze; although she calls on God of her own initiative, thus becomes an independent agent briefly, Daniel's intervention reduces her again to an object. Women readers might be caught between identifying with her as object or with the gazers (male, elders, authoritative) as subjects. This gender representation appears to be supported by the gendered ideology inscribed by and in the text. It constructs our understanding of it though the gendered seeing/visualization of the narrative situation (cf. Bal on Judith).

Susanna is a victim. Is she, however, an altogether blameless victim? In '"Hemmed in on Every Side": Jews and Women in the Book of Susanna', Levine clearly sets out her agenda: she is a Jewish woman scholar in the diaspora who reads ('views') a text about a Jewish woman who represents a Jewish diaspora community. The woman/community position is tenuous and ambiguous; and while blame should not be attributed to 'her', a certain responsibility cannot be ignored. Susanna is pious, but also a lady of leisure without a care or thought for less fortunate members of her community. Her daily walk in the garden is shown to lend herself to being viewed. As an object of desire, she is an occasion for sin. Her husband becomes effective only after she is cleared from the accusation of adultery. Levine recalls a list of intertexts and sources for motifs featuring in Susanna: from the Hebrew Bible (like Joseph and Potiphar's wife; the Garden of Eden; David and the bathing Bath Sheba; Solomon's judgment) and postbiblical ones (*Testament of Reuben*; *m. Soṭa*) in order to demonstrate that Susanna, after being gazed at and accused, will need to be reintegrated into her community even though she is innocent. Although she is educated and religious and beautiful and functions as symbol for the community, her relationship with the divine remains indirect and mediated. Susanna's position is and remains ambiguous even after her formal redemption, and so is the position of the community in its exilic garden.

Part I
ESTHER: WHEN GENDER POLITICS
REPRESENT POWER POLITICS

ESTHER: FOLKLORE, WISDOM, FEMINISM
AND AUTHORITY*

Susan Niditch

It is appropriate to follow the study of the Joseph narrative
with a study of Esther, for several scholars suggest that the
two narratives are associated by virtue of shared literary form[1]
and/or by direct interdependence through borrowing.[2]
Though Rosenthal and Gan base arguments for Esther's
dependence on portions of the Joseph narrative largely on linguistic similarities, Arndt Meinhold bases his case for dependence on correspondence between patterns of content.[3]

Meinhold's comparative charts reveal a variety of weaknesses. As Berg notes, Meinhold is guilty of superimposing patterns on the tales, reordering 'the sequence of verses in each
story to conform them to his delineation of structures'.[4] It is
questionable, moreover, whether in content and structural
function his motifs really do correspond at the detailed level

   *   From *Underdogs and Tricksters: A Prelude to Folklore* (San Francisco:
Harper & Row, 1987), pp. 126-45, 168-70.
   1.   For example S. Talmon, 'Wisdom in the Book of Esther', *VT* 13
(1963), p. 455.
   2.   Talmon, 'Wisdom', pp. 454-55; L.A. Rosenthal, 'Die
Josephsgeschichte mit den Buchem Ester und Daniel verglichen', *ZAW* 15
(1895), pp. 178-84 and 'Nochmals der Vergleich Ester–Joseph', *ZAW* 17
(1897), pp. 126-28; M. Gan, 'The Book of Esther in the Light of Joseph's Fate
in Egypt', *Tarbitz* 31 (1962), pp. 144-49 (Hebrew). So also A. Meinhold, 'Die
Gattung der Josephsgeschichte und des Esterbuches: Diasporanovelle, II',
ZAW 88 (1976), p. 75. S.B. Berg agrees in a nuanced way with dependence
theories. See her careful discussion in *The Book of Esther: Motifs, Themes and
Structure* (SBLDS, 14; Missoula, MT: Scholars Press), pp. 123-43.
   3.   Meinhold, 'Die Gattung', I (*ZAW* 87 [1975], pp. 306-24), II.
   4.   Berg, *Esther*, pp. 135-36 and 157-58 n. 52.

suggested by Meinhold. Gen. 40.14, 20, 23; 41.9-13, the outcome of Joseph's dream interpretation and the baker's remembering him to Pharaoh, is for Meinhold the same in its narrative role as Esth. 4.1–5.8; 6.14–7.6; 8.3-6, Mordecai's mourning and communicating with Esther about Ahasuerus's decree and Esther's revelations and requests to Ahasuerus. All are listed by Meinhold as 'activity of hero to ward off danger'.[1] The Genesis passage has to do with Joseph's rise but is not precisely action to avoid danger. Some motifs, moreover, are described with a certain degree of detail, for example, 'activity of hero to ward off danger', whereas others are quite general, 'proof of constancy'. Some are major items in the plot, for example, 'elevation'; some mere details of denouement, 'cause for success is recognized'.[2] Meinhold's study is not without merit and does touch upon some key comparisons. Its weaknesses, however, point to the dangers of superimposing external patterns on literature, to the importance of exploring motifs at various degrees of specificity, and to the value of dividing a complex story such as Esther into its various episodes. Meinhold's chartings are rough-hewn and, as Berg notes, do not confirm a theory of dependency.[3] The chartings, however, begin to hint at the workings of a shared tradition of storytelling. So, too, Rosenthal's examples of linguistic dependence. It is difficult to speak of formulas in our limited corpus. Nevertheless, to the folklorist, the parallel language describing the heroes' elevation at Gen. 41.42-43 and Esth. 6.11 and describing the king's making a party at Gen. 40.20 and Esth. 1.3; 2.18; 8.2 is suggestive of the traditional ways in which a composer describes comparable images in tales with comparable content.[4] Note that the parallel language is not precisely the same language, as one would expect with copying or borrowing, but shows flexible variation on comparable language and syntax. Such is the sign of traditional-style composition. Other examples of shared terms,

---

1.   Meinhold, 'Die Gattung', I, p. 316; II, pp. 82, 84, 85.
2.   See the chart in 'Die Gattung', II, pp. 88-89.
3.   Berg, *Esther*, p. 136.
4.   Cf. similar findings in ch. 2 of Niditch, *Underdogs and Tricksters*; and in S. Niditch and R. Doran, 'The Success Story of the Wise Courtier', *JBL* 96 (1977), pp. 179-93.

phrases, or syntax point to the gray area where idiom meets formula. Thus, annoying, haranguing harassment at Gen. 39.10 and Esth. 3.4—*wayhî kᵉdabbĕrāh 'el yôsēp yôm yôm*, 'though she spoke with Joseph day in day out'; *wayhî bᵉ'āmrām 'ēlâw yôm wāyôm*, 'though they spoke with him day in day out'—finds another variation in the lament at Ps. 42.11—*bᵉ'āmrām 'ēlay kol hayyôm*, 'in their saying to me all day long'.

The language and content that Esther shares with the Joseph narrative confirms its place in the traditional-style literature of Israel. The book of Esther also should be viewed within a wider range of traditional-style literature. In fact, the book of Esther appears a most obvious candidate for folkloristic approaches. Its characters seem to be drawn from a veritable motif index of treacherous villains, fair maidens of lowly status who become wives of kings, upright and wise heroes, stupid and ineffectual kings. Its magiclike setting is plush with the trappings of court: servants, purple furnishings, fetes, food and magnificent clothing. Its literary patterns follow well-worn models at generic, morphological and typological levels, patterns found in the tales of Abraham, Jacob and Joseph and sharing much with the tales of other cultures.

Esther places in bold relief themes implicit in studies of the wife-sister tales and the lives of Jacob and Joseph: (1) the view of authority (often unjust authority) and relations to it, and related questions concerning (2) the place of women in Israelite worldview (What is women's relation to authorities, divine and human?), and (3) the attitude of Israelites to the outside, non-Israelite world.

An exploration of these sociologically and anthropologically based questions, together with a study of style and structure, lead, of course, to suggestions about authors and audiences for whom Esther is meaningful and to the continuing critique of some traditional scholarly assumptions. One is also led to interesting conclusions concerning the social ethics of Scripture vis-à-vis legitimate and illegitimate authority, conclusions holding significance for later appropriators of the biblical tradition.

Style

Esther evidences a distinctive comic-hyperbolic style beautifully appropriate to its content, tone and themes.[1] The comic-hyperbolic style shares much with the sort of traditional-style writing found in Genesis 12 and the Jacob narrative, but also evidences some of the more expansive, ornate or baroque touches found in Genesis 20 and the Joseph tale. In style, as in content, the book of Esther is traditional with a twist.

One occasionally finds in Esther sentence constructions worthy of modern-day bureaucratese:

> And when arrived the turn of Esther daughter of Abihayil, uncle of Mordecai who took [her] to himself as a daughter, to go to the king...(2.15).

Such sentences are not usual in the book of Esther, however, which more often exhibits the brief, sometimes parallelistic, phrase-by-phrase constructions typical of the other biblical narratives mentioned.

> And the king became very angry
> and anger burned in him (1.12).

See also 2.17; 2.23; 3.8, 15; 6.8 for other good examples. This brief phrase style encapsules a wonderful image of 'fiddling while Rome burns' at 3.15:

> The courtiers went in haste at the king's command
> and the decree was issued in Susa, the capital.
> The king and Haman settled into drinking
> while the city of Susa sat dumbfounded.

This style serves to contrast the seriousness of what has happened with the portrait of apathy and petty self-absorption. The powerful parallel phrases at 4.1 in turn contrast Mordecai's response of horror, mourning and panic with the self-satisfaction of the perpetrators of evil just seen at their drinking (4.1):

---

1. Gunkel points to qualities of 'exaggeration' (H. Gunkel, *Esther* [Religionsgeschichtliche Volksbucher, II, Reihe, 19.20; Tübingen: Mohr, 1916], p. 50) and the style of superlatives (p. 51) in Esther, suggesting parallels with Daniel, Judith and *3 Maccabees*.

When Mordecai realized all that had been done,
he ripped his clothing
and dressed in sackcloth and ashes.
He went forth into the midst of the city
and cried out a great and bitter cry.

Traditional-style repetition is found frequently in Esther. There are ways to describe the king's accepting a suggestion by courtiers (1.21; 2.4),[1] to describe his formally allowing someone to enter his presence (4.11; 5.2; 7.4), and to indicate the sending of court decrees (3.12-13; 8.9-10). The king's recalling the assassination plot is reported in very much the same language at 6.2 as the plot was described at 2.21. The king's effusive promise to Esther that she ask and it will be granted is phrased in the same way at 5.3, 6; 7.2; 9.12. The frame of Esther's response is also found at 5.4; 5.8; 7.3; 9.13, but whereas 'if it please the king' introduces an invitation to dinner in the first two instances, at 7.3 it introduces a request that her life and her people's existence be spared, and at 9.12 a request that Haman's sons be hanged. The use of the formulaic frame makes the request to be spared all the more dramatic, highlighting the climactic moment of revelation in the narrative. It makes the response to the request for vengeance the more inevitable as the tale's theme of just deserts unfolds. Similarly, language of the decree that the Jews be 'destroyed, killed and annihilated' (3.13) appears in Esther's revelation to Ahasuerus (7.4) and in the counterdecree that the Jews in turn may destroy their enemies (8.11). In a situation of reversal, this repeated language of destruction effectively creates irony, underscoring the theme of just deserts.

The dense repetition in 6.3, 6, 7, 8, 9, 10, 11 (language of dressing in royal clothing, wanting to honor, setting a person to ride on a horse) is essential to the ironic scene in which the king asks Haman's advice about the ways to honor a hero. The king, of course, is planning Mordecai's elevation in thanks for his

---

1.   The phrase 'and the matter was good in the eyes of' (i.e., 'it pleased') found at 1.21, 2.4, is found at Gen. 41.31, Josh. 22.30 and 33, 1 Kgs 3.10 and elsewhere, and is one of the examples of the boundary where idiomatic speech meets formulaic construction. In any event, this particular idiom is the preferred mode, in Esther, of expressing approval of a decision (see also 5.14).

having foiled a plot to kill the king. Haman, however, thinks the honor is to be his and makes suggestions for bestowing honor appropriately fulsome. When it turns out that the honor is to be paid to Mordecai, Haman and Mordecai essentially change places. Whereas Mordecai had been in ashes and away from court (4.1), Haman now dresses in mourning and absents himself (6.12). The prediction of Haman's wife, Zeresh, further marks this turning point in the narrative. Dense repetition enhances the irony of the situation in ch. 6, building the puffed-up Haman for his fall and involving the reader, a 'fly on the wall' who is fully cognizant of Haman's self-delusion while Haman himself is ignorant. This form of repetition is strongly reminiscent of that of Genesis 39, where the seductress accuses Joseph of being the seducer. It is a baroque, hyperbolic form of repetition rather than evidence of economical style.

Economical style is not always the norm in Esther. For example, in two places where one would expect traditional-style repetition, one finds instead abbreviated allusion. The maidens tell Esther about Mordecai's condition briefly (4.4), not employing the description of 4.1. Similarly, 4.7, 8 is a much briefer version of 3.9-14. Mordecai reports to Esther 'all that happened', not what happened in traditional style, that is, fully. Compare Rebecca's reports to Jacob about the words of Isaac and the plans of Esau. Thus, though Esther evidences fine traditional style, it evidences also the sort of elaborative touches characteristic of the Joseph narrative and the tendencies to summarize typical of nontraditional-style literature.

The most distinctive feature of style in Esther is the extensive use of elaborative chains of synonyms, the tendency to say precisely the same thing two, three, or four times. This is the parallel style of Hebrew narration pushed to the hyperbolic, a style entirely appropriate to the exaggerated extremes of good and evil, wise and foolish, imminent destruction turned to instant salvation found in Esther.

Thus we have the full lists of seven eunuchs and seven princes in 1.10 and 1.14. The king plans not merely to kill the Jews but *lᵉhašmîd lahᵃrōg ûlᵉ'abbēd*, 'to destroy, to kill, and to cause to perish' (so 7.4 and 8.11). The people's mourning is described, *wᵉṣôm ûbᵉkî ûmispēd śaq wā'ēper*, 'and fasting, and weeping, and wailing, sackcloth and ashes...' (4.3), and the kitchen sink for good measure. Esther asks that the people fast over her and not eat and not drink (4.16). The rejoicing at 8.16 is described, 'for the Jews there was light and rejoicing, joy and honor'. They are to celebrate *bᵉkol dôr wādôr mišpāḥâ ûmišpāḥâ mᵉdînâ ûmᵉdînâ wᵉ'îr wā'îr*, 'in every generation, every family, every province, and every city' (9.28; cf. 8.17).

Esther's style, frequently economical in repetition, thus also waxes more ornate and more hyperbolic. An examination of narrative structures leads back to the underdog and the trickster, to familiar morphologies and especially to traditional-style typologies.

Status and Wisdom in Four Parts

Esther contains four major plot moves: (1) the story of Vashti's banishment, (2) the story of Esther's becoming queen, (3) the brief story of Mordecai's saving the king, (4) the most important story of Esther's saving Mordecai and her people.

Scholars have suggested that some of these 'moves' are based on individual stories, perhaps specific Persian tales, borrowed and reformulated by the author of Esther.[1] Bardtke goes so far as to posit a source book of Persian tales from which the author made selections.[2] Again we encounter the image of the scholar at work in the scriptorium rather than the composer creating in a story-telling tradition. It is certainly true that any of the four plot lines could and do make for a good traditional tale, but it is equally true that folktales—even orally composed tales—are often made of combinations of such plots, as is Esther. As Bickerman and Berg note, the book of Esther, the whole, is beautifully balanced and unified as it now stands.[3] Others have looked for evidence of different sources in the seeming 'doublets' of content, the two lists of court officials, the two

---

1. E. Bickerman, *Four Strange Books of the Bible* (New York: Schocken Books, 1967), pp. 172-81.

2. H. Bardtke, *Das Buch Esther* (KAT, 17.5; Gütersloh: Gerd Mohn, 1963), pp. 248-52.

3. On a unified quality in Esther, see Bickerman, *Four Strange Books*, pp. 172-81; Berg, *Esther*, pp. 31-35, 72.

banquets, and so on.[1] Such repetitions, however, are part of the traditional-style woof and warp of the tale, as are instances of repetitive, economical language. The book of Esther divides into sources only by the most wooden exegesis. The folklorist and composition-critic again find allies in each other.

The Fall of Vashti

The book of Esther is about the status quo, maintenance of it, and finding a proper place within it. Vashti's actions mark her as a threat to the status quo, and she is eliminated. The 'banished queen' (S416) and 'banished wife' (S411) are common folk motifs appearing in various traditional typologies.

Such banishments are often of innocent women, falsely accused and later rehabilitated by their husbands. The dismissal of 'arrogant' wives assumed guilty by the tradition is no less common in folklore: one thinks of the misogynistic Norwegian tale of the husband who kills his shrew wife and throws her in the river, where her body floats upstream.[2] The presence in folklore of the 'uppity' wife is in itself interesting and exposes a male-chauvinist tendency shared by the author of Esther and the larger folk tradition. Gender-related issues emerge strongly in the book of Esther. Its heroine is a woman who offers a particular model for success, one with which oppressors would be especially comfortable. Opposition is to be subtle, behind the scenes, and ultimately strengthening for the power structure. A number of modern feminist writers have, in fact, found their heroine in Vashti, their empathy with her, while regarding Esther as a weak collaborator with tyranny, an antifeminist[3]— a subject to which we will return. For the writer of Esther, however, Vashti's foolishness is the foil for Esther's wisdom,

1. H. Cazelles, 'Notes sur la composition du rouleau d'Esther', in H. Gross and F. Mussner (eds.), *Lex tua veritas: Festschrift für Hubert Junker* (Trier: Paulinas, 1961), pp. 17-29, esp. p. 28; J.C.H. Lebram, 'Purimfest und Estherbuch', *VT* 22 (1972), pp. 208-22; C. Schedl, 'Das Buch Esther', *Theologie und Gegenwart* (1964), p. 90.

2. See the Norwegian tale 'The Old Woman against the Stream', a tale collected by P.S. Asbjørnsen, found in P.C. Asbjørnsen and J. Moe, *Norwegian Folktales* (New York: Viking, 1960), pp. 112-14.

3. For example M. Gendler, 'The Restoration of Vashti', in E. Koltun (ed.), *Jewish Women* (New York: Schocken Books, 1976), pp. 241-47.

her dismissal justified and, indeed, from a narrative point of view, the spark that commences the story.

On the other hand, the man, the king who banishes Vashti, receives no sympathy from the writer. He eats, and drinks, and follows willy-nilly the advice of others. His courtiers fear that Vashti will become a model of resistance for all wives. Others have pointed justifiably to the humorous tone here; it is the humor of those in control. It is easy to laugh at a potential loss of power when there is no real threat. Vashti must be put away.

Generic	Morphological	Typological
Problem	Threat to status quo	Queen refuses to appear before king
A plan	Exercise of wisdom	Courtiers advise banishment
Resolution	Threat eliminated	Queen banished (new problem)

The king's decision to find a replacement for Vashti may be introduced here by an erotic suggestion, 'the king remembered what Vashti used to do' (2.1), presumably 'for him'. He does not miss a person or a personality but a function. This under-lines his shallowness, of course, but the portrait of the king is fully in tune with another traditional motif, that of the stupid, impotent king. Such kings, who have something in common with the patriarchs as senexes portrayed in Genesis,[1] have no control of the situation around them. As fathers to princesses desired by dragons, they have no idea how to resist. (For other examples, see Thompson Motif J1705.4.) Thus Ahasuerus, the surface mover of the story, is a manipulated, passive tool as much as Esther is, and he remains so throughout the narrative. Again the folk character has his equivalent in what Old Testament scholars generally assign to Near Eastern wisdom tradition. As Talmon has shown, Ahasuerus exemplifies how not to be a good ruler and wise.[2] Though the Ahasuerus of Esther is somewhat akin to the buffoon Pharaoh of Genesis 12, the portrait is much fuller here and the implicit attitude to authority more complicated. He is less respected than Joseph's Pharaoh,

---

1.   On old men and foolish kings, see Talmon, 'Wisdom', pp. 450-51.
2.   Talmon, 'Wisdom', pp. 441-43.

who at least knows enough to have good men around him, and certainly less respected than the rulers of Genesis 20 and 26, who are so ethically scrupulous. Ahasuerus may be molded; he can be made good or evil. A wise person never trusts such a leader, nor does he or she openly oppose or trick him. He is a given, and his power is a given; one must learn to make the most of the fool. Haman, Mordecai and Esther all try their hand at controlling the king for their own advantage. In this first move the king's advisers direct him to find a new queen, and, of course, he follows their advice. The banishment of Vashti thus leads to a new problem and the story of Esther's rise.

The Rise of Esther

If one tells the story from Ahasuerus's point of view, the plot deals with the lack of a family member and the need to make the family whole, as do the birth episodes in the narratives of Jacob and Joseph; yet as the morphological outline indicates, the book of Esther presents not merely a matter of marginal or incomplete status but of status quo interrupted:

Generic	*Morphological*	*Typological*
Problem	Status quo upset	First wife banished
Plan	Search	Beauty contest to find a new one
Resolution	Restoration of status quo	An underdog selected to become new wife

As in Genesis 20, concern with the status quo is extremely important in the book of Esther. The work is largely about the status quo and how to become and stay a part of it. From Esther's point of view, the tale traces a familiar morphological pattern: underdog status, for Esther is an adopted orphan, a member of an exiled people instructed by her cousin not to reveal her identity as a Jew; intervention by helpers, that is, Mordecai's wise advice to keep silent (2.10) and Hegai's advice not to ask for too much (2.15); rise in status, as Esther becomes queen.

Very much like Joseph, Esther is a passive character at the beginning of her story who will become an active character later. Helpers, Mordecai and Hegai, guide her career as God guided that of Joseph. Like Joseph, she finds favor with her overlords (2.9). Her major asset is her beauty, a gift of nature. It might be suggested that as a woman, Esther does display already hints of an author's notion of the exercise of wisdom by a wise woman. She knows enough to take good advice and to be self-effacing, humble and even-tempered. In Scripture it is noticeable that Esther's helpers are human beings and not God, but it is perfectly usual in folk narration. The morphology, as Dundes would remind us, works well no matter how the general motifs are specified.[1] A difference in the sort of helpers, however, is an important indicator of the interests of author and audience.

Most noticeable about this move in the book of Esther, whether explored from the point of view of the controller of the action, Ahasuerus (as much as he controls anything), or that of the one controlled, is how typical of folklore the typological motifs are at a quite specific level. Thus, the 'beauty contest' by which the heroine of low status becomes royalty finds many folk parallels in Cinderella tales and their ilk (see Thompson motifs T91.6.2; T121.8). As we have shown, the details of the first two moves, characterizations, actions and settings are quite compatible with folk literature.

Does any detail make Esther distinctive? The one thread that is distinctively Israelite is the most obvious: Esther's lowly status is largely defined by her being Jewish. Her fear to reveal her identity is most significant and points to a strong us–them quality in the work. The underdog tales explored in chs. 2–4[2] distinguish between haves and have-nots—those with status and wealth versus those without, those with the rights of primogeniture versus those without such rights, those with parents' love versus those without—all status issues, to be sure. In Esther, however, the clearest marker of us versus them is whether one is a Jew or not. To be Jew is to have marginal status.

Lee Humphreys, Arndt Meinhold, Shemaryahu Talmon and others have pointed to the exilic mentality in Esther, drawing parallels between worldview in this work and in the tale of

---

1. A. Dundes, *The Morphology of the North American Indian Folktale* (Helsinki: Suomalainen Tiedeakatemia, 1965), pp. 59, 80, 98.
2. Of *Underdogs and Tricksters*.

Joseph.[1] It is certainly true that Potiphar's wife describes Joseph as the Hebrew slave (Gen. 39.14, 17) and that Joseph is introduced to Pharaoh as a Hebrew (Gen. 41.12),[2] but his ethnic otherness is not strongly emphasized in the work, whereas it is central in Esther. 'Hebrew' may in fact mean '*apiru*, that is, 'stateless person', in the Joseph story and emphasize his marginality rather than his ethnicity.[3]

The book of Esther is indeed an early example of Jewish folk literature with important implications for the developing tradition. This emerges in 'Esther's rise' and especially in the 'saving of Mordecai'. The most significant and final move of Esther is preceded by another that serves as an important transition in the tale.

How Mordecai Saves the King
This typological pattern is found not only in countless traditional tales but also in popular film and television:

Generic	Morphological	Typological
Problem	Threat (to status quo)	Plot to kill king
Intervention	Exercise of wisdom	Wise man spies on perpetrators and reports them
Resolution	Threat eliminated	Perpetrators hanged

The 'espionage' story is, perhaps, the modern equivalent of the court conflict/intrigue tale. As in the banishment of Vashti, the direct affront to authority leads to downfall. Mordecai's wisdom emerges not only in his loyalty but also in letting no information escape his attention, a wise activity for the courtier, as Talmon has emphasized, but also for the folk hero who succeeds by using his head (See motif K1956.7: sham wise man

1. W.L. Humphreys, 'A Life-Style for Diaspora: A Study of the Tales of Esther and Daniel', *JBL* 93 (1973), pp. 211-23; Meinhold, 'Die Gattung', I and II; Talmon 'Wisdom'.

2. Contra Meinhold, who emphasizes the importance of the hero's ethnic identity in Joseph ('Die Gattung', I, p. 311-13; II, pp. 76-78).

3. See G. Mendenhall, *The Tenth Generation* (Baltimore: Johns Hopkins University Press, 1973), pp. 122-41, esp. 136-41; N.K. Gottwald, *The Tribes of Yahweh: A Sociology of the Religion of Liberated Israel 1250–1050 BC* (Maryknoll, NY: Orbis Books, 1979), pp. 213-19, 401-25.

utilizes overheard conversation, a trickster tale.) Again, except for the fact that Mordecai is a Jew, this tale has a stock quality. It is a necessary episode in the larger narrative; the king's recollection of Mordecai's help will commence the evil Haman's downfall.

The Saving of Mordecai and the Jews
The morphological pattern is the same as that of Mordecai's saving Ahasuerus and the fall of Vashti, but now the threat is directed against Mordecai and his people. Each of these typological elements finds parallels in Thompson's Motif Index. The Motif Index is rich in treacherous counselors (K2290), servants (K2250.1), slaves (K2251), and rivals (K2220). Haman finds a place among this traditional stock, as does his end: to be 'condemned to the punishment he has suggested for others' (Q581). Themes of wisdom and lack of wisdom again intertwine with folkloristic characterizations, for tales about wise and foolish are narrative manifestations of folk wisdom. In this case, wisdom is offered for dealing with persons of higher status.

Generic	*Morphological*	*Typological*
Problem	Threat	Evil courtier seeks to eliminate rival and rival's nation and convinces the king to assist him
Intervention	Exercise of wisdom	Queen cleverly reveals matters to king and changes his mind
Resolution	Elimination of threat	King's orders altered, perpetrator hanged, and enemies defeated in reversal of evil courtier's plans

Haman's obsequiousness to the queen, his advice giving, are attempts to appear the good and wise counselor, but his self-absorption, his overwhelming self-love grounded in insecurity, is often the same thing. The combination of a foolish king and a villainous adviser makes for special mischief. Ahasuerus is oblivious to the rivalries around him and presumably unconcerned that the Mordecai who saved him is a Jew threatened by

Haman's proposed edict of annihilation.

Esther, though initially guided and motivated by her cousin (4.8, 13-14), finally becomes an independent wisdom heroine. She invites the king and Haman to two dinner parties, revealing her own identity and exposing the villain at the second of these. The queen 'intervening for a condemned courtier' is found in Thompson's Motif Index (P21), as is the daughter who intercedes with the king to save her father.[1] Esther's cleverness emerges in the way she employs womanly wiles to seduce Haman and Ahasuerus to wisdom. Like a Judith or an Abigail, Esther dresses for success; she speaks in sweet words of flattery and is self-effacing in demeanor ('if it please the king...'). Like these women, she employs wine and good food to set up her situation, reaching a man through his stomach. In short, she is an altogether appealing portrait of women's wisdom for the men of a ruling patriarchate, but hardly an image meaningful or consoling to modern women. She is, as such, not peculiar to Israelite imagery, nor to Near Eastern or biblical 'wisdom' traditions, but fully typological, reminding us nevertheless of the ways in which traditional literature reflects and affects a prevailing culture. This sort of tale is about maintenance of status quo, about working from within the system, and serves to reinforce such values. Esther contrasts with the rash Vashti, who would insolently and overtly dare to challenge a king in direct contradiction to the advice of folk wisdom.

The narrative goes to great lengths, in fact, to show that it is not only Esther who is 'wise' in this self-effacing sense but all the Jews. To be wise is to be a good citizen. Haman's charges of Jewish rebelliousness and tricksterism are refuted, for Mordecai saved his king; Esther wins the king over not by confrontation

1.   See the Turkish tale 'The Daughters of the Broom Thief' for a good example of this motif (W.S. Walker and A.E. Uysal, *Tales Alive in Turkey* [Cambridge, MA: Harvard University Press, 1966], pp. 135-39). For an example of the interceding queen, see 'The Unjust King and the Wicked Goldsmith', in J.H. Knowles, *Folk-Tales of Kashmir* (London: Kegan, Paul, Trench, Trubner, 1893), pp. 229-32. In this tale, the intercession of the good queen becomes a cause for her banishment, which in turn leads to other adventures. Work with the Motif Index instructs one about the stuff of traditional tales, the many combinations of motifs possible, the process of variation and multiformity that is traditional-style composition.

but by begging for her life.[1] The Jews defend themselves only because they have the king's permission to fight (Esth. 8.11-12). They fight a just war, killing only in proportion to that plotted against them, taking no booty. Not taking booty not only evokes holy war theology but also underscores the non-self-aggrandizing and defensive nature of the war. In Robert Gordis's translation of 8.11, the Jews are not about to slaughter their enemies' children, wives and so on but to defend themselves against those who are about to slaughter the Jews' children.[2] His suggestion could be correct, but even if the more usual translations of 8.11 are correct, Jewish vengeance in Esther does not reflect a debased spirit peculiar to 'post-prophetic Israel', that is, to Judaism, or evidence Jewish 'ethnocentricism', as some would suggest.[3] Drawing parallels with events in 1916 Russia, Gunkel considers the book of Esther to be about the first pogrom against the Jews.[4] It is ironic that such a work has been the target of misunderstandings. These insensitive descriptions of Esther fail, at any rate, to appreciate its folk-literary qualities. Folktales of Esther's type go this way; violence rounds out a theme of just deserts. (See motif Q581: *lex talionis*.) What is remarkable about the Jacob and Joseph narratives is that a violent conclusion to a pattern of rivalry between brothers is avoided; these underdog tales are family narratives with messages of wholeness and healing. Esther deals with a stronger theme about us and them, insiders and outsiders, and the traditional pattern goes as one would expect. It is no coincidence that all the wise and good characters in Esther are Jews, the foolish, rash, and evil ones non-Jews. Esther is a strongly ethnic tale. Even so, the message of this victory of 'us' over 'them' is a careful, cautious one that does not advocate direct and open rebellion against injustice—quite the contrary. One begins to see that Esther is not only about wise and foolish, good and evil but also about attitudes to authority and methods

1.   Berg emphasizes the theme of dual loyalty to state and people found in Esther (*Esther*, p. 100). See also Meinhold, 'Die Gattung', I, p. 319.

2.   R. Gordis, 'Studies in the Esther Narrative', *JBL* 95 (1976), pp. 49-53.

3.   For a striking example of this point of view see B.W. Anderson, 'Esther', *IB*, III (1954), pp. 828-30.

4.   Gunkel, *Esther*, p. 1.

of dealing with unjust authority,[1] central questions in Jewish ethics as old as the founding myth tradition of the exodus.

Underdog Tales and Social Ethics

The response of the book of Esther to injustice has implications not only for Jews' relations with an often hostile world but also for women's relationship to Judaism. The book of Esther encourages attempts to work from within the system, to become an indispensable part of it. This model personified by Esther is strongly contrasted with that of Vashti. Direct resistance fails.

The trickster and the wisdom hero/heroine have much in common: the stealthy, home-based power of the women; the emphasis on clever, behind-the-scenes manipulation of those of higher status to secure for oneself benefits. And yet the trickster tales have a clear anti-establishment bent. Tricksters toy with the establishment and when uncovered escape, elude authority, and trick again. They embody chaos, marginality and indefinability. The wisdom heroes and heroines seek to become a part of the system that threatened them and, like Esther and Joseph, enjoy being a part of the establishment, deriving much benefit from it. They personify order, neatness, a world in which everything fits.[2]

How does one evaluate this model for and of dealing with unjust authority? Some in later Jewish tradition are rather uncomfortable with Esther. Whereas Judith can brag (over and over) that the heathen Holophernes never laid a hand on her, Esther cannot be so proud about her accomplishments. Hence the Zohar's suggestion that Esther never lay with Ahasuerus, for God would send a female spirit to the king in her place (*Zohar* III, 275b-276b). Clearly, the folktale writer has no qualms about women's using sexuality to obtain benefits for themselves or others. The later exegetical tradition shows some ambivalence. Some of the rabbis praise Vashti for her resistance, suggesting that the hedonistic Ahasuerus had wanted Vashti to

1.   See Berg on themes of obedience and disobedience in Esther, which she sees as recurring and unifying in the work (Berg, *Esther*, pp. 72-82, 100).
2.   See in this context Humphreys, 'A Life-Style', p. 223.

dance naked before his friends (*Esth. R.* 3.13-14). The rabbis, of course, are not proponents of women's liberation. Much as the Moral Majority and the National Organization for Women might agree on issues of pornography, so the rabbis appear to take a feminist position. Nevertheless, the issue of unjust authority is raised. Fine studies such as David Daube's *Collaboration with Tyranny* explore this issue in rabbinic political ethics.[1] Relations to unjust authority remain hotly debated issues in post-Holocaust Judaism. Interesting for our purposes is that the underdog tales provide various models for dealing with authority: tricksterism, self-inclusion in the power-structure and/or collaboration. Were tales of Samson and David included in our study we could add another: direct confrontation.

Author and Audience

Where does our study of Esther—its style, structures and themes—lead in dealing with questions of author and audience? Do the concerns of the folklorist lead us away from answers of traditional biblical scholarship concerning the date and provenance of Esther?

Style in Esther does not provide as clear a guide as it does in Genesis 12 and 20 or the Jacob narrative and Joseph narrative. A style that is quite traditional combines with baroque nuances to produce a style all its own, characterized in particular by hyperbolic chains of synonyms. It may well be that in Esther, distinctions of 'courtly' versus 'popular' style relevant for a pre-exilic or early post-exilic Palestinian setting have no meaning. We are clearly dealing with postmonarchic literature and probably with non-Palestinian Jewish literature.[2]

It is not surprising that scholars who have been most sensitive

1.   D. Daube, *Collaboration with Tyranny in Rabbinic Law* (The Riddell Memorial Lectures, 1965; Oxford: Oxford University Press, 1965). See also M. Greenberg, 'Rabbinic Reflections on Defying Illegal Orders: Amasa, Abner, and Joab', in M.M. Kellner (ed.), *Contemporary Jewish Ethics* (New York: Sanhedrin, 1978), pp. 211-20.

2.   See my review article, 'Legends of Wise Heroes and Heroines', in D. Knight and G. Tucker (eds.), *The Hebrew Bible and its Modern Interpreters* (Chico, CA: Scholars Press, 1985), pp. 445-46.

to the folk quality of Esther's content and structure—for example, Gaster and Bickerman—have been least willing to find in Esther hints of specific Persian period history.[1] Other scholars have employed archaeological information from the excavations at Susa to suggest that details in the work are historical;[2] Ungnad published a cuneiform text mentioning Marduka, a high official of the Susa court during the reign of Xerxes I.[3] Clause Schedl attempts further to argue away problems in Esther such as the age of Mordecai, who would have been about 150 years old in the time of Ahasuerus-Xerxes—if deported in the time of Nebuchadnezzar.

Talmon describes the consensus of scholarly opinion thus:

> The author of the Esther-story generally shows an intimate knowledge of Persian court-etiquette and public administration. He must have had some personal experience of these matters or else was an extremely well-informed and gifted writer.[4]

The author of the book of Esther does employ Persian local color, Persian names and words, a setting in Susa, and mention of court personnel and is aware of the setup of the Persian kingdom in provinces and so on, but I question whether this sort of knowledge is intimate or based on personal experience at court. A Persian period date seems logical; it is from this setting that the author draws local color, but it would not have been necessary to be of the court to do so.

Talmon reads into the text one example of Esther's realistic portrayal of the counselors attached to Near Eastern courts when he suggests that Mordecai and Haman are portrayed as multilingual and thus modeled after real court officials.[5] The

---

1.   T.H. Gaster, *Purim and Hannukah in Custom and Tradition* (New York: Schuman, 1950), p. 35; Bickerman, *Four Strange Books*, pp. 199-200; Gunkel suggests that a more folkloristic work has been redacted by a later scholastic writer concerned with historical detail (*Esther*, pp. 53-54).

2.   C.A. Moore, *Esther* (AB, 7b; Garden City, NY: Doubleday, 1971), p. xli; Anderson, 'Esther', pp. 827-28.

3.   A. Ungnad, 'Keilinschriftliche Beiträge zum Buch Ezra und Esther', *ZAW* 58 (1964), pp. 20-24. See also S. Horn, 'Mordecai, A Historical Problem', *BR* 9 (1964), pp. 20-24.

4.   Talmon, 'Wisdom', p. 422.

5.   Talmon, 'Wisdom', p. 436.

language these men speak may be as irrelevant to the audience of the Esther tale as the fact that Frenchmen in 1948 war films always speak to one another in English with Austrian accents.[1] We suspend disbelief about these matters when participating in narrative experiences.

Zeroing in on the date of court wisdom portrayals in Esther, Talmon suggests further that the wisdom heroine is a uniquely biblical phenomenon in the ancient Near East until possibly the Persian period.[2] The commonness of wise women in plots such as those of Esther in world folklore casts suspicion both upon the uniqueness of Esther in the Near East and upon her relation to Persian motifs of a particular period. The same must be said of the suggestion that the book of Esther reveals 'the courtier-counselor's psychology'.[3] It is a wisdom tale in which underdogs succeed via proverbial wisdom exercised at court, but are comparable wisdom tales filled with powerful dupes, wise women, and themes of just deserts always from a courtier-class author?[4]

Finally, folklore, the literature and the field, cautions us to be careful in our descriptions of wisdom literature as a genre. Many of the traits Talmon finds in wisdom works—for example, the *ad hoc* mentality and lack of historical depth, the undeveloped characterizations[5]—scholars such as Olrik and Lüthi claim to find in a whole range of folklore.[6] Does Talmon observe the wisdom quality of the book of Esther or its folkloristic quality?

Thus although Esther certainly is about the wise and the foolish, about wisdom as the means to succeed and become a member of the 'ruling class', and though it does have a court setting and strongly Persian local color, it need not have been composed by a member of a courtly elite, as Meinhold

1. See H. Gunkel, *Das Märchen im alten Testament* (Religions-geschichtliche Volksbucher, II, Reihe. 23.26; Tübingen: Mohr, 1917, 1921), p. 158, for some relevant observations.
2. Talmon, 'Wisdom', pp. 452-53.
3. Talmon, 'Wisdom', p. 433.
4. Talmon, 'Wisdom', pp. 441, 452, 446.
5. Talmon, 'Wisdom', pp. 431, 433.
6. A. Olrik, 'Epic Laws of Folk Narrative', in A. Dundes (ed.), *The Study of Folklore* (Englewood Cliffs, NJ: Prentice–Hall, 1965), pp. 131-41; M. Lüthi, *The European Folktale: Form and Nature* (Philadelphia: ISHI, 1982), p. 56.

suggests;[1] nor is it easily assignable to one period in Persian history, as others suggest.[2]

An important indicator of Esther's author and audience is its attitude to authority as part of a larger worldview. In this context one might also explore suggestions that a historical kernel is to be found in the escape of the Jewish community from a threat to its very existence.[3]

It is as impossible to ascertain whether or not this escape has a historical kernel as it is to answer the same question about the exodus. We can say for Esther, as Gerleman has noticed, that the people's narrow escape from oppressors in exile is a favorite, indeed central, Israelite literary *typos*.[4] It is through this specification of cross-culturally found narrative patterns, the threat morphology and the evil courtier typology, that the Jewish author makes this work meaningful to an audience, giving it special power of identification for the reality of a people caught in a particular historical and sociological setting.

I am inclined to believe that the work was written in diaspora, for a cultural group surrounded by overlords in an alien setting, for a minority rather than for a conquered and culturally threatened majority in Palestine. In this I agree with Humphreys, Meinhold and others.[5] What mode of relating to authority is offered? It is the way of Jeremiah, as Humphreys notes (Jer. 29.4-7), to build homes, raise families, be good citizens, but more. It suggests becoming a full part of the system, all the while acknowledging the stupidity of those who run the system. We must not forget, moreover, that the book of Esther is comedy, as Samuel Sandmel saw so well.[6] It is meant to be amusing as well as uplifting and is ultimately optimistic, if

1. Meinhold, 'Die Gattung', II, p. 92.
2. See Niditch, 'Legends', p. 446.
3. See Niditch, 'Legends', p. 446.
4. G. Gerleman, *Studien zu Esther: Stoff-Struktur-Stil-Sinn* (Neukirchen–Vluyn: Neukirchener Verlag, 1966), pp. 10-28; *Esther* (BKAT, 21; Neukirchen–Vluyn: Neukirchener Verlag, 1973), pp. 11-23.
5. Humphreys, 'A Life-Style'; Meinhold, 'Die Gattung', I, II.
6. S. Sandmel, *The Hebrew Scriptures: An Introduction to their Literature and Religious Ideas* (New York: Oxford University Press, 1978), p. 450. See also B.W. Jones, 'Two Misconceptions about the Book of Esther', *CBQ* 39 (1977), p. 177.

sobering. The author of Esther is more audacious and insulting to authority than the respectful author of the Joseph story, who is more likely to have written in the context of Israelite royalty than foreign lordship. The author of Esther is at the same time more accepting of authority than the authors of the trickster tales. One deals with life in exile as members of an insecure, sometimes persecuted minority by steering a course of survival somewhere between co-option and self-respect and by holding to the conviction that to be wise and to be worthy are the same. Critical also are the psychological release of humor and the enactment of ultimate vindication in lively literary and cultic traditions. The plot of the folktale, in which one knows all will turn out well for the heroes whether via their wisdom or 'some other source', thus makes real suffering bearable and helps to bridge the gap between the way things are and the way they should be.

AN ORIENTAL BEAUTY PARLOUR:
AN ANALYSIS OF ESTHER 2.8-18 IN THE HEBREW,
THE SEPTUAGINT AND THE SECOND GREEK TEXT

Kristin De Troyer

1. *Introduction*

The book of Esther contains the story of a Jewish girl who becomes the queen of the Persian empire. In that same period Haman, a dignitary, is forging a plan to exterminate the Jews. He rolls the dice and decides to destroy the whole Jewish population in one day. Esther and her uncle, Mordecai, try to foil his assault on the Jews. To do this, Esther must convince the king to nullify the decree which made Haman's extermination plan into law.

Esther's story is initially idyllic. Esther, a common Jewish woman, becomes queen, as in a fairy tale. The ingredients are promising: an Eastern palace, a king who chooses a simple girl, eunuchs and a harem, enough elements to fill a story along the lines of the Thousand and One Nights.

However, a story for the Thousand and One Nights does not fit into the Bible well. At least, other types of stories are expected, an opinion evidently shared by the story's translators into Greek. From the third century BCE, as a result of the exploits of Alexander the Great who conquered most of what was then the 'civilized' world, Greek became the spoken language of the Mediterranean area, including the East. It thus became necessary to translate the books of the Bible into the new everyday language: Greek.

But the translators not only translated, they also altered Esther's story. For example, they added God's name; they had Esther utter a prayer before approaching the king—a prayer that was more than necessary, since those appearing before the king without being summoned were condemned to death. In fear and trepidation Esther pleads for the Lord's help, 'Help me who stands alone and has no helper but You'. She appeals to God's justice, to his protecting hand (Appendix C.14-29 [= NRSV Esth. 14.3-19]).

The Greek translator is now apparently in his element, for he—the translator's perspective seems to be male—increases the drama and religious tone of the next scene. When the need is greatest, salvation is near. So the author first makes the need greater. Esther is in her finest array when she approaches the king, but she is also in fear for her life: 'her heart contracted with fear'. Here the thriller really starts: she must first pass through many doors before she finally reaches the 'very awesome' king. 'In flaming anger' he glances up with 'eyes full of majesty'. He looks at her 'seething with fury'. Most people would take to their heels at less and, sure enough, Esther faints (Appendix D.7 [= NRSV 15.7]). Now the Greek translator has to add more religious polish to the deliverance. He has God intervene: 'God softens the king's heart and the king takes Esther in his hands'. A moment later Esther tells the king she saw him 'as an angel', something normal in this situation, but she piously adds 'as an angel *of God*' (Appendix D. 8, 13 [= NRSV 15.8, 13]).[1]

There is much less tension in the Hebrew version. Esther comes uninvited before the king. However, she finds grace in his eyes, and the story continues (5.1-3). No trembling, fainting queen, no furious king, but also no delivering God or saving angel in the form of the king.

The Greek translator adds a religious ingredient to the story. Moreover, he heightens the tension, he increases the need by placing the female protagonist in a frightening position. Esther must surmount more obstacles before she finds grace with the king. The reader perceives her fear immediately. In the Greek story she trembles and faints. The 'weak little woman' is portrayed as even more frail. This makes the king appear even more fearsome. God himself provides the deliverance. Among other things, this increased tension has ramifications for the image of women. The 'weak' aspects are emphasized. To focus

1.   It is noteworthy that tractate *Megillah* mentions that three angels support Esther when she faints: cf. *b. Meg.* 15b.

on this more clearly, we will examine 'what a woman looks like' in the Hebrew and Greek texts. And where can we have a better 'look' at a woman than in an Oriental beauty parlour?

Esth. 2.8-18 describes how Esther is prepared for the royal bed. An analysis of this passage can provide an idea of who wrote this text. Was it a man or a woman? Which way is the wind blowing? Does the text have a feminine or masculine perspective? Whose world is described in the text: a man's or a woman's? And even more important than these questions are the following: with whom must the reader identify? With which norm should one agree? Which world is presented here as normative?

2. *The Hebrew Story*

The Hebrew text is simply constructed. Verse 8 explains why and how Esther came to be in the royal palace. Verses 9-11 introduce the background of people and events. Verse 9 depicts Esther's connection to Hegai, while vv. 10 and 11 tell of Esther's background and relation to Mordecai. Verses 12-14 describe the ritual to which Esther, and all virgins, are subject, while vv. 15-16 show it applied concretely to Esther. Verses 17-18 portray the king's reaction to Esther and round off the scene.

We can present the structure in a schema, as follows:

v. 8:	General introduction:
	Girls are brought to the palace
	Specific introduction:
	Esther is brought to the palace
vv. 9-11:	Esther–Hegai
	Esther–Mordecai
vv. 12-14:	General ritual
vv. 15-16:	Specific application of the ritual to Esther
vv. 17-18:	Specific reaction of the king to Esther
	General reaction of the king to the events at hand

Discussion

Verse 8. At the king's command many girls are brought to the harem in Susa (ובהקבץ נערות רבות אל־שושן הבירה). Esther is one of them. However, the author mentions that Esther is not brought to Susa but to the king's house (אל־בית המלך). Does the author want to suggest a difference between Esther and the other girls? Does the author already know the result of the beauty contest? Esther and the other girls are put in Hegai's custody. Hegai is presented as the guardian of women (הגי שמר הנשים). In half a verse, the 'girls' have become 'women'. It appears that 'putting girls in Hegai's hands' means the same as 'becoming a woman'. Hegai evidently has something to do with the transition from girlhood to womanhood.

Verse 9. Esther appears to please Hegai, who is the central figure, the norm, in v. 9. He represents the 'demands' of society and the king. In this verse Esther passes a first 'test': she enters the palace and obtains the favour of Hegai, the guardian of women. What does she do to obtain this favour? Nothing. We read, 'and the maiden pleased Hegai', and thus, 'won his favour' (ותיטב הנערה בעיניו ותשא חסד לפניו).

Because Esther pleases Hegai, he immediately gives her all the necessary adornments and food. She is over the first hurdle, and has obtained all she needs to take the second. That food is necessary is understandable, but she also needs the adornments. These, too, she receives. This gives the impression that a woman thrives on food and adornments (לתת לה את־תמרוקיה ואת־מנותיה).

Hegai, the guardian, is generous. He gives her the seven best slaves from the royal palace and the best quarters in the harem (ואת שבע הנערות...וישנה ואת־נערותיה לטוב בית הנשים). Esther is now in the king's house, with the best rooms and slaves. Hegai plays the key role here: he acts, he rewards those who please him. This verse is written completely from his point of view. As far as he is concerned, Esther is already the king's property.

Verse 10. Another normative person is Mordecai. He has forbidden Esther to speak of her origins, and she obeys. Esther listens to Mordecai. By her very movements, that is, 'telling nothing', she obeys the *order* and *norm* of a man. In this verse there is a contrast between Esther's '(not) telling' and Mordecai's 'orders'.

Verse 11. Esther now has beautiful quarters, good slaves, food and all types of adornments. What does she do with them all? Mordecai knows the answer. He apparently knows all that is to be done with women. Whenever he visits he never fails to ask about two things: how she is, and what is being done with her (לדעת את־שלום אסתר ומה־יעשה בה).[1] How she is, is one thing. How she is being prepared for the night with the king is another. And that latter business is determined by food, adornment, slaves and good quarters.

Verse 12. Mordecai apparently knows that something must be done with Esther. But the reader is not yet aware of all that is involved. To make clear what is to be done with the girls, the author of v. 12 describes the beauty treatment. Each girl must undergo this twelve-month-long treatment: for six months she is treated with oil of myrrh and for six months with feminine spices and ointments (בבשמים ובתמרוקי הנשים).[2] The use of the specification 'of women' with 'spices' emphasizes the distance between the male writer and the female world in question.

After the description of the ritual, the average reader knows at least why Mordecai not only wanted to know 'how' Esther was but also 'what' was being done to her. She was being given a thorough treatment, beauty parlour style.

But there is still another problem. Literally, the first part of

---

1.   We find this combination of questions nowhere else in the Bible. It is striking that the word *šālôm* is translated by 'good health', 'peace' and 'prosperity' (Gen. 29.6; 43.27; 1 Sam. 10.4; 17.18; 17.22; 25.5; 30.21; 2 Sam. 8.10; 11.7; 20.9; 2 Kgs 4.23; 4.26; 5.21; 5.22; 9.11; 9.31; 10.13; and it has the same meaning in the noun form in Gen. 37.14; 41.16; Isa. 27.5; 45.7; Esth. 10.3. Only in Ezra 2.12 are two different words used to denote 'peace' and 'good health': שלום and טובה. Moreover, the verb עשׂה, 'do', is here in the *niphal*, which indicates that something is being done *to* Esther. A nice parallel for the second part of the question can be found in Exod. 2.4: Moses' sister watches from afar to see what would happen, 'be done', to him.

2.   Cf. W.F. Albright, 'The Lachish Cosmetic Burner and Esther 2.12', in H.N. Bream, R.D. Heim and C.A. Moore (eds.), *A Light unto My Path: Old Testament Studies in Honor of Jacob M. Myers* (Philadelphia: Temple University Press, 1974), pp. 25-32. See also C.A. Moore, *Studies in the Book of Esther* (New York: Ktav, 1981), pp. 361-68.

v. 12 reads as follows: 'Now when the turn came for each maiden to go in to King Ahasuerus, at the end of the time of /the being for her, as/according to the law of women, the twelve months...'. Normally after the expression 'at the end of' (מקץ), there follows a reference to time, for example at the end of so many days or years. Here, instead of following immediately and completely, the indication of time is split up. First, we find an infinitivus constructus of היה and we translate: at the end 'of the time reserved for her' (היות לה), and only further on in the verse follows the real indication of time: '(of) twelve months' (שנים עשר חדש). In between, we find 'according to the law of women' (כדת הנשים). The ritual is presented as something pre-scribed *by* women. The ritual is 'according to the law of women'. But two readings are possible: in addition to 'the law *of* women' we can also read 'the law *for* women'. In Esther we find expressions such as 'the laws of the Medes and Persians', the law of the king, the law of the Lord, and the like.[1] But this text speaks about a rule, familiar to the eunuch and probably Mordecai, but not to the public (including the girls?). It appears more a law for or about women, prescribed by men; and not a law prescribed by women for themselves.

The ritual is described in some detail. Once the ritual has been performed on the women, 'everyone' is satisfied. The ritual

---

1. The book of Esther speaks either of law in the abstract (1.8, 13, 15; 3.14, 15; 4.8, 11, 16; 8.13, 14; 9.14) or of a specific law: the law of the Persians and Medes (1.19), the word of the king and his laws (4.3; 8.17; 9.1; 2.8), the law of the king (3.8), the law of today (9.13), their (i.e. the Jews') laws (3.18). Ezra 8.36 refers to the laws 'of' the king. In all these cases we are dealing with laws of kings, peoples or institutions. In the ancient East legislative power lay in the hands of men. In general, women were not presupposed to participate in legislative work. The reference to the 'laws of women' in Esth. 2.12 is therefore surprising. Does it refer to a tradition of laws made by women? Or should 2.12 be interpreted as a slip? Or does the author 'merely' mean that what is happening to the girls is totally in accordance with the law of the land? It seems that the term 'laws of women' must discourage the girls from opposing their fate, and from opposing their beauty treatment. It is more a law *for* women than *of* women.

On the rare cases of a ruling queen, see A. Brenner, *The Israelite Woman: Social Role and Literary Type in Biblical Narrative* (The Biblical Seminar, 2; Sheffield: JSOT Press, 2nd edn, 1989).

appears to be 'of' women, but it in fact prescribes 'for' the women.

Verse 13. The author informs us that after the beauty treatment, the candidate may bring with her what she desires when she goes to the king (את כל־אשר תאמר ינתן לה). Everything she requests is given to her when she leaves the harem for the king's house. The girl's activity is limited to 'asking'. She does not 'take' any-thing, she asks. The active person is the one who gives. The anonymous giver has a role in determining the girl's lot. Esther may choose her own weapons. When it is her turn to appear before Ahasuerus, the king, all she desires from the harem will[1] be given to her. Esther, like the other women, may 'ask'.

Verse 14. Verse 14 relates Esther's test. In the evening she will go to the king and in the morning she will return. When she returns she will go to another harem where she will be under the care of Shaashgaz, the king's eunuch who is in charge of the concubines (שמר הפילגשים). In other words, after one night with the king, Esther no longer belongs with the maidens, but with the (real) concubines. The author is clear about that. From then on she will not return to the king unless[2] he is pleased with her and summons her by name. That is the lot of women in a harem.

The beauty treatment, together with the night with the king, is the second and last test which Esther must pass in order to be crowned as queen. The beauty treatment is essential, it is the primary means of passing the test. As was said, Mordecai seems to know of the procedure. The men know the procedure; the girls undergo the procedure. The women undergo the beauty treatment, may sleep with the king, are put under the charge of another guardian, and may return to the king only when sum-moned. All the active roles clearly belong to the men. They determine the course of the story. They invent the norm for the girls' lives.

1. To aid a more fluent reading of the text, 'would' is consistently replaced with 'will'.

2. For the translation see A. Aejmelaeus, *On the Trail of the Septuagint Translators: Collected Essays* (Kampen: Kok Pharos, 1993), p. 176.

Verses 15-16. Esther's turn comes in v. 15. The author relates what she does. She brings with her to the king only what the eunuch advises. Hegai knows what the king likes. Men know the norm. Esther conforms to this norm by taking only what Hegai recommends. Apparently his choice is not so bad, for she finds favour in the eyes of all who see her. Thus, the first to see her are already enthusiastic. Hegai knows the king and his court. He expresses what 'everyone'—and this probably means all the men—considers acceptable. Hegai functions as the norm-holder for the ritual.

Of course, Esther is also active here: she goes to the king. Yet, even here in her 'active' role she is identified as 'daughter of...'. It is Esther, the daughter of Abihail, the uncle of Mordecai, who goes to the king. She is defined by her relationship to the men in her life. She remains in Mordecai's shadow.

Verse 17. Then it happens, the king is smitten: 'The king loved Esther more than all the other women, and she found favour and compassion in his sight more than all the virgins'. He takes a fancy to her. It is no longer Hegai but the king who is the central figure. The king assumes the normative role from Hegai. The result is that Esther becomes queen: 'he set the royal crown on her head' (וישם כתר־מלכות בראשה). In a way, this act also settles the Vashti affair. The author is also very clear on this in what follows, '[and the king] made her queen instead of Vashti' (וימליכה תחת ושתי). All is well that ends well, or so it seems.

Verse 18. The king now organizes a great feast for all his princes and servants. This feast is further characterized in the Hebrew text as Esther's banquet (ויעש המלך משתה גדל ל...את משתה אסתר). Matters are now settled. The men's feast has become the feast of the woman Esther. Order is restored.[1]

Conclusion
This short passage describes the gauntlet run by women before being admitted to the king. The norm for admission is beauty.

---

1.   In ch. 1 there is a strong contrast between the men's feast and the women's. This is no surprise, since the chapter operates within a framework of inequality between men and women.

The girl has only to be pretty. *Sois belle et tais-toi!* It seems that this text is written by a man who states what women must be if they want to please men.

The book of Esther is a magnificent short story. Yet it also has a hidden agenda. Between the lines it transmits a code, a norm of behaviour for women. This code and norm is delivered completely from a male point of view. Therefore this part of the book is in all likelihood written by a man or, at the very least, from a male perspective.[1]

3. *The Greek Story (The Septuagint or B-Text)*

The Septuagint version has a simple structure. In 2.8 the king's command is heeded: girls are brought to Susa, Esther among them. She is put under Gai's authority. In vv. 9-11 we read how Gai reacts to Esther and what Esther's relationship to Mordecai is. In vv. 12-14 the author describes the ritual the women must undergo in order to be admitted to the king for the chance of being chosen queen. Verses 15-16 narrate Esther's turn. We learn of the king's reaction to Esther in v. 17. His further reaction is depicted in v. 18.

A schema of vv. 8-18 looks as follows:

v. 8:	What does Esther have to do with the story?
	One command: The king's precept is heeded
	A double action:
	Girls are brought to Susa
	Esther is also transported
vv. 9-11:	Introduction of the protagonists and their relationships:
	Gai–Esther
	Mordecai–Esther
vv. 12-14:	General summary of the ritual
v. 15-16:	Application to Esther
v. 17-18:	Double reaction to Esther
	Specific reaction
	General reaction

Although the oscillation between general and specific, typical of the Hebrew Esther story, has been adopted by the Greek

---

1.   Chapter 1 may possibly have been written by a woman, but that is another story. At the very least, a woman's perspective might be in evidence there.

translator, our attention here will be primarily directed toward the differences between the Hebrew and Greek texts.

Discussion
Verse 8. There are numerous passive verbs here. The king's command is *heeded*. Many girls *are brought* to Susa and *are put* under Gai's authority. Esther *is* also *transported*. The reader hears, as it were, the king's command and undergoes the events. Many girls also undergo the command. They *are brought* to Susa. Susa is further defined as 'in Gai's hands' (συνήχθησαν κοράσια πολλὰ εἰς Σουσαν τὴν πόλιν ὑπὸ χεῖρα Γαι). Consequently the girls come into his hands.

It is noteworthy that when Esther is brought, she comes 'directly' to Gai (καὶ ἤχθη Εσθηρ πρὸς Γαι). In her case no mention is made of Susa. We also learn who Gai is: the guardian of women. In the Hebrew text we noted that Esther was brought to the king's house while the other girls were taken to Susa. This marked a difference between Esther and the other girls. This distinction was already known to the author. Esther is destined for the palace and the king. She stands above the others. The distinction between Esther and the other girls, made in the Hebrew text, is maintained in the Greek text. But in the Greek text Gai is taking the place of the king. Gai is the first to examine the girls, the king comes later. Gai is the first member of the jury in the beauty contest.[1]

Again Gai is called the guardian of women (Γαι τὸν φύλακα τῶν γυναικῶν). The 'girls' will become 'women' in his hands. Esther, in his hands, must become *the* woman.

In this verse the women are not represented as active individuals. They are transported. Not one woman opposes this passive pattern. Or should we assume that the text does not reflect any sign of protest? We can, of course, always wonder why the girls did not spontaneously go to the palace. Perhaps this did not fit in with the culture. Yet in ch. 5 Esther does go to

---

1. Do Esther and the other girls know they are involved in a sort of beauty contest? The author does not even wonder whether the girls are aware of this, let alone whether they consent. Both Hebrew and Greek authors assume that everyone agrees with the selection procedure.

the king uninvited.[1] Must we assume from the passive mode that the girls did not go to the palace of their own free will?

Verse 9. In the Greek text we read that Esther pleases the eunuch (καὶ ἤρεσεν αὐτῷ τὸ κοράσιον).[2] She finds favour in his eyes (καὶ εὗρεν χάριν ἐνώπιον αὐτοῦ), and he hurries to give her 'her requirements': 'cleansing creams',[3] her share of the food and seven maids (τὸ σμῆγμα καὶ τὴν μερίδα καὶ τὰ ἑπτὰ κοράσια τὰ ἀποδεδειγμένα αὐτῇ ἐκ βασιλικοῦ). The eunuch repays Esther for pleasing him. Again he knows what Esther needs.[4] What it amounts to is that a man knows what a woman needs. The author does not doubt that: what the man thinks that the woman needs, she needs. There is no room for what the woman thinks. To the author it is evident that the woman shares the opinion of the man, of Gai.

Esther is also assigned seven royal maids. The eunuch takes good care of her and her seven maids. They remain in the harem.[5] In the Hebrew text, Esther and her maids stay in the best rooms of the palace. In the Greek text, Esther stays in the

---

1.   Some biblical women do approach the man of their choice. Tamar's story is an obvious case (Gen. 38). Ruth also takes advantage of an occasion to sleep with Boaz (Ruth 3). But in Esther we are concerned with the unusual situation of a king seeking a wife. Cf. K. van der Toorn, *Van haar wieg to haar graf: De rol van de godsdienst in het leven van de Israëlitische en Babylonische vrouw* (Baarn: Ten Have, 1987), pp. 52-53. (ET: *From her Cradle to her Grave: The Role of Religion in the Life of the Israelite and the Babylonian Woman* [trans. S.J. Denning-Bolle; Biblical Seminar, 23; Sheffield: JSOT Press, 1994]).

2.   Is Esther active here? The verb αρεσκω is in any case used in the active voice. Only in the passive or medial can it have the meaning of 'she pleased him'. In the active the verb means 'give pleasure to'. Αρεσκω is the translation of the Hebrew expression בעיׂ טׂוב. I translate: 'And she pleased him', with which the options—active or passive—are left open.

3.   The Hebrew uses the root *mrq* (to 'polish'). This word indicates clearly what needs to be done. The translator modified the verb 'polish' into ' clean'. The king wants a 'clean' woman; one's imagination can run wild at the possible implications.

4.   As in the Hebrew text.

5.   In v. 10 we read that Esther tells nothing of her origins. I will not go further into this aspect since it has little importance for the discussion of the norms of female appearance.

harem. There is no mention of the best apartments. This 'lack' is more than made good by the note that Gai took very good care of Esther and her maids (καὶ ἐχρήσατο αὐτῇ καλῶς καὶ ταῖς ἄβραις αὐτῆς). Gai's care is on a royal level. Esther has no reason to complain.[1]

Verse 10. As in the Hebrew text, v. 10 informs us that Esther reveals nothing about her ethnic origins, since Mordecai has forbidden her to do so. The Greek version does nothing to undermine Mordecai's authority.

Verse 11. Mordecai also perambulates in the Septuagint version of the story. However, he does not seek information about two points as in the Hebrew version, but only about one: what is happening to Esther (ἐπισκοπῶν τί Εσθηρ συμβήσεται). In the Septuagint Mordecai only wants to know about matters important for the story and leaves the rest aside.[2] Not how Esther *is*, but what is happening to her is important.[3] So far Gai is the only one who knows what is going on behind the closed doors of the harem.

Verse 12. Now the reader is finally introduced to the women's world, to 'Gai's world'. Neither the women nor Gai speak directly here. What happens *is related*. It is the narrator who informs the readers. 'This' is what is happening to the girls. The beauty treatment which the girls must undergo is described. As

1.   Throughout the whole passage Esther utters not one word. This is the remarkable position ascribed to Esther, and women in general, in this beauty parlour description.

2.   The Greek verb συμβαινειν may be the translation of the Hebrew verb עשה, 'do'. In the parallel of Exod. 2.4, the Greek translation αποβαινειν is used. This verb can, however, render עשה, as well as היה, 'be' and יצא, 'go out'.

3.   For the sake of completion, let us also mention how Josephus treats this point. In his version he relates how Mordecai spent some time every day in the palace and 'wondered about his darling, how she spends her life'. Josephus does indeed mention two actions but they are not joined by a conjunction. This gives the impression that Mordecai wonders about one thing only: he asks how Esther spends her time. This is closer to 'What is Esther doing/what is happening to her' than 'how she is'. Cf. Josephus Flavius, *Ant.* 11.6-2.

in the Hebrew text, the story is clear. Still, a few details are worth noting.

In the Septuagint there is an obvious connection between 'the completion of the treatment'[1] and 'the completion of time' (οὗτος δὲ ἦν καιρὸς...ὅταν ἀναπληρώσῃ μῆνας δεκαδύο). This arises from the use of the verb 'to complete'. The women must go to the king when the twelve months *are complete*, that is when the days of the 'therapy', 'treatment', are complete: six months of anointing with myrrh and six months of female aromas and cleansing creams (ἐν τοῖς ἀρώμασιν καὶ ἐν τοῖς σμήγμασιν τῶν γυναικῶν).[2] Only then may they go to the king. In the Hebrew text we read that fulfilling the twelve months was in accordance with the law of women (כדת הנשׁים). The phrase 'the law of women' is not found in the Greek text. This may, of course, be due to the difficult Hebrew. While Hebrew requires an indication of time after the words 'the end' (מקץ [היות לה]), we find first 'of the (for her reserved) time' and next, the strange expression 'in accordance with the law of women' (כדת הנשׁים) and only thereafter the specific indication of time (שׁנים עשׂר חדשׁ). The Greek text gives a complete indication of time in a correct way and writes: 'after the completion *of the twelve months*' (ὅταν ἀναπληρώσῃ μῆνας δεκαδύο), omitting the words 'in accordance with the law of women'. This omission, however, can arise from something other than grammatical ambiguity, since the Greek translator could have inserted 'in accordance with the law of women' in another place in the text. I offer the following explanation. The women were anointed with female cosmetics. The Hebrew text sees this as 'in accordance with the law of women'. But is this so? Is this beauty treatment not rather the law and desire of men? The translator could have

1. Literally, 'therapy'. In Dutch (and English) this word has other associations than in the Hebrew: 'therapy' refers to a radical healing process as in 'chemotherapy'. To translate the Hebrew word with 'therapy' would have the effect of Esther being transformed from girl/sick to beautiful woman/healthy. And it is unlikely that such a radical treatment is either meant or necessary.

2. It is no wonder that the Greek translation omits part of the Hebrew sentence here. The Septuagint reads, 'at the end [of] the twelve months'. Cf. the problem of the reference to time in the discussion of the Hebrew text (above).

realized that this law is more a law of men then of women and, therefore, omits the words here and also refrains from inserting them elswhere.

Verse 13. When they appear before the king, the women are accompanied by those who have received the order to bring them (καὶ ὧ ἐὰν εἴπη, παραδώσει αὐτὴν συνεισέρχεσθαι αὐτῷ). This element is absent from the Hebrew text.

The Greek text-critical apparatus must be closely examined here. In the Hanhart edition we read, 'and she went to the king, and to whom he [the king] spoke, will she be given to go in together with him'.[1] In Rahlfs's Septuagint edition we find the following sentence,[2] 'and that over which they spoke, she will take with her, when they come together to go with her...'. In Hanhart's edition, Esther goes with the man ('somebody') who had received the order to bring her in. In Rahlfs's edition Esther is given the freedom to take 'something' with her. The difference is important. In Hanhart's edition Esther remains passive to the last moment, submitting to what she is told she may or may not do. In Rahlfs' s text she here has, for the first time, an active role. She chooses what she brings.

These two possibilities perforce influence the translation of v. 15 where we read, literally, 'Esther refused nothing of what the eunuch commanded' (οὐδὲν ἠθέτησεν ὧν ἐνετείλατο ὁ εὐνοῦχος).[3] Esther refuses nothing; this may mean that she takes along something or someone. Both alternatives are possible: the relative pronoun gives no indication whether a 'person' or a 'thing' is involved. ὧν can refer to both persons and things. I leave the problem open.[4] A passive Esther who

---

1. See also Hanhart, *Esther*, p. 80.
2. Hanhart's Göttingen Septuagint edition of Esther contains this sentence as a variant.
3. Rahlfs adds, 'of that which the eunuch had commanded *her*'.
4. For the sake of completion I will outline the whole problem here. In the Hebrew text we read that Esther 'asked nothing unless Hegai the eunuch said so' (for the translation 'unless' see the Hebrew grammars: J.P. Lettinga, *Grammatica van het Bijbels Hebreeuws* [Leiden: Brill, 8th edn, 1976], § 80 l. and § 76 g.; and P. Joüon, *Grammaire de l'hebreu biblique* [Rome: Pontifical Biblical Institute, 3rd edn, 1965], § 172 c. and § 173 b; as well as A. Kropat, *Die Syntax des Autors der Chronik verglichen mit seinen Quellen:*

takes nothing and is herself 'taken' along fits better into the whole picture. The emphasis in this verse is on the eunuch. As Esther has listened to Mordecai, she now listens to the eunuch.[1]

Verse 14. Verse 14 briefly describes the rule of going in to the king in the evening and returning in the morning. The women merely return to the second harem. In the Hebrew text the girls move to another type of harem, to the harem of the concubines where they come under the control of another guardian. The Greek author simplifies all types of harems, all harems being controlled by Gai, and that is that (εἰς τὸν γυναικῶνα τὸν δεύτερον, οὗ Γαι ὁ εὐνοῦχος...).

Another element of the Hebrew text which the Greek omits involves the subsequent naming process. After one trial night, the girl no longer returns to the king unless he is pleased[2] with her and calls for her by name. The Greek has only the 'calling by name' (ἐὰν μὴ κληθῆ ὀνόματι), omitting the 'being pleased with her' element. It appears that the Greek author keeps to a strict description of the ritual, adding no grain of emotion.

Ein Beitrag zur historischen Syntax des Hebräischen [Giessen: Töpelmann, 1909], p. 31). In the Septuagint we read οὐδὲν ἠθέτησεν ὧν ἐνετείλατο ὁ εὐνοῦξος ὁ φύλαξ τῶν γυναικῶν, which Brenton translates, 'and Esther neglected nothing which the chamberlain...commanded' (L.C.L. Brenton, *The Septuagint Version of the Old Testament, with an English Translation* [London: Samuel Bagster, 1844; Grand Rapids: Zondervan, 1970]). The Greek verb comes from the root αθετεω, to 'consider worthless', 'attach no importance to'. The verb ἀθετέω can easily be confused with τίθημι, which we would translate 'to place'. The Vulgate struggled with these two words (αἰτέω and τίθημι) and translates, 'quae non quaesivit (αἰτέω) *muliebrem cultum,* sed quaecumque voluit Egeus eunuchus custos virginum, haec ei *ad ornatum* dedit (τίθημι, in the background of the interpretation). The italicized words are an addition to the Hebrew text and are clearly an interpretation and further addition to the Septuagint. The Latin translator tries to offer both possibilities in one sentence: Esther asks nothing—but takes a bauble, that is, places it on herself. The A-text omits this sentence.

1.   Again the question is raised: is Esther an active agent at this point? In v. 13 we can translate, 'and the one to whom *he* [the king] spoke', or 'him to whom *she* [Esther] spoke'. In the latter case, Esther would choose the one to lead her in, whereas in the former, the king (or eunuch) would do so. I shall leave this problem open, without supplying any solution.

2.   The Hebrew text uses the verb חפץ.

Verse 15. Like the Hebrew text, the Greek text repeats part of v. 12. This repetition makes it immediately clear to the reader that we have now reached the application stage. Esther's time has come, the beauty treatment is behind her.

In the Hebrew text Esther is called 'the daughter of Abihail, uncle of Mordecai'. In the Greek text we now read of Esther that she is 'the daughter of Aminadab, the brother of Mordecai's father'. The Hebrew text mentions specifically that Mordecai has adopted Esther as his daughter. The Greek text omits this further definition.[1]

We are not at all sure whether Esther takes something along with her. Verse 15 does not solve the problem of v. 13. At first glance this does not make much difference to the story. The first reaction to Esther is self-evident, 'For Esther found favour in the eyes of all who saw her'. As in the Hebrew text, Esther is the object of public (male) gaze, be it the gaze of the textual figures or the cooperative reader. Again Esther is the viewed object, not the subject, of her story. She is not asked for her opinion and does not give it.

Verse 16. Esther now goes in to the king. This is the apex of twelve months of preparation.

Verse 17. The king loves Esther who finds favour in his eyes above all the other virgins (καὶ ἠράσθη ὁ βασιλεὺς Εσθηρ, καὶ εὗρεν χάριν παρὰ πάσας τὰς παρθένους), and he places the 'diadem of women' on her head (καὶ ἐπέθηκεν αὐτῇ τὸ διάδημα τὸ γυναικεῖον; we shall come back to this point in a moment). In the Hebrew text it is said twice that the king chooses Esther above all other women. The Greek text limits this to one statement.

The Greek also alters an element of the repetitive, parallel Hebrew description 'and she has found "favour" (חן) and

---

1.   Has Mordecai raised Esther as a daughter? Or as a future wife? On this see M.V. Fox, *The Redaction of the Books of Esther: On Reading Composite Texts* (SBLMS, 40; Atlanta: Scholars Press, 1991), pp. 27-28. The passage in Esth. 2.7 is discussed in the context of the dependence of the A-text on the Hebrew text and its independence of the Septuagint. This discussion should also take 2.15 into consideration.

"compassion" (חסד), in his eyes'. The Septuagint replaces this with a new parallelism. Esther finds favour in the king's eyes as she found favour in those of the eunuch. It appears that what is good for the eunuch is good for the king.

As the eunuch has given 'gifts' to Esther, so the king gives her a diadem. But this is not the 'royal crown' (כתר מלכות) of the Hebrew text. In the Greek text the crown has become 'the diadem of women' (τὸ διάδημα τὸ γυναικεῖον). In my opinion this change is not mere caprice. Royal power is not to be compared with the power of women. The royal crown belongs to the king. The diadem of women is in another class. Just as the author of the Greek text omits the reference to the 'laws of women' earlier, here the author avoids giving women anything to do with the symbols of government or royal power.

Finally, there is one more omission in the Septuagint that is worth noting: the Hebrew text ends with the sentence, 'And he made her queen in the place of Vashti'. The Greek translator eliminates this statement.[1]

Verse 18. The king's reaction is mirrored by the response of the rest of the population. He gives a week-long feast for his friends and dignitaries. The mention of 'friends' seems somewhat strange. So far we have only heard of 'important people' with no reference to 'friends'. The Hebrew original, 'all princes and servants' (לכל־שריו ועבדיו), is rendered 'friends and dignitaries' (πᾶσιν τοῖς φίλοις αὐτοῦ καὶ ταῖς δυνάμεσιν). The question is, who are the king's friends, the princes or the servants? We will not pursue this matter further here.

At any rate, the king 'honours' Esther with a (wedding) feast (καὶ ὕψωσεν τοὺς γάμους Εσθηρ). The Greek text adds the element of 'honouring his wife Esther' to the Hebrew, while it omits the Hebrew text's reference to the king's feast being Esther's feast (ויעש המלך משתה גדול...את משתה אסתר). Honouring Esther can be seen as a sort of compensation for the omission of

---

1. In my opinion this too is not accidental. Vashti does not agree with the king's laws and refuses to obey. She has her own norms, whereas Esther adapts herself to the laws of the king and his court. Esther does not really function as a replacement for Vashti. Thus the author does not translate that Esther took Vashti's place.

the identification of the feast of the king as the feast of Esther.[1]

In addition, in the Greek text, the king clearly remits taxes. In the Hebrew text there was a mention of giving gifts *and* of remitting taxes. The gifts seem forgotten in the Greek text. Honouring Esther (with a wedding feast) must sufficiently compensate for not giving gifts.

Conclusion

The Greek translator simplifies the Hebrew text. The whole procedure is described more succinctly. Repetition of verbs, for instance, is avoided. And changes are introduced to the story line.

The translator obviously interprets the story. The link between the duration of the beauty treatment and the completion of time before going in to the king is made more obvious. Mordecai asks about what is happening to Esther. He asks about what is most essential to the story, about what helps the story move along. This fits in with the translator's simplification. A subtle link is made between king and eunuch; Mordecai becomes less central to the plot than he is in the Hebrew source text.

I consider it important to note the perspective from which the Greek translator writes. The 'cleansing' which the women must undergo is not described as 'in accordance with the law of women'. Moreover, the translator is resoundingly silent about Esther's replacement of Vashti. The change of 'royal crown' to 'diadem for women' confirms this perspective. These omissions and changes might indicate that the translator gives, as it were, a covert critique or exposure of the Hebrew text's hidden agenda.

---

1. The Septuagint does not maintain the order of events for a normal marriage (and as we shall see later, neither does the AT). Normally there is first a period of acquaintance, then—if all goes well—a long marriage feast after which the bride is led to the house of her parents-in-law and still later to her own (her husband's) house. (Cf. van der Toorn, *From her Cradle to her Grave*, pp. 59-76). However, Josephus respects the 'normal' chronological order and has Esther in the king's house only after the wedding feast. To do this Josephus does have to change the order of the Septuagint (and AT) story. Cf. Josephus, *Ant.* 11.6.2.

4. *The Second Greek Story (The A-Text)*

Esther is brought to the house of the king. Bougaios, the eunuch guardian, sees the girl (Esther), and she pleases him more than all the other women (v. 8). Esther finds favour and mercy in his eyes; he hurries to care for her; he gives her, in addition to the seven maids, her own girls. When Esther is brought to the king, she pleases him enormously (v. 9). When evening comes, she will be brought to him and will leave in the morning (v. 14). After the king has examined all the girls, Esther is judged the best. She finds favour and mercy in his eyes, and he puts the crown of the kingdom on her head (v. 17). The king marries Esther in all glory, and remits the taxes of the whole country (v. 18).

The second Greek story relates only to vv. 8, 9, 14, 17 and 18 of the MT.[1] The narrative structure is not too transparent. The alternation between general and specific in the Hebrew and Septuagint texts is no longer recognizable. In v. 8 Esther is brought to the palace. The other girls are referred to only vaguely in vv. 2 and 4. Verse 9a-c describes Esther's relationship with Bougaios. Mordecai is not mentioned at all. By the end of this verse Esther has already been brought to the king (v. 9d) and we are told that she pleases him. Only then do we take up the description again (v. 14). In v. 17 we read of the application stage to the other girls and to Esther. The end of v. 17 contains, once more, the king's reaction to Esther. This is continued in v. 18.

Schematically, then:

v. 8:	Esther is brought to the palace
	v. 9a-c: Esther and Bougaios
	v. 9d: Esther and the king
v. 14:	Ritual
	v. 17: Application
	General: to the girls (vague)
	Specific: to Esther

1.   Every comparison of the A-text with the Septuagint and the MT must take into consideration the variant verse numbering in the A-text. I have used the Hanhart edition and follow the numbers given there. Concretely this means that the comparison with v. 9 (MT) begins at v. 8b of the A-text.

v. 17d-18:   The king's reaction
                    Specific: to Esther
                    General: to the whole country.

Discussion

Verse 8. Esther is taken to the king's house. She is referred to as 'the girl'. This recalls the Septuagint, in which many girls are brought to Susa. In the second Greek text Esther is brought directly to the king's house (καὶ ἐλήφθη τὸ κοράσιον εἰς τὸν οἶκον τοῦ βασιλέως).

Bougaios, the eunuch, 'sees' her immediately (καὶ εἶδε Βουγαῖος). Bougaios sees and the reader sees with him. The reader collaborates by gazing at Esther with Bougaios. What Bougaios must do is evident: he must see, watch carefully. This is why he is the guardian, the overseer.

Verse 9. And Esther pleases him more than the other women. The same verb as in the Septuagint is used here, but she pleases him 'more than the other women' (Septuagint, 2.17: καὶ ἠράσθη ὁ βασιλεὺς Εσθηρ; AT, 2.9: ἤρεσεν αὐτῶ σφόδρα). Suddenly the other women are mentioned again. In the A-text these others are less clearly defined than in the Septuagint and Hebrew texts. In the Septuagint text, the women are taken to Susa. The A-text submits the women immediately to the eunuch's judgment. Esther found favour and mercy in his eyes (face). The reference to favour was also met in the Septuagint and Hebrew texts. The author adds 'mercy' (καὶ ἔλεον) here. These words are repeated again later in the story.

The eunuch hurries to take care of Esther. And what does she get this time? Six maids and her own girls (καὶ ἐπέδωκεν ὑπὲρ τὰ ἑπτὰ κοράσια τὰς ἄβρας αὐτῆς). In the Hebrew text Esther receives the seven best slaves and the best rooms (ואת שבע הנערות...וישנה ואת־נערותיה לטוב בית הנשים). In the Septuagint the rooms are omitted, but by way of compensation the good care of the eunuch is emphasized (καὶ ἐχρήσατο αὐτῆ καλῶς καὶ ταῖς ἄβραις αὐτῆς ἐν τῶ γυναικῶνι). The A-text retains the maids and adds—apparently as compensation for the rooms—

another set of girls (καὶ ἐπέδωκεν ὑπὲρ τὰ ἑπτὰ κοράσια, τὰς ἄβρας αὐτῆς).[1]

This should apparently suffice for a queen, for the author continues, 'And when Esther went to the king, he loved her very much'. The king loves Esther, as the eunuch loves Esther. The parallel between the eunuch and the king, which we have already met in the Septuagint, is maintained in the A-text and developed further.[2]

It is worth noting that there is no sign of a 'beauty salon' routine or the twelve months of treatment here.[3]

Verse 14. Here the author changes the order of both the Hebrew and Septuagint texts. In those texts the ritual was first described in general and then applied to Esther before she goes to the king. Then the king's reaction follows in both texts. In the A-text this chronological order is broken. The author anticipates the end of the story in v. 9, and describes the king's reaction. In this verse Esther goes in to the king, and the king already loves her. However, the author waits for v. 14 to describe (part of) the procedure: 'when the time comes, they go in the evening to the king and come back in the morning'. Esther is, as it were, delivered to the king first, before the other girls. Then we read about the procedure.

Verse 17. When the king has examined all the girls (ὡς δὲ κατεμάνθανεν ὁ βασιλεὺς πάσας τὰς παρθένους), Esther appears to outshine them all. That this is so cannot be deduced from the Septuagint. The latter is simpler: 'and he loved Esther, and she found favour more than the other girls'. Esther's magnificent appearance is highlighted in the A-text: 'dazzling Esther shines [above them all]' (ἐφάνη ἐπιφανεστάτη Εσθηρ). The application of the ritual is described from the king's point of view. He examines the girls as the eunuch has done before him. The reader presumably knows that Esther has already been with the king, but that the other girls will also have to be

1. The word for the 'extra' girls is the same word the Septuagint uses for the maids.
2. See v. 17.
3. The beauty treatment in Josephus's *Antiquities* lasts only six months.

examined. Esther, who has already enjoyed the king's favour before the other girls are seen, seems to be the best of them all. Unfair advantage, one may suspect. From the beginning it is clear that Esther will be the one chosen. This had already been suggested in the Hebrew text and the first Greek translation (Septuagint). Esther finds favour and mercy in the king's eyes. The author intentionally uses the same words that have described the eunuch's reaction. The king and the eunuch respond in the same way. They *look* at women in the same way.

Next, the king puts the crown of the kingdom on Esther's head. It is neither the diadem of women nor the royal crown, but the crown of the kingdom (καὶ ἐπέθηκε τὸ διάδημα τῆς βασιλείας ἐπὶ τὴν κεφαλὴν αὐτῆς).[1]

This verse repeats what the readers of the A-text already know: the king loves Esther. This is now said with more, and plainer words than in v. 9d. Finally, it should be mentioned that the A-text, like the Septuagint, omits the comparison of Esther with Vashti.[2]

Verse 18. The king marries Esther in all glory and remits the country's taxes.

1.   The AT author does not use the term 'royal', but 'of the kingdom'; surely this is similar to the Hebrew כתר מלכות. Here the Septuagint author uses the expression 'the diadem of women'. Elsewhere he uses the words 'of the king' or 'royal' (6.8 and 2.17). In the only parallel passage, 6.8 (on the horse's royal diadem) the Septuagint does not translate the phrase. The author of the AT uses the adjective 'royal' in 6.11 (MT and Septuagint 6.8), but refers to—as does the Septuagint—something other than the horse's royal diadem. In 2.17 the author of the AT does not follow the Septuagint's unique translation but, rather, chooses the MT, although without using the word 'royal' (as in other places). It is worth noting that the author explicitly mentions that the crown is put 'on her head'. This is also found in the Hebrew text.

It would seem, therefore, that on the one hand the AT author avoids the Septuagint reading, while on the other hand he wants to imply that the expression (τὸ διάδημα τῆς βασιλείας) has another source. Therefore, he consciously avoids using terms found elsewhere in the story, while relying on the MT.

2.   In v. 4, however, it is said that the new wife will take Vashti's place. Here the author seems again to refer to the Hebrew text.

Conclusion

The author of the A-text eliminates much of the story.[1] The author narrates that the eunuch cared well for Esther (v. 9b-c), but the whole beauty treatment is deleted. Esther does have to go to the king, but this takes place immediately (v. 9d).

Again it should be said that the king makes a choice. For this reason, an element of the story as found in the first Greek translation—the going in in the evening and returning in the morning—is taken up again. Here the author uses a different technique than that of the Hebrew and Septuagint writers. The author narrates first what happens: 'Esther goes to the king', then he offers the king's reaction: 'the king loved Esther'. Only later does he describe (part of) the preparation procedure. The author of the second Greek narrative is not interested in Esther, but in the broader outline of the story. Esther has to be introduced into the story somehow or other, and then it can continue. There is no long-spun description of her arrival at the palace and selection as queen. That is not indispensable for the story. Esther must arrive at the palace, and then she is where she should be. Esther is just a necessary tool.

As far as the figure of Esther is concerned, the author describes her as a 'sharp number', without the extensive beauty-parlour treatment. Without any of the fuss and bother of a beauty contest the king puts the crown of the kingdom on her head. Thus the A-text has no hidden agenda, as does the Hebrew text which transmits between the lines a code of behaviour for women. On the other hand the A-text does not follow the Septuagint, which criticizes this agenda. The A-text just tells a story without the double meaning of the Hebrew text or the criticism of the Septuagint. The author of the A-text

1. H.J. Cook considers part of this material (2.8a and 2.10-11) as 'irrational material', not belonging to the AT and the original pre-Masoretic text (H. J. Cook, 'The A-Text of the Greek Versions of the Book of Esther', *ZAW* 81 [1969], pp. 369-76). D.J.A. Clines agrees in general with this statement: 'The A-text presents a coherent narrative of a plot that is slimmer than the MT' (D.J.A. Clines, *The Esther Scroll: The Story of the Story* [JSOTSup, 30; Sheffield: JSOT Press, 1984], pp. 76-78). Cook and Clines view the AT as older and representing a text form that is older than the MT (and the Septuagint).

presents what is important for the story line: Esther has to become queen. That is what matters.

But is the A-text merely a story with no double meaning or criticism? The author agrees with the procedure for selecting women. The king examines *all* the women, and Esther seems to be the best. The text allows the selection procedure solely to the king (ὡς δὲ κατεμάνθανεν ὁ βασιλεὺς πάσας τὰς παρθένους). There is no double meaning in the A-text, but a straightforward agreement with the state of affairs. The Hebrew text here uses more sophisticated tactics (girls have to pass a double test: the eunuch's and the king's; the ritual is first generally introduced to the reader, next Esther is going through it). This compliance with the state of affairs could also explain why the perambulating and questioning Mordecai is absent from the A-text. The figure of Mordecai is not needed here. On the contrary, he is avoided in order to elude complications.

5. *General Conclusions*

1. The Hebrew text is written from a male perspective. It imposes a norm on women. It appears to have been written by men for men, and for women.

2. The first Greek translator (the Septuagint translator) softens this perspective and in some ways criticizes its male bias.[1]

3. The second Greek translator (the A-text translator) is not interested in criticism at all. Esther has to be introduced only because she is necessary for the story line. The A-text has no problems with the male perspective and thus confirms it. It appears to have been written by men for men.

1.   One may state that the Septuagint could have been written by a woman. But at the end of the Septuagint of the book of Esther there is a strange colophon, stating that this Greek text has been made 'by Lysimachus, *son* of Ptolemy, one of the residents of Jerusalem'. A lot has been written on this colophon, it being the only one found in the Septuagint, whereas colophons are very common elsewhere in the Greek literary world (cf. E. Bickerman, 'The Colophon of the Greek Book of Esther', *JBL* 63 [1944], pp. 339-62). A feminist could become suspicious. Why has this note been added to the Septuagint of Esther? In order to indicate and to stress that the translator was indeed a 'son'? To avoid critical questions on this topic? Further study is called for.

LOOKING AT ESTHER THROUGH THE LOOKING GLASS*

Athalya Brenner

Symmetries and repetitions are characteristic features of the book of Esther.[1] Indeed, how can it be otherwise when the underlying theme is an inversion of fate, an overturning of destinies? Such an inversion is a common enough theme in the Hebrew Bible. Let's mention in passing the stories of Joseph (Gen. 37–48, 50), Daniel (esp. chs. 2, 4–5), Ruth, King David (1 Sam. 16–2 Sam. 1), the exodus from Egypt and Hannah's poem (1 Sam. 2.1-10).[2] However, in none of these are symmetries and duplications as much in evidence as they are in all levels of Esther—in the style, semantic stock, plot and characters. I shall therefore begin by exploring the duplication and multiplication techniques in Esther; and then proceed to read Esther as a hall of mirrors with the aid of an obvious intertext, Lewis Carroll's *Alice through the Looking Glass*.[3]

Style and Language

Duplications and parallelisms abound in Esther, so much so that one wonders whether the primary style of the Scroll was not

* This article grew out of a paper presented at the SBL/AAR Annual Meeting in Washington, November 1993.
1. Cf. Susan Niditch's article in this volume.
2. There are numerous examples of the inversion-of-fate theme in the Psalms. However, these are outside the scope of this article because they do not constitute a narrative elaboration of the theme. The Hannah poem, be its origin as it may, is appended to the narrative as its summary, hence belongs to the theme discussed.
3. I used *The Annotated Alice* (with Introduction and notes by M. Gardner and the original illustrations of J. Tenniel; London: Penguin, 1970). The text and illustrations are from the Macmillan edition (London, 1865).

poetry or the so-called 'poetic prose'. However, the accumula-
tion and diversity of duplication, and its exaggeration into multiplication, are such that their attribution to poetics alone is not
adequate. Elsewhere,[1] I have classified twelve categories of
stylistic and semantic phenomena of such duplications; I am sure
that more categories of instances can be added to the classified
list. Some of the items noted are listed here, each with at least
one characteristic example to illustrate it. The examples adduced
will include noun phrases and verb phrases in order to convey
the wide range of the duplication or multiplication of linguistic
stock.

1. Hendiyadic pairs of linked noun phrases and/or verb
phrases: פרס ומדי, 'Persia and Media' (1.3); הרגו...ואבד,
'killed...and destroyed' (9.6).

2. Substitutions (unlinked but repetitive synonyms, or part-
synonyms): החכמים ידעי העתים, 'the wise [men], the knowers of
times'.[2]

3. Doubled pairs: בכי ומספד שק ואפר, 'wailing and mourning,
sackcloth and ashes' (4.3);

4. Triplets, even doubled triplets: עשר כבוד מלכותו//יקר תפארת גדולתו,
'the richness of the honour of his kingdom//the opulence of
the grandeur of his greatness' (1.4); להשמיד להרג ולאבד, 'to exterminate and kill and destroy' (3.13).[3]

5. Noun phrases with a repeated noun, meaning 'every...',
such as מדינה ומדינה, 'every town' (8.13), with or without כל
('every', 'each': בכל יום ויום, 'each day', 2.11). A chain of such
pairs appears in 9.28: בכל דור ודור משפחה ומשפחה מדינה ומדינה ועיר ועיר,
'in every generation, family, province and town', undoubtedly
signifying 'always and everywhere'.

6. Division of a synonymous pair between two cola, as usual
in poetry: איביהם//שנאיהם, 'their enemies//their adversaries' (9.16).

7. Repetition of ideas in larger phrases and/or sentences:

---

1.   A. Brenner, 'Esther in the Land of Mirrors', *Beth Miqra* 3.76 (1981),
pp. 267-78, esp. pp. 268-74 (Hebrew).
2.   That is, the 'astrologers'.
3.   A combination of a noun phrase and a verb phrase is ויכו...מכה חרב
והרג ואבדן, 'and they struck...a strike of the sword and killing and destruction' (9.5). On the repetition of the same root-sequence in two words
('struck...a strike'), cf. point 9 below.

לכל העם...למגדול ועד קטן , 'to the whole population, [that is], from the greatest to the smallest' (1.5; for a repetition of a whole sentence cf. 1.12: 'and the king was extremely angry, and his wrath burned within him').

8. Phrases of inclusio, that is, mirror images, such as 'from the greatest to the smallest' or מנער ועד זקן, 'from boy to old [man]' (3.13), signifying 'all'.

9. Repetition of root-sequences within an utterance, as a noun or verb or a combination thereof: ויפקד המלך פקידים; 'and the king appointed appointees' (2.3); or מחשבתו...אשר חשב, 'his thought... that he thought' (9.25).

10. Various combinations of these techniques, or straight-forward repetition: כאשר אבדתי אבדתי, 'and if I perish, I perish' (4.16); or repetition with a minimal change introduced: מה זה ועל מה זה, 'what is it and for what is it' (4.5).

11. Finally, verbatim repetitions of expressions obtain on both sides of the inverted plot (that is, before and after the turning point of the plot in 6.1, 'on that night' when the king suffered from insomnia).[1] R. Weiss has shown, and convincingly so, that the differences between the two parts of the Scroll are well served by the utilization of the *same* idioms and linguistic combinations for *different* effects.[2] Some scholars therefore advocate the recognition of a chiastic structure for the Esther Scroll, that is, a highly structured inversion of plot items, signified by repeated catch-phrases.[3]

To summarize the linguistic phenomena: none of these repetition devices is unique to Esther. Nonetheless their cumulative weight, quantitatively and qualitatively, is quite exceptional. It would be naive to assume, I think, that such repetition techniques do not constitute a message as well as a medium.

1. Cf. the following pairs of utterances: 3.7 and 9.24; 3.8 and 7.4; 3.10 and 8.2; 3.11 and 8.8.

2. R. Weiss, 'The Language and Style of the Esther Scroll', *Mahanayim* 104 (1966), pp. 56-63 (Hebrew).

3. For the symmetrical or chiastic structure see Y.T. Radday, 'Chiasm in Joshua, Judges and Others', *Linguistica Biblica* 3 (1973), pp. 6-13.

Plot and Figures

In an inversion story, where events turn out diametrically opposite to original intentions and apparent 'heroes' exchange places with 'anti-heroes', symmetry is a functional device. The mirrored or chiastic structure emphasizes the direction of the unfolding plot. A victimizer becomes a victim whereas the victim flourishes; the doomed people fights for its life and wins; there is a Hollywood-style happy ending. Some secondary plots—such as Vashti's feast which complements the feast given by Ahasuerus (1.1-9), the substitution of Esther for Vashti (chs. 1–2), the conspiracy (2.21-23) and Mordecai's exposure of it against Haman's later defeat and Mordecai's victory (ch. 6)—function as thematic props, another kind of mirror for the mirror structure. They reflect stages and movements in the central plot. This repetitive structure places both readers and textual characters inside a metaphorical hall of mirros. These mirrors are of various sizes and properties and, therefore, produce an assortment of images and contortions.

However, not all secondary plots in Esther contribute to the main story line. Some are less than functional in terms of dramatic movement or plot unfolding. Esther's double feast can be excused because it is divided between the two parts of the plot (5.8; 7.1), each lying on a different side of the proposed equator of inversion (6.1). But why would virgins be gathered twice to the harem (2.19), and have their preparations divided into two periods of six months each (2.12)? Why should the narrator mention twice that Mordecai asked Esther to deny her ethnic origins and she obliged (2.10, 20)? The tautologies climax in ch. 9. Why are Haman's sons killed twice, differently each time (9.7-10; 14)? For both Mordecai and Esther to send letters to the Jewish diaspora about the Purim feast (9.20-22; 29-32, with an effort in v. 29 to harmonize the two passages) is superfluous. Is the explanation about the two dates on which Purim is celebrated, according to location, convincing (9.16-19)? And more examples of seemingly unnecessary repetitions on the plot level can be easily adduced.

Scholarly explanations for repetitions of plot movements

vary.[1] Some scholars appeal to source theories: when in doubt about a biblical text, refer to its editorial or redactional pre-history. But the repetitions, both the apparently functional and the non-functional ones, are too numerous to be accounted for in this manner. Some scholars argue for a discernible utilization of folk-tales or motifs, the combination of which causes some non-functional reduplications. A morphological analysis, Proppian-style, might account for some twists and back-tracking on the plot level, but not for most or all of them.

Ultimately, no single theory explains the necessity for the doubled, even tripled infrastructure which is echoed by the style and semantics. Let us have a look once more at the cast of figures. On the primary plot level, we get three pairs: two male figures in competition; two female figures are juxtaposed;[2] a kingdom against a nation. On the secondary, complementary plot level pairs are much in evidence too.

Although the chief figures of the Scroll (apart from Ahasuerus, to whom we shall return later) are paired off, they do not represent uncomplicated contrasts of light and darkness, good and evil, moral and amoral. The symmetry principles are quite sophisticated. Mirror twins, twins of destiny, and shadow (Doppelgänger) twins or their equivalents have various roles. Although most of the figures have doubles of sorts, those and the appositions/oppositions they embody are far from simplistic. Mordecai and Haman are paired-off competitors, but neither is an 'either/or' figure: each mirrors the other's ambitions and intrigues; if the one triumphs and the other loses, this does not qualify either loser or victor as 'evil' or 'great'. Esther mirrors Vashti: she does voluntarily what Vashti has refused to do (she comes to the king unbidden, 5.1). Thus the joke, finally, is on

1.   Cf. S.B. Berg, *The Book of Esther: Motifs, Themes and Structures* (SBLDS, 44; Missoula, MT: Scholars Press, 1979); E. Bickerman, *Four Strange Books of the Bible* (New York: Schocken Books, 1976), from p. 172; D.J.A. Clines, *The Esther Scroll: The Story of the Story* (JSOTSup, 30; Sheffield: JSOT Press, 1984); C.A. Moore, *Esther* (AB, 7b; Garden City, NY: Doubleday, 1971); L.B. Paton, *Esther* (ICC; Edinburgh: T. & T. Clark, 1951).

2.   Although, to be sure, Esther and Vashti do not compete: the one is removed before the other comes on the scene. The reader, however, cannot help but compare the two. The results of this comparison are of course motivated by the beholder's gaze.

the males in the story: see what a seemingly obedient female can achieve (as against 1.19-22)? Bigtan and Teresh (2.21-23) mirror—in different ways—both Mordecai and Haman, and also the eunuchs Hegai (ch. 2)[1] and Harvona (7.9).[2] There is a play here on loyal and disloyal, ostensibly successful and truly successful. The cooperation between Mordecai and Esther is mirrored by that of Zeresh and Haman, where Zeresh is the wise[3] counsellor (5.10-14; 6.13). Once again, a 'hall of mirrors' is a suitable metaphor. Ambiguities, ambivalences and dualities are rife.

What about Ahasuerus? He has no parallel, neither a mirror-image nor a shadow—that is, unless we consider the absent God, the 'other place' of 4.14, as his counterpart. Ahasuerus is a veritable paradox. Of nearly absolute power (only the Word is above him), he is passive more than active, drinks more than rules, is easily influenced and sensual. A caricature of a king, one would think, although when he suffers from insomnia he attends to state business rather than finding solace in creature comforts (6.1). He is busy with his counsellors and his women. Ultimately, women and 'wise men' and 'eunuchs' determine the fate of kingdom, Jews and their own selves by their own moves. And this leads us directly to Lewis Carroll and his *Alice*.

Alice through the Looking Glass

Reading *Alice* as an elucidating intertext for Esther requires prior knowledge of both. I shall therefore try to summarize the tale's structure, plot and characteristics at this point.

Ostensibly a children's tale, *Alice* raises serious problems of logic and ethics. Hence, it has been deeply psychoanalysed and

---

1.   A double of Hegai is probably active too. Thus, in ch. 4, another eunuch serves as a go-between for Esther and Mordecai (vv. 5, 6, 9-10).

2.   Whose wise advice with regard to Haman is asymetrically mirrored by Memuchan's ludicrous suggestions concerning the control of wives (1.16).

3.   Wiser than her husband, in fact. This can be read as a subversive comment on the 'wise' advice of the king's 'wise men' concerning wives in 1.16-22.

extensively scrutinized for philosophical implications.[1] The book
deals with the problematics of defining 'reality', of matter and
anti-matter, of reversals and inversions, of the relationship
between image and source, of absurd and coherent, of rational
and irrational, of shadow and reflection, of life and death. In
short, the book deals with the problematics of language as it is
mirrored in the world and vice versa. It also contains parodies
(mirroring of a literary piece),[2] caricature and political satire
(mirroring of human behaviour).[3] The chosen vehicle for presenting this non-Platonic vision of multiple reflection is an eclectic
and not always consistent hall of mirrors. The inconsistencies
are held together by the framework of a chess problem. Chess
is a game with well-specified rules. These rules are sometimes
broken but, ultimately, the game goes on until it ends; that is,
until Alice becomes queen and then 'unqueens' herself by
waking up from the narrative 'dream'.

After Carroll's Alice goes through her living room's mirror in
a dream, she enters the strange world of yet more mirrors and
chess. Naturally, in chessland there are kings and queens about,
two of each gender and one of each colour (white and red).
And there are pawns. There are Tweedledee and Tweedledum,
mirrored twins. There are two knights. The White Knight, who
has a special relationship with Alice, is apparently a caricatured
(thus reflected) shadow figure of Carroll himself. The strange
mirrorland is inhabited by fabulous creatures (such as talking
flowers and insects and a unicorn) who perceive themselves as
normal and Alice as fabulous. She meets queens who are more
active than their spouses (and this conforms with the rules of
the game, of course): a nice but dumb White Queen, a more
active but much harsher Red Queen. The Red King spends his
time sleeping; he dreams of Alice. The White King walks around
with a memo book, to signify his active political function and to

1. Cf. for instance J. Pudney, *Lewis Carroll and his World* (London:
Thames & Hudson, 1976); or *The Philosopher's Alice*, an edition introduced
and annotated by P. Heath (London, 1974).
2. For instance, according to Gardner's notes, Wordsworth is parodied
on pp. 307-13.
3. Again according to Gardner, the politicians Gladstone and Disraeli
are satirized on pp. 279, 287-88.

remember by (cf. Esth. 6). Otherwise he is not distinguished by courage or anything else apart from his appetite. Naturally, the king has two messengers. Alice allies herself with the 'white' faction although the other side is not evil or 'black'.

Fights and falls are just a game. Nobody gets terribly hurt, although there is a moody atmosphere of passage and change in many places. After Alice realizes her dream and becomes queen by advancing to the other side of the (imaginary) board, the game is over. She soon wakes up in her living room. Which is 'real', which is a dream, the looking-glass world or the perceived world, remains unresolved. Ambiguities, existential and political, are not explained away.

Esther and Alice

I have claimed earlier that the duplicated and multiplicated phenomena of style and language in Esther reflect, and are reflected in, the mirrored-symmetrical alignment of plot and figures in *Alice through the Looking Glass*. I find support for this claim in the knowledge that in *Alice*, a self-declared text about mirrors and reflections, language is also put to extraordinary uses (although these are much more sophisticated and, to my taste, entertaining than the Esther ones). The intertext helps me realize that the Esther style is essential (I tread the dangerous ground of author's intent here), and cannot be waved aside simply as poetry, or the combination of sources.

We can read *Alice* as a looking glass for Esther on the plot-and-character level, although it is not necessary to look for precise correspondences between the two tales. In both the action does not always move smoothly forward. In both, time is a little blurred. In both, the king is weak and his wife stronger: this is the natural order of the game. The knights are more active than the kings; so are wise men and counsellors. The White Knight (Carroll, Mordecai) beats the Red Knight (Haman). The White Knight supports the chief female protagonist, Alice or Esther, so that she can become queen. The Red and White Queens (Vashti? Zeresh?) disappear at the end of the game/tale. All through the *Alice* game, pieces reflect themselves in their same-colour counterparts, while being mirror-imaged by their other-colour figures. The same obtains in Esther. All the pieces are active; the kings are relatively passive but remain kings. In Esther, ministers and counsellors—and women—initiate the action and promote it.

I would like to conclude by outlining a few more reflections on how *Alice* may help us further in reading Esther.

Nobody is wholly evil in mirrorland, although the reds are ultimately inferior and losers, as preordained by the symbolism of 'white'. Similarly, no one is wholly evil (Haman) or good (Mordecai) in Esther, although Mordecai is 'ours', and thus superior. A non-simplistic tale of mirrors excludes simplistic morality. Thus, an ideo-moralistic reading of Esther can be rejected in favour of a phenomenological or political reading. The winners are those whose side we are on, not necessarily saintly but our favourites. Thus read, Esther is not a morality tale. It can be read as a politico-philosophical guide to life and survival. What does it take, in a diaspora framework, to survive and succeed as a Jew? The answers given are not altogether comforting: you have to mutate into your former adversary, or nearly that.

If we recognize that almost everybody, including the Jewish figures, is satirized in Esther, we may have to give up a Jewish-chauvinistic reading of it. This would cut both ways. It would unsettle traditional Jewish celebration of the narrated events while, simultaneously, undercutting some Christian criticism of the chauvinistic sentiments allegedly expressed in the book (see Luther).

Caricatures, parodies and satires are reflections, modified imitations of originals whose properties they illuminate. These are to be expected in a mirror text. Does it not make sense to examine, for instance, how political (male) rule—both foreign and Jewish—is caricatured in the brief ch. 10 of Esther, instead of resorting to other solutions concerning the status of the chapter?

Both texts are quite funny, while also containing elements of cruelty and morbidity. In the Bible, the humour component is often and too easily overlooked. Let us stress once more that the joke in Esther is not merely on the other side, be it the side of the 'foreigners' or the 'Jews' or the 'males' or the 'females' or the 'eunuchs' or whatever; neither is it so in *Alice*.

Female authority and the actions of well positioned or titled males who are in fact subordinate and inferior by performance feed the plot in *Alice*; the same goes for Esther. Criticisms of the dominant, institutionalized system? Should we feminists rejoice? Let us remember that both texts depict mirror worlds. As in Alice's final predicament: which is real, which is a dream? The situation remains unresolved.

Should we continue to look for the historical provenance and background of Esther? Or may we rather conclude that the story is a mirror tale, its link to Purim notwithstanding? The Scroll might have been produced with Purim as its surface *raison d'être*, with a mirrored (once more), imaged never-never kingdom and king which scholarship dooms itself to look for. The celebration of Purim is not attested before Maccabean times; this is a clue often underestimated in the quest for Esther's history and historicity, while its significance for social and political issues is relatively neglected.

Finally, a didactic note. For my generation Lewis Carroll's *Alice* tales were a cultural must. Most of our students are probably acquainted with *Alice* through Walt Disney's *Alice in Wonderland*, which also incorporates a few scenes from *Alice through the Looking Glass*. Those who do know the looking-glass *Alice* better might profit from using it as an intertext. Looking at Esther through Alice, they might be able to read it for reflection, philosophy and politics instead of for ethics, hate and revenge. There is no reason why Esther should not be read as a didactic game too.

MIRROR, MIRROR IN THE TEXT:
REFLECTIONS ON READING AND REREADING

Alice Bach

Last spring I presented a workshop at a Jewish feminist
conference on the book of Esther. When I asked the
participants to imagine Esther, they offered glimpses of their
fantasy looking glasses: Esther was blond (unanimous), Esther
was petite and doll-like, Esther was tall, stately and elegant,
Esther was blue-eyed, green-eyed. Esther in their eyes seemed
to fit the Personal Columns description of a perfect woman. In
the looking glass of my workshop, Esther appeared as an
American dream. Grace Kelly perhaps. What occasioned this
odd reflection? Probably the desire for all heroines, even
ancient Persian queens, to mirror film heroines. After all, my
workshop members had gazed at the standard of beauty
projected on the big screen and internalized the Hollywood
ideal of the bad and the beautiful. Remember Hollywood's
'sword and sandal' biblical films of the fifties? Rita Hayworth
was a sanitized Salome threatened by Herodias, played by the
fearful Judith Anderson, Hedy Lamarr was a pouty Delilah and
Angela Lansbury glistened as the ill-fated Timnah wife. Gregory
Peck was an elegant King David, opposite Susan Hayward's
flirty Bathsheba. Charles Laughton played a gluttonous Herod,
a sort of Semitic Falstaff, and Victor Mature invented a Samson
who could have been born only in Brooklyn.

I have found no fifties Esther. Thus, one would have to
imagine Esther. In keeping with Israelite narrative tradition, the
book of Esther has not provided us a precise physical
description of its heroine. The reader is told only that Esther is
beautiful. While we do not know the specifics of her beauty, we
know that she must be the most beautiful young woman at

court because she is the king's choice. She does not do anything to become queen; she is chosen not because of lineage (like Michal), or wealth (like Abigail), but because of her beauty. Esther is the object of the king's gaze much as Bathsheba has been. And the women in my workshop told me what a gazed-at heroine looks like to them.

Athalya Brenner has escorted us through a glass lightly in her article 'Looking at Esther through the Looking Glass'. She has challenged us to a game, invited us to question the old rules in which biblical texts may be read solely intratextually. In the traditional game biblicists comment on the Bible and are forbidden to play outside its canon. Outsiders can't play without being subject to ridicule. Brenner insists that the Bible be fair game. What Brenner proposes is that biblical narrative be read against a Victorian exploration of linguistic logic disguised as a children's fantasy. Instead of taking up arms in the academic turf wars, Brenner has turned playful.

What does playful have to do with the discipline of biblical studies? Clearly neither of us is arguing from the traditional perceptions of biblical methodologies. Admittedly the two texts under consideration share neither linguistic, geographic, nor cultural properties. The reader may share one or two properties with the texts, but probably not all three. Because Brenner has challenged her readers to play a new game, I am standing on a different playing field, in which narratives can be compared by looking at tropes and themes, such as mirror images, body images, the power of the gaze.

What could be further from the biblical book of Esther than the *Alice* books?[1] The books bear some parallels, particularly for readers who might dream of being the heroic Queen Esther while wishing for the magical adventures of Alice. I was such an Alice, intrigued by the visual delight of seeing my name Alice Alice Alice binding me forever to the Victorian Alice Liddell. Along with the mirrored images of the two heroines, however, I also see a distorted image when I try to reconcile the genres. The book of Esther purports to be a historical narrative, one

1.   L. Carroll, *Alice's Adventures in Wonderland and through the Looking Glass* (New York: Bantam Books, 1981; originally published in 1865 and 1871 respectively).

that extol the virtues and beauty of a Jewish heroine, a once-upon-a-time story of hope and possibility. Like most didactic literature, it pleases us with certitude. There is a sturdy solution that assures us of triumph.

The two *Alice* books, on the other hand, are classic examples of the genre of fantasy, that is, they are stories controlled by violations of what is generally accepted as possible. If there is pleasure to be had from this literature of disillusion, it is that of anxiety, of uncertainty, of eyeing a problem without a solution. If Carroll's fantasy has an ancient Mediterranean literary source it would be the *menippea*, fictions that move easily between the human world and the divine realms.[1] Works such as Apuleius's *Metamorphoses*, Petronius's *Satyricon* and Lucan's *Strange Story* conflate present and past, allow dialogues with the dead, states of dream, hallucination, personal transformation, extraordinary situations. They are clearly works of dis-possibility. Bakhtin connects these *menippea* with the notion of carnival, in which

> everyone is an active participant, everyone communes in the carnival act…The carnival act is life drawn out of its usual rut, it is to a degree 'life turned inside out', 'life the wrong way round'.[2]

One of the major clues that informs the reader that our notions of reality are being challenged is the chessboard itself. Brenner has set her characters to playing the game, but she does not examine the image of the chessboard itself. Chessboards are regular, as precise as the Victorian hedgerows and topiary that enclosed Alice Liddell's waking world.

Tilting the looking glass this way and that, one finds both Esther and Alice at the center of narratives in which girls or women might be seen as subjects as well as objects of the gaze. The title of Brenner's article informs us of a ground rule: she will be controlling the gaze; she will be looking at Esther (of course Brenner sneaks the figure of Alice into the picture although she is allusory in the title). Carroll is gazing at Alice all the time. As an amateur photographer, he gazed at Alice

1. F. Jameson, 'Magical Narratives: Romance as Genre', *New Literary History* 7.1 (Autumn 1975), pp. 133-36.
2. M. Bakhtin, *Problems of Dostoevsky's Poetics* (trans. R.W. Rosel; Ann Arbor, MI: Ardis Books, 1973), p. 101.

Liddell, the object of his visual fantasy as well as his textual one. I suggest that Brenner's game involved reading the book of Esther as if it had the form of *Through the Looking Glass*, taunting the biblical author to play Carroll's game. In this response I shall try to push Brenner into an even more ludic rematch, to see how the real world described in the book of Esther compares to the fantasy world of Lewis Carroll.

Let's examine some basic differences between our heroines. When she faces the court of the Red King and Queen, Alice is faced with the end of the world as she knows it. Esther is in a more liminal period when she faces King Ahasuerus. She is facing opportunity. Alice is in a dream state, set against grotesque grinning apparently cruel monsters, caucuses, caterpillars and pigs. Esther's world is inhabited by real enemies of the Jews, Haman and his political cronies. Esther does not want to escape her story.

Alice is faced with linguistic intrigue, wordplay. Her enemies are part of her dream, as she is part of Carroll's dream. She confronts this impossibility when she sees the Red King dreaming:

> 'He's dreaming now,' said Tweedledee, 'and what do you think he's dreaming about?'
> Alice said, 'Nobody can guess that.'
> 'Why, about you!' Tweedledee exclaimed, clapping his hands triumphantly: 'And if he left off dreaming about you, where do you suppose you'd be?'
> 'Where I am now, of course,' said Alice.
> 'Not you,' Tweedledee retorted contemptuously. 'You'd be nowhere. Why, you're only a sort of thing in his dream.'[1]

Carroll's text multiplies incertitude. He unnerves the reader while he frustrates Alice. The White Queen taunts her, 'jam yesterday, jam tomorrow, but never jam today'. As Alice learns time and again a sign can mean anything.

In my game, one tries to look at both Esther and Alice, while proposing possibilities for what each of these young literary figures saw while gazing in her glass. While Esther is aware of her beauty and of being the object of the gaze and her power in directing that gaze, Alice is not. The Victorian girl is presexual,

1. Carroll, *Through the Looking Glass*, p. 222.

not being prepared as a tasty treat for the king of anywhere. Rather she has an intellectual dual with the Red Queen, an older, also asexual female, who rules with a power that does not derive from the looking glass.

Buxom and broad, the Queen's game is comprised of the fast moves and irrelevant diagonals of the most powerful chess piece on the board. Not the prettiest. But how would such a queen play in Persia? We have a clue from the older queen, Vashti, who no longer wants to be a reflection in the looking glass. In 'Persia' there is no such choice for a queen, no victory for a Victoria, whose maternal figure bears a sly resemblance to Tenniel's illustrations of the domineering Red Queen who knocks the other creatures off their squares. The contest between women in the book of Esther is a contest of conventional beauty, of who will be the prettiest of them all. The battle of wits in the Looking Glass is a battle for the power to escape the tyranny of that same glass.

Alice goes through the looking glass; she is not reflected in that glass. Alice has the power to slip past the fixed gaze of the male spectator. Esther is caught in that gaze although, like the Red Queen, she then uses whatever power the rules of the game have given her to checkmate her foe. If Alice is reflected in the book of Esther, I suggest that her congruent image might be closer to Vashti, who has gone through the looking glass and is no longer a vision to be ogled by men. While Vashti may be relieved to have become an invisible body, Alice is frightened when her body plays telescope tricks on her. After drinking from the bottle tagged Drink Me (seemingly a simple sign) she becomes excessively tall, then, after another swig, tiny enough to swim in a puddle of tears. Her body makes her a victim, not a prize like Vashti and Esther. Alice's body has no stable identity.

Clearly I find pleasure in this play, reflecting unruly texts off each other. What is immediately apparent is that I am not solving any of the traditional puzzles posed by the Guild, and nor is Brenner. I do not think this makes our endeavor less worthy, just a different puzzle. By comparing the characters of Esther and Alice, I have perceived what the Persian Jewish queen's story might look like had she been a presexual dreamy sort of girl trying to escape the strictures of an oppressive adult society. Because the reader never has a fixed picture of Alice's image—it is her voice rather than her body that remains consistent during her dream—it is more difficult to imagine her story in the world right-side-up. Alice travels outside the normative world, the one in which a beautiful girl and her uncle from a subjugated population can dazzle a king and his court with her beauty and win safety for her people. Or is that the story that challenges reality?

TRACING ESTHER'S BEGINNINGS

Timothy K. Beal

In biblical narratives, beginnings can make all the difference. Of course, there can be no decisive beginning, no 'fresh start' for biblical narratives and their readers, for readers have always already begun.[1] That is, I the reader am always already 'located' politically, socially, economically, ideologically, sexually and so on (in ways that go mostly unrecognized or at least insufficiently scrutinized) before I ever begin to locate myself in the text. And yet, while I come to the text already vested, I also, nonetheless, in-vest in the story as I begin a new relationship with it. Thus it is not inappropriate to continue asking questions that struggle with issues of determination—determinations of the reader and determinations of the text. For example, how might the beginning of the biblical narrative set the stage? How might the beginning of the story work to position, or 'recruit',[2] the reader as subject within a particular social

1. Likewise, if, as has become clear in the last few decades, every text is intertextual (an intersection of other textual surfaces, a field of transpositions, a dialogical space), then there is no point of beginning *ex nihilo* for the biblical text, and it is impossible to trace it back to a single origin. This issue will emerge again in the final section, below.

2. On the power of a biblical text to 'recruit' its reader into a particular androcentric subject position, see C.A. Newsom, 'Women and the Discourse of Patriarchal Wisdom: A Study of Proverbs 1–9', in P.L. Day (ed.), *Gender and Difference in Ancient Israel* (Minneapolis: Fortress Press, 1989), pp. 142-60. This conception of recruitment is drawn from L. Althusser's 'interpellation' (see esp. *Lenin and Philosophy* [trans. B. Brewster; London: Monthly Review, 1971]), which refers to the power of a text to position the reading subject within a particular ideological system to representation. Newsom's study and the work of M.C. Parsons ('Reading Beginnings/Beginning a Reading: Tracing Literary Theory on

and symbolic order, and what are the possibilities of resistance to such recruitment? How might it serve to frame the world of the narrative? Or, more subtly, might there be traces of this beginning remaining throughout the subsequent narrative?

This paper focuses on ch. 1 of the Masoretic Text (MT) of Esther. In addition, attention is given to two other versions of the story—the LXX and the so-called Alpha Text (AT). In all this, the main task is an ideological-critical reading of Esther's beginnings—that is, how these beginnings work to position the reading subject within a particular social and symbolic order, and how that positioning is, nonetheless (in the end), always problematic and never entirely secure.

The basic argument falls into three parts. First, I offer an exegetical analysis of the first chapter of MT Esther, exploring how this beginning of the Esther narrative supports an alignment of the reader with a non-Jewish woman (Vashti) as heroine in a gender-based conflict. In conversation with Simone de Beauvoir and Luce Irigaray, among others, I argue that as a way into the world of Esther, this conflict indicates, on the one hand, the vulnerability of its particular form of patriarchal domination,[1] and, on the other hand, the extremes to which the male subject will go in order to maintain his position over against the woman-as-object. In the process of opening the story, then, MT

Literary Openings', *Semeia* 52 [1991], pp. 11-31) on narrative beginnings in the Gospels have been highly influential on the direction of the present study.

1.   The effort to establish a universal definition for patriarchy or patriarchal domination as a hegemonic structure that is basically identical in every cultural-historical context has become increasingly problematic in recent years, along with the binarisms of male/female, subject/object and so on that such definitions require. See esp. J. Butler, *Gender Trouble: Feminism and the Subversion of Identity* (Thinking Gender; New York and London: Routledge, 1990), pp. 3-5; and C. Meyers, *Discovering Eve: Ancient Israelite Women in Context* (Oxford: Oxford University Press, 1988). Thus while I find, for example, Irigaray's discussions of Freud and the 'logical of the same' to be suggestive (see below), there will be no effort to draw a universal definition of patriarchy from an engagement between that work and Esther. In fact, Irigaray is noteworthy for her own care in avoiding such universalizing tendencies, with regard to patriarchy as well as gender.

Esther 1 opens the possibility of a critique of the very gender-coded order it is introducing.

Secondly, I explore how MT Esther's beginning might serve a reading of the rest of the narrative. This beginning may be understood to function in terms of what formalist Boris Uspensky and others call a *frame*, which situates the reader within the world of the narrative. As such, it would be peripheral to the 'main body' of the story, which is about different characters and, to some extent, a different struggle. And yet, as Derrida's writing on the preface and supplementarity suggests, the formal boundaries that would separate the 'peripheral' frame from the 'main' story are not very stable or secure. Rather, traces, or erasure marks, left by that beginning may be found throughout the subsequent narrative. When attended to, traces of the erasured characters from MT Esther 1 build a subtext of gender-based conflict into the more explicit struggle for deliverance of the Jewish people. In this sense, the Esther narrative may be understood as a sort of narratological *palimpsest* (a text written over an earlier, erasured writing).

Thirdly and finally, I compare MT Esther's beginning with the beginnings of the Esther story in the two Greek recensions (LXX and AT). While diverging from each other in important ways, these two Greeks texts are both *transgressions* of the MT beginning; in them Mordecai appears from the very beginning to be aligned with the king (as his savior), and Vashti's character is denigrated while the king's is elevated. In these alternative beginnings, the cause of Jewish deliverance is aligned with the king *against* Vashti. Thus a positive identification with Vashti as heroine is strongly resisted. Moreover, those elements that open the possibility of a critique of gender codes in the story are greatly diminished. As a result, a reading such as the one I undertake in MT Esther 1 is almost entirely refused.

Honor, Pleasure and Other Difficult Objectives

Chapter 1 of MT Esther may be broken down into the following three parts: (1) a sketch of the setting for the story in vv. 1-3a; (2) the three drinking parties in vv. 3b-9; and (3) two interchanges (Ahasuerus–Vashti and Ahasuerus–Memucan), each initiated by the king, and each concluded with the king's reaction, in vv. 10-22.

Verses 1-8 quickly sketch the setting and then describe the first two drinking parties, both of which are hosted by King Ahasuerus. The fact that drinking is the primary focus of these festivals is clear not only from the word designating them (מִשְׁתֶּה), but also from the details describing them. Other than the descriptions of the decor in v. 6, all the details given about the parties have to do with drinking: the goblets in which the drinks were given, the potency of the wine, and the kind of drinking ('without constraint') that the king wishes his guests to enjoy.

The first drinking fest lasts 180 days and includes all the king's high officials and nobility. The host's interest, explicitly related in v. 4, is to display his unequaled honor, greatness and wealth. The kingdom is so secure that all its high officials can party on at the king's open bar in Susa for over half a year! When this party is over, the king then directs his attention to the other strata of his royal dominion, namely, 'all the people who were found in the acropolis of Susa, from greatest to least' (v. 5).[1] It would be naive to assume that the king throws this party strictly out of the goodness of his heart. Rather, this works to secure the next strata of the social order.

Throughout these first eight verses, emphasis on the security and greatness of Ahasuerus's reign is excessive, pushing, it would seem, any doubts about its security to the margins.[2] There are, for example, five references to the king's rule (מלך in

---

1.   While clearly related to 'house' (בַּיִת), בִּיתָן occurs only in Esther. The Akkadian *bitânum* suggests 'palace' as the least problematic translation here (cf. 'pavilion' in C.A. Moore, *Esther* [AB, 7b; Garden City, NY: Doubleday, 1971], p. 7).

2.   As others have noted (M.V. Fox, *Character and Ideology in the Book of Esther* [Studies on Personalities of the Old Testament; Columbia, SC: University of South Carolina Press, 1991], pp. 16-17, following Ibn Ezra; and H. Striedl, 'Untersuchung zur Syntax und Stilistik des hebräischen Buches Esther', *ZAW* 55 [1937], p. 86), the description of the decor and the drinking in vv. 6-7 involves a peculiar 'one-membral' sort of sentence structure. Fox (*Character and Ideology*, p. 16) comments, 'The exclamatory listing creates a mass of images that overwhelm the sensory imagination and suggest both a sybaritic delight in opulence and an awareness of its excess'.

nominal or verbal forms); and territorial references are made repeatedly,[1] along with several other words or phrases suggesting preeminence or security ('resting securely [כשבה], v. 2; 'glorious' or 'weighty riches', 'honor', 'splendor of his greatness', 'numerous', v. 4; high numbers; and lavish descriptions of the party decor, vv. 6-7). Perhaps most significantly, the purpose of the festivals is explicitly to demonstrate the king's *honor* (v. 4). Indeed, honor, most closely associated in Esther with יקר, is a central theme throughout the entire narrative, and emerges already here as an important means for consolidating power.[2] As will soon become clear,

---

1.   The sense is that the king rests securely (בשבה) over the entire known world, 'from India to Ethiopia, 127 provinces'. See L.B. Paton, *The Book of Esther* (ICC; New York: Charles Scribner's Sons, 1908), pp. 123-24; and Fox, *Character and Ideology*, pp. 14-15; cf. Moore, *Esther*, p. 4. The translation of מדינה as 'province' rather than 'satrap', the latter being the standard governmental division in the Persian empire, is supported by the fact that there were probably less than 30 satraps. These provinces, therefore, are best understood as subdivisions of the satraps (so Fox), each of which was governed by an appointed *sar*. That this expansive description suggests something like 'the entire world' is supported by *b. Meg.* 11a.

2.   יקר, 'honor', occurs 10 times in the book of Esther (1.4, 20; 6.3, 6 [2×], 11; and 8.16)—more than anywhere else in the Hebrew Bible. The next most frequent usage is in the Aramaic material of Daniel (2.6, 37; 4.27, 33; 5.18, 20; 7.14), where it is likewise best translated in terms of honor. In another related study, 'It's a Shame about Vashti: Messing with Honor in the Book of Esther' (paper presented to the Emory University Graduate Division of Religion Department of Hebrew Studies, 4 May 1993), I have drawn from anthropological studies (esp. J. Pitt-Rivers, *The Fate of Schechem or the Politics of Sex* [Cambridge: Cambridge University Press, 1977]; J.G. Peristiany and J. Pitt-Rivers [eds.], *Honor and Grace in Anthropology* [Cambridge: Cambridge University Press, 1992]; J. Davis, *People of the Mediterranean* [London: Routledge & Kegan Paul, 1977]; and J. Schneider, 'Of Vigilance and Virgins', *Ethnology* 9 [1971], pp. 1-24), as well as from M. Foucault's analytics of power (see esp. *The History of Sexuality Volume 1: An Introduction* [trans. R. Hurley; New York: Vintage, 1978]), in order to argue that honor is a central means of consolidating power in the book of Esther—one that Esther is able to manipulate and problematize to her advantage. יקר proves to be an important element in this system, as does the phrase 'in the presence of' (see above) and 'pleasing' or 'good' (see below). In all this, it is clear, as it is in anthropological studies, that honor is closely related to social power, especially male dominance. On the integral

moreover, the king's honor is not unrelated to every man's honor, especially in relation to their status over against women.

The language of proximity in this narrative, already prevalent in vv. 1-8, deserves special notice. The phrase 'in the presence of' (the construct לִפְנֵי or something closely related) occurs nine times in ch. 1 alone, all in reference to the king. In each case, it connotes control: to be in the king's presence is to be under his control and easily manipulated. The hierarchical social order, on top of which the king 'rests securely' (v. 2), can only be maintained if other members of that order remain 'in his face'—or at least as long as they can be easily brought here. This will be especially important when it comes to Vashti.

In addition to proximity/distance—which itself implies inside/outside as well—the narrative is dominated by the discourse of pleasing/displeasing. This is developed in ch. 1, and in the chapters that follow, primarily through verbal and adjectival forms of the word טוב ('good', 'pleasing', 'to be good', 'to be pleasing'), and is especially prevalent at key junctures in the narrative action involving the king. For example, it occurs five times in the interchanges of 1.10-22, with four of those occurrences concentrated around Vashti's refusal to come and her subsequent dishonorable discharge (vv. 11, 19 [twice] and 21; see the subsequent discussion). To 'be pleasing' is to confirm, or at least appear to confirm, the order of things. For Vashti in particular, as will soon be clear, it means remaining accessible as object for the pleased male ogle.

One might well suspect that while 'from greatest to least' (v. 5) covers several classes of people within the social order, it may not include women. Indeed, that suspicion is confirmed in v. 9: 'Also, Queen Vashti threw a drinking fest [for the] women of the royal house that was King Ahasuerus's'.[1]

In the otherwise entirely male homosocial (i.e., hom[m]osocial)

---

relationship between patriarchy and socio-economic hierarchies of power more generally, see esp. Davis, *People of the Mediterranean*; and Schneider, 'Of Vigilance and Virgins'.

1.   I read this relative plus a *lamed* of possession as a qualifier on Vashti's party, indicating exactly whose property we are talking about, and anticipating further problems. Cf. *Targum Sheni*, which appears to take its cue from this same phrase (see below).

series of events described in ch. 1 (all apologies to the eunuchs),[1] Vashti's party stands out, both literally and figuratively. That is, it takes place elsewhere and is thrown by the other sex. Contrasted against the descriptions of the two previous festivals, moreover, the details given about this one are extremely scant. Yet this verse is freighted with significance. It is introduced with the particle גַם ('also'), which has the rhetorical force within the narrative of emphasizing a turn in the story while maintaining an association with the previous material. As such, it draws attention to a new acting subject. Up to this point, every active verb has had the king as its subject. He has 'displayed' his honor, 'ordered' his officials, and (twice) 'thrown' or 'done' (עשׂה) drinking fests. Now, it is Queen Vashti who is the acting subject. Moreover, she acts in precisely the same way the king has acted: she 'throws [or does] a drinking fest' (עָשְׂתָה מִשְׁתֵּה).

While these women are in the king's house (v. 9b), they are not really in his presence. Neither fully outside nor fully inside, both inside and outside, they are not fully in his control. Yet since they are not entirely outside, they cannot simply be dismissed as beyond his concern. How to exclude without losing control? This is a perennial question for any form of patriarchal domination. What might they be doing? Well, drinking, for one. What might they be talking about? *Targum Sheni* may elicit the anxiety best when it suggests that during her party Vashti brings the women into the king's most intimate quarters—his bedroom—and answers all their questions about his private life.[2]

---

1. On the dynamics of male homosocial desire in literature, see esp. E.K. Sedgwick, *Between Men: English Literature and Male Homosocial Desire* (New York: Columbia University Press, 1985).

2. Throughout the history of interpretation in MT Esther, many readers have treated this scant notice of Queen Vashti's party as one large gap in the narrative, and have gone about the business of trying to fill it. Some of these readings/fillings have shown very high regard for the queen. See, for example, *Targum Sheni*, where the queen lectures the king about her higher nobility, and scolds him for suggesting that she be degraded by displaying herself naked before a party of drunken men. Others have rendered her abominable. Rashi's commentary, for instance, cites a rabbinic tradition claiming that because she used to strip Jewish girls naked and do work with

Settling Differences

On the last day of the king's second drinking party, whether
out of insecurity or a desire to show off to the other men or
some combination thereof, the drunken king asks his seven
eunuchs to 'bring' (להביא) Vashti the queen 'into the presence of'
(לפני) the king.[1] While there may be some other more ritualistic
aspect to this bidding that is lost to us,[2] the text does give one
explicit motive: 'to show (להראות) the people and the chiefs her
beauty, for she was pleasurable to look at (טובת מראה)' (v. 11).
Just as he was displaying (בהראתו...את) his honor and unequaled
greatness in v. 4, so now he intends to display (להראות...את) his
queen's good looks. Given this close parallel, it is reasonable to
understand the king's request here as another attempt to assert
his secure control over every aspect of his reign—that is, his
secure subject position as the true patriarch and absolute center
of the entire social and symbolic order. For, as will soon become
clear, maintenance of male subjective power in the household
economy (*oikonomia*) is integrally related to the maintenance of
power in the larger order of things. In all this, Vashti is treated
exclusively as an object: she is to be brought by the eunuchs and
stared at by the king and the other men for pleasure. The fact
that seven eunuchs are sent for her on the seventh day, moreover, may suggest that this will be the impressive finale of the

---

them on the Sabbath, she was punished by being stripped naked on the
Sabbath herself (cf. *b. Meg.* 12b). This kind of misogynistic treatment of a
foreign woman who is perceived as threatening recalls biblical and extrabiblical traditions concerning Jezebel, among others. It should be noted,
however, that these same traditions often view Ahasuerus as a profaner as
well (see for example *b. Meg.* 12a; *Panim Aherim* 58; *Abba Gorion* 9; cited in
L. Ginzberg, *The Legends of the Jews* [Philadelphia: Jewish Publication
Society, 1941], IV).

1.   This more literalistic translation is intended to make the interests and
desires of the king more blatant. She is to be displayed for male entertainment, not art appreciation. Moore (*Esther*, p. 2) recognizes that the LXX and
AT list Haman here among the eunuchs, but regards this as a mere error
(since Haman has a wife and sons). By rendering it thus, Moore misses the
function this emendation serves for the LXX. See below.

2.   Fox, *Character and Ideology*, p. 20.

king's display and will conclusively confirm his secure resting place on the throne.

The queen's response, however, undermines any such desire (v. 12a). In fact, her refusal to come at the king's bidding marks the first and only point in the narrative where the royal impetus is brought low. Just when his 187-day-long demonstration of honor and power is about to come to its final climax, the party is cut short. The pleasure of an appropriate finish is frustrated. And, as is typical when male dominance and control are threatened, the queen's refusal is met with burning rage.[1]

As already pointed out, the narrative world of ch. 1 would be exclusively male, except for Vashti. That certainly is an exceptional exception. Once recognized, the utter dependence of this narrative's primary male subject on her—as well as the related dependence of the other male subjects on other women—rapidly becomes clear. Ironically, however, it is not Vashti's *presence* that makes this clear, for she is never really fully present in the narrative. Rather, it is her willful *absence*, her refusal to come, that throws a wrench into the machinery and leads to her dishonorable discharge. So long as she can be construed to be absent by exclusion, there is no problem. But eventually, the male subject requires a special object, something to bounce off in order to remind him of how solid he is, a negative image, something to reflect his own self-made image back at him ('who's the potentest of them all?'). And, as Simone de Beauvoir so aptly put it over half a century ago, in literature as in society woman inevitably 'appears as the *privileged Other*, through whom the subject fulfills himself: one of the measures of man, his counterbalance, his salvation, his adventure, his happiness'.[2] Yet there is certain irony in this situation, since it reveals the male subject's

1. The LXX and AT transpose the MT's 'wrathful' (קָצַף) to something more like 'grieved' or 'vexed' (Greek *elupēthē*). This should not influence the reading here, however, since, as will be argued later, these two Greek versions take a much more sympathetic stance toward the king (whom Mordecai saves in Addition A).

2. S. de Beauvoir, *The Second Sex* (trans. H.M. Parshley; New York: Vintage, 1989), p. 248. For an excellent study of Genesis to 2 Kings as a whole in relation to this idea, see D.M. Gunn and D.N. Fewell, *Gender, Power and Promise: The Subject of the Bible's First Story* (Nashville: Abingdon Press, 1993), especially the concluding chapters.

special and highly problematic dependence on her as fixed object. As Luce Irigaray writes, she is 'a bench mark that is ultimately more crucial than the subject, for he can sustain himself only by bouncing back off some objectiveness, some objective'.[1] From v. 10 onward, Vashti is clearly the objective, and it is equally clear from the parallel with v. 4 (להראות...את ;בהראותו...את) that her objective status is linked to his subjective status. Needless to say, then, her refusal to come and be pleasing to look at does not reflect well on him.

The second interchange follows (vv. 13-22), as the king turns to those 'wisemen' (חכמים) who are already 'in his presence'. The text emphasizes their close proximity to the king: they are 'near him' (הקרב אליו), they 'look upon the king's face' (ראי פני המלך), and they are the ones 'who sit first (הישבים ראשנה) in his kingdom'. These men are *not* marginal. They are inside and up close. They are, moreover (or better, therefore), expert advisors in law and judgment, who know what is 'appropriate' (v. 13).[2] And what precisely is appropriate? Whatever will reassert and restabilize

1.   L. Irigaray, *Speculum of the Other Woman* (trans. G.C. Gill; Ithaca, NY: Cornell University Press, 1985), p. 133. It is a mistake to conflate the writings of de Beauvoir and Irigaray, for there are highly significant differences between them. Irigaray has noted (*Je, Tu, Nous: Toward a Culture of Difference* [trans. A. Martin; New York: Routledge, 1993], pp. 9-11) that one major difference is her training in and commitment to psychoanalysis for theorizing sexual difference. Ironically, the aspect of Freudian psychoanalysis that Irigaray has the most occasion to criticize, namely the view that the sexual development of girls and boys unfolds in the same way, is largely assumed by de Beauvoir (see, for example, *Speculum of the Other Woman*, pp. 25-26; and *This Sex Which Is Not One* [trans. C. Porter with C. Burke; Ithaca, NY: Cornell University Press, 1985], pp. 34-35; and cf. de Beauvoir, *Second Sex*, pp. 267-68). Indeed, this assumption is a corner stone in Irigaray's analysis of the phallocratic 'logic of the same', by which alterity is violently reduced and objectified. Another difference between the two writers, on my reading, is Irigaray's less dismissive treatment of various forms of female subjectivity within phallocracy that de Beauvoir condemned as delusional (for example, the mystic's effort to 'transform her prison into a heaven of glory, her servitude into sovereign liberty' [de Beauvoir, *Second Sex*, p. 628]; cf., on the other hand, Irigaray on *La Mystérique* in *Speculum of the Other Woman*, pp. 191-202).

2.   The more literal sense of עתים is 'times'. Thus they 'know the times'. Perhaps Vashti's refusal is a sign of the times!

the hierarchical, patriarchal social order, with the king balanced at the top. The king asks (v. 15),

> According to the law, what ought to be done with Queen Vashti on account of her not doing what the king told her to do by way of the eunuchs?[1]

Memucan responds 'in the presence of (לפְנֵי) the king and the chiefs' (v. 16).[2] Here one finds the most obvious evidence of anxiety and vulnerability among the men in the story with regard to their own subjective status over against women. Memucan begins in v. 16 by making clear the broad ramifications of the queen's transgression.[3] He says,

> Vashti the queen has transgressed not only against the king, but also against all the chiefs, and against all the people in every one of King Ahasuerus's provinces.

Like a pebble dropped in a puddle, the queen's offense is first against the king, but moves out 'against all the chiefs' (על כל הַשׂרים), and ultimately threatens to upset the entire social order.[4] Male fixation on/of her is central.

Memucan then goes on in vv. 17-18 to describe what could happen when news of the queen's transgression gets out 'to all

1. Literally, 'by the hand of the eunuchs' (cf. v. 12).
2. Reading the *qere* to agree with v. 14.
3. Many interpreters have commented on the ridiculous panic expressed in Memucan's speech (for example, Fox, *Character and Ideology*, pp. 21-22; Moore, *Esther*, p. 14; and Y.T. Radday, 'Esther with Humour', in *idem* and A. Brenner [eds.], *On Humour and the Comic in the Hebrew Bible* [JSOTSup, 92; Bible and Literature Series, 23; Sheffield: Almond Press, 1990], pp. 297-98). Without dismissing it, I wish to read the humor in all serious-ness. Ahasuerus may be ridiculous, but so was Ronald Reagan, and look what harm he and his חכמים, 'wise men', caused (in Washington, Hollywood and the 'Third World')! It should be noted, moreover, that any ridiculousness attributed to the characters of the king and his officials only alienates the reader from them even more. Thus the reader's positive identification with Vashti is further encouraged.
4. The phrase 'all the people' in Memucan's speech is, referentially speaking, at least *double*. First, given the use of 'all the people' in v. 5, one may understand it to be signifying all the *male* people in every province. Secondly, in the plural, it may be understood in relation to 'all the provinces' as signifying all the 'peoples' under the king's dominion (cf. v. 22).

the women' (על כל הנשׁים; note the parallel with 'all the chiefs', from v. 16). In reality, however, he appears more concerned with his own particular social location, for the scene quickly moves to the insurrectional words and actions of the 'women of the chiefs of Persia-Media' (v. 18).

> For word of the queen will go out among all women, and they will despise their lords[1] with their eyes, saying[2] 'King Ahasuerus said to bring Vashti the queen into his presence, and she did not come'. On that day the women of the chiefs of Persia-media will talk to the chiefs of the king concerning the word that they heard about the queen, and there will be plenty[3] of contempt and wrath.

It is a Persian lord's nightmare. In Memucan's depiction of the avalanche Queen Vashti may have started, he describes two instances in which there will be contempt (להבזות בעליהן and וכדי בזיון וקצף),[4] and two instances in which the women will 'talk' (אמר). The sequence is contempt–talk–talk–contempt. At the heart of this sequence one finds two male nightmare-fantasies of women speaking. Thus far in the narrative, no one but the king and Memucan have spoken (אמר; vv. 10, 13 and 16). Women have had no voice—not even Vashti. Ironically, it is at the center of Memucan's speech, which is intended to reassert the proper deferential position of women, that male anxiety about their power to speak finds a way into the discourse.[5]

---

1.   The more literal translation 'their lords', rather than 'their husbands', maintains a sense more hospitable to my reading.
2.   Given its context (concerning what the women will say), the masculine plural form of the verb (באמרם) must be read impersonally (i.e., 'they will say' or 'it will be said').
3.   One might also read 'there *is* [already] enough'. Given that this phrase appears at the conclusion of a hypothetical description of what may happen, the future sense is more likely.
4.   It is noted that קצף ('to be wroth') was used in v. 12 to describe the king's reaction to the queen's refusal. Given this connection, and its indefinite subject here, it may read as a reference to the wrath of the chiefs in reaction to the insurrectional behavior of their women. Thus, just as the king was wroth at his woman's transgression, so will the chiefs be wroth at the behavior of their women.
5.   Irigaray writes (*Speculum of the Other Woman*, p. 135), 'But what if the "object" started to speak? Which also means beginning to "see", etc. What

Memucan concludes, in vv. 19-20, with a recommendation. He proposes that the word that will get out concerning the queen's transgression (יצא דבר המלכה) be closely followed by a 'royal [written] word' that 'will go out from his [the king's] presence' (יצא דבר מלכות מלפניו). Thus the spoken word that could undo the androcentric social and symbolic order must be followed by a written word that would wipe out the threat and, quite literally, reinscribe that order.

The content of the recommended royal word actually falls into two parts. First, Vashti (no longer referred to as 'Vashti *the queen*') shall never again 'come into the king's presence' (לפני המלך),[1] and her status shall be given to another who is 'more pleasing than her' (הטובה ממנה; cf. 2.2-4). She has become, quite literally, *abject*: that which can be neither subject nor object within the social and symbolic order, and therefore must be pushed outside its boundaries.[2] Up to the point of her refusal, her place was ambivalent. As already observed, she was neither totally inside nor totally outside (i.e., her party took place elsewhere, but nonetheless in the palace 'that was King Ahasuerus's'). She was, furthermore, throwing a party just as the king was, and the narrative uses identical language to describe the actions of both subjects (עשתה משתה/עשה; vv. 3, 5 and 9). She was more than—or rather, *other than*—an object. Within the world of the narrative, then, the king's demand that she be brought into his presence and be the good-looking object of the male ogle was an attempt to settle and reduce that ambivalence and excess once and for all—to pin things down, and thereby to secure the

disaggregation of the subject would that entail?' To be sure, in this passage in Esther, the 'talk' is a projection by the self-same male subject, a 'secula(riza)tion' as Irigaray would call it, but not an altogether comforting or 'pleasant' one. Rather, it is a projection of the male subject on trial, on the verge of instability.

1. This is certainly ironic, since Vashti had refused to come (לבוא) into his presence in the first place (v. 12).

2. This definition is drawn from J. Kristeva, *Powers of Horror: An Essay on Abjection* (trans. L. Roudiez; New York: Columbia University Press, 1982). For a more thorough discussion and critique of Kristeva's essay on abjection as it relates to the Hebrew Bible, see T.K. Beal, 'The System and the Speaking Subject in the Hebrew Bible: Reading for Divine Abjection', *Biblical Interpretation* (1994), forthcoming.

king's own subjective status over against her. Refusing to come and be looked at, thereby rejecting the status of fixed object (perhaps finding it objectionable, as *Targum Sheni* suggests), and being refused the status of full subject, she must be banished, abjected.[1] Oblivion will be her 'place'.

In the second part of his recommendation, Memucan describes what will happen when news of this decree concerning Vashti is disseminated (v. 20). Put simply, the disastrous scenario imagined in vv. 17-18 will be reversed. Women will once again 'give rightful honor to their lords'—the same honor (יקר) that the king has been eager to display since the beginning of the story (v. 4).[2]

As with the interchange between the king and Vashti (vv. 10-12), this second interchange concludes in vv. 21-22 with the king's reaction: his 'pleasure' returns (וייטב). Royal dispatches are sent throughout the kingdom. The proper order of things—a proper grammar, so to speak, with all its subjects and objects straight—is reinscribed on every territory. Boundaries are re-established. And the message is the same, no matter what language or what script is used to communicate it: every man will 'act as chief' (שׂרר) in his household, 'from greatest to least'. As above, so below.

Thus Vashti has been erased, ironically, with an edict. (There is indeed a kind of writing that erases.) After helping to erase Vashti, Memucan also disappears. Others will fill the blank spaces they leave. Yet, as with an ancient palimpsest, might there still be traces of the former in the latter? Might there remain erasure marks that will be 'read' into the subsequent story about their replacements?

1.   It is intriguing in this regard that some rabbinic traditions understood her refusal to be due to the fact that 'leprosy had broken out on her' (noted in Rashi's commentary on 1.12).

2.   This is rendered in a way that agrees with v. 4 (p. 91 n. 2). It also emphasizes the issue of social status. Vashti hampered the king's display of his honor and greatness. This has threatened the entire patriarchal social fabric (see discussion, below). Action must be taken so that women once again will give יקר to their lords.

Frame Work

Formally speaking, the beginning of a narrative such as MT Esther 1 may be understood as one side of what Boris Uspensky and others have called the narrative 'frame'.[1] This would suggest that it establishes a boundary separating the 'real' world outside from the world of the narrative inside, and marks the movement of the reader into that alternative world, replete with its own ideological order and its own codes for 'proper' behavior. Uspensky writes,

> In a work of art...there is presented to us a special world, with its own space and time, its own ideological system, and its own standards of behavior. In relation to that world, we assume (at least in our first perceptions of it) the position of an alien specta-tor, which is necessarily external. Gradually, we enter into it, becoming more familiar with its standards, accustoming our-selves to it, until we begin to perceive this world as if from within, rather than from without. We, as readers or observers, now assume a point of view internal to the particular work.[2]

In this sense, the frame of the narrative would work to frame the reader as well, who is persuaded, enticed, or otherwise compelled to enter this *other* self-enclosed world.

This model for narrative analysis is compelling, not least of all because it is useful for ideological criticism. That is, it allows one to conceive of a narrative in terms of its function as an ideologi-cal 'strategy of containment',[3] or system of representation, for its readers. Yet there are certain structuring principles in this model that are problematic. First, on the level of the text, it is presumed that the 'world' of the narrative is closed off, self-contained and internally coherent. This is most evident in the external/internal binary opposition, which allows the formalist critic to see a clear move by the reader from without to within, so that the reader does not bring along anything that might

1.   See B. Uspensky, *The Poetics of Composition: The Structure of the Artistic Text and Typology of a Compositional Form* (trans. Z. Savarin and S. Wittig; Berkeley: University of California Press, 1973), pp. 137-67.

2.   Uspensky, *Poetics of Composition*, p. 137.

3.   The phrase is from F. Jameson, *The Political Unconscious: Narrative as a Socially Symbolic Act* (Ithaca, NY: Cornell University Press, 1981), pp. 52-53.

complicate the closure and coherence of the internal world and its ideology.[1]

Secondly, in addition to the external/internal opposition, there is the opposition of periphery/center. The frame, which serves as a transition between the external and the internal worlds, is not part of the story proper. It belongs, rather, on 'the periphery of the artistic text'.[2] In this sense, the frame is not part of the 'real' story, just as the picture frame is not part of the actual picture. This second oppositional structure, of course, makes the first one (external/internal) more plausible, because it allows for some liminal point as the reader moves inside. In other words, it protects the sanctity of what Uspensky calls the 'borders of representation'[3] between the two distinct worlds.

Such programmatic oppositions establish sharp formal boundaries, without which the edges of frames and main bodies become rather blurred. Jacques Derrida's first essay in *Dissemination*, which focuses mostly on Hegel's use and understanding of the preface, is particularly suggestive in this regard.[4] There he writes,

> Prefaces, along with forewords, introductions, preludes, preliminaries, preambles, prologues, and prolegomena, have always been written, it seems, in view of their own self-effacement. Upon reaching the end of the *pre-*..., the route which has been covered must cancel itself out.[5]

In this way, such beginnings, like the narrative frame, remain peripheral to and distinct from the self-enclosed 'real' world of the writing—whether that 'real' world is a totalizing philosophy

---

1.   Uspensky uses the external/internal opposition on other levels in his model as well. Point of view, for example, can be either external or internal. Usually, according to Uspensky (*Poetics of Composition*, p. 165), the point of view for the frame is external, since the world of the narrative has not been fully entered at that point.

2.   Uspensky, *Poetics of Composition*, p. 165.

3.   Uspensky, *Poetics of Composition*, p. 165.

4.   For an excellent survey of the influences of Derrida and Uspensky, among others, on various trends in biblical studies, see the excellent study in Parsons, 'Reading Beginnings', pp. 11-31.

5.   J. Derrida, *Dissemination* (trans. B. Johnson; Chicago: University of Chicago Press, 1981), p. 8.

of history such as Hegel's,[1] or a story about a struggle to deliver the Jews of Persia from an anti-Jewish pogrom. They cancel themselves out before things 'really' get started.

And yet, that 'peripheral' beginning can never be entirely removed by the time the 'main body' of the narrative begins. A remainder (*restance*) always traces itself into the rest of the writing. As Derrida puts it, 'this subtraction leaves a mark of erasure, a remainder which is added to the subsequent text and which cannot be completely summed up within it'.[2] The clear boundary between the periphery and the center—the 'opposition between pre-text and text'[3]—is therefore blurred, even displaced.

As the reader moves out of ch. 1 and into the narrative proper, the beginning *'leaves the mark of erasure'*. This is an especially intriguing metaphor for a story like Esther, which is about erasing people and writing laws.

It is quite common in studies of Esther to bracket off ch. 1 from having a significant role in the subsequent story. In fact, the structural approach that understands Esther in terms of a system or pattern of plot reversals has no significant place for ch. 1.[4] Indeed, given that most of its characters disappear by ch. 2, it seems natural to understand this chapter as peripheral, even superficial in relation to the conflict driving the 'main' plot line and establishing its 'basic' structure. That is, the first chapter draws the reader into the story world, introduces the king and his ingratiatingly festive persuasions, makes a space in the royal court for Esther, and then erases most of itself before the 'real' story begins.[5]

---

1. The primary writings Derrida reads in this essay are the series of 'prefaces against the necessity of a preface' in Hegel's *Phenomenology of Spirit*.

2. *Dissemination*, p. 9.

3. *Dissemination*, p. 41.

4. On reading Esther in terms of plot reversal patterns, see esp. S.B. Berg, *The Book of Esther: Themes, Motifs, Structure* (SBLDS, 44; Missoula, MT: Scholars Press, 1979), pp. 103-13; and Fox, *Character and Ideology*, pp. 158-63. The discussion is expanded in terms of multiple ironies by S. Goldman, 'Narrative and Ethical Ironies in Esther', *JSOT* 47 (1991), pp. 15-31.

5. It would actually be truer to Uspensky's conception of the narrative

But erasure marks remain on the surfaces that cannot necessarily be perceived in terms of deep structure. One may find
traces of Vashti in the one who replaces her. Most obviously,
Esther is the queen and Vashti was the queen. And although
Vashti was banished to oblivion, the king does not forget her.
Indeed, it is actually the memory of Vashti and not lack of a
queen that motivates the pageant-search for a replacement (2.1-
2; cf. 2.17).[1]

The actions of both Vashti and Esther, moreover, are often
described in ways that play on the king's actions. As noted
already, Vashti is the first acting subject in the narrative other
than the king, and she throws a drinking party just as he did.
Similarly, in 4.16-17 Esther commands Mordecai in rather royal
fashion, and Mordecai 'did everything that she commanded
him' (ויעש ככל אשר צותה עליו). In 8.2, furthermore, Esther 'placed'
(ותשם) Mordecai 'over (על) the house of Haman', just as the king
had 'placed' (וישם) Haman's seat 'over (מעל) all the chiefs' in 3.1.
She is even given the royal seal. Thus they possess similar characteristics as royal acting subjects. And of course, their status as
privileged objects is also similar. Both Vashti and Esther are
described (at least for a time) as 'pleasing to look at' (טובת מראה)
'in the presence of' (לפני) the king (see, for example, 1.11; 2.2, 3,
9). The fact that they are similar both as subjects and objects,
moreover, suggests a third kinship: the ambivalence and excess
of their place in the order of things. That is, they are not red-
ucible to one or the other side of binary ordering principles such
as subject/object, I/Other, inside/outside, honor/deference,
which found the patriarchal economy. As a result, they expose
the limits and the uncertainty inherent in those binarisms,
suggesting that they are neither natural nor ontological, but

frame to include the first phrase of Esth. 2.1 as well ('After these things...').
In fact, this phrase might be read along with 'It was in the days...in those
days...' (1.1) as a sort of framing of the beginning, or a framing of the
frame.

1. Kristeva's words about abjection generally are suggestive in this
regard: Vashti is 'the *land of oblivion* that is constantly remembered. Once
upon blotted-out time, the abject must have been a magnetized pole of
covetousness' (*The Powers of Horror*, p. 8).

rather are quite problematically *produced* by androcentric political operations.[1]

Of course, Vashti and Esther go about their existence under and within the limits of that patriarchy in very different ways, due partly to choice and partly to compulsion. Whereas Vashti, at least by the time she is brought to the reader's attention, refuses to come before (לפני) the king (1.12), Esther often presents herself before (לפני) him; and each time she makes requests on behalf of her people and against her enemy Haman (see esp. 8.3-8; 9.13; 9.25). In the Vashti–Memucan–Ahasuerus triangle, Memucan was the only one making suggestions introduced by 'if it pleases the king...' (1.19; cf. 1.21). In the Esther–Haman–Ahasuerus triangle, both Esther and Haman make such requests (3.9; 5.4, 8; 7.3; 8.5-8; 9.13) in a life or death game of hiding and revealing.

Vashti refused the status of fixed object, whether intentionally or accidentally. Esther takes the place that had been envisioned for Vashti.[2] In fact, she appears to be put there—that is where she finds her start in this fictive world. In the long run, however, she is able to exploit her position and its inherent ambivalence (not fully fixed, not entirely without subjective power, not altogether 'in his presence') in order to lead the male subjects away, somewhere other than where they thought they were (that is, on the verge of a Jewish pogrom).

Esther plays the game Vashti refused. Esther fills the space from which Vashti was erased—but not entirely. Vashti is the

1. For a trenchant analysis of one of the most unproblematized examples of biblical (divine) discourse objectifying women into currency for male power plays and fantasies, see T. Linafelt's study of 2 Sam. 12, 'Taking Women in Samuel: Readers/Responses/Responsibility', in D.N. Fewell (ed.), *Reading between Texts: Intertextuality and the Hebrew Bible* (Louisville, KY: Westminster Press/John Knox, 1992), pp. 99-113.

2. Her place is, to borrow from Irigaray, 'rigorously postulated by the pursuit of a certain game for which she will always find herself signed up without having begun to play' (*Speculum of the Other Woman*, p. 22). H. Cixous writes, 'The prisons precede me. When I have escaped them, I discover them: when they have cracked and split open beneath my feet...This is a thought, that we Jewomen have all the time, the thought of good and bad luck, of chance, immigration, and exile' ('We Who Are Free, Are We Free?', *Critical Inquiry* 19 [1993], pp. 203, 204).

supplement that Esther requires. Her erasure marks on Esther's character re-member the extremes to which this ridiculous patriarchy will go in order to maintain itself, and the extremes to which women must go to resist it. Vashti refused to come. Esther hides, but she learns to hide even while coming into the king's presence. אסתר: 'I will hide'. The Talmud (*b. Ḥul.* 139b; cf. *Meg.* 71) saw in her name a dialogical relation with Deut. 31.18, where God declares, 'I will surely hide (הסתר אסתיר) my face from them'.[1] Yet the name is telling with regard to Esther's own (non)place as well. Esther is, from the start, in plain view of the king and the other Persians, but not entirely. There are necessary supplements to her subjectivity that are, so to speak, closeted, as Eve Kosofsky Sedgwick suggests in her reading of Racine's *Esther*.[2] And her strategic coming-out party in chs. 7–9 proves to be a real doozy (7.6-8).

Memucan, too, traces himself into Haman, another advisor to the king who seeks ill for our protagonists. Here the relationship is closer than that between Vashti and Esther. So common are their characters that *Targum Rishon* introduces Memucan as 'Memukhan, who is Haman, grandson of Agag the evil one' (1.16; see also *b. Meg.* 12b and *Midr. Esther Rabbah*). Still, they diverge ultimately. Memucan finishes his part in the story by pleasing the king (1.21); Haman, by contrast, is terror-stricken before (מלפני) both Esther and a very displeased king (7.6-8). His end is a shameful death. Whereas a word went out from the

---

1.   I am grateful to Professor D.R. Blumenthal and his paper, 'Where God Is Not: The Book of Esther and Song of Songs', for the Talmud references.

2.   See E.K. Sedgwick, *Epistemology of the Closet* (Berkeley: University of California Press, 1990), pp. 78-82. Sedgwick is correct to distinguish the dynamics of the 'closet' and 'coming out' in Racine's *Esther* from those of people who are gay or lesbian in contemporary culture. The same holds true in any analogy with or metaphor-borrowing for the biblical story. And yet, on the other hand, her reading tends to mitigate the *risk* involved in hiding and coming out for a Jewish woman in the book of Esther. The fact that Esther was advised to hide her familial and ethnic identity, and the fact that a high-ranking official in Ahasuerus's court hates Jews and is supported in his instigation of genocide, both indicate a strongly anti-Jewish context. And one need only remember Vashti to recognize the risks involved in refusing objectification by the preeminent male subject.

presence of the king to write off Vashti's offense at the end of ch. 1 (see above), in 7.8 'the word went out of the king's mouth' (הדבר יצא מפי המלך) and covered 'Haman's face' (פני המן). Thus, in the game of pleasing the king in his presence, Memucan defeats Vashti, while Esther defeats Haman.

In ch. 1 of MT Esther I have read Vashti as a (non-Jewish) heroine in a gender-based conflict within a very vulnerable patriarchal order. In the subsequent narrative, it is difficult to imagine a reader identifying with Haman or the king over against Esther. Thus, insofar as there may be traces of Vashti in Esther, and traces of Memucan in Haman, there are traces of that gender-based conflict and the problematics of gender politics it entails in the Esther–Haman–Ahasuerus dynamic, as well as in the more obvious struggle of the Jewish people against its murderous, anti-Jewish enemies. Erasure marks remain.

Transpositions

What about the other recensions of the story of Esther (LXX and AT)? How might one read their beginnings? And how might one read the intertextual relations between these beginnings and the beginning of MT Esther?

Julia Kristeva describes intertextuality in terms of *transposition*.[1] 'Every signifying practice,' she writes, 'is a field of

1.   In fact, Kristeva was the first to use the term 'intertextuality', which she developed in relation to Bakhtin's notion of *dialogism* (*Desire in Language: A Semiotic Approach to Literature and Art* [trans. T. Gora, A. Jardine and L. Roudiez; New York: Columbia University Press, 1980], pp. 64-91; repr. from *Semeiotike: Recherches pour une sémanalyse* [Paris: Seuil, 1969]). Later, in her 1974 thesis *Revolution and Poetic Language* (trans. M. Waller; New York: Columbia University Press, 1984), intertextuality comes to play a major role in her understanding of the revolutionary character of poetic language. Primarily by means of transposition, poetic language produces a new symbolic order that transgresses the symbolic order of the discourse it transposes. While acknowledging this potential, I am arguing that transposition in the LXX and the AT has accomplished just the reverse, by undermining the likelihood of a woman-identified reading of the story of Esther. For a fuller discussion of how I understand Kristeva's theory of intertextuality in relation to ideological criticism and biblical studies, see T.K. Beal, 'Ideology and Intertextuality: Surplus of Meaning and Controlling the

transpositions of various signifying systems (an inter-textuality)'.[1] Such relationships of intertextuality are not neces-sarily (or rather, are necessarily not) friendly. The 'passage from one signifying system to another' results in the production of a new text that *transgresses* the symbolic order of the former.

As it has become clear in the past two decades, the AT is genealogically related more closely to the MT version than to the LXX.[2] Therefore one might assume that the AT and MT versions of Esther would line up over against the LXX. However, the additions (A–F) were added to both Greek versions at a much later time; and the texts of both recensions have been reworked

Means of Production', in D.N. Fewell (ed.), *Reading Between Texts: Intertextuality and the Hebrew Bible* (Louisville, KY: Westminster Press/John Knox, 1992), pp. 27-39.

1.   Kristeva, *Revolution in Poetic Language*, p. 60.

2.   Less than a century ago, the dominant scholarly view was that the AT was the Lucianic recension of the LXX (most fully developed on text-critical grounds by Paton [1908]). Major differences between the two ver-sions were explained as being a result of the poor copy Lucian was using for his source. Since C.C. Torrey's 1944 essay ('The Older Book of Esther', repr. in C.A. Moore [ed.], *Studies in the Book of Esther* [New York: Ktav, 1982], pp. 1-40), however, most have agreed that the AT derives from a Semitic *Vorlage* quite distinct from that of the LXX (see also C.A. Moore, 'A Greek Witness to a Different Hebrew Text of Esther', repr. in *idem* [ed.], *Studies*). More recently, D.J.A. Clines (*The Esther Scroll: The Story of the Story* [JSOTSup, 30; Sheffield: JSOT Press, 1984]) and M.V. Fox (*The Redaction of the Books of Esther: On Reading Composite Texts* [SBLMS, 40; Atlanta: Scholars Press, 1991]) have offered very well-developed arguments that nuance Torrey's early claims significantly. Both of these redaction critics argue that there was an original AT to which material from the LXX was added, as well as additions A–F (see Fox, *The Redaction of the Books of Esther*, p. 16). More importantly, they provide a wealth of data indicating that, while the LXX is basically a translation of MT Esther, the AT derives from a different *Vorlage*. This 'proto-AT', as both scholars call it, is on a par with MT Esther, both of which derive from a Hebrew 'proto-Esther' (Fox, *The Redaction of the Books of Esther*, p. 9; Clines, *Esther Scroll*, p. 140; cf. K.H. Wynn, 'The Sociohistorical Contexts of the Recensions of Esther' (PhD dissertation, Southern Baptist Theological Seminary, 1990). All agree that the additions were added to both the LXX and the AT at a much later date (see also C.A. Moore, 'On the Origins of the LXX Additions to the Book of Esther', repr. in *idem* [ed.], *Studies*; and *idem, Daniel, Esther and Jeremiah: The Additions* [AB; Garden City, NY: Doubleday, 1977]).

significantly in order to accommodate those additions. This is of utmost importance, for addition A (about Mordecai's dream and his warning the king about the eunuchs' planned assassination) changes the beginning of the story significantly. Intertextually speaking, the final-form beginnings of LXX Esther and AT Esther *transpose and transgress* the beginning of MT Esther.

In both Greek recensions, the story of Esther begins in Addition A with a Jewish male hero, Mordecai. Following his apocalyptic dream of Jewish deliverance, both recensions go on to relate how Mordecai overheard two eunuchs plotting to 'lay hands' on the king (AT adds 'to put him to death'). Mordecai then reports this plot to the king. The king, acting independently and assertively, without advice from any 'wisemen', interrogates and executes the eunuchs. He then has Mordecai's good deed recorded in the official annals, and gives him an official post as a palace guard (the LXX adds that Mordecai wrote it all down for himself as well).[1] Thus, in this version of the story the male hero is, from the start, on the side of the king, and judging from his actions in this first episode, the king may not be so insecure, drunk or impressionable as a reader of the MT might expect.

At the end of Addition A, moreover, one learns that Haman had been a compatriot of the two insurrectional eunuchs, and that he wishes harm for Mordecai. (In the AT, he is given over to Mordecai as a servant.) Thus, as one moves into the story about Vashti's rebellion, the Jewish hero Mordecai is aligned with the king over against Haman.

Still, is it not possible that Mordecai and Vashti could both be regarded as protagonists in what follows? Is this necessarily a displacement of Vashti as heroine? Indeed it is. For it would be logistically impossible to keep Vashti, who is subversive against the king, aligned with Mordecai, who has saved the king from another subversion. Where, then, will Vashti stand in relation to

---

1. The AT adds that he was to 'keep watch conspicuously on every door' (*pasan thuran epiphanos tērein*). It also adds that the interpretation of the dream became clear to him (*epikrisis diasaphēthēsetai autou*) when he heard the eunuch's plotting, thus linking Jewish deliverance even more closely to an alliance with the king.

these other characters? More with Haman and the eunuchs than with anyone else.

Not surprisingly, therefore, the king's portrayal is nuanced more positively in the Greek versions of Vashti's rebellion.[1] In the AT, for example, his festivals are in celebration of his deliverance (*sotēria*) as well as his greatness. In the LXX, he summons Vashti not only to display her beauty but also to 'make her queen' (*basileuein autēn*) and to 'crown her' (*peritheinai autē*; v. 11). In both versions, when she refuses to come, he is 'grieved' or 'vexed' (*elupēthē*) as well as angered. The AT includes nothing like vv. 17-18 of the MT, where the high chiefs express their panic concerning what might happen as a result of Vashti's rebellion (i.e., how women will talk and rebel). By doing so the AT further diminishes the theme of gender politics.

As Kristeva writes, transposition always involves 'the destruction of the old [subject] position and the formation of a new one'.[2] I have read MT Esther 1 as a text that positions the reader on the woman's side within a patriarchal social order, and that, in the process, insinuates the limits and rupture-points in the order of patriarchal domination it is introducing. Furthermore, I have suggested that there are traces, or erasure marks, of Vashti and Memucan in the characters who fill their blanks. Insofar as there are traces of these two erasured characters in Esther and Haman, one may also find traces of a gender-based conflict and (to borrow Judith Butler's title) the 'gender trouble' it entails (ch. 1) throughout the subsequent race-driven conflict about Jewish deliverance (chs. 2–29). The *transposition* of this story by the LXX and the AT virtually destroys the possibility of such a reading. One might say that my reading of the MT text is erased in the process of its transposition. Thus Vashti takes it on the chin both within the world of the MT narrative (that is, by Memucan and Ahasuerus) and within the story (that is, its literary history).

1. And note that Haman is not the one who recommends Vashti's removal in either the LXX or the AT.
2. Kristeva, *Revolution in Poetic Language*, p. 59.

ESTHER: THE INCOMPLETE EMANCIPATION OF A QUEEN

Bea Wyler

The book of Esther is among the best known texts of the
Hebrew Bible, particularly within the Jewish community. It is an
eminently Jewish book, perhaps even the most Jewish book of
all. It is a book about Jews for Jews, as reflected in many commentaries. Robert Gordis writes in the introduction to his new
translation,

> The Book of Esther is one of the Five Megillot, or Scrolls, in the
> Bible and, by all odds, the best known and most popular, so that
> it is frequently referred to as 'The Megillah' par excellence...The
> theme of the book is the first extensive plot in history to annihi-
> late the Jewish people by wholesale massacre...Haman's plan
> failed...[1]

Elias Bickerman hints to a hidden God acting in the background
when he opens his analysis of Esther with the words,

> The Scroll of Esther narrates how the plan to slay all the Jews in
> the Persian Empire was thwarted by a providential interposition,
> how the Jews in self defense annihilated their enemies, and how a
> feast of deliverance was instituted. This feast, Purim, is still cele-
> brated by the Jews.[2]

Jack M. Sasson, too, understands Esther to be a book about a
nation's successful attempt to liberate itself from the threat of
extermination, when he writes,

---

1.   R. Gordis, *Megillat Esther with Introduction, New Translation and
Commentary* (New York: The Rabbinical Assembly, 1974), p. 1 (all texts are
quoted from this translation).
2.   E. Bickerman, *Four Strange Books of the Bible* (New York: Schocken
Books, 1967), p. 171.

The Book of Esther tells Jews that their national liberation festival originates in an historical event. It explains to them why such a festival bears the non-Hebrew name Purim and instructs them how to observe it. It also seeks to imbue them with pride at the accomplishment of Jewish ancestors who lived in a strange land and faced ruthless foes.[1]

Even Sandra Beth Berg, in her dissertation, understands the book of Esther first of all to be a book about Jews, and to her the deity seems to be very distant:

The narrative tells of the dramatic rescue of the Jewish people from threatened destruction, and without any discernible assistance from Yahweh. The narrated events seem to stand outside Yahweh's control of history and to result from 'fate'.[2]

I. Greenberg, in his wonderful and rich guide on how to live the Jewish holidays, follows in the steps of those who see Esther as a Jewish book:

Purim is deceptively simple. On the surface, Megillat Esther...is a charming melodrama...No wonder the atmosphere of synagogue and the community on this day is all fun and games, masquerade and mummers, drinking, partying and gift-giving.[3]

However, Greenberg nuances the first observation by looking at an important issue, even though Esther remains in his view throughout and exclusively a book about Jews:

Yet appearances can be deceptive. Purim...may well be the darkest, most depressing holiday of the Jewish calendar. Its laughter is...a hair's breadth away from despair...it is really the holiday that grew out of Jewish history...it is the holiday of the Diaspora; it reflects and affirms the experience of the Jewish people living as a minority outside the land of Israel. In its own way, it offers a special guide to Jews who plan to continue living in the Diaspora...[4]

1.   J.M. Sasson, 'Esther', in R. Alter and F. Kermode (eds.), *The Literary Guide to the Bible* (Cambridge, MA: Harvard University Press, 1987), p. 355.
2.   S.B. Berg, *The Book of Esther: Motifs, Themes and Structure* (Missoula, MT: Scholars Press, 1979), p. 1.
3.   I. Greenberg, *The Jewish Way: Living the Holidays* (New York: Summit Books, 1988), p. 224.
4.   Greenberg, *The Jewish Way*, p. 224.

Arthur Waskow too sees not only joy and merriment in the festival of Purim, when he observes:

> But the laughter of Purim is not a gentle laughter: it is a kind of angry, blood-red humor that celebrates the tyrant's overthrow...Purim...remembers, that his [i.e. Haman's] own stupidity and greed would not have been enough to save us without the courage and tenacity of Mordecai and Esther. So even as a festival of merriment, Purim has its bloodier, darker underside of fear and fury.[1]

Indeed, the book of Esther is about the Jewish people (not the 'Israelites!') in the Persian empire at a time somewhere between the early fifth and late fourth centuries BCE, and about their deliverance from an endangered existence. Furthermore, it portrays personal initiative as a crucial—although not the only—ingredient of that deliverance; and the value of solidarity between people with comparable fates should not be underestimated. Nevertheless, the solidarity theme requires further attention. It is also true that the majority of the ten chapters deal with the 'Jewish question'. However, the plot against the Jews begins only in ch. 3, after the two Jewish protagonists, Mordecai and Esther, are introduced almost en passant (2.5-6).

Mordecai is described as a refugee, one of the exiled from Jerusalem. His genealogy causes some trouble for the dating of both the book's plot and the book itself. In any case, Mordecai is introduced at this place in the book because he encourages his adopted cousin Hadassah, alias Esther, to participate in the royal beauty contest for the replacement of the vacant position of queen. After his family relationship to the later Queen Esther is established (2.7), the emphasis shifts immediately to the young beautiful woman, and that remains so to the end of ch. 2. It seems, in other words, that Mordecai is only introduced for the purpose of Esther's subsequent introduction. His presence in close vicinity to the royal palace hints at a probable connection to the court, even though that is not mentioned explicitly (2.5, 19, 21). Mordecai's Jewishness is an aside, which at this time in the narrative seems to be of minor importance. At first sight this

---

1. A. Waskow, *The Season of Our Joy: A Celebration of Modern Jewish Renewal* (New York: Bantam Books, 1982), p. 115.

piece of information appears totally superfluous.

It is not yet known what kind of a Jew Mordecai is. His genealogy discloses nothing about his identity as a Jew. One may assume that, in spite of the experience of his own expulsion from Jerusalem, he is fairly well acculturated, if not to say assimilated, in Shushan, the capital of the Persian empire. His favorite post is by the gate of the royal court: perhaps he even holds an official position. In any case, it is not at all obvious why he advises Esther, who acquires a good position in the royal court through the beauty contest, to conceal her ethnic-religious background (2.10). After she wins the contest and is crowned as the new queen (2.17), the feature of her hiding her Jewishness is surprisingly repeated (2.20). What does this repetition signify?

The repetition itself is the answer to the question why the concealment is mentioned altogether. The emphasis in both verses (2.10, 20) is not on the fact of Esther's being a Jew, but on the fact that Mordecai pronounces a command to her and she obeys. Esther obeys Mordecai's commands, whether she is under his direct rule as an adopted orphan (v. 10) or under the king's rule as queen of the Persian empire (v. 20). That is indeed surprising! It is also surprising that a woman's identity, as it is related to her ethnicity, is not very important at this point of the story—a woman can even become queen while the king does not know where she originally comes from. On the other hand one could also argue that, at this point, Esther's identity in general is developmentally on such a low level that it is an easy task to have her hide even her ethnic background. Sasson remarks:

> She is pretty and winsome; but she responds to what others expect of her. She becomes a Queen because she lets others make decisions crucial to her future, and she can be browbeaten by Mordecai's threat even when assured of her husband's attachment (4.13-14).[1]

Hiding her Jewishness and thus following Mordecai's command is indeed astonishing, particularly when compared to the commander/commandee relationship she has with her royal husband, who never explicitly dictates anything to her; rather,

---

1. Sasson, 'Esther', p. 227.

all their direct encounters are accompanied by his friendly asking what her desires are and his readiness to give her half of the empire (5.3, 6; 7.2). Only indirectly is it made known to the reader that there is a force in the king's commands which even lets the (new) queen refrain from simple disobedience: Esther reminds Mordecai that it is well known in the entire empire by every single servant of the king that one enters uninvited into the king's chambers only at one's own peril. 'It is the law', she emphasizes (4.11).

Two chapters of the book—one quarter of the whole text—pass before the book 'turns Jewish'. Obedience and disobedience are established as major motifs;[1] the introduction of anything Jewish at this point is slightly distracting, though meaningful for what is about to transpire. Esther is a book about an empire ruled by absolute power, where imperial laws are irreversible (1.19; 8.8); Esther is also a book about how the king, as the personification of that absolute power, and the ruling class around him deal with those who dare to disobey, whatever motivation drives them to do so. The Jews, in the person of Mordecai, are instrumental in demonstrating this—but so are the women, in the person of Queen Vashti!

In its main plot the book of Esther narrates the anti-Jewish pogrom ordained and sanctioned by the state. But by then the Persian empire is already in a state in which executive power is established by way of subjugating a whole 'class' of society. It is interesting to notice that the absolute power in the Persian empire of this brilliant novella is established as a response to the disobedience of one individual. The fact that the disobedient individual is no one less but the First Lady marks a first-rate scandal which renders the book into a drama attracting the readers' or listeners' attention at its very beginning.

When the king, after an extensive period of feasting and drinking (one hundred and eighty plus seven days, 1.4, 10), orders his wife to present herself with the royal diadem (1.11), she refuses without giving any explanation (1.12), whereupon the king immediately gets furious. 'Her refusal,' says Bickerman, 'poses a grave legal question'.[2] Since there has never been a

---

1. Berg, *Esther*, pp. 72-82.
2. Bickerman, *Four Strange Books*, p. 186.

case like this, a new law has to be established, and the king reaches out for advice from his experts. Memuchan understands that the boldness of the queen's refusal puts into question not only the king's supreme position in his vast empire, but also all the men's supreme positions in their little empires of family. 1.17-18 illustrates Memuchan's worst fears that Vashti's example could be followed by both ordinary womenfolk and noble ladies of Persia and Media. What a distinctive and subtle notion, parallel to the king's two feasts, one for the nobility (1.3-4) and one for the common people (1.5). Memuchan therefore suggests to the king that he issue a royal, hence irrevocable decree that Vashti should no longer be queen (1.19). But this is not enough—such a decree cannot serve as sufficient example on its own if the issue at stake is the establishment of absolute (royal, male) power in the empire. Memuchan comes up with an incredibly chauvinistic proposal (1.20-21): The 'class' to be punished, which is represented by Queen Vashti, is made up of no less than half of the people, namely all the women, in spite of the fact that she alone has exercised disobedience against the king.

The special treatment meted out to Vashti deserves additional attention. According to Bickerman,[1] married women could participate in Persian feasts but, when the drinking began, they would leave and give way to concubines and courtesans. 'By coming to the king's party, Vashti...would degrade herself to the position of a concubine.'[2] Thus, it is not only the human dignity of the woman Vashti that is affected by the king's involving her in (male) party entertainment, but also her vocational role within the hierarchic structure of the empire.

To make sure that the message is understood, namely, that from now on every man is not only entitled but actually *commanded* by royal law to be the master in his own household and speak the language of his own people, the letters sent out to the provinces are written in indigenous scripts and languages. Gordis remarks that, apparently, in the Persian empire,

> when an intermarriage took place...the mother's language would normally prevail...The book of Nehemiah explicitly complains

1. Bickerman, *Four Strange Books*, p. 185, esp. n. 10.
2. Bickerman, *Four Strange Books*, p. 186.

that when some Jews married foreign wives, their children spoke the language of their mothers (Neh. 13.23-24). Ahasuerus' edict was designed to make the father's language dominant in the home.[1]

In other words, language used as an instrument of power is the means to show how far-reaching male dominance may be: women will literally have nothing to say anymore. When men use a language foreign to the women's, women are silenced. Thus the absolute power in Ahasuerus's empire is established as male power. And every man in the empire, from the king to the lowest peasant, is affected by it. Men dominate, women are dominated; men oppress, women are oppressed; men subjugate, women are subjugated—women obey, men are obeyed.

Two linguistic details in this section are remarkable. The first concerns the designation of the queen. Queen Vashti is mentioned seven times in ch. 1, either as 'Vashti, the queen' (וַשְׁתִּי הַמַּלְכָּה) or else as 'Queen Vashti' (הַמַּלְכָּה וַשְׁתִּי). In the first form, 'queen' is the attribute to modify 'Vashti'; in the second, 'Vashti' gives some additional information about the 'queen'. Since the result of ch. 1 is that the disobedient Vashti is no longer queen, it is worthwhile to check if there is any significance in the applied designation in each occurrence. It is 'Vashti' who organizes a feast for the women (v. 9) and who is ordered to appear before the king (v. 11). In both instances her womanhood is more important than her queenship: a particular woman, namely the queen, organizes a party for women, and the king wants to see a particular woman, namely the queen, wearing the royal jewelry. In the next two instances the order of the wording is reversed. It is 'the queen' who refuses to follow the king's command (v. 12), thus creating the scandal at court; and it is again 'the queen' whom the king does not know how to deal with (v. 15) after the scandal has become public knowledge. Here her function as queen overwrites her womanhood. Most significant is Memuchan's explanation (v. 16), that it is 'Vashti' who has wronged not only the king but all noble men: her transgression is that of a 'woman'. That she also functions as the queen is of lesser, albeit not minor, significance. Most

1. Gordis, *Esther*, pp. 24-25.

surprising is his repeated emphasis on Vashti's womanhood,
when he ponders (v. 17) what the noble women throughout the
empire will eventually use as justification for their own disobedience. This exposes Memuchan's deep concern. The noble
women would hardly refer to the queen as 'Vashti' but rather
as 'the queen'; for him as a man, however, 'Vashti' is dangerous
precisely because she is a woman rather than because of her
queenship. Finally, in her last appearance in the chapter (v. 19),
she is only designated as 'Vashti', her queenship (מלכוח) having
been stripped from her name by three words—the queenship is
literally taken away from her. Furthermore, she is removed
from the king's presence. Where is she? What has happened to
her? Is she chased away or hidden somewhere in the furthest
corner of the court? Since she refuses to be degraded to the
position of concubine, says Bickerman,[1] the phrase 'Vashti shall
not appear before King Ahasuerus' (1.19)[2] means exactly that
she was degraded to the status of concubine. The text certainly
does not say that she is dead—the death penalty is reserved for
those who appear uninvited before the king (4.11), and that is
precisely not what she did. Many commentators, though,
understand her sentence to be a death sentence.

The second linguistic detail is found at the beginning of ch. 2
(2.1). It opens with the words 'after these things', a formula
used frequently in Genesis. It often refers to the previously
narrated results of a specific development as firmly established.
'After these things' opens the curtain on a new stage, from
where the text develops towards the next, often even more
dramatic events. For example, after the wars with the local
kings (Gen. 14), where Abraham takes a stand, a new political
order in the region is established. 'After these things' God
speaks to Abraham in a vision (Gen. 15.1-4), announcing the
birth of the long expected offspring. Or, after Joseph is accused
of the attempted rape of Potiphar's wife and put in jail (Gen.
39), the prison manager soon recognizes Joseph's excellent
organizational talents and entrusts him with the management of
the prison. 'After these things' two new inmates arrive,

1. Bickerman, *Four Strange Books*, p. 186.
2. Gordis, *Esther*, p. 25.

Pharaoh's butler and baker (Gen. 40.1), and the narrative eventually leads to Joseph's liberation from prison. In Esther 'after these things' is used in a slightly irritating, though revealing manner: Vashti is disposed of, the throne of the queen is vacant; but, since this is not good order, a new queen needs to be appointed. One would expect 'after these things' to introduce the royal beauty contest, but 'after these things' the king first remembers (!) 'Vashti', who is no longer queen, and what she has done to him (and this is actually the very last time she is mentioned). Only then is he ready to focus on her replacement. Thus, it is not the vacant throne of the queen which symbolizes the new order yet to be established, but the fact that the king remembers a (fallen) woman: the new queen should not be someone like Vashti, a person with a well-developed sense of (her own) human dignity and the boldness to stand up against royal power that has turned violent but, rather, someone nice, smooth and accommodating, for whom obedience and obeisance are part of her character.

If it seems that absolute power is expressed mainly as the power of men over women, the process of appointing a new queen may well add to this impression. Hundreds if not thousands ('all', 2.3) of lovely virgins from over the whole empire are brought to the harem, where they undergo a year-long treatment of bodily beautification to suit the king's desires. Hadassa alias Esther is among them, and when she wins the contest and becomes the new queen (2.16), it is already the seventh year of Ahasuerus's reign. William Phipps points to this striking element of time:

> Evidently Ahasuerus enjoys judging the contest, for four years elapse from the time that Vashti is deposed until someone is selected to take her place. He perhaps deflowered hundreds of virgins before deciding which damsel had given him the most pleasure.[1]

Esther is the one but, as mentioned above, even as queen she obeys her cousin Mordecai's commands. In the Persian empire of King Ahasuerus the men hold absolute power over the women

---

1. W.E. Phipps, *Assertive Biblical Women* (Westport, CT, and London: Greenwood Press, 1992), p. 96.

and, against this sexist backdrop, an ethnic drama unfolds.

But once more 'after these things' (3.1)—a murderous plot against the king has been revealed by Mordecai (2.21-23)—the plot changes direction. Haman is promoted to vizier. His genealogy and his first decree are given but not his merits for the promotion. It is now royal law that everybody has to bow down before the vizier. Mordecai, who has earlier been introduced as a Jewish refugee present in the gate almost all the time and who has advised his adopted cousin to conceal her Jewishness, does not follow this royal law (3.2). We have a new case of disobedience, although the parallels to the first case are not yet visible. Nevertheless, from what the reader has already learned from Vashti's (feminine) non-compliance, this case of (Jewish) non-compliance is going to cause trouble. Day after day the royal attendants, as if they wanted to warn Mordecai, ask him for the reasons of his refusal; day after day he gives the same reason for not obeying the royal law: his Jewishness. It is important to understand that Mordecai's non-compliance is only against the king's rules, not against the Jewish rules. Rachel Rosenzweig remarks that 'in this case it is the deed of inner freedom and not the crime of an individual Jew which gives rise to the catastrophe for Israel'.[1]

Bickerman understands the source of the tension between Haman and Mordecai to lie elsewhere. Even though Mordecai denounces the plot against the king, nothing is done for him. Bickerman points out that

> the right reward for Mordecai would be to promote him to chief minister, but the forgetful king exalts Haman...the royal minister, who has appropriated the rank which rightfully belongs to Mordecai. So Mordecai never bows or pays homage to Haman...In fact, Mordecai fights for his honor. A man from whom the due reward is withheld by the king protests even if it should cost him his life...[2]

---

1.   R. Rosenzweig, *Solidarität mit den Leidenden im Judentum* (Berlin and New York: de Gruyter, 1978), 'Die Konkubine des Königs: Solidarität eines Einzelnen mit der Gemeinschaft', p. 114: 'In deisem Falle ist es aber gerade diese Tat der inneren Freiheit und nicht das Verbrechen eines einzelnen Juden, welche die Katastrophe für Israel heraufbeschwört'.

2.   Bickerman, *Four Strange Books*, pp. 178-80.

Would Mordecai dare to confront the vizier openly? Yes, as a further encounter between Haman and Mordecai shows (5.9). Bickerman continues: 'Now he [i.e. Haman] has lost face. He consults his friends (5.14) and decides to hang Mordecai on a gallows.'[1] Bickerman sees Mordecai as being forced into an unjustified career competition with Haman, and this is the reason for his not bowing down before Haman. The textual notice about Mordecai's Jewishness, according to Bickerman,[2] functions only as a link between the two plots, that of Mordecai and that of Esther.

It is not because of a one-time transgression of royal law that the attendants report the issue to Haman, who immediately becomes furious (3.5). Becoming furious becomes a state affair—there is a first hint that Vashti's and Mordecai's cases might be somewhat parallel. Haman has quickly become an ally in thought of Memuchan, when he expresses his fears that punishing Mordecai alone would not solve the problem (3.6), for Haman, in his sickly fantasies of grandeur, believes that it is the Jew in Mordecai who signifies the danger. Such eagerness in a political position of such influence, however, cannot be taken lightly. Indeed, Mordecai's alertness will soon become crucial.[3]

Interestingly enough, Haman comes up with the idea of collective punishment only after he learns about Mordecai's ethnicity (3.6).[4] In his plans Haman extends the future punishment of the initial transgressor to the whole group of those who might perform the act of disobedience in question, that is all the Jews. Thus Haman has also become an ally of Memuchan in respect of the measures recommended when he suggests that the king should take care of this obnoxious and stubborn people as a whole. What looked in 3.6 to be a plan for a preventive

1. Bickerman, *Four Strange Books*, p. 180.
2. Bickerman, *Four Strange Books*, p. 180.
3. 4.7-8. Mordecai seems to know more than the average Jew; he also seems to possess a copy of the official letter (3.13). Is this an additional piece of implicit information that he holds an official position in the court?
4. Special punishment for the *individual* Mordecai is only much later taken into consideration, when he refuses to rise (!) before Haman (5.9). The gallows built for Mordecai is thus thought of as an extra punishment for the repeated opposition at a moment when the fatal decree against the Jews is already in operation.

step becomes in 3.11 an edict, approved and financed by the politically not very alert king. Executive power in this empire wants to be respected. Non-compliance with royal rules, that is, not to be at the king's disposal, entails heavy consequences. When individuals practice resistance, the punishment is extended to the whole of their—innocent—identity groups. And the parallels between chs. 1 and 3 are emphasized further by the same means undertaken to spread the new law to the furthest provinces in the empire (3.12-15).

Preventive measures, however, are not a new feature in the book of Esther, even though there is an important difference in the level of the punishment: the women in the Persian empire have their rights curtailed by being restricted in their husbands' houses; the Jews are doomed to extermination. Preventive measures seem to be unavoidable to Memuchan and Haman, the two ministers in charge, for otherwise the king's interest will be affected: it might occur to all the women in the empire to 'look with scorn upon their husbands' (1.17),[1] just as it might occur to all the Jews 'not to obey the king's laws' (3.8).[2]

Even though this difference between the two cases is important, it is not the only one. While Vashti's challenge lies in her opposition, Mordecai's is in his existence. Vashti refuses to do something which in some way corresponds with her role, Mordecai to do something which is not within the realm of his normative behavior. While hers is an act out of character, his is perfectly consistent with his tradition. Furthermore, the decree of ch. 1 has a very broad impact: it literally affects every single household in the empire, while the death sentence for the Jews directly affects 'only' this small nation, scattered but distinctive, in all the provinces (3.8).

However, in spite of the many differences between the two cases, the parallels between them add a sobering touch to the plot. Those who have smiled about the funny, even farcical, setting and the totally exaggerated reaction of male chauvinism in ch. 1 are given a shock in ch. 3. The exercise of power as presented in ch. 1 can still be accepted as fairly normal, particularly by an audience not sensitive to gender issues. This does not

1.   Gordis, *Esther*, p. 25.
2.   Gordis, *Esther*, p. 35.

apply to the execution of power as presented in ch. 3, where 'execution' is to be taken in its most literal sense. Chapter 1 needs ch. 3 in order to uncover the pattern of power abuse, whereas ch. 3 can do without ch. 1, since the abuse is so obvious. The equal patterns of consequences for transgressions different in character unmask the proportions of executive power in this empire in the most frightening way. How can such disaster be averted? Is there any hope?

So far the person who gives the book its name has not had her grand appearance, but now her time has come. What is known about Esther? She is very beautiful (2.7-9, 15-17), which marks the initial impulse for her appointment as queen; she has been rather passive, most probably she lives a fairly protected court life. Her only role is to be the king's playmate, and she does not seem to fill (other) political roles. On the advice of her cousin Mordecai she successfully hides her Jewish background (2.10, 20) and therefore, for the time being, is not affected by the fatal decision against the Jews. Even though she has been appointed queen after the subjugation decree against all women, she obeys her husband Ahasuerus *and* her cousin Mordecai (2.7, 10, 20). In ch. 4 everything except her beauty is challenged, but her beauty is shortly to play a major role.

The Jews in every province are mourning, fasting, weeping, lamenting (4.3). Mordecai cannot come inside the gate since, due to the Jewish mourning custom, he is dressed in sackcloth (4.1-2), which makes it very difficult to make contact with Esther. Esther becomes very agitated when she hears of it (4.4). What do her maids and the eunuch tell her (4.4) that she makes her so agitated? The answer lies in her first action: she sends decent clothes to Mordecai (4.4), which indicates that she is agitated because of her cousin's appearance, not because of the decree against the Jews, of which she is presumably ignorant. His wailing, tearing clothes and putting on sackcloth are traditional Jewish expressions of mourning. In contradistinction, Esther's reaction as a Jew is quite assimilated, as Greenberg observes: 'she vacillated at first—just the reaction one would expect from a marginal Jew who was reluctant to lose her place in society'.[1]

---

1.   Greenberg, *The Jewish Way*, p. 228.

However, in the given context it is understandably dangerous to have Jewish relatives, even for an assimilated queen. Only after Mordecai returns the clothes she sends does she reach out for information. In the following passages (4.5-9, 10-14, 15-17) the narrative shifts several times from Esther to Mordecai and back again.

Mordecai reports via Hathach everything he knows about the decree against the Jews. He even sends a copy of the letter to Esther, which shows that he is better informed than the average Jew in Shushan. 'All that had happened to him' (4.7) is worthy of being reported. It seems that Mordecai understands that he alone is the source of the moral danger for the Jews, because he alone has refused to bow down before Haman. Rosenzweig points out that innocent people, as listed in 3.16, are included in the liability for Mordecai's behavior:

> An individual person therefore cannot afford to do whatever occurs to his mind, even if he has a deed of heroism and faithfulness towards religion and conscience in mind. Perhaps the whole community will have to bear the consequences of his deeds...Could Mordecai have acted differently? Should he have bowed down? These questions must not be evaded, if the awfulness of the laws of liability are to be understood.[1]

Mordecai is ready to take responsibility for his 'mistake' of overrated faithfulness, overrated because it has brought mortal danger to his fellow Jews; and he is consequently ready to do something about it. However, in order to divert the threatening catastrophe, he needs to make contact with the king himself,

---

1. Rosenzweig, *Solidarität*, p. 115: 'Mit dieser Detailierung von Menschenkategorien (wie in 3.6, 13) stellt die Bibel stets die Unschuldigen heraus, die von der Haftung betroffen werden, ganz gleich ob die Haftung durch Menschen oder durch Gott in Funktion gesetzt wird. Der Einzelne kann sich also nicht erlauben zu tun, was ihn in den Sinn kommt, selbst wenn er eine Tat des Heldentums und der Treue zu Religion und Gewissen im Sinn hat. Denn die Folgen seiner Taten muss möglicherweise seine ganze Gemeinschaft tragen...Hätte Mordecai anders handeln können? Hätte er sich niederwerfen sollen? Man darf dieser Frage nicht ausweichen, will man das Gesetz der haftung in seiner ganzen Furchtbarkeit erfassen'. Rosenzweig then goes into a lengthy discussion of whether Haman's was a decree to idol worship, which brings the question of martyrdom into the picture, but denies that the Esther story touches this issue (pp. 115-16).

and for this plan to be successful, Esther is needed as the crucial mediator. He requests, even demands, that she intercede.

So far Esther has been loyal—as a woman, for the king, warned through the experience with Vashti, has surely paid attention to her feminine loyalty when he appointed her queen. As a Jew she does not have to initiate loyalty, since her cousin did all the thinking for her. How is she going to react now, in this difficult situation? Is she going to act as a Jew, or as a woman? Even though she holds the throne as Persian queen, she is the only representative of both discriminated-against classes in the whole book. Esther is, as Letty Cottin Pogrebin describes herself, 'twice over marginal';[1] and, as such, she is almost obliged to disobey somebody! Is she going to deny her compliance as a Jew, which would be against Mordecai? Or as a woman, which would be against the king? Well, Esther has by now thoroughly internalized her cousin's earlier advice to conceal her ethnic background. At court she is not a Jew, thus her first response is that of a woman. However, hers is a complicated case of conflicting loyalties. She informs Mordecai about the factor which is common knowledge throughout the empire—it is indeed remarkable who in this book lacks which

1. L.C. Pogrebin, *Deborah, Golda and Me* (New York: Crown, 1991), p. xv: 'I chose to identify with the categories I find most meaningful, "women" and "Jews", two groups that manage to be simultaneously significant yet intractably marginal. What do I mean by marginal? Neither of my chosen affinity groups is a cultural norm. The...American norm is white Christian male and as long as Americans are measured against the standards of the white Christian male, both women and Jews will be seen as the Outsider—the Other—and the Jewish woman as the Other twice over...Discrimination and bigotry are intrinsic hazards of Otherness; so is invisibility. Invisibility results when a word is used to describe a class of people in which you count yourself—American, for example—but you discover that the person using that word doesn't mean you. To test Jewish and female invisibility, ask the next ten people you meet to describe "an American". Chances are not one will conjure up a female of any persuasion or a Jew of either sex...That's what I mean by double marginality.' Thus, a new element in both Vashti's and Mordecai's opposition is their attempt to overcome their 'invisibility' because, for both of them, different norms and rules obtain. Queens do not appear before drunken kings; Jews do not bow down before human masters, which conflicts with the standard, that is male Persian, norm.

piece of information!—that entering the king's chambers without a personal invitation inevitably means execution, except when the king shows mercy through his scepter: and, since she has not been invited for a whole month, her chances of escaping the death penalty are minimal (4.11). Therefore, Esther concludes, there is nothing she can do for the Jews and, if she tried, she would endanger her own life. Thus she exercises loyalty towards her husband the king but, in so doing, she is—conversely—hard-pressed to disobey Mordecai. She designates King Ahasuerus 'Lord over Life and Death', or at least master over comings and goings, with whom she, as a servant, has no power whatsoever to initiate an encounter. Rosenzweig understands Esther's lack of solidarity with her people as an expression of cowardice; however, she concedes that this cowardice will later enable the queen to save the people.[1]

Mordecai reacts to Esther's self-distancing from his request very aggressively (4.13-14), with the only direct speech attributed to him in the whole book. He—of all people!—reminds Esther sharply of her Jewishness and warns her that her fate will certainly catch up with her sooner or later, even within the court. 'For if you remain silent at this time, relief and deliverance for the Jews will arise from another quarter': this fierce statement is his male reaction[2] to Esther's feminine non-compliance. What irony. Mordecai forces Esther's emancipation as a Jew by practicing male power over her! In a significantly distorting way he comes back to his former advice (concerning the concealment of her origins), as if he wanted to say, 'You have dared to take my advice literally and not only hide your Jewishness but also to do away with it!' With menacing undertones, he pronounces nothing less than a ban by claiming that she and her father's house will surely disappear because of her non-compliance towards him. This implies that he, Mordecai, her adoptive father, would not come to her rescue in case of necessity—by the force of his word she is literally excommunicated from the Jewish people. Esther now experiences what her predecessor Vashti has gone through.

And this brings Esther to reason. She understands that she is

1.   Rosenzweig, *Solidarität*, p. 117.
2.   Gordis, *Esther*, p. 41.

lost, both as a Jew vis-à-vis Haman and as an assimilated queen vis-à-vis Mordecai and the Jewish people. Unless she is loyal to the identity group which currently suffers the greater danger, she has no chance of survival. At this point in the plot, if she separates herself from the fate of her Jewish people, she will perish. Greenberg adds color to the terseness of the biblical text:

> For Esther, these days are the long night of the soul. All around her in the court she sees the sharpening of the knives. Since people do not know that she is Jewish, they talk freely of the coming bloodbath and gleefully anticipate the rich spoils of the dead Jews. She cannot trust anyone, nor dare she betray her own tremendous anxiety for her people. So she must sit with fixed smile while the courtiers roar with laughter, anticipating how cowardly, helpless Jews will run around like drugged cockroaches in a bottle.[1]

But since the situation is so much without prospect, she might as well take her stand: she can only win. 'If I perish, I perish',[2] are her moving words, and they mark the turning point. Rosenzweig observes: 'Esther indeed takes responsibility upon herself, though rather out of despair than out of solidarity'.[3] And, further,

> even a person who is presumably not affected with the liability of his community...may recognize his dependence and draw the consequence to exercise solidarity. The very fact that Esther had a special position outside her community enabled her to convert passive into active liability. It is not Mordecai, who bears responsibility for the approaching pogrom, who can save the people. Esther, who embodies everything a proud Jew disdains, has to learn that the survival of the people depends on her.[4]

1. Greenberg, *The Jewish Way*, p. 240.
2. Gordis, *Esther*, p. 41.
3. Rosenzweig, *Solidarität*, p. 119: 'Ester nimmt denn auch die Verantwortung auf sich, wenn auch mehr aus Verzweiflung denn aus Solidarität'.
4. Rosenzweig, *Solidarität*, p. 117: '[Der zweite Akt wird zeigen,] wie selbst ein Mensch, der augenscheinlich nicht durch diese Haftung betroffen wird, weil er von seiner Gemeinschaft isoliert ist und die Illusion haben kann, nicht von ihr abhängig zu sein, diese seine Abhängigkeit erkennen und aus ihr die Konsequenz der Solidarität und der Sendung ziehen muss.

She will, from now on, appear as the liberator of the Jews and—who knows?—perhaps women's liberation will be a by-product.

The development of the queen begins with an invitation to her people to fast for and together with her. By the three-day fast all energies are concentrated in her, her metamorphosis is packed into one single, incredibly dense verse (4.16): 'Go, assemble all the Jews to be found in Shushan and fast for me. Do not eat or drink for three days, night or day, and I and my maids will also fast like you. Then I will go to the king, though it is against the law, and if I perish, I perish.'[1] The fast not only clears her mind, but also sets a truly impressive process of emancipation in motion. Esther's decision to break the royal law in spite of the mortal danger for herself echoes Vashti's failed resistance; in this way, Vashti's discontinued story is taken over and away from the power holders. Esther accepts the loser's story and liberates herself by/from it. After this, things really change and the changes are expressed in the language too: when Mordecai leaves he does 'all that Esther had commanded him' (4.17).[2] When, on the third day, she stands in the inner courtyard (5.1) in order to begin her resistance against the king's or rather Haman's anti-Jewish decree, she is dressed in 'royalty'.[3] By mobilizing all her feminine qualities, she wins the king's favor and he stretches out his scepter. With her new identity which, in its own way, is new beauty too, Queen Esther approaches the king and quickly diverts the catastrophe for the Jews.

During the second dinner at the queen's rooms, Haman is unmasked as the evildoer who schemes against the queen's people (7.6) and is brought to the gallows (7.10). On the same day the king gives Queen Esther Haman's house (8.1). In terms

Gerade die Tatsache, dass Ester eine besondere Stellung ausserhalb ihrer Gemeinschaft einnahm, ermöglichte ihr, passives Haften in aktives Bürgen zu verwandeln. Nicht Mordecai, der Schuld an dem bevorstehenden Pogrom trägt, kann das Volk retten, sondern gerade Ester, die all das verkörpert, was ein stolzer Jude verachtet, muss lernen, dass von ihr das Leben des Volkes abhängt.'

1. Gordis, *Esther*, p. 41.
2. Gordis, *Esther*, p. 41.
3. No translation captures the precise meaning of the Hebrew, ותלבש אסתר מלכות (5.1).

of its political value, this outcome is certainly more than the offered half-kingdom, thus exceeding by far the king's generosity of the previous chapters, when he has no idea what Esther's particular desires are (5.6; 7.2). And that is not all; Mordecai, too, is allowed to visit the king. It is indeed intriguing that Mordecai is entitled to come before the king for no other reason than being Esther's relative; his previously narrated personal merits (2.21-23; 6.2-3) are not mentioned again at this juncture of the plot. While Esther gets Haman's house, Mordecai is honored by the king with the ring withdrawn from Haman and, surprisingly, Esther appoints Mordecai over Haman's estate (8.2). In other words, Mordecai has not only gained access to the king but also finally holds the long-desired court position, all thanks to a woman. Queen Esther as ruler with Mordecai as acting director: now that Jews are in charge, are the imperial problems resolved?

Indeed Haman, the man of evil deeds, is finished, but the same does not apply to his deeds. The irrevocable decree against the Jews is still valid (8.8), hence the danger for the Jews has not vanished. And since the selected day of execution is approaching fast, Mordecai and Esther have to take care of that urgently. With no invitation to a fancy dinner this time, Queen Esther talks again to the king, requesting him to annul the decree. But the king, again backing away from responsibility, delegates the power of attorney for finding a solution to Mordecai and Esther (8.7-8), who allow the Jews self-defense (8.11-12). It is again Esther who talks to the king, even though Mordecai now occupies Haman's former position. She has to finish her job and, as long as her people, with whom she now fully identifies, is not safe, she has to pursue her goal.

The king, as usual, assumes a strange position in this episode. He claims that royal decrees, once released, cannot be annulled, since this is the structure of the law. But who decides about the legal structure in this empire?! The structure of power in the Persia of King Ahasuerus has not changed, because he does not want to change it. This means that, even though the Jews are saved for now, at any other time another people can be annihilated if the king willingly supports the plans of some courtly villain. As long as decrees cannot be annulled, nothing has changed. This, then, sheds new light on Vashti's refusal to appear before the king: it constitutes a serious challenge to the system, because it unmasked its weakness and has caused so much turmoil that power abuse by the leading class has become the only way to save the system. The second decree concerning the Jews, allowing them to defend their lives on their own, marks a special privilege (!). It indeed breaks the totalitarian system, albeit modestly, that is, in this singular case alone. The system itself remains intact.

Although it is not clear whether the king recognizes Esther's initiative as resistance, it is not a very good sign for the quality of power if Esther's 'subversive' methods lead faster to the aimed-for goal than Vashti's and Mordecai's open ones. When the right woman appears illicitly the king, pleased by the appearance of a beauty queen, willingly shows his merciful side. Thus the resolution of the Jewish problem is only possible by a temporary loosening of the patriarchal structures. This hints at the right direction, namely that the liberation of one discriminated segment of society, the Jews, is in the end not possible without the liberation of the other subjugated segment of the same society, the women, and vice versa. If one group's attempt at liberation yields a breakthrough, the other will eventually be successful too. Esther, who has meanwhile become a liberated Jew but remains a discriminated-against woman, would be in her privileged position as queen the ideal figure to pursue that goal.

However, this does not happen within the framework of the book of Esther. Two sources for the failure are to be mentioned, namely Vizier Mordecai's ascent to power and Queen Esther's failed emancipation. In connection with the governmentally permitted revenge of Persian Jewry against their persecutors, Mordecai's influence keeps growing (8.7-9), although it is Esther who remains in personal contact with the king. The letters are hardly on their way when Mordecai is already dressed in a robe of royalty (8.15).[1] After the fight ends victoriously for the Jews, there is a new decree sent out which designates the festive commemoration day of Purim. This decree

1. Cf. 5.1, where Esther, after her successful metamorphosis into a queen, appears before the king wearing 'royalty' too.

is signed by Mordecai exclusively (9.20); only in the confirmation letter for establishing the Purim holiday as a permanent institution is Esther the first to sign; Mordecai, however, remains a co-signatory (9.29). And in the very last verse of the book (10.3) it is made unambiguously clear that the male vizier, and not the queen, is second to the king. Male bonding allows Mordecai to assume the absolute power he has inherited from Haman, which is a male power.

Esther's incomplete emancipation is tragic. After the crucial encounter with Mordecai (Esth. 4), it seems that she understands what discrimination and liberation are about. Her original refusal to entreat for the Jews makes her for a moment almost a collaborator with Haman, even though her reasons are weighty. At the right time, however, she understands that the decree is directed against her too, and that standing up against it is merely an act of self-defense, with a welcome potential of positive outcome for the others affected. When she visits the king (5.1), she acts as a spiritually liberated Jew, whose physical liberation will eventually follow. The experience of successfully living through a life-endangering liberation process should have opened her eyes to the subjugation of women, particularly since she herself is subject to it. But since she understands only the more imminent discrimination against Jewishness, her act of solidarity with the oppressed remains an act of solidarity with the oppressed Jews only. Within this context, it is remarkable that— as a matter of fact—Esther is discriminated against first and foremost as a woman. She has been subjugated as a woman before her Jewishness becomes a problem or, better still, she gains her exclusive position only because of the general subjugation of woman. Is this subjugation accepted by her? Is it firmly internalized? Or is it just not recognized?

Queen Esther has learned only one lesson, the Jewish one. As mentioned before, Mordecai's challenge to the Persian empire lies in his existence as a Jew, while Vashti's lies in her opposition as a woman. Is Esther's standing up as a Jew against threatening annihilation undertaken only because the threat is lethal? What infringement of her dignity as a woman might have made her take a similarly oppositional stand? Under what circumstances would Queen Esther fight as a woman for human dignity, for allowing one to live according to one's wishes? As a Jew, she fights for the right to self-definition; as a woman, she tragically gets stuck in a system where others decide about right and wrong. Queen Esther remains bound to the decrees of men, written in the script and language of her own husband the king (1.22). She has no influence to bring to bear on this state of affairs either for herself or for other women, due to her blindness about her situation as a woman; at the single moment when all the power is concentrated in her feminine hand (8.1), she hands it all over to Mordecai (8.2). Esther's insights about how to fight subjugation come to a dead end there. What she has learned about discrimination as a Jew is apparently not applicable to her situation as a woman in a male-dominated world. Her emancipation is one-sided and thus incomplete.[1]

The book of Esther presents two problems of subjugation which the established classes in the empire have to deal with. Since absolute power is at work, the methods applied are methods of violence—actual imprisonment for the women, extermination for the Jews. At the same time, this shows that the absolute state is highly vulnerable. First, there is a violent demonstration of the ruling male class against women, which makes Esther a book with a theme of sexism. Secondly, there is an even more violent demonstration of the ruling Persian[2] class against Jews, which makes Esther a book with a theme of racism. Only the ethnic problem is resolved and, as an extremely

---

1.   Since, as a Jew, Mordecai has gone through the same liberation process as Esther, he too should have developed a sensitivity to the discrimination of woman although, in the given context, this is admittedly asking for a lot.

2.   Bickerman differentiates the decree against the Jews as of Haman's origin only, not the whole upper Persian political class: 'the author goes out of his way to isolate Haman, to show that his decree was an act of personal vengeance. Even his wife and his advisers warn him (6.13). The king was deceived by Haman: it is significant that Haman does not name the people he wants to slay in his report to the king. When Haman's edict was published, the city of Susa was grieved (3.15), and the same city rejoiced at Mordecai's appointment (8.15)' (*Four Strange Books*, p. 196). Greenberg makes a similar observation: 'Nowhere is there a hint that all Gentiles were like Haman' (*The Jewish Way*, p. 237). Ironically Haman, like Mordecai, is *not* of Persian background.

important feature, self-initiative leads to a (more or less) happy ending.

The gender problem is not mentioned again after ch. 1. Sasson's conclusion that 'any audience...including all those who now read the tale purely for pleasure, will find in it...fully resolved situations',[1] neglects completely the fact that the problem presented is about authority as applied in a totalitarian system; and that the mortal danger for the Jews is just one of the means for illustrating this. If it is true of Esther that the process of her emancipation is discontinued before completion, this is also true for the book that bears her name. Esther's liberation as a Jew is a marvelous example of emancipation, containing all elements from insight to action to success. But if the book of Esther is also a book about liberation from bondage in general, then it simply 'lacks' two chapters, which I am now going to speculate upon.

The 'missing' two chapters, which would have transformed the book of Esther into a book with a truly happy ending, would have included the following features.

Chapter 11

Esther recognizes her subjugation as a woman, inasmuch as she herself and her 'people' (i.e. other women) are concerned. After a period of fasting, she takes steps to change this situation. Since private dinner parties have been a successful means in the previous case, she once more issues invitations for one or two dinners in her private chambers. Her guests this time are her husband King Ahasuerus and her cousin Vizier Mordecai, the present holder of all the power in the empire. Both men are receptive to Esther's suggestions—they, too, have learned their lesson. The king again offers her, in imitation of the first case, half the empire. Esther accepts it so that, from now on, women would have their own opportunity to share responsibility for the welfare of the state.

1. Sasson, 'Esther', p. 341.

Chapter 12

Esther sends out a decree, signed by the king and herself, in all languages of all the provinces,[1] allowing women to gather, organize themselves and stand up for their human rights—in imitation of 8.11 (but not that bloody, please!). The goal of this last decree is of course not the subjugation of men, but the removal of the subjugation of women. The book ends with Queen Esther offering amnesty for her predecessor ex-Queen Vashti and inviting her for a festive banquet. Vashti's rehabilitation is celebrated with an empire-wide feast for the whole people, men and women alike. Esther gives Vashti the diadem as a sign of acknowledgment of the latter's achievements as spokesperson for human dignity and, in addition, honors her by appointing her as the queen's personal adviser.

All this is certainly midrashic wishful thinking. Far be it from me to suggest such a bold emendation of the text—after all, the book of Esther has been part of the canon for a long time. But Scripture in its timelessness should speak to today's readers too, as it actually does in a fairly strong way to many people. The book of Esther bears a rich lesson which is worthy of embrace. From a Jewish point of view, does it not teach that courageous initiative at the right moment in the right form and setting are crucial for God to eventually grant intervention?[2] The book, however, does not speak to me only as a Jew, but also as a woman. On this count the message is not such a happy one. As Jews, we have good reasons to celebrate Purim, as described in 9.21-22. As women, we have no reasons to celebrate, for, following 1.22, our subjugation still stands. We are still struggling for our rights as human beings and our place in public life. And as female Jews, the Esthers of the Esther novella, does not the story present to us an unresolvable dilemma? Surprisingly, that is not necessarily so! In fact, the Jewish calendar already has a

1. In such circumstances, even linguistic gender issues would be considered.
2. I deliberately exclude here the horrendously gruesome episodes of self-defense as portrayed in ch. 9; I need to think some more on that.

commemoration day, right before the feast of Purim, which is called 'the Fast of Esther' (Ta'anit Esther[1]). But, since it is one of the 'minor' fast days of the liturgical year, its observance has largely fallen out of practice. I think that, as Jewish women, we need to reinterpret the Fast of Esther. We can give it a new meaning, as a fast of current mourning for the lasting discrimination against and subjugation of women, Jewish and non-Jewish alike. Esther fasts (4.16) because she has to come to terms with the danger of being a Jew who is deprived of the freedom to simply be and live like a Jew. As Jewish women, we ought to fast in our own time because, even though things have drastically changed for the better in the past thirty-four decades or so, we are still deprived of the complete freedom to simply be and live like women, the way women are: with all our peculiarities, skills, beliefs and rights.

1. In imitation of 4.16.

ESTHER AND THE QUEEN'S THRONE

Zefira Gitay

Scenes from the book of Esther are depicted on a wall panel of the Dura Europos synagogue (236 CE; see Figure 1). In one of these illustrations Esther herself appears seated, dressed like a Tyche.[1] This depiction suggests that Esther is projected as a monarchic figure.[2] She occupies a throne which appears to be situated somewhat behind King Ahasuerus's elaborate throne. Such a depiction of the queen, who is represented as slightly secondary to the king, is not unique to the wall paintings of the Dura Europos synagogue. It reflects a common tradition of iconographic composition, as revealed by illustrations of Mesopotamian and Egyptian monarchs.[3] It seems that the artists are not interested in portraying realistic images. Rather, they focus on representational portraits expressing persons' roles, and the actual importance of those persons' political or military position within the monarchic hierarchy. Thus, the artist utilizes a political vocabulary that focuses on status rather than on what could represent an actual realistic scene.[4]

1. Goddess of luck and chance in Greek and Hellenistic culture. For a brief definition and selected bibliography, cf. M. Leach, *A Guide to the Gods* (London, Detroit and Washington: Gale Research International, 1992).

2. According to E.R. Goodenough, *Jewish Symbols in the Greco-Roman Period* (New York: Pantheon, 1964), IX, p. 179, Tyche equals Atargatis, a Near Eastern mother-goddess of—variously—fertility, fish and the moon (cf. Leach, *Guide to the Gods*, pp. 238, 430, 569 and literature cited). Goodenough stipulates that Esther is a projection of Atargatis. But cf. M. Avi-Yonah, 'Goodenough's Evaluation of the Dura Paintings: A Critique', in J. Gutman (ed.), *The Dura Europos Synagogue* (Missoula, MT: Scholars Press, 1973), p. 123.

3. R. Wischnitzer, 'From My Archives', *Journal of Jewish Art* 6 (1979), p. 15.

4. E. Panofsky, *Meaning in the Visual Arts* (Garden City, NY: Doubleday, 1955), p. 62.

Figure 1. *Ahasuerus and Esther*, detail from the Esther panel, Dura Europos
Synagogue (Yale University, Dura Europos Collection, New Haven, CT,
USA).

One wonders whether the depiction of Esther in the Dura
Europos synagogue, and the royal status attributed to her in
that depiction, indeed reflect her position as presented in the
biblical text. It may be conjectured that the portrayal of Esther
in almost the same proportions as Ahasuerus, and having her
situated almost next to him, has a purpose. The artist may have
intended not to portray Esther solely as a beauty queen who is
totally subordinate to the king's desire. The artist may have
wished to reflect on Esther's ability to practise her formidable
authority over the empire. Thus, the portrayal focuses on the
role Esther actually plays in the king's court. Can this depiction,
traditional but also deviant, be read as a definitive comment on
Esther's status in the king's court? Was Esther a 'queen' by title
only, or so addressed in the text because of her active role in
the political arena?

Artists like Filippino Lippi, of the Italian Renaissance, did not
follow in the footsteps of the painter from Dura Europos, in

Mesopotamia. Lippi's depiction of Esther in his *La Derelitta*
(1475; Figure 2)[1] does not contain a definitive artistic statement
on the question whether Esther was granted a title void of
political authority, or whether she was a reigning queen whose
subjects accepted her authority. Lippi focuses on presenting
Esther as a beautiful maiden, at the moment when she is being
introduced to Ahasuerus (2.13). Esther, who is being brought
to the king, bows her head gracefully. She is modest and does
not expose herself too much. In Lippi's painting, her modest
appearance is noticeable since she is in line with the other
maidens, all of whom walk under the king's gaze. The other
participants in the pageant raise their heads, proud and self-
assured. Esther, however, lowers her head and does not face
the king directly. The artist creates the impression that Esther is
not expected to become a leading figure. She is depicted as a
subordinate future spouse, destined to serve her husband the
king rather than practise her own authority.

Interestingly, not only artists are puzzled with regard to
Esther's role in Ahasuerus's court. Bible critics also express two
diametrically opposed views concerning Esther's role. Some
view her as a fully fledged queen, whereas others maintain that
the crown on her head (2.17) has decorative value only. The
dispute about the biblical text revolves around the function of
the Hebrew word *timlōk* (literally 'reign', 'be queen', 2.4). Does
it simply mean, in the context of Esther, that she becomes the
wife of the king (Heb. *melek*), suggesting that her way of con-
ducting affairs does not justify an occupation of the throne?
Thus Moore:

> Esther was called queen, but she did not rule; even after being
> queen for five years (see 3.7), Esther still occupied a weak and
> precarious position—in her own eyes at least, for she was most
> uncertain about her fate and her powers over the king.[2]

Paton views things differently. In his commentary to the book
he does not view Esther as just the king's wife. Referring to the
word *timlōk*, he translates the relevant sentence (2.4) as 'let the

1.   On whether this painting is Lippi's or Botticelli's, see R. Lightbown,
Sandro Botticelli (London: Paul Elek, 1978), II, pp. 208-10.
2.   C.A. Moore, *Esther* (AB, 7b; Garden City, NY: Doubleday, 1971), p. 18.

Figure 2. Filippino Lippi, *The Virgins Appear before Ahasuerus*, detail from *La Derelitta* (Chantilly, Musée Condé, No. 19, France).

girl ...reign',[1] thus emphasizing her role as a figure with ruling power extending to the whole empire.[2]

It seems that the two alternatives—Esther is simply the king's wife; Esther occupies the queen's throne and is politically influential—can be read into 2.4. The instruction is to look for a girl who will be queen and/or will reign. The issue is not yet resolved: it is open-ended, it can turn out to be either/or. Had Esther not succeeded in becoming fit for the throne, she would have served merely in her capacity of king's wife. However, she will be prepared and trained for the role of ruling queen. And if it transpires that her personality is of such dual capacity, then her role will be transformed and she will reign together with her husband, the king. Therefore, the question is whether Esther can back the title of queen by substance. Will she be able to transform her role from that of a beauty queen to that of a reigning figure?

The biblical text suggests that Esther has been well prepared for her role in Ahasuerus's court. Her introduction focuses on her genealogy, which connects her (through Mordecai, her cousin) to Kish, the father of Saul, the first king of Israel (Esth. 2.25; 1 Sam. 9.1-2). Such kin relationship is significant: it suggests that Esther is a queen by blood (she is related to a royal family). In addition, she is also trained for twelve months to become the king's wife (2.12). The process of teaching Esther how to please the king follows the palace protocol: she is entrusted to the hands of Hegai, who is in charge of the women (2.8). Esther passes the text and pleases Hegai (2.9), following his instructions to the letter (2.15).

It appears, therefore, that the biblical text contains an awareness of the two possibilities: of Esther being a queen in title

1.   L.B. Paton, *The Book of Esther* (ICC; Edinburgh: T. & T. Clark, 1976), p. 165.
2.   Paton in fact notices that accepting Esther as a reigning queen entails some difficulties since, according to Persian custom, the king's wife must be of Persian stock. Also, there are references to the custom that the queen must be a member of one of seven noble families. But, to offset these arguments, Paton also wonders why there was a need to choose a queen from outside the court when any of the other royal wives could have been elevated to that position (*Esther*, p. 165).

only; and of her taking an active role in ruling the land of Ahasuerus. The story is designed to verify the nature of Esther's place in the Persian court. The point is that she manages to establish herself as authoritative queen not only by her beauty, but also by her personality and wisdom. Esther knows how to communicate with people: she finds favour in the eyes of her attendants (2.7). Her discretion with regard to revealing her ancestry and identity (2.10) suggests that she knows what can and should be done, and what is forbidden, in the diplomatic arena. As an orphan (2.7), her family ties are not visible, thus she can act freely in court. At the same time, she is portrayed as the daughter of a monarchic family, which means that she has the genealogical background for becoming a queen.

Artists have chosen both approaches for the portrayal of Esther. Many of them, however, have been fascinated by the long preparatory process Esther has to undergo in order to become the king's wife, emphasizing the toiletries, cosmetics and rich wardrobe (2.12-14). She is supposed to become a companion to the king, hence is being groomed for her role in keeping with traditions of the Orient. Theodore Chasserieu's image of *Esther Preparing to Meet Ahasuerus* (1842; Figure 3) depicts a

> captive of another world brought into our civilization, clad in striped garments, sparkling with barbaric jewels, and resistant, like caged gazelles, with attitudes of wild grace.[1]

Esther's noble roots have been referred to in the biblical text; it appears that she is expected to justify her title by wisdom and back it by authority. At the beginning, however, when she is presented to Ahasuerus, it is not at all certain that she will be able to accomplish this goal. Rembrandt, an artist with an instinct for dramatic portrayal, shows Esther at the moment she is presented to Ahasuerus by Hegai. In his drawing *Esther is Presented to Ahasuerus* (1655; Figure 4), Rembrandt focuses on possible relationships. He presents Esther in a simple composition, with no rich background. The introduction emphasizes the relationship between Esther and her presenter and raises the

---

1. W. Griffith (ed.), *Great Painters and their Famous Bible Pictures* (New York: Wise, 1925), p. 80. Chasserieu was a native of the West Indies; cf. Griffith.

Figure 3. Theodore Chasserieu, *Esther Preparing to Meet Ahasuerus*
(Maison Ad. Brown & Cie, Paris, France).

Figure 4. Rembrandt, *Esther is Presented to Ahasuerus* (The Louvre, Paris, France).

question: will she rise to the challenge? The artist leaves the question open. He does not supply an answer, even though he might be supplying a clue: the king, who is rising from his throne, is standing next to the kneeling figure of Esther, while the throne remains empty in the background. Hence, it is up to the audience or viewers to fill in the details and to meditate on the outcome of this encounter.

Artists have left the audience to reflect on Esther's future role in Ahasuerus's court in other instances too. Konrad Witz seems to have bestowed upon Esther the full power of regnal authority. In his painting of *Esther and Ahasuerus* (fifteenth century; Figure 5), the king is crowning his queen while she is seated beside him. For Witz, Esther is the queen who succeeds in gaining power in Ahasuerus's court. She is an equal partner whom the king views as fit to partake in his political activities. However, in his portrayal of Esther, Witz's interpretation might have been influenced by the idea of attributing to Esther the role of mediator on behalf of her people. When imagined thus, Esther is compared with Mary and becomes the latter's prefiguration. It is possible that what Witz had in mind was not Esther queen of Persia but, rather, Mary mother of Christ. But whatever the capacity he attributes to Esther in his altar piece, her portrayal remains equivalent to that of the king's: the king grants the crown to Esther and she accepts it from him.[1] In this interpretation, Esther does seem to have become a woman whose throne is not simply adjacent to Ahasuerus's; she has acquired an independent personality. She appears to have succeeded in filling the throne. Her wisdom, perhaps inherited by this descendant of Saul's house from her monarchic line, is combined with the knowledge she could acquire when trained at the Persian palace for that particular position. She might have also learnt a lesson from her predecessor, Queen Vashti. As a result, she appears to be acting wisely and carefully.

Esther, whose main task is to become a messenger to the king on behalf of her people, has to calculate her moves in her husband's, the king's, court. At the same time, when the need arises she has to find a way of expressing herself skilfully—to

---

1.   J. Gantner, *Konrad Witz* (Vienna: Anton Schroll, 1943), p. 22.

Figure 5. Konrad Witz, *Esther and Ahasuerus*
(Öffentliche Kunstsammlung, Basel, Switzerland).

approach the king not as a subordinate figure but as an authoritative person who possesses a personality of her own and is, like the king, capable of running the country. It is fascinating to note how an artist of the third century CE already succeeds in portraying Esther in the Dura Europos synagogue as a figure who does not only carry a title because of her beauty, but is also a person and true ruler in her own right.

Strikingly enough, a modern Jewish artist follows the trend introduced by the Dura artist. In his illustration of Esther, L. Baskin (1978; Figure 6) neglects her beauty almost completely. Instead, he focuses on her pillar-like qualities. The visual image he creates is powerful. Esther's people rely on her, and she responds by becoming a tower of strength (ch. 4 onwards). There is no room then for dwelling upon beauty and jewellery. Since Esther is the person to act, she has to be at the centre of the picture. Baskin's portrayal of Esther is of a woman standing erect. She looks like an overwhelming tower, raised above the crowds. She is dressed in simple grey attire. The artist depicts Esther as a person who promises to do the best that can be expected; one hand is placed on her heart, and the other points downwards.[1] Esther is being perceived here as a queen who does not even need the throne in order to represent the authority of her regnal power.

In sum, the queen's throne has been filled by Esther. A wife of Ahasuerus, she might have been adored as a beauty queen. But her genealogical affiliation to the house of King Saul, together with her training at the house of King Ahasuerus and her personality, brought to the throne a woman capable of reigning. That mandate was given to her by her husband. However, she herself was capable of interpreting the role and creating an image of a queen with power to change her people's destiny.

It is fascinating to see how artists such as the Dura Europos painter and Baskin were able to express this visually, regardless of the differences in time and culture. Witz's approach is most interesting, for he points to the further developments Esther's image has undergone when the figure of Esther

---

1. Cf. Esth. 4.15-16.

Figure 6. Leonard Baskin, *Queen Esther*
(Central Conference of American Rabbis Press, New York).

became a prefiguration for the portrayal of Mary. However, artists like Chasserieu and Lippi were enchanted by the image of a subordinate female figure. Nonetheless, the debate engaged in by Bible commentators concerning Esther's role is echoed in Rembrandt's drawing. This drawing presents both possibilities: was Esther a queen by title only? Or did she in fact acquire the power to rule for herself?

HONOR AND SHAME IN ESTHER

Lillian R. Klein

Introduction

The book of Esther is held to offer a paradigm for Jewish life in the diaspora, as stated by Sidnie Ann White.[1] But this is only part of the picture. As exiles, the Jews are in a 'dependent' position, one associated with females, whereas autonomy and power are associated with males. These male and female 'roles'—representing, respectively, honor and shame—not only permeate the text of Esther, but are also used pointedly, to 'shame' the culture in which the Israelites are exiled and, by comparison, to 'honor' the Israelites. The Persians may not, historically, have responded to the same honor/shame codes as the Israelites, but the text suggests that they did, and the narrative ridicules the dominant culture, personified by the king, in terms of communal values or those of the minority culture. It does so through the agency of a woman, apparently because women are normally identified with shame.[2]

To support this claim of honor/shame as a definitive cultural value among the Israelites in the text of Esther, current cultural anthropological theories and sociological field studies are invoked, correlating similar social groups which demonstrate analogous features of economic life and economic constraints.[3]

1. S.A. White, 'Esther: A Feminine Model for Jewish Diaspora', in P.L. Day (ed.), *Gender and Difference in Ancient Israel* (Minneapolis: Fortress Press, 1989), pp. 161-77.
2. L.M. Bechtel, 'Shame as a Sanction of Social Control in Biblical Israel: Judicial, Political, and Social Shaming', *JSOT* 40 (1991), p. 63.
3. Cf. the illumination of ancient anthropological artifacts through contemporary sociological fieldwork in C.L. Meyers, 'Everyday Life: Women in the Period of the Hebrew Bible', in C.A. Newsom and S.H. Ringe (eds.),

Unlike those studies, the focus here is not on equating two social groups—one ancient, one modern; instead, honor/shame in contemporary sociological fieldwork is invoked to illuminate an ancient text. Working 'backwards', reading biblical texts through the paradigms of contemporary research, establishes an analogy. An analogy is not a mirror, however, and absolute consistency is not to be expected. Indeed, the deviations are provocative and rewarding.

Today, 'honor' is a term describing an obviously desirable condition involving recognition of self-worth and respect from others. In ancient (and some more recent) cultures, however, the term is involved with more specific conditions; and the primary condition for achieving honor is autonomy. One of the principal determinants of honor is sexual autonomy, and in the sexual sphere, only men could be autonomous. Women are marked as sexual beings by public awareness of menses and pregnancy, while men bear no outward witness of sexual activity. Therefore, in such a social structure, only men can be fully autonomous and be worthy of honor. Other elements of masculine honor involve providing for and protecting the reflected honor of the family, social prominence, manly courage and virility. Males can demonstrate their sexuality, even aggressively, but they are ostensibly capable of having that sexuality under control, whereas women, who menstruate and become pregnant, are not.

Women are not utterly denied honor, but usually they can only achieve it through 'shame'. In this context, shame achieves a positive value akin to honor, albeit not so obviously honorific. According to Bechtel, shame 'relates to failure or inadequacy to reach or live up to a socio-parental goal or idea';[1] and since women cannot achieve the honor associated with autonomy,

---

The Women's Bible Commentary (Louisville, KY: Westminster Press/John Knox, 1992), p. 245. See also C. Delaney, 'Seeds of Honor, Fields of Shame', in D.D. Gilmore (ed.), *Honor and Shame and the Unity of the Mediterranean* (American Anthropological Association Special Publication, 22; Washington, DC: American Anthropological Association, 1987), pp. 35-48; B.J. Malina, *The New Testament World: Insights from Cultural Anthropology* (Louisville, KY: Westminster Press/John Knox, rev. edn, 1993).

1.   Bechtel, 'Shame', p. 49.

they take pride in contributing to their males' honor through preservation of feminine modesty, that is, 'shame'. Furthermore, 'shame' is to be clearly distinguished from 'guilt' and from 'being shamed'.[1] Feminine 'shame' as a positive value is characterized by deference and submission to male authority, by docile and timorous behavior, by hiding nakedness, by sexual exclusiveness, and by modesty in attire and deportment. The absence of these qualities renders a woman 'shameless' and dishonors her family—particularly her husband, who cannot 'control' his wife—in the eyes of the community: 'a shameless person is one who does not recognize the rules of human interaction, who does not recognize social boundaries'.[2] A husband who fails in his obligations is likewise 'shamed'. To protect his honor and social reputation from his wife's shameful behavior, a husband has socially recognized strategies: segregation of his women, insisting that they remain veiled in public, and restricting their social behavior to 'women's spaces'.

Female spaces and female things are centered around the family residence and 'face toward the inside', and all things remaining within the home are identified with the female; those taken from the inside to the outside—the male 'space'—are identified with the male. Places of contact between the genders are 'male when males are present' or when females are 'properly chaperoned'.[3] Accordingly, women are excluded from male social assemblies.

In her chapter on 'Modesty, Gender and Sexuality', Lila Abu-Lughod points out that feminine modesty associates denial of sexuality with morality: 'the more [women] deny their sexuality, the more honorable they are'. Significantly, 'The woman [who is modest] does not allow herself to be seen by men [and] does

---

1. Quoting Bechtel: 'guilt relates to the *internalized, societal and parental prohibitions or boundaries* that cannot be transgressed (as opposed to the internalized goals and ideals [of shame]' (author's italics). 'Guilt' is imposed from *inwards* (conscience) and reinforced by social pressure; 'shame' arises predominantly from *external* pressure and is intensified by the internal apprehension of being shamed. 'Being shamed', which Bechtel does not distinguish, is a negative aspect of shame. The passive voice emphasizes its *external* origin. See Bechtel, 'Shame', p. 53.
2. Malina, *New Testament World*, p. 51.
3. Malina, *New Testament World*, p. 49.

not appear when guests or strangers visit her household'.[1] A modest woman forbears eating and talking in the presence of men. By suppressing her sexuality in front of men, a woman shows deference to and dependence upon males, thus validating their honor and prestige in the community. In this way, shame allows women to partake vicariously of honor.

These social values—honor and shame—constitute a 'basic pattern of affect, of what is symbolically meaningful' in societies where social approval of authoritative figures is characteristic of their patriarchal, segmentary structure.[2] These honor/shame codes are most effective in group-oriented societies, which tend to stratify social status, defining ranks of authority: king, elders, parent, husband, wife. Each class has a subordinate from whom it claims deference.[3] The individual or group that fails to uphold community honor is shamed by publicly exposing his, her or their failure to realize the internalized ideals of the society. The passive construction—'is shamed', 'being shamed'—conveys the lack of autonomy involved.

In ancient Israel, being shamed functioned in a range of contexts: judicial, political (including both warfare and diplomacy) and social. Tellingly, captive warriors of all ranks were stripped and led off naked and bound. Such nakedness exposed the prisoners to the elements and also exposed their genitals to public view. 'Walking naked entailed double shame...Part of the socialization process in Israel involved an awareness that public nakedness was inappropriate and unacceptable behavior'.[4] Exposure of the genitals depicted people as powerless and susceptible, putting males in the position of 'shameless' women, robbing them of their self-respect and pride, and demeaning them in the community.

1.   L. Abu-Lughod, *Veiled Sentiments: Honor and Poetry in a Bedouin Society* (Berkeley: University of California Press, 1986).
2.   Malina, *New Testament World*, p. 54.
3.   Malina, *New Testament World*, p. 54.
4.   Bechtel, 'Shame', p. 66.

The Palace Milieu

Because the cultural value of honor/shame is diffused through the entire book of Esther, the book will be treated as a unit, disregarding recent studies in the structure of the narrative which are valuable in another context. It is noted, however, that the exposition of the book is a self-contained narrative unit which provides background material for the rest of the book and, in so doing, establishes foil characters and foil situations, including honor/shame, against which the main action can be interpreted.[1] Significantly, the abuse of honor/shame in the exposition presages later developments. These developments do not necessarily polarize honor/shame in inflexible patterns; instead, elements of honor/shame shift and combine, revealing all-too-human individuals and a sophisticated text.

The narrative takes place in the royal palace of Persia; Ahasuerus's name may have been a title: 'chief of rulers'.[2] Apparently to assert his power, his autonomy, his honor, this 'chief of rulers' gives two banquets, distinguished by duration and by those who attend. The guests at the first banquet are the courtiers and nobles of the far-flung kingdom. As part of the aristocracy, these guests comprise a 'natural' group based on degree of honor or power; and the festivities last 180 days—approximately six months. The second banquet recognizes a more intimate 'natural' group, the 'family' of the palace, without regard for hierarchy.[3] The king's honor is enhanced by the opulence of both banquets and by his apparent authority over both kinds of natural groups: the ruling class of the far-flung hierarchy and the inclusive palace contingent.

The first insinuation that the king's autonomy is not consistent with his title occurs when these very banquets, which suggest redistributive banquets of tribal societies,[4] make no mention of

1. The king is the only character who bridges both actions.
2. W.J. Fuerst, *The Books of Ruth, Esther, Ecclesiastes, the Song of Songs, Lamentations: The Five Scrolls* (Cambridge: Cambridge University Press, 1975), p. 44.
3. Malina, *New Testament World*, p. 45.
4. M. Harris, *Cannibals and Kings: The Origins of Cultures* (New York: Random House, 1978), p. 113.

food. In fact, the honor sought in relating the costly accoutrements of the palace is subtly undermined by the excessively
protracted banquets (1.6-7)—which fail to mention food—and by
the emphasis on drink (1.7-8).[1] This innuendo of inconsistency is
reinforced when the king invites his courtiers to drink as much
as they want: Ahasuerus places no restrictions on their drinking
and thereby relinquishes his authority over their consumption.[2]
They are not invited to eat as much as they want, which does
not lead to loss of control, but are legally *decreed* to drink as
much as they want, even to become drunk:[3] 'And the drinking
was by law without restraint, for the king had ordered his
palace officials to do as each [man] wished' (1.8). Ahasuerus
legally relinquishes his autonomy over his guests in this sphere
and invites all of them—great and small—to do the same:
relinquish autonomy over themselves. Since autonomy is
essential to honor, the king's action undermines himself and his
people. Thus, from the outset, the Esther narrative subtly (and

1.   Persian drinking celebrations are historically verified; nevertheless,
the narrative renders ironic the redistribution not of nourishing food but of
alcohol, which, when consumed in the excessive quantities associated with
Persian banquets, is detrimental to life.

2.   I disagree with David Clines's claim that 'on every other front [except
the battle of the sexes] he [Ahasuerus] is masterfully supreme' (*The Esther
Scroll: The Story of the Story* [JSOTSup, 30; Sheffield: JSOT Press, 1984], p. 32).

3.   According to Israel Bettan, a midrash explains that the king issues an
order allowing the guests to drink at their own discretion. 'On festive occasions the Persian rulers used to serve wine in large cups which guests were
duty-bound to drain.' This time they were not so constrained (*The Five
Scrolls: A Commentary on the Song of Songs, Ruth, Lamentations, Ecclesiastes,
Esther* [Cincinnati: Union of American Hebrew Congregations, 1950],
p. 205). See also G.M. Lamsa, *Old Testament Light: The Indispensable Guide to
the Customs, Manners and Idioms of Biblical Times* (San Francisco: Harper &
Row, 1964), p. 404. The midrash makes it seem that the king is protecting
his guests from overindulgence. This is not supported by the statement that
the king's 'heart was merry with wine' (1.10). Surely his guests drank as he
did. M.V. Fox has a clearer analysis: 'The point is that no one was forced to
drink, but that no one was kept from drinking when and as much as he
wished, and that *this* was the king's "law" or edict: to let everyone do as he
wished' (author's italics) (*Character and Ideology in the Book of Esther*
[Columbia: University of South Carolina, 1991], p. 17). In any case, the control of drinking is shifted from the king to the guests.

repeatedly) proclaims the power and honor of Ahasuerus and his kingdom—and immediately, insidiously, undermines it.[1]

The king's questionable autonomy is further demonstrated after Ahasuerus uses his authority to command seven eunuchs to bring his queen Vashti to appear before the assembled non-kin males.[2] Bickerman observes that 'By custom, the wedded wives could be present at Persian dinners (Neh. 2.6). But they left when the drinking bout was to begin. At this time, concubines and courtesans came in.' Bickerman implicitly acknowledges the element of honor/shame: 'By coming to the king's party, Vashti would lose face, she would degrade herself to the position of a concubine'.[3] Losing face, we recall, is one of the major elements of the honor/shame system.

Actually, the king's command is contrary to the basic tenets of honor/shame, for he commands his wife to enter masculine space inappropriately, forbidden a woman who values her sense of shame; and his command only specifies that she wear her royal crown. Rabbinic commentary has interpreted that command to specify that she wear only her royal crown and appear naked, and gives her credit for refusing.[4] The degree of clothing accentuates a basic problem. Even fully clothed, Vashti is faced with a dilemma: whether to relinquish her claim to honor through abandoning her modesty and appearing in a forbidden masculine space, or through defying her husband's authority. She chooses the latter.

When Vashti acts autonomously and refuses, the king again does not manifest his royal control or leadership in his response; he asks for the judgment of his wise men. These men are described as knowing 'the times' (1.13), and the text suggests that this is the king's customary response. His 'customary'

1. This pattern of elevation and denigration initially includes Haman, as part of the Persian court, but Haman will be distinguished from the Persians.

2. This is virtually the only specific command the king initiates on his own; and it is impulsive, shortsighted and probably drunken. All other such royal commands follow the advice of others—servants, court advisors and even a woman, his queen—until the conclusion.

3. E. Bickerman, *Four Strange Books of the Bible* (New York: Schocken Books, 1967), pp. 185-86.

4. *Est. R.* 3.13-14 (trans. M. Simon; London: Soncino Press, 1951).

response reinforces the image of the king as one who does not exercise his autonomy or authority independently but seeks sage advice. Despite the expectations of autonomic honor, Ahasuerus's practice of consulting sages can be taken as an encouraging sign (that he is not a tyrant, that he is seeking wisdom)—until the judgment of these 'sages' reflects negatively on the king. Indeed, elements of this negative view of the king have been noted in scholarly literature. For instance, David Clines says, 'The satire is against the king, Persians, men', and he even acknowledges that the king has 'lost face'.[1]

The 'wise men' advise the king to dismiss Queen Vashti because, if her behaviour is tolerated, the other wives (especially the wives of these courtiers?) might behave in a similar way and refuse to defer to their husbands. The whole honor/shame edifice might tumble if women were to assert their own autonomy, even to protect their own shame. The king acquiesces: he 'leads' by following his courtiers.

When the king's wrath against Vashti has subsided, it is the king's servants who, in effect, initiate the search for a replacement. The servants direct,

> Seek beautiful young virgins for the king
> And the king will appoint officers...
> And the young woman who pleases the king shall rule
> instead of Vashti (2.2-4).

Once again, the authority of the king is undermined by others' autonomous words, this time words of relatively insignificant members of the palace household, words which direct not only what shall *be done* (seek virgins) but also what the king shall *do* (choose officers). Most surprising is the statement that the chosen woman will 'rule instead of Vashti'. It may be that the reader is to assume that the queen will 'rule' over the harem, but the ambiguity, especially in light of Esther's subsequent actions, is provocative. The text has already delineated a paradoxically non-autonomous king, and this verse prefigures an (equally paradoxical) autonomous queen. Consistent in his character, the king once more follows the lead of his followers.

---

1.   Clines, *The Esther Scroll*, p. 32.

The Beauty Contest

At this juncture, Mordecai is introduced with full genealogy and history to explain his presence in Susa and his relationship with his niece, Esther, all of which serves to present Mordecai as a man of honor. Mordecai, we note, does not direct Esther to enter the beauty contest and remains uninvolved in this un-Jewish behavior. Nevertheless, he does nothing to interfere with Esther's entering into a situation foreign to Jews or her potential loss of shame. On her part, Esther's participation is passive, as befits a modest woman and a Jew in a foreign culture: 'Esther was also brought to the king's house' (2.8). The question remains how Jewish values can be assimilated to a beauty contest and the possibility of harem life. I suggest that this episode foreshadows other events of the narrative which tacitly posit and approve that the Persian (diaspora) Jews maintain a 'low profile', by publicly assimilating to the practices of the host culture and, in this instance, by not refusing to give up their virgins to the king's command. The narrative suggests that group survival supersedes even a 'basic pattern of affect' such as honor/shame. (The conclusion affirms that the Jewish community and Jewish identity is to be maintained intact, presumably in the seclusion of the Jewish home and community.)

This bid to judge women by their physical appearance recalls the king's command to Vashti to appear before and be admired by his courtiers. We may ask what the difference is between Vashti's display of her beauty and Esther's (and the other virgins'). Rabbinic commentary notwithstanding, the maidens' clothing—or lack thereof—is unknown. To my knowledge, no one has questioned the exposure required in the beauty contest; and it seems likely that Mordecai accedes with Esther's entering into a situation in which her beauty of body as well as face will be judged—probably as fully exposed as Vashti, or more so.[1] A basic difference is that Vashti is *one* woman confronted in *male space* with *many men* as judges; Esther is among *many* women confronted in *female space* with *one man* as judge. In both

1. Modern beauty contests expose as much of the body as is socially acceptable. Of course a king can establish his own rules of exposure.

circumstances, the females are unveiled and implicitly exposed before males who are not male blood relatives (patrikin) and are not husbands, thus threatening the female sense of shame—their perception of their own reputations. Vashti refuses to defer to her husband, protecting her shame; and she is summarily dismissed from her title and from the narrative, never to be heard of again. Esther, unlike Vashti, does not protest; it is implied that she is obedient to her patrikin when she reveals her beauty to the king.[1] Certainly Vashti is confronted with a much more shaming situation; but Esther is also faced with behavior not in accord with her (Jewish) values. The connotation is that women should obey their patrikin or husbands even if their shame is threatened. Female obedience to male authority is shown to be preferable to insistence on established communal values.

The modesty code of feminine shame requires discriminating women to deny sexual interests and to avoid men who are not kin, by not allowing themselves to be seen by men and by acting and dressing to avoid drawing attention to their beauty.[2] The beauty contest—suggested by the servants to find Ahasuerus a mate—violates the values of honor/shame more blatantly than Vashti's refusal does, but in ways which dishonor the women, not the men.

Esther's deference to Mordecai's command that she not 'reveal her people or her kindred' (2.10) is consonant with loyalties in patricentered systems: the women remain bound to their patrikin even in marriage.[3] Mordecai, as the responsible patrikin, is sufficiently concerned about his charge that he 'walked to and fro every day [for twelve months!] in front of the court of the women's quarters in order to learn of Esther's

1. A beauty contest demands greater than normal exposure, especially in a society which demands that its women be covered and veiled. Even uncovering of the face is 'exposure', though more disrobing is presumed in a beauty contest. Nakedness is not.
2. Abu-Lughod, *Veiled Sentiments*, pp. 152-53.
3. Abu-Lughod observes that the sexual bond is threatening to the kinship bond: it can break up male-determined kinship lines. To counter this, females are conditioned to remain primarily loyal to patrikin (*Veiled Sentiments*, pp. 148-49).

welfare and what would be done to her' (2.11). Mordecai's perambulations emphasize the normally strict separation of male and female spaces and make the king's command to Vashti to appear among the men seem all the more capricious. Similarly, Esther's 'modesty' in this immodest situation is underscored by passivity: in 2.8, Esther 'was brought to the king's house'; and in 2.11, Mordecai is concerned with 'what will become of her'.

After a twelve-month period of beautification, each young woman 'goes in to' the king, leaving the women's quarters in the evening and returning in the morning (2.13-14). There is no doubt that a sexual encounter takes place, that the virgins return to the women's quarters unsuitable for marriage or any alliance outside the king's harem.[1] The honor/shame of life in the king's harem may excuse the loss of shame the virgins suffer and even justify unchaste sex for a Jewess living in exile.[2] Esther is spared this dilemma by being chosen queen and duly married, albeit to a non-Jew. Recognizing a preference for low public profile as exiled Jews (shame) and outward assimilation with the dominant culture (honor) clarifies Esther's un-Jewish behavior and explains Mordecai's cautioning Esther to keep her Jewish heritage secret.

With the king's choice of Esther as his queen, mention is first made of Mordecai's sitting 'in the king's gate' (2.19), an honorific position. The very next verse (2.20) reminds the reader that Esther has not revealed herself as a Jew because 'Esther obeyed the command of Mordecai, as she did when she was supported by him'. As expected, despite her marriage to the king, Esther's primary loyalties remain with her patrikin.

Mordecai's newly-augmented honor positions him to overhear the plot of two eunuchs against the king. Surely the fact that eunuchs—feminized, hence non-autonomous 'males'—are plotting against the king, the epitome of male power, suggests

1.   Fox proposes that 'the actual competition, to take place after a year of beauty treatments is a *sex* contest, with the winner being whoever can most please the king during her night with him' (author's italics) (*Character and Ideology*, p. 28).

2.   White suggests that the reader 'accept the worldview of the text' which makes Esther 'a more sympathetic character'. Honor/shame helps understand that worldview ('Esther', p. 168).

that the 'normal' honor/shame values of the community are ironically skewed. Curiously, despite the strict separation earlier, Mordecai is somehow able to relate the plot directly to the queen: there is no mention of transmission by messenger (2.22). Esther, still modest and obedient, gives credit to Mordecai and does not assert herself in relaying the message. Significantly, at this juncture there also seems to be no problem with direct access to the king: 'And Esther told the king in Mordecai's name' (2.22). The culprits are punished, and the events are 'written in the book of the chronicles before [לִפְנֵי, 'in the face of'] the king' (2.23). The presence of the king emphasizes his knowledge and approval of the entry.[1]

Jews (Mordecai) versus Amalekites (Haman)

The king's leadership is immediately brought into question when he elevates not Mordecai, who has saved his life, but Haman, the son of Hammedatha the Agagite. Like Mordecai, Haman is provided with a genealogy and family identification, one which invokes the enmity between their respective peoples—Jews and Amalekites.[2] (It also implicitly differentiates between Haman the Agagite and the Persian ruler in whose kingdom he resides.) It is against the background of Mordecai's life-saving deed that the king, without any apparent grounds for doing so, honors Haman to sit over all the other courtiers, who must now bow and worship him.[3]

This action increases Haman's honor vis-à-vis Mordecai (and all the other courtiers); but Mordecai, unlike the other courtiers, refuses to recognize Haman's position. Mordecai apparently justifies his refusal by identifying himself as a Jew (3.4). Haman responds by including *all* the Jews in his revenge: he 'scorned to lay hand on Mordecai alone for they had revealed to him the people of Mordecai' (3.6).

---

1. It also hints that although he dictates laws and commandments, the king does no reading or writing on his own, further poking fun at his autonomy.

2. See 1 Sam. 15; 27.8; 30.1, 18; 2 Sam. 1.1; 1 Chron. 4.43.

3. '"Worship" originally meant "worthiness", a recognition of worth' (Malina, *New Testament World*, p. 48).

What is it that necessitates Mordecai's abandoning his well-preserved public anonymity? Nothing less than his perception that his honor has been affronted. Esther may lose her shame, but Mordecai the Jew will not bow before an Amalekite, the prototypical enemy of the Jew.[1] The effect is that Mordecai the Jew refuses to acknowledge the position of Haman the Amalekite, implying that the latter is a lesser man. Haman is enraged that his honor is decried and decides to revenge himself not only on Mordecai but also on all Jews. Mordecai has publicly shamed Haman; and Haman seeks to avenge himself by destroying Mordecai and his entire people, thereby reasserting his (Haman's) honor in the eyes of the community.

In response to Haman's complaint against 'a certain people' and promised economic advantage, the king takes off the royal ring, his seal of authority, and gives it to Haman.[2] The king has acceded without question and without verification (a form of control) of Haman's claims, with 'feminine' impulsiveness instead of 'masculine' consideration. By handing over the royal ring, the authority which the king has consistently been ambivalent about exercising is symbolically relinquished, again bringing his autonomy (honor) into question, and establishing the lax ('feminine', as opposed to 'masculine' control) manner with which the king exercises the authority of his position. The royal signet ring and power of decree, symbol of consummate masculine autonomy, is ceded to one of lesser degree in a paradoxically 'feminine' reaction.

A few verses later, Haman issues commands to the king's lieutenants and to the provincial governors. The runners are hurried out by the 'king's word [commandment]' (3.15), for the king's seal-ring proclaims the king's word, even if it originates with someone else. (The linguistic motif of 'hurry' links Haman's rise and fall: here he hurries others with the power of the king's ring; later, he will be hurried.) With Haman's word under the king's seal, the two men—the king, a leader shamed by his lack of autonomy, and Haman, a subject who 'leads' the king—sit

---

1.   As in the verses cited above (n. 2 p. 159), and also Exod. 17.8-16, esp. v. 16b: 'for YHWH wages war against the Amalekites generation after generation'.

2.   Haman is here specifically identified as an enemy of the Jews (3.10).

down to drink. Once again, drink is associated with the king's inappropriate want of autonomy.

To this point in the narrative, Mordecai has represented the honor/shame of the assimilated Israelites, and Ahasuerus has exemplified the paradoxically foolish (shamed) leader (honor) of the Persians. With the crisis precipitated by Haman's actions against the Jews, these roles shift: Mordecai's autonomy seems displaced to Esther, who acts autonomously but modestly, never seeking the male prerogative of public honor; and Haman usurps the role of shame, surpassing and, by comparison, somewhat redeeming the Persian king.

Esther Honors Shame

Mordecai's response to the warrant for genocide is to shame himself openly by tearing his clothes, by putting on sackcloth and ashes, and by crying publicly, loudly and bitterly (4.1). Esther's reaction is dramatic: 'she writhed in pain exceedingly' (4.4) and immediately sends clothing to reassert his honor; for Mordecai's abasing himself shames not only himself but also his family, including Esther. After all, with Mordecai's self-abasement, Esther's kinship male-authority figure has been made weak, 'feminized'. This creates a paradoxical position for Esther: she is outwardly honored as queen and inwardly shamed by her uncle's shame. Naturally, she seeks to restore honor to her uncle (and herself) by sending him proper clothing.[1] It is also clear that, in the protection of the harem, Esther does not know of Haman's and Ahasuerus's edicts against the Jews and the cause of Mordecai's shaming himself.

Upon Mordecai's refusal, Esther gives Hatach the eunuch an order (צוה) to ascertain the reason for Mordecai's aberrant behavior, confirming that she does not know of the edict (4.5). Despite self-dishonor, Mordecai retains authority; he uses a string of verbs and verbal phrases directed to Esther: 'give',

---

1. Without insight into honor/shame, R. Lubitch questions 'How narrow-minded could she [Esther] possibly have been to send clothes for Mordekhai before investigating the matter!' ('A Feminist's Look at Esther', *Judaism* 42.4 [1993], p. 440).

'show', 'declare', 'command', 'order (צוה) her to go', 'make supplication', 'seek help' (4.8). Esther's response gives Hatach the eunuch an order (צוה) to deliver a message to Mordecai but does not command her relative; she merely reminds Mordecai (and informs the reader) of the danger involved in appearing before the king without express summons (4.9). Mordecai abandons honor but retains authority; Esther assumes authority but maintains deference. Consistent with the established separation of authorized male and female spaces, all communication between Esther and Mordecai is not direct but through a eunuch—a 'safe' demi-male—as messenger. Mordecai does not risk approaching Esther but wants Esther to approach the king. An element of ruthlessness—or is it disdain for women?—in Mordecai's character may be inferred.

Although Esther protests that she cannot approach the king without his having called for her, the narrative shows that she has approached him earlier to tell him of Mordecai's discovery of the plot (2.22) without any mention of the sceptre of approval. Is this a device to increase narrative tension? This conjecture seems validated by Esther's descriptive emphasis on what is assumed to be common knowledge about the rules of the inner court. Along with increased suspense, this narrative tactic also allows the danger of Esther's mission to ennoble her.

Initially, Mordecai interprets Esther's response as refusal. He maintains his 'command' (צוה) form (4.13) to the eunuch(s) and uses a threatening tone to Esther, even implying that her role as queen may have the intrinsic purpose of saving the Jews from this predicament (4.14). Esther then breaks the series of 'orders', using the milder 'speak' (אמר) to direct the messengers; and this time her words, without specific mention of command (צוה), do convey an imperative to Mordecai: 'Go, gather...and fast' (4.16). These astute variations toy with autonomy and dependence—honor and shame.

Subtly, Esther maintains her feminine 'shame' even as she assumes increased responsibility. I suggest that she manages this by shifting her allegiance from Mordecai to a higher male authority, God. Although God is never mentioned in this book, Esther summons a traditional avenue of prayer and supplication:

fasting, including abstinence from all drink.[1] She asks all the
Jews to fast for her, as she will do with her maidens, for three
days. Offering the epitome of effacement, Esther is willing
to surrender her own life for the sake of the community,
to save her people: 'If I die, I die' (4.16). Mordecai's response
is to do 'all that Esther had commanded him' (4.17). In paradoxical tandem, Esther remains outwardly deferential, but
Mordecai acknowledges her power.

Despite her autonomous decision, Esther does not act as an
independent agent. She ritualizes by fasting and communalizes
by involving all the people and her maidens at the court. These
are Jewish responses to be tacitly compared with the banquets,
especially with the non-ritualized, unrestrained drinking of the
Persians. The apparatus of honor/shame suggests that power
and honor do not shift from Mordecai to Esther; they pass from
Mordecai to a greater power through whom Esther works.
Esther's response subtly compares the Jewish greater power
with the Persian kingly power, to the detriment of the Persian
ruler of the Jews.

Esther dresses herself in royal clothing for her unexpected
visit to the king. By so doing, she calls attention to her beauty
and her sexual appeal, not denying them in the manner of feminine modesty and shame. It seems that individual abuses of
honor/shame may be acceptable but communal honor must be
maintained.[2] This behavior can be seen as a paradigm for the
Jews in exile.

Ahasuerus assumes that there is a request (בקשה) attached to
Esther's appearance and makes exaggerated promises. The
beautifully-dressed (shameless) Esther answers with extreme
modesty (shame), seeking the king's approval ('if [it seems]
good to the king' [5.4]) before inviting him and Haman to a
banquet prepared for him.[3] This banquet, unlike the earlier

---

1.   'Normally [fasting] involved abstinence from all food to show
dependence on God and submission to his will' (J.N. Suggit, 'Fasting', in
B.M. Metzger and M.D. Coogan [eds.], *The Oxford Companion to the Bible*
[New York: Oxford University Press, 1993], p. 225).
2.   This also accords with her participation in the Persian beauty contest
and its sexual consequences.
3.   Both men are invited, but the banquet is prepared for the king.

ones, is private, in the queen's quarters, and prepared by Esther herself, thereby reinforcing her feminine shame by acting as 'servant' to the men.[1] Ahasuerus sends a message to hurry (מהר) Haman to do the queen's bidding, which subtly shifts authority from the king to his queen: Haman is to follow the directives of a woman. Since it is 'inappropriate' for a 'dominant' male to be commanded by a 'submissive' female, the narrative discreetly ridicules Haman.[2]

At the banquet, Ahasuerus once again seeks to learn what Esther will ask, her petition (שאל); and he repeats his exaggerated promises. As before, the king's hyperbole is an effective contrast with Esther's even more humbled response. This time, two conditional subjunctive phrases ('if I have found favor in the eyes of the king', and 'if [it seems] good to the king' [5.8]) precede her petition (שאלה) and her request (בקשה), which is for their attendance at a second banquet which Esther will prepare. Esther concludes her request by submitting her authority to the king's: she will act 'according to the king's word' (5.8). Esther's words and actions all support her claim to shame. They also draw attention to the authority of the king's word, providing a foil for his actions.

With the king's acquiescence implied, the narrative shifts temporarily to a omniscient point of view. Until now, it has been objective, rendering what could be seen or heard but offering no inner feelings or thoughts. Suddenly the reader is invited to perceive Haman's shifting inner responses to the honor of a second invitation and to Mordecai's refusal to honor him. This brief change of perspective allows the reader to experience Haman's barely-controlled fury and, since control is tantamount to autonomy, Haman's equivocal honor. Once more objective, the narrative shows Haman at home with his wife and friends, to whom he brags about the various kinds of honor he has accrued, culminating in Esther's banquets. He flaunts the fact that Esther herself prepares them and that he is the only (outside) man invited. Ironically, Haman depicts himself as honored by a woman's invitation to table. Even as he

1. It also reverses Vashti's non-appearance in a male space by inviting Haman to a female space.
2. Bechtel, 'Shame', p. 61.

claims honor, he diminishes that honor.

Yet all the honor 'avails [Haman] nothing' in the light of Mordecai's presence at the king's gate (5.9). Mordecai's refusal to honor Haman, in fact, effectively counters all the honor Haman has received and evokes shame. Haman does not know how to thwart Mordecai; only advice from his wife and his friends generates a pleasing plan of action (to build an execution scaffold). The advice Haman takes is primarily from his wife, named first and followed by 'his friends' (5.14), pointedly in reverse order from an earlier passage (5.10). It is implicitly shameful that a man rely on his wife for advice about public matters; thus the narrative shames Haman even as it displays his pride. Haman's reliance on the advice of others is consistent with that of a group-oriented, honor/shame-motivated person, who 'simply needs another continually in order to know who he or she really is...Such persons internalize and make their own what others say, do, and think about them because they believe it is necessary...to live out the expectations of others'.[1]

In a shift of scene (6.1-4), Ahasuerus's sleeplessness, which he seeks to relieve by being read to from the chronicle records, makes him aware of Mordecai's honorable action in protecting the king. Even this event slyly pokes fun at the king. Although it was written 'to his face', this most honored figure in the land commended someone else and only now, inadvertently, recognizes the need to reward. Ahasuerus has to ask what has been done to honor and dignify Mordecai. The implication is that he does not know what is going on in his palace, let alone in his kingdom. Ahasuerus's dependence is stressed by his immediately seeking advice when he learns that Mordecai has not been rewarded:

> Nothing has been done for him [Mordecai].
> And the king said, who [is] in the court? (6.3b-4).

The king's leadership—honor—has been consistently presented ironically.

Situational irony adds zest to the developments. Haman happens to be in the outer court, seeking permission to hang Mordecai on the newly-constructed scaffold, when Ahasuerus

---

1. Malina, *New Testament World*, p. 67.

consults him on how to honor 'the man whom the king wants to honor' (6.6). Haman naturally thinks he is to be honored, so he advises public recognition—essential to honor—in the king's robes, attired by 'one of the king's most noble courtiers' (6.9). There is no royal consideration or evaluation: the king impetuously wants the advice he has received followed immediately—'Hurry!' (מהר)—as he earlier directed Haman to hurry (מהר) to come to Esther's banquet, another subtle erosion of his honor.

The irony becomes multidimensional when Haman, as 'one of the king's most noble courtiers', must dress Mordecai, lead him through the streets and proclaim him as recipient of the king's honor. Haman's honor as a noble courtier actually shames him when he must honor Mordecai, his enemy. The Mordecai–Haman (Jew–Amalekite) opposition is reinforced when Mordecai returns to the king's gate, royally attired, but Haman 'hurried to his house mourning' (6.12), just as Mordecai was earlier in the mourning attire of sackcloth and ashes and Haman was honored by the king. Even Haman's counselors, his friends and his wife, predict Haman's defeat 'if Mordecai [is] of the seed of the Jews' (6.13). With these words, the narrative foreshadows the culminating triumph—honor—of the Jews. In so doing, the opposition of good (Mordecai, Jews) and evil (Haman, Amalekites) avoids directly involving the Persian kingdom in which the Jews are exiled. Ahasuerus may be diffident and impetuous but he is not associated with evil.

With this prognosis of doom from his wife and friends, Haman is rushed by the king's eunuchs to Esther's banquet. The delightful play on honor/shame ironically represents Haman's 'honor' as he is being 'hurried'—without the autonomy of his own time—by eunuchs to a woman's banquet. He does not enter alone; the king must accompany him to Esther's quarters in the restricted women's area of the palace.

As before, the king seeks to know Esther's request (בקשׁ) and makes promises of generosity. Esther's long-postponed enunciation of her wish is preceded by two deferential phrases similar to the ones she used at her earlier banquet (7.3), and this time her wish is not directed toward the narrow sphere of her two guests, Ahasuerus and Haman. In a surprising shift from the inner, woman's sphere to the outer, political, male sphere,

Esther pleads for her people, all the Jews exiled in Persia. In answer to the king's query after her request (בקשה), Esther personalizes and dramatizes her wish by first asking for her own life by petition (שאל) and then for the life of her people by request (בקשה). She identifies her people with herself, as queen and as the king's beloved, by saying 'We are sold, my people and I' (7.4). The planned genocide is dramatically tripled in expression: 'to be destroyed, to be killed, and to perish' (7.4). In conclusion, Esther emphasizes her humility (shame) by insisting she would not speak were they to be sold as slaves, as Haman had slyly implied, even though the damage to the king would far exceed the reparations (the ten thousand talents of silver paid by Haman) made by the enemy.[1]

The king naturally wants to know whose heart is so filled (with pride, self-honor) to do this. Esther again triples her answer and adds a fourth expression, surpassing the three forms of death with four qualities of the enemy: 'A man, an enemy, a hater—Haman! This evil [one]' (7.6). Implicitly, Esther has identified herself as a Jew, and she has done so without permission from Mordecai, her patrikin. She apparently acts on her own initiative, but humbly, seeking no honor for herself. Indeed, Esther's decisiveness (power, honor) coupled with humility (shame) is in sharp contrast to masculine indecisiveness (Ahasuerus) and pride (Haman). Even Mordecai is powerless to protect the Jews. This woman—whose traditional claim to (vicarious) honor is through feminine shame and by ennobling her male kinsmen—achieves what her patrikin cannot. Paradoxically, Esther gains honor through her opportune practice of shame.

The king's response is consistent with his character. Without an able advisor nearby to tell him what to do, he does nothing—that is, he seeks to vent his anger by leaving the scene and walking in the palace garden. When he returns, he misinterprets Haman's prostrating himself before the queen as 'ravishing' her; and, to add to the affront, Haman has not even waited until the king has left the house. The king not only jumps to conclusions which offend his honor but, consistent with his character, does

---

1.   See S.B. Berg's cogent analysis of Haman's petition to Ahasuerus and Esther's response in her plea in *The Book of Esther: Motifs, Themes and Structure* (Missoula, MT: Scholars Press, 1979), pp. 100-103.

not investigate his suspicions, voicing what appears to be a purely rhetorical question (7.8). Ahasuerus's impetuous response contributes to his image as ineffectual ('feminine') even as it reinforces the honor/shame values of the culture.

Instead of improving his situation, Haman has insured his own demise. It is noteworthy that Haman, who was brought into the queen's quarters by the king, has his face *covered* to leave.[1] The strict exclusion of the harem, broken only on Esther's request, is restored, and Haman's right to sight of forbidden (female) spaces is revoked. The royal anger is not dispelled until, at the recommendation of a eunuch, Haman is hanged on the scaffold he had prepared for Mordecai.

Ahasuerus does give Haman's house to Esther, but this narrated action does not permit knowledge of the king's dependence or autonomy. On the other hand, Mordecai is invited to appear before the king because 'Esther had told what he was to her' (8.1). Esther had earlier revealed herself as a Jew; now she reveals her relationship to Mordecai—again apparently autonomously. The king, consistently impetuous, gives Mordecai the ring (and the honor) which he had withdrawn from Haman. Ahasuerus apparently relinquishes his authority and his honor rather lightly, which emphasizes once again his impotence, his inadequacy, his deficiency in honor, as leader.[2] Indeed, it is Esther, not Ahasuerus, who 'set[s] Mordecai over the house of Haman' (8.2).

Esther's power (honor) is quickly and characteristically mitigated by humility (shame) as she prostrates herself before the king (8.3).[3] Her deference to the king's authority is heightened

---

1.   In the Hebrew of 7.9, the last sentence (וּפְנֵי הָמָן חָפוּ) may be understood as 'his face was covered' (but cf. suggestions in *BHS* to emend, following the LXX). The 'covering' of Haman's face, however, is *not* in preparation for the gallows (as our knowledge of European custom might tempt us to assume). In any event, the king has no knowledge of the already-prepared 'tree' until he is informed by Harvona the eunuch in the next verse (7.10).

2.   Autonomy is closely identified with sexual prowess, and a slight to a male's honor implies a slight to his sexual competence.

3.   Her presence does raise the question of the danger involved in an unsummoned appearance. The verse (8.3) begins, 'Esther added and spoke before the king', which conveys the impression that her comments

by her tears as she 'begs favor' of him to countermand Haman's plot. Significantly, Haman, whose name has not been otherwise qualified since 3.1, is suddenly and consistently referred to as 'Haman the Agagite' or 'Haman the son of Hammedatha the Agagite', which emphasizes Haman's role as prototypical enemy of the Jews and also separates him from the Persian king and his people. This and the following passages subtly mark the shift of authority from Mordecai to Esther (who nevertheless remains modest) and a shift of shame from the king (who retains leadership) to Haman.

To couch her plea with utmost intensity, this time Esther uses four separate phrases of supplication:

If it pleases the king,	(shame)
and if I have found favor in his sight,	(shameless)
and the thing is right before the king,	(shame)
and I [am] pleasing in his eyes (8.5)	(shameless)

To her modest (shame) phrases, Esther adds clear reminders of her (sexual) appeal to Ahasuerus, including a 'shameless' coda recalling the earlier and less pronounced 'if I have found favor in [the king's] sight' (7.3). Esther's clever balance of shame and shamelessness in her actions is succinctly expressed as she seeks to redress Haman's edict.

Esther wants to retrieve the letters sent by Haman with the king's authority (seal-ring) to forestall the planned genocide. She pesonalizes her plea in terms of the pain it will cause her:

For how will I face the evil which my people will find?
And how can I face the slaughter of my kindred? (8.6).

Esther reiterates the patriarchal kinship bond, the foundation of Jewish honor/shame cultural values, in her appeal.[1] The king

occurred at the same sitting. It may be that Esther was present when Mordecai was honored and that she uses the opportunity to introduce her own interests. To counter this assumption, the text also says, 'the king held out the golden scepter toward Esther' (8.4), suggesting a separate appearance. Bettan says that the king's holding out his sceptre is not a sign of audience but of favor to her petition (*The Five Scrolls*, p. 236).

1.   'Honor might be described as socially proper attitudes and behavior in the area where the three lines of power, gender status and religion intersect' (Malina, *New Testament World*, p. 31).

responds by reiterating what he has done (given Esther Haman's house and hanged Haman) 'because he [Haman] laid his hands on the Jews' (8.7), but he cannot rescind what has been written with his authority. Instead, he advises Esther and Mordecai to write for the Jews, 'as it pleases' them, 'in the king's name and seal it with the king's ring' (8.8). Ahasuerus's advice is an apparently autonomous move, without counsel, which begins to restore his authority and honor. His independent action avoids characterizing the king as in the power of the Jews and also emphasizes that Ahasuerus does not save the Jews; the Jews do.

The scribes are called in, but it is Mordecai, not Esther, who dictates the letters to be sent out in the name of Ahasuerus and sealed with his ring. Esther, who has employed autonomy and power to save her people, does not seem to strive for power or to accrue masculine honor for herself. She reverts to modest shame, and Mordecai increasingly resumes authority and honor.

Mordecai cannot undo the edict permitting attack on the Jews, but he can direct the Jews to assemble and to avenge (נקם) themselves. Haman's edict had not permitted the Jews self-defense: they were reduced to the (feminine) position of helplessness (shame), unable to protect their own families and their honor. Mordecai's edict permits them to congregate and not only defend themselves (as powerless women) but also to avenge themselves (as honorable men)—but they may kill only those who attack them, including women and children. The text suggests that if women and children assume the male prerogative of autonomous aggression, they will be treated as males. The Jews are also authorized to plunder those who are killed, just as Haman encouraged the people to plunder the Jews. Plundering is an expression of autonomy and authority over another, but the Jews decline to exercise this form of power (9.9, 16).[1]

Only when the Jewish population has been notified does Mordecai celebrate his elevated position and honor. Since honor must be recognized publicly, Mordecai's prominence is again

1. Their refusal 'reverses' the sin of the Israelite war with the Amalekites (1 Sam. 15), when Saul disobeyed by allowing the people to take booty.

proclaimed by public parade in royal accoutrements. Whereas the city of Susa was 'troubled' with Haman's edict, it rejoices with recognition of Mordecai. The narrative repeatedly attributes unwarranted pride, honor-grabbing and enmity toward the Jews to Haman and his people, and separates those qualities from the Persian population.[1]

> For the Jews there was light and gladness and joy and honor.
> ...the Jews had joy and gladness, a feast[2] and a good day (6.16-17b).

The Jews have honor (8.16)—autonomy and power—through Mordecai's honorific position even though they are in exile, in a dependent situation. This passage highlights a major thrust of the book: how diaspora Jews can achieve honor and autonomy within a foreign culture in which they are an ineffective—if not scorned—minority. The outward assimilation to the dominant culture is developed in the closing chapters to emphasize the cohesiveness of the Jewish community.

On schedule, on the day when 'the enemies of the Jews hoped to have *power* over them', the reverse occurs, and the 'Jews had *rule* over the ones who hated them' (9.1). The Jews are depicted as invincible: 'no one would withstand them'; and part of their power is the people's awe of the Jews. Even the provincial ruling nobles come to the aid of the Jews, and the awe shifts from the Jews en masse to Mordecai (9.3). Symbolic leader and representative of the Jews, Mordecai personifies the people; and his honor in Susa gives honor to the people. With Mordecai's public honor, the narrative also continues the transference of honor from Esther to Mordecai so that the conclusion specifies a male symbol of honor for the patriarchal Jews. The text emphasizes that this is a struggle not only for life but also for autonomy; and the Jews, even in exile, are accorded independence and honor as they 'rule over' their attackers by avenging themselves but not taking spoil (9.10).

1.   Nevertheless, there must have been some segment that thought as Haman did if the numbers of people killed by the Jews (9.5-6, 16) are indicative of an opposition.
2.   Contrary to all the drinking parties of the Persians, no drink is mentioned here. Nevertheless, Purim traditionally includes plenty of drinking.

The text celebrates the Jews' autonomy and honor in details of the narrative resolution: a round number of five hundred men 'killed and destroyed' is given veracity by adding named individuals, enemies of the Jews in the palace of Susa, including the sons of Haman (9.6-10). Ahasuerus is duly notified and suddenly, apparently without being summoned, Esther is again in the king's presence. No formality of sceptre-touching occurs here (which adds to scepticism about the earlier drama). The king tells Esther what has happened in Susa and asks for her further requests. Although he does ask for information ('What have they done in the rest of the king's provinces?' [9.12]), Ahasuerus does not ask for advice and thereby retains his autonomy and honor.

This time, Esther's requests are prefaced by only one phrase of humility ('If it pleases the king' [9.13]). Perhaps this and her unsummoned appearance attest to her newly-attained confidence (but not transgressing deferential shame) with her husband and king. She asks that Haman's already-dead sons be hanged in public disgrace, presumably to shame utterly the enemies of the Jews; and that the following day also be designated for the Jews' avenging themselves against their enemies. Her request is granted. Three hundred enemy men are killed in Susa on the second day and an additional seventy-five thousand in the provinces; and again the Jews 'did not lay their hands on the spoil' (9.16). To celebrate their deliverance with honor, the Jews feast in Susa and in the provinces and establish the fourteenth of Adar as a day 'of sending portions to one another' (9.19). No mention of drink is made, and the non-redistributive feasts of the opening chapter are rectified to correspond with Jewish tradition.

Mordecai is given the recognition—honor—of being literate (9.20, 23) and of establishing a holiday to celebrate deliverance 'by sending portions to one another and gifts to the poor' (9.22). Whereas scribes wrote all the messages for Ahasuerus and Haman, the text explicitly states that Mordecai himself wrote about the events and sent letters to the Jews in outlying areas of the kingdom, and that Esther and Mordecai wrote 'to confirm this second letter of Purim'. Against the background of Ahasuerus's questionable literacy, the Jewish community is honored through its learned (symbolic) leaders. In this milieu of honor/shame, it is notable that Esther is given equal credit with Mordecai for writing (that is, for literacy and authority); and that the 'decree of Esther' (9.32) accords her a distinctly 'masculine' (public and legal) role. Esther *receives* (feminine) rather than *seeks* (masculine) recognition, once again merging honor/shame without blurring their distinctive functions.

Structurally, the festivities of the Jewish deliverance *correspond* to and *reverse* those of the Persian introduction: public honor, feasts, sending messages, distributing portions; but whereas honor/shame are initially polarized, they are merged in some characters and shared between the sexes in various degrees by the conclusion. Only the 'appearance' of honor/shame remains paradigmatic for females: Esther retains the demeanor of female shame even as she invokes honor.

After a recapitulation explaining the origin of Purim (9.20-28), both Esther the queen and Mordecai the Jew are recognized for their deeds, and a 'decree of Esther' confirms the ritual observance (9.29-32). In the concluding chapter, even King Ahasuerus is redeemed. He makes decisions without recourse to advisors ('laid a tax') and his 'acts of...authority and of his might' (10.2) give him honor, adding complexity to his earlier shame. The king's honor is underscored by the honor given to the 'greatness of Mordecai' by the king:

> For Mordecai the Jew was second to King Ahasuerus, and great among the Jews, and pleasing to his many kinsmen,[1] seeking the welfare of his people and speaking peace to all his seed (10.3).

Esther, for whom the book is named, is not mentioned in the concluding verse. Instead, Mordecai, who depends on Esther in the crisis he himself causes by his refusal to bend his pride (and his knees) to honor Haman, is restored to his place as dominant male with all due honor. Esther, as a modest female who protects her shame when possible and is shameless when necessary, is once again subsumed in Mordecai's honor. Honor/shame permeates the action in the book of Esther and offers substantive support for reading the book as a paradigm for the Jewish

---

1. This phrase may also be translated 'and pleasing to many of his kinsmen', implying a veiled criticism of Mordecai.

diaspora. Paradoxically, the narrative supports and satirizes sexual politics through an intelligent and resourceful woman who uses—and abuses—the system to achieve her purpose: to allay threats to the existence of the community of Jews and restore to their lives a sense of autonomy within dependence. This interpretation teaches that Jews in a dependent position in exile can maintain their honor by *outwardly* observing the customs and laws of the host country while still maintaining their communal solidarity. Thus the *appearance* of feminine shame masks Esther's actions in the masculine world just as Mordecai's *appearance* of feminine shame is actually an action of masculine power directed to involve Esther. The text allows that, in threatening situations, social paradigms may be creatively interpreted as long as the prescribed gender role is publicly observed. Powerless women—and Jews—can invoke power as long as they maintain required appearances.

Esther has been championed as an example of an enterprising woman. Nevertheless, the text demonstrates how she acts behind the mask of 'feminine shame'. Thus Esther epitomizes the book's message and manipulation of the honor/shame theme.

ESTHER REVISITED: AN AGGADIC APPROACH

Leila Leah Bronner

Contemporary studies of the book of Esther have tended to concentrate on the history, provenance, plot and contents of the scroll.[1] The focus of this paper will be on the character of Esther, her actions, and those figures of the story interacting with her. We will take our lead from the aggadic sources, which concern themselves with precisely these aspects. The sages of Talmud and Midrash appear to be interested not only in what the Megillah contained, but also in what it lacked—the name of God and other religious concepts are strikingly absent. Indeed, apart from the mention of fasting, there is no *direct* reference to divine providence, the covenant, the land of Israel, the Jerusalem Temple, Judaism or Jewish religious practices.[2] The ancient rabbis fill in the gaps, even suggesting that the apparent omission of these subjects is intentional, part of the 'hiddenness' of the book.[3]

1.   See, for example, L.B. Paton, *The Book of Esther* (ICC; Edinburgh: T. & T. Clark, 1908); S.B. Berg, *The Book of Esther: Motifs, Themes and Structure* (SBLDS; Missoula, MT: Scholars Press, 1979); D.J.A. Clines, *The Esther Scroll: The Story of the Story* (JSOTSup, 30; Sheffield: JSOT Press, 1984); and C.A. Moore, *Esther* (AB, 7b; Garden City, NY: Doubleday, 1971).
2.   I refer here to the Masoretic Text. The LXX version does inject some of these themes into the story, discussion of which can be found in numerous articles on the Greek text contained in C.A. Moore (ed.), *Studies in the Book of Esther* (New York: Ktav, 1982).
3.   M.V. Fox, *Character and Ideology in the Book of Esther* (Studies on Personalities in the Old Testament; Columbia, SC: University of South Carolina Press, 1991), pp. 244-46, observes that the silence of the book speaks volumes, 'but,' he queries, 'what does it say?' In other words, how conscious was the book's religiosity? If the failure to find evidence of the book of Esther at Qumran was not purely accidental, it is possible that the Qumran sect omitted Esther from its canon because the book was insufficiently religious in emphasis and its heroine insufficiently pious.

In studying the character of Esther, they transform her into a pious Jewish woman punctiliously observing the commandments (*mitzvot*) incumbent on a woman. In this paper I shall demonstrate that the rabbis' exegesis is dominated by their preoccupation with giving Esther a strong Jewish identity, a factor not explicit in the scroll. Furthermore, my analysis will also note their partiality towards a celebrity in contrast to other, more mundane women figures in the Bible. Finally, we will see that rabbinic exegesis of Esther highlights her multifaceted qualities, in keeping with the actual character development that takes place in the biblical book, as Esther moves from beauty queen to determined leader.

Before proceeding to our analysis, it is fitting to take note of the galaxy of late midrashic works amplifying the book of Esther. The earlier sources include the *First Targum*, *Esther Rabbah 1* on the first two chapters of Esther, and tractate *Megillah*. The *Second Targum*, considered to be more midrash than targum, is later than the *First Targum*.[1] Then there exists an array of works dating mainly from the tenth through the thirteenth century: *Panim Aherim, Abba Gurion, Esther Rabbah 2* (on Esth. 3–8),[2] *Aggadat Esther, Leqah Tov on Esther, Yalqut Shimoni on Esther*, and *Midrash Aher*. Midrashim devoted to other topics, such as *Midrash Tehillim, Yosippon*, and *Pirke deRabbi Eliezer* also provide details about Esther in passing. Such collections are later manifestations of the phenomenon of scriptural expansion represented in the apocryphal additions to Esther and the paraphrase of Josephus. Most of these later midrashim take their cues from earlier Talmudic discussions of Esther, particularly the Talmudic tractate *Megillah*, and perhaps also the two versions of *Esther Rabbah*.[3] The exact relationship between these overlapping

1. Dated anywhere from the fourth century CE to the eleventh; see the discussion of B. Grossfeld (trans. and ed.), *The Two Targums of Esther, Translated, with Apparatus and Notes* (The Aramaic Bible, 18; Collegeville, MN: Michael Glazier, 1991), pp. 8-24, who prefers the early seventh century. Most would consider them to be post-talmudic.

2. Part of the reason for an early dating of *Esther Rabbah 1* is that it evidences knowledge of the Palestinian Talmud but not the Babylonian; see M. Herr, 'Esther Rabbah', *EncJud*, VI, p. 915.

3. Herr, 'Esther Rabbah'.

sources is a complicated subject that has engaged scholars for over a century and cannot be resolved within the compass of this paper.

The provenance of the biblical book of Esther has been variously placed in Egypt, Palestine and Persia. The earlier view that the work was Hellenistic is giving way to the growing consensus that it is actually earlier, either from the late Persian or early Hellenistic period.[1] The rabbis, however, accepted the book as a unified work that authentically related actual events taking place in the court of the Persian king and dating from that time.

The Story in the Esther Scroll

The story of Esther opens with Ahasuerus, one of the most powerful rulers of the ancient world, holding a munificent banquet. With drunken enthusiasm he commands Queen Vashti to be brought forth so that he may display her beauty before the party attendees. (In rabbinic tradition, she was ordered to appear naked.[2]) Without further explanation being provided, Vashti disobeys the royal summons and is summarily dismissed from court. (Rabbinic consensus held that she was put to death.[3]) An empire-wide search for a replacement queen ensues. Esther, the lovely orphan girl who had been raised by her uncle Mordecai, is selected to be the new queen. Mordecai apparently holds a position in the royal court and now offends the high official Haman by not bowing down to him, as was Haman's due.[4] As a result, Haman plots revenge against all Jews throughout the realm. A royal decree is issued, and the doom of the Jews seems certain.

Mordecai prevails upon Esther to intercede on behalf of her people before the king. Esther, whose true identity as a Jew is

1. R. Gordis, 'Studies in the Esther Narrative', in Moore (ed.), *Studies in the Book of Esther*, pp. 408-409; C.A. Moore, 'Book of Esther', *ABD*, II, p. 641; S.A. White, 'Esther', in C.A. Newsom and S.H. Ringe (eds.), *The Women's Bible Commentary* (Louisville, KY: John Knox, 1992), pp. 124-25.

2. E.g. *Esth. R.* 3.13-14; and further below.

3. *First Targum* 1.19; 5.1; *b. Meg.* 10b, 11b, 16a; 19a; *Esth. R.* Proem 12 and 3.9; 3.15; 4.8; 5.1. For a fuller discussion of why the rabbis maintained Vashti was put to death, see below.

4. Compare Esth. 2.21 and Dan. 2.49.

unknown at court, is reluctant to expose herself but ultimately agrees. Commanding that the Jews fast for her, she risks her own life by defying Persian protocol and appearing before the king uninvited. However, she finds favor with the king, who grants her an audience. Thereupon, she requests that he come with Haman to a special banquet that will be prepared for the three of them. At the party, Ahasuerus is charmed and offers to grant whatever Esther desires. She asks only that he and Haman return for a second banquet the following night. At the second banquet, she reveals that Haman's machinations would undo her along with the rest of the Jews, since she too is a Jew. Incensed, the king orders Haman's execution; and allows the Jews to defend themselves, since the original order against them cannot be rescinded. Mordecai, Esther and the Jews emerge victorious; and the holiday of Purim is proclaimed, the events being recorded in a book.

Esther in Aggadic Sources[1]

Etymologies of her Names

Rabbinic sources place great emphasis upon the meaning of names as keys to the personality of their bearers. Esther was unusual in that she had two names (Esth. 2.7), providing the rabbis with an opening for describing Esther as a multifaceted personality.

Tractate *Megillah* employs the question of Esther's two names as a tool for revealing her attributes:[2]

> She is called Hadassah and she is called Esther. It has been taught: Esther was her proper name. Why then was she called Hadassah? After the designation of the righteous who are called myrtles,[3] for so it says, *And he stood among the myrtle trees* [Zech. 1.8].[4] R. Judah says: Hadassah was her name. Why then was she called

---

1.   A comparison of Esther in rabbinic sources and in Josephus can be found in L.H. Feldman, 'Hellenizations in Josephus' Version of Esther', *Transactions and Proceedings of the American Philological Association* 101 (1970), pp. 143-70.
2.   B. *Meg.* 13a.
3.   Heb. *hadas*.
4.   See also *Panim Aherim* 63 for further elaboration.

Esther? Because she concealed [*masteret*] the facts about herself, as it says, *Esther did not make known her people or her kindred* [Esth. 2.20]. R. Nehemiah says: Hadassah was her name. Why then was she called Esther? All peoples called her so after *Istahar*.[1] Ben 'Azzai said: Esther was neither too tall nor too short, but of medium size, like a myrtle. R. Joshua b. Korha said: Esther was sallow ['greenish', like a myrtle], but endowed with great charm.

This etymological discussion relates in large part, but not solely, to Esther's physical appearance. 'All peoples called her *Istahar*' (Venus, Ishtar) highlights her ultra-feminine quality. Associating her other name Hadassah with the qualities of a myrtle further promotes her attractiveness by indicating that her height was 'just right'; but another opinion uses her supposed 'greenness' to downplay all the emphasis on her physical beauty and instead promote her appealing personality. In this vein, another statement uses the myrtle to bring a prooftext demonstrating not only her beauty, but also her righteousness.

The *Second Targum* elaborates further on the myrtle theme in order to catalogue Esther's virtues.[2] It relates that, as the myrtle's fragrance is pleasant throughout the world, so Esther's good deeds were spread throughout the world.[3] As the myrtle does not dry up summer or winter, so the righteous ones have a share in this world and the world to come.[4] Then, too, her good deeds continued throughout her life, when she was young and when she was old.[5] The verse 'instead of the nettle, a myrtle shall rise' (Isa. 55.13), is taken as a sign that Esther was destined to reign in place of Vashti, the nettle.

Finally, the name Esther is explained by *b. Megillah* as demonstrating Esther's essential quality of 'concealment'. She hid her true identity from Ahasuerus until the right moment for self-revelation. The hidden causality guiding the book of Esther is a leading motif for rabbinic interpretation. It is best illustrated in the heroine's name: Esther *masteret*—Esther 'concealed'. Tractate *Hullin* more fully develops the idea. The verse 'and I

1.   Also found in *Second Targum* 2.7.
2.   *Second Targum* 2.7.
3.   In a variation on this theme, *Panim Aherim* 63 states that as the *hadas* smells good, so her deeds were good.
4.   Also found in *Panim Aherim* 63.
5.   Also found in *Panim Aherim* 63.

will surely hide ('*astir*) my face' (Deut. 31.18) is said to refer to Esther, thus implying that Esther would come to redeem them at a time when God hid his face.[1] A further development of this theme is found in *Midr. Tehillim*:[2]

> The 'Light of Israel' [Isa. 10.17] refers to Esther, who lit up Israel like the light of dawn...she remained hidden until she lit up Israel. She and Mordecai were a light to the Jews, but darkness to the nations. Her name was Hadassah because she had a sweet smell to the Jews, but a bitter taste to the nations...[as it is said] 'the Jews had light'...[Esth. 8.16].

In *Midr. Tehillim*, the name Hadassah is a guide not merely to her character, but to her destiny. The concealment theme, as embodied in the name Esther, would increasingly be understood to set the pattern for life in the diaspora, when God's providence would assume a more subtle mode.

Esther's Allure
Esther's great beauty is mentioned in three places in the biblical account: Esth. 1.11; 2.3, 7. Her appeal is also emphasized in a number of midrashim. Midrashic embellishment of a few biblical clues is directed at underlining her charisma, charm and beauty. For example, Tractate *Megillah* notices that similar phrasing, 'and Esther obtained favor', is used both in reference to Hegai the eunuch (2.9) and Ahasuerus the king (2.17). *Megillah* understands this as meaning that every man took her for a member of his own people.[3] *Abba Gurion* informs us that she had grace in everyone's eyes.[4]

Panim Aherim relates that she was extremely charming, even more so than the popular Joseph, and everyone tried to curry favor with her because they knew she would be queen.[5] Although Ahasuerus put beauties on each side of her, Persians on one side and Medeans on the other, Esther outshone them

1.   B. *Ḥul.* 139b.
2.   *Midr. Tehillim* 22; cf. *Second Targum* 2.8.
3.   B. *Meg.* 13a.
4.   *Abba Gurion* 18.
5.   L.A. Rosenthal and M. Gan are among those asserting the influence of the Jacob cycle upon the account of Esther; see the discussion of Moore, *Studies in the Book of Esther*, pp. xliii-xlv.

all.[1] The biblical text introduces us to Esther by telling us that she was 'shapely and beautiful' (Esth. 2.7). According to the *Megillah*, she was one of the four notable beauties of all time: 'There have been four women of surpassing beauty in the world—Sarah, Raḥab, Abigail and Esther'.[2]

Some accounts give Esther divine help in boosting her charm at key moments. *Megillah* tells us that three ministering angels assisted her when she went in to the king uninvited: one to hold her head erect, a second to give her charm and a third stretching forth the scepter to grant her entrance.[3]

Esther's Sexuality

Part of Esther's appeal was her sexuality. *Megillah* states that she recited Psalm 22 on her way to see Ahasuerus.[4] This psalm has the colophon 'on *'ayyelet haśśaḥar'*, 'dawn star', but literally 'the hind of the morning'. Tractate *Yoma* questions:[5] 'Why was Esther compared to a hind? To tell you that just as a hind has a narrow womb and is desirable to her mate at all times as at the first time, so was Esther precious to King Ahasuerus at all times as at the first time.'[6] A more allegorical interpretation adds: 'Why was Esther compared to the dawn? To tell you that just as the dawn is the end of the whole night, so is the story of Esther the end of all the [biblical] miracles.'[7] Here again is the motif of concealment. The implication is not that miracles would cease, but that henceforth they would take a different form, hidden from the naked eye. God's providence would nevertheless continue to guide them, as it were, from behind the veil.

Abba Gurion provides us with a portrait of a regretful Ahasuerus, who retained images of Vashti over his bed. When women entered his quarters he would look at them, and then at

1. *Panim Aherim* 64.
2. B. *Meg.* 15a.
3. B. *Meg.* 15b.
4. B. *Meg.* 15b.
5. B. *Yom.* 29a.
6. B. *'Erub.* 54b makes the same comparison between *words of Torah* and the hind in order to show that Torah study retains its eternal freshness and allure.
7. B. *Yom.* 29a.

the images of his former queen; but there was none to compare with Vashti. When Esther entered, however, he tore down Vashti's image and put up Esther's.[1]

Further details about Esther's sex life are provided: '*In the evening she went and on the morrow she returned* [Esth. 2.12]. From the discreditable account of that wicked man we can learn something to his credit, namely, that he did not perform his marital office by day'.[2] Thus, even an undesirable person like Ahasuerus is found to have one positive attribute.

How Could She Marry Him?

Rabbinic literature, as we have seen, does not attempt to cover up the sexuality entailed in Esther's marriage to the foreign king. They were troubled not by the sex, but by her marriage to a non-Jew.[3] Concern over the marriage is demonstrated as early as the LXX Additions to Esther,[4] which has Esther defend her modesty before God in the following terms: 'You know that I hate the splendor of the heathen, I abhor the bed of the uncircumcised or of any Gentile'. The question repeatedly surfacing throughout the rabbinic sources is: why did Esther not suffer martyrdom rather than marry him?[5]

Tractate *Sanhedrin* discusses when one must choose to be martyred.[6] Certain *mitzvot* may not be transgressed even at the cost of one's life.[7] In the course of *Sanhedrin's* discussion, it broaches the topic of ravaged girls, stating that a betrothed maiden must be slain rather than allow herself to be violated. The discussion continues by stating that in a time of 'royal decree',[8] that is, religious persecution, one should be killed rather than transgress even a light commandment in public. The

---

1. *Abba Gurion* 19; a less elaborate version is found in *Panim Aherim* 65; also *Esth. R.* 6.12.

2. *B. Meg.* 13a; also *Midrash Aher* in A. Jellinek, *Bet ha-Midrasch* (Hebrew; Jerusalem: Wahrmann, 1967), p. 24; and *Panim Aherim* 64.

3. The only roughly analogous situation is Sarah's abduction by Pharaoh (Gen. 12.15-16).

4. Add. Esth. 14.15 (NEB).

5. *Aggadat Esther* 11.9 (see also 20-21).

6. *B. Sanh.* 74 a-b.

7. Idolatry, incest/adultery and murder.

8. The word used in *Aggadat Esther* is 'crisis'.

implication is that at a time when one's very religious identity is at stake, even the small observances represent a higher principle and must be defended.[1] The question is then posed whether Esther transgressed in public when confronted with a royal decree. Yes, is the response; but 'she was the ground of the earth (*qarqaʻ ʻōlām*)', that is, she just lay there and was tilled. Moreover, the monarch did not order it to violate her religion, but for his pleasure, so she did not have to die for it.

One approach to defending Esther's honor was prompted by the theme of her hiddenness, emphasizing that she did her best to avoid notice by the king's emissaries. The *Second Targum of Esther* relates that Mordecai hid her, but her qualities were already known to the messengers of the king. When they were unable to find her, the king issued a decree that any virgin found hiding would be executed, whereupon Mordecai panicked and brought her out.[2] The *First Targum to Esther* explicitly states that she was taken *forcibly*.[3]

Panim Aḥerim relates that while Gentile girls flaunted themselves for the king's emissaries, Esther hid for four years. God remarks that because she hid herself, she would be the one to enter royalty, rather than they.[4] Whereas most sources view the marriage in a negative light, this midrash views it as a reward for Esther's modest virtue. In this way, her marriage is given divine validation. *Aggadat Esther*[5] provides similar details but does not view the marriage in the same favorable light. While the Gentile girls were adorning themselves for the king's emissaries, Esther hid herself for four years. She was eventually taken against her will, as Sarah was taken to Pharaoh. Unlike *Panim Aḥerim*, however, *Aggadat Esther* then discusses whether

1. See further Maimonides, *Yad, Yesodei ha-Torah* 5.3, who states that even in private one must not breach any commandments in a time of national danger. Halakhah on this subject is complicated and beyond the purview of this paper.

2. *Second Targum* 2.8.

3. *First Targum* 2.10.

4. *Panim Aḥerim* 63-64 in S. Buber, *Sammlung Agadischer Kommentare zum Buche Ester, enthält Midrasch Abba Gorion; Midrasch Ponim Acherim; Midrasch Lekach Tob* (Hebrew; Vilna, 1886); cf. *Aggadat Esther*.

5. *Aggadat Esther* 2.8, found in S. Buber, *Midrasch Aggadat Esther* (Cracow, 1897); repr. in *Midrash Leqaḥ Tov* (Jerusalem: Wagshall, 1989), p. 20.

she should have allowed herself to be killed rather than transgress, introducing the previously mentioned discussion from *Sanhedrin*.

The *Zohar* takes the most radical approach to the intermarriage, denying that Esther ever really lived with Ahasuerus. Instead, God sent as a substitute a spirit (*šîdâ*) that looked like her.[1] This view contradicts the talmudic remark in *Sanhedrin*, which states that, lying there like the ground, she passively tolerated the sex. The *Zohar* certainly contradicts the view in certainly contradicts the view of *Yoma* that Ahasuerus enjoyed sex with her every time as though it were the first. It is also difficult to reconcile with the midrashic view that Esther was the mother of Darius.[2]

Esther's Jewish Identity

Esther's alleged unhappiness with her marriage to a non-Jew was only part of the larger projection of Jewish piety built up for her by the rabbis. In commenting upon Esther's supposed recitation of Psalm 22 ('My God, my God, why have you forsaken me'), *Midrash Tehillim* provides an unusually personal plea: 'Sarah was in the house of Pharaoh only one night and you helped her, while I have been in the house of this *rāšā'* [wicked man] all these years and you have given me no miracles'.[3] She pleads her piety, having observed all three women's *mitzvot* 'even in the house of the *rāšā'*. In this context, Esther protests her abandonment into the hands of the king. Moreover, she claims that she was undeserving of such a fate, having properly observed a woman's obligations, even under duress.

The LXX is only the first in a line of commentators ensuring that Esther had ritually fit food to eat in the king's palace. In pleading her merits, Esther prays: 'I, your servant, have not eaten at Haman's table; I have not graced a banquet of the king or touched the wine of his drink-offerings...'[4] The *Second Targum*

---

1. *Zohar*, III, 275b-267b. *Tiqunei Zohar* 20-21 states even more clearly that she never had relations with him.
2. *Lev. R.* 13.5; *Esth. R.* 8.3.
3. *Midrash Tehillim*, *mizmor* 22, 16 (S. Buber, *Midrash Tehillim* [Vilna, 1891], p. 188).
4. Add. Esth. 14.17 (NEB).

to Esther states that Esther gave the gifts she received to her Gentile handmaidens because she did not want to taste of the palace wine.[1] According to the *First Targum*, however, Esther's attendants were also pious and worthy, so much so that food and drink could be given to her through them from the royal palace.[2] The implication is that they could be trusted to ensure its ritual suitability. *Pirke deRabbi Eliezer* relates that the reason Mordecai sat in the gates of the city was to be sure that Esther and her handmaids were not defiled with forbidden food (answering the question of what he was doing sitting in the gate), and it was then that he heard the conspiracy against the king.[3]

In *Panim Aherim*, the eunuch is said to have brought her adornments and food from the king, because he was concerned that she was not trying to beautify herself. Nevertheless, Esther only ate her own food, like Hananiah, Mishael and Azariah in the book of Daniel. Although Daniel is expressly stated in the biblical book to have refused the king's food, no such provision is found about Esther.[4] Consequently, much of this line of commentary on Esther is no doubt based on comparison with the piety expressed in the book of Daniel but omitted in Esther and therefore supplied by the rabbis.[5]

Esther is also said to have observed the Sabbath. According to Tractate *Megillah*, Esther had seven handmaids so that she could count the days of the week by them, apparently so as to know which day was the Sabbath.[6] The *First Targum* provides the actual names for her seven maidens, one for each day of the week.[7]

Esther's decision to declare a fast is among the first overt

1.   *Second Targum* 2.9.
2.   *First Targum* 2.9. B. *Meg.* 13a also states that she was given kosher food in the palace.
3.   *Pirke deRabbi Eliezer* 50.
4.   'Daniel resolved not to defile himself with the king's food or the wine he drank, so he sought permission of the chief officer not to defile himself' (Dan. 1.8).
5.   *Panim Aherim* 64.
6.   B. *Meg.* 13a; L. Ginzberg, *Legends of the Jews* (Philadelphia: Jewish Publication Society, 1941), IV, p. 386-67; Grossfeld, *The Two Targums*, p. 44 n. 26.
7.   *First Targum* 2.9.

signs of religious sensibility to be found in the biblical book, and it is also the first time she asserts independence of thought and action. The LXX is not the only source to elaborate the presumed prayer that she would have pronounced on such an occasion. The *First Targum* contains a succinct and not very lofty prayer, speaking of Haman's ambitions and asking God that the Jews not fall prey to him:

> Lord of the Universe, do not deliver me into the hand of this uncircumcised one, and let not the will of the wicked Haman be carried out against me as he did against Vashti, when he gave advice to the king to have her killed as he wanted (him) to marry his daughter...You, too, in Your abundant mercy, have compassion on your people and do not deliver the descendants of Jacob into the hands of Haman...son of the wicked Esau.[1]

The prayer in the *Second Targum* is much longer. Filled with biblical citations and allusions, it is heavily dependent on the theme of the merit of the fathers (only hinted at in the *First Targum* prayer) and other traditional piety, including reference to the expulsion from Jewish land. All these are themes virtually absent from the biblical book.

> You, Who are the God of Abraham, Isaac and Jacob, as well as the God of my ancestor Benjamin, it is not because I am worthy before You that I am going in to this foolish king, but only so that Your people, the House of Israel, should not be destroyed from this world. For the sake of Israel You created the entire world, so if Israel will be destroyed from the world who will say, 'Sanctified, Sanctified, Sanctified' [Isa. 6.3] three times every day?...Remember in this hour the merit of Abraham, Isaac and Jacob. Do not turn away from my request...[2]

The *First Targum* also answers the unvoiced question: why did Esther not ask for the rebuilding of the Temple when Ahasuerus had said that she could have up to half the kingdom?[3] It adds to the narrative that the king told her she could have up to half the kingdom, *but not the Temple*, since he had already sworn to

---

1.   *First Targum* 5.1, cited from Grossfeld, *The Two Targums*, p. 63.
2.   *Second Targum* 5.1, cited from Grossfeld, *The Two Targums*, pp. 159-63.
3.   *First Targum* 5.3-7. R. Yohanan b. Zakkai is subject to a similar difficulty, because he did not ask for enough from Vespasian when given the opportunity; see *b. Giṭ.* 56b.

Sanballat, Tobiah and Geshem that he would not allow it to be rebuilt to serve as a base for Jewish rebellion against him. This elaboration assumes that Esther, in her piety, could not have overlooked such an important matter, hence there must have been another reason why she did not make the request.

Whether because of her piety, or because of the important role she had to play, Esther is granted divine assistance by the rabbis in the form of angels. We have already noted that in Tractate *Megillah* three angels were present when she approached Ahasuerus: one to make her head erect, one to give her charm, and one to stretch forth the royal scepter.[1] *Panim Aḥerim* relates that at first Ahasuerus turned his face so that he would not see her. Nevertheless, his eyes, which were blind, lit up when he turned to her, so that he could extend the scepter to her. She, however, was so weak with fear that she could not take it, and so the angel Michael helped, making it reach her.[2] *Midrash Tehillim* says that the king was about to make a derogatory remark, when an angel came down and hit him on the mouth, saying 'Wicked one, your spouse stands outside and you sit inside'. Against Ahasuerus's will, God made him attracted to Esther.[3] In all these instances, it is not only her own charm, beauty and courage that caused her to succeed, but God's succor. Without God's assistance, Esther would not have been selected over the thousands of other maidens, let alone have been able to carry out her task of redemption.

Vashti and Zeresh
It is worth mentioning that Vashti was made a foil to Esther regarding piety. The constantly negative portrayal of Vashti in rabbinic sources served to highlight the contrasting virtues of Queen Esther. Unlike Esther, who was a Sabbath observant, Vashti had forced Jewish girls to violate the Sabbath; and ultimately it was for this reason that she had been punished.

1.   *B. Meg.* 15b.
2.   *Panim Aḥerim* 71, *parašah* 5, paragraph 151. *B. Meg.* 15b says that the scepter grew in length, so that it would reach her; *b. Meg.* 16a has an angel guide Esther's hand so that she pointed at Haman. Cf. the stretching of Pharaoh's daughter's hand to assist her in reaching Moses; see *b. Soṭ.* 12b and Rashi on Exod. 2.5.
3.   *Midr. Tehillim* 22 [136] (Buber, p. 194).

Just as she caused the daughters of Israel to be stripped naked and work on the Sabbath, so was the command to appear naked her downfall.[1] This talmudic passage consistently demeans Vashti. The biblical story provided no reason for Vashti's refusal to appear. In rabbinic tradition, her motivation for refusing Ahasuerus's command had nothing to do with noble virtues such as modesty. Instead, she did not come because she had been stricken with various maladies that made her unattractive; and she did not want to be seen that way.[2]

Midrash Esther Rabbah, too, is almost entirely negative in depicting Vashti. One midrash creates for her a vicious character, stating that the reason Memuchan (Haman)[3] hated her is because she was wont to strike him across the face with her shoe. A variant says that it was because she failed to invite his wife to her women's banquet. Another example states that even without her act of rebellion she was deserving of punishment, implying the vast extent of her shortcomings.[4]

Only a few rare instances show Vashti in a more favorable light. In one case, she fights against the humiliation of being displayed naked without the text making any moral judgment against her.[5] Another instance wryly comments upon Ahasuerus's foolishness in thinking that men could force their will upon women: 'If a man wants to eat lentils and his wife wants to eat beans, can he force her? Surely she does as she likes'.[6] This statement at least acknowledges women as beings possessing an independent will. Then again, two examples indicate that Vashti herself was not really deserving of death. According to the *Second Targum*, Vashti suffered because it had been decreed by heaven that the descendants of Nebuchadnezzar would be expunged.[7] *Panim Aḥerim* suggests

---

1. *B. Meg.* 12b.
2. *B. Meg.* 12b.
3. According to *b. Meg.* 12b, the character Memuchan, who is mentioned in Esth. 1.16, was in fact Haman.
4. *Esth. R.* 4.6-7.
5. *Esth. R.* 3.14.
6. *Esth. R.* 4.12.
7. *Second Targum* 2.2. For Vashti as a descendant of Nebuchadnezzar, see further *Esth. R.* 3.8.

that she was killed not because of her actions per se, but because she would become a role model of a rebellious wife and threaten the dominance of husbands throughout the realm.[1]

A final example of rabbinic treatment of Vashti turns the standard Vashti–Esther dichotomy upside down. Ahasuerus's opinion of Esther's boldness is forthrightly presented: as compared with Vashti, who would not come at all, Esther came uninvited like a prostitute.[2] The rabbis, however, did not view Esther as the real prostitute in the story. Ahasuerus's comments are ironic, because the reader of the midrash knows the true virtue in Esther's appearance before the king.

While rabbinic tradition was almost consistently derogatory in its depictions of Vashti, modern feminists have been highly sympathetic toward her plight. Vashti's rebellion has made her a new role model for the contemporary woman.[3] Despite the considerable attention that her character has drawn, both in the rabbinic and modern world, Vashti is to a great extent simply a necessary plot device without which there could be no Esther. Nevertheless, that it was this particular means—a woman's rebellion and subsequent downfall—that was selected for Esther's rise to power is in itself quite telling.

The only other named female character in the book of Esther is Haman's wife Zeresh. Ironically, the Bible actually describes a very cordial relationship between Haman and Zeresh. On two separate occasions he turns to her for advice, demonstrating that within her limited role of wife, a woman could influence her husband. In rabbinic literature, however, Zeresh, like Vashti, was usually a model of wrongdoing and impiety: when Haman went to his lovers, Zeresh went to hers (cf. Esth. 3.14). In this way, the midrash categorizes all idol-worshippers as promiscuous

---

1.   *Panim Aherim* 61.

2.   A modern author conveys a similar idea; see R.J. Weems, *Just a Sister Away: A Womanist Vision of Women's Relationships in the Bible* (San Diego: LuraMedia, 1988), p. 99; and B.W. Jones, 'Two Misconceptions about the Book of Esther', *CBQ* 39 (1977), pp. 171-81; repr. in Moore, *Studies in the Book of Esther*.

3.   M. Gendler, 'The Restoration of Vashti', in E. Koltun (ed.), *The Jewish Woman* (New York: Schocken Books, 1976), pp. 241-47; and White, 'Esther', p. 127; cf. also Timothy Beal's article in this volume.

(unlike the virtuous daughters of Israel).[1] Strangely, Zeresh gives wise, if evil, counsel, telling Haman that God has already saved the Jews from all kinds of dangers, fire, slaughter, imprisonment. He should therefore try a form of attack for which God has not demonstrably come to the rescue in the past, and she recommends crucifixion (i.e. hanging).[2] In this way, the midrash makes Zeresh the evil partner of Haman.

A different instance is predicated upon Esth. 6.13, where Zeresh tells her husband that he is destined to fall. In this midrash, upon hearing that Mordecai is a Jew, she advises her husband to abandon his efforts because attacking a Jew is like falling upon a stone. The one falling is hurt, not the stone. Haman, however, listens to his friends rather than his wife and proceeds to build the gallows. This alternative version is more favorable to wise Zeresh than the first example.

Whereas the Bible mentions only Haman's ten sons, the rabbis introduce yet another female character to the tale—Haman's devoted daughter. This midrash returns to the more dominant theme of the wickedness of Haman's family:

> As he [Haman] was leading him [Mordecai] through the street where Haman lived, his daughter who was standing on the roof saw him. She thought that the man on the horse was her father and the man walking before him was Mordecai. So she took a chamber pot and emptied it on the head of her father. He looked up at her and when she saw that it was her father, she threw herself from the roof to the ground and killed herself...'But Haman hastened to his house, mourning...' [Esth. 6.12], mourning for his daughter...[3]

Although Zeresh, a woman giving wise counsel, has gone oddly unnoticed by feminist scholarship, Vashti has been rehabilitated. Rabbinic literature does not usually share this favorable view of Vashti. Highlighting her negative pagan qualities, the rabbis drew no positive moral messages from Vashti's character. On the other hand, Zeresh fits the rabbinic dictum: 'Whoever says a wise thing, even if he is a non-Jew, is

1. *Panim Aherim* 72.
2. *Panim Aherim* 36; cf. 71-72, where Haman realizes this himself.
3. *B. Meg.* 16a; cf. *First Targum* 5.1 and especially 6.1; and the references cited by Grossfeld, *The Two Targums*, p. 72.

called wise'.[1] Zeresh's first round of advice is evil, but she did ultimately recognize the futility of her husband's efforts to harm the Jews before he himself did.

Esther the Prophet
According to the sages, Esther is not only queen but also prophet. She is listed as one of the seven female prophets of ancient Israel:

> Our rabbis taught: Forty-eight prophets and seven prophetesses prophesied to Israel...Seven prophetesses. Who were these?—Sarah, Miriam, Deborah, Hannah, Abigail, Hulda and Esther...[2]

Esther's inclusion among the female prophets evokes our curiosity. What quality was it that prompted this elevated status? Several of the women listed are expressly named as prophets in the Bible, and thus pose no problem. Four of those listed, namely Sarah, Hannah, Abigail and Esther, bear no such biblical appellation. Why were they included? Probably because all four display qualities of the 'wise woman' type. Sarah and Abigail are women who advise men (Gen. 21.12; 1 Sam. 25). A considerable tradition views Hannah's prayer as having been a prophecy, perhaps as an explanation of why it was significant enough to have had its text included in the biblical account. Esther, too, can be viewed as a personification of typical wisdom virtues.[3]

Despite recognizing the wisdom of these four women, the rabbis were reluctant to call them 'wise women'. ḥākām ('wise man') was a term they applied to themselves and their own leadership group. The Talmud states that when the spirit of prophecy departed from Israel, it went into the ḥᵃkāmîn, the sages.[4] The title ḥākām came to mean 'someone learned in certain texts' rather than wise per se; and the term was restricted solely to the male elite of teachers and sages. Since the talmudic teachers take the title of 'the Wise' for their own elite class of male scholars and teachers, they do not apply it to women, not even biblical women who were treated with greater respect than women of their own time. For this reason, when they wanted

1.   *B. Meg.* 16a.
2.   *B. Meg.* 14a.
3.   S. Talmon, '"Wisdom" in the Book of Esther', *VT* 13 (1963), pp. 419-55.
4.   *B. B. Bat.* 12a; *b. Soṭ.* 48b.

to note the achievements of women of the past, the rabbis crowned them with prophecy rather than wisdom.[1]

Esther's inclusion among the prophets in the talmudic source is based on the verse: 'on the third day she clothed herself in royalty' (Esth. 5.1). The verse did not say 'royal *apparel*', according to the commentary, in order to show that it was the holy spirit clothing her, and not normal apparel. A later source similarly states that God dressed Esther with the 'heavenly kingdom'.[2] What moved the rabbis to crown Queen Esther in particular with prophecy? After all, there is no real hint of this in the text. In part it was probably that her success and talents were viewed as an indication that she must have had special divine favor. When the biblical text says that Esther found favor in the eyes of the king, some midrashim suggest that the king referred to is none other than the King of Kings.[3] Her status is surely related to the success of her mission. The rabbis saw in Esther a spirit of prophecy (*rûaḥ haqqōdeš*), which strengthened her and enabled her to wield power to save her people. No doubt the word 'prophetess' was applied to her because she was an important woman, a queen, who delivered her people from oppression.

Esther's prophetic inspiration is also interconnected with the divine inspiration accorded her book. The book bearing Esther's name is surprisingly secular, never mentioning the name of God.[4] There was some dispute about the canonical status of the book, but the Talmud states that Esther was composed under the inspiration of the holy spirit. Certain elements of the book, argues the Talmud, could have become known only by the holy spirit, for example, 'and Haman said in his heart'; 'and Esther obtained favor in the eyes of all that looked upon her'; 'and the thing became known to Mordecai [by the holy spirit]'.[5] *Seder*

1. For more details on the rabbinic transformation of the wise woman, see my book *From Eve to Esther: Rabbinic Reconstructions of Biblical Women* (Gender and the Biblical Tradition; Louisville, KY; Westminster Press/John Knox, forthcoming).

2. *Panim Aherim* 71, *parašah* 5; paragrah 151.

3. *Esth. R.* 9.1.

4. Nevertheless, *b. B. Bat.* 15a attributes the authorship of Esther to the men of the Great Assembly.

5. *B. Meg.* 7a.

'*Olam* bases the tradition of Esther as prophet on the verse 'Then Esther the Queen, daughter of Abihail wrote...' (Esth. 9.29).[1] That is, her writing was divinely inspired. The rabbis' attribution of prophetic powers to Esther indicates that the high esteem they held for royalty was translated in their religious conceptualization into prophecy.

Esther as Leader
In granting Esther prophecy the rabbis were, to a certain extent, acknowledging her leadership; but what did they have to say about the most obvious leadership role she fulfilled—that of queen? It is important to note the growth in leadership ability undergone by the Esther character, because until recently she has been viewed solely as a passive figure who obeys Mordecai. The feminist literature dealing with Esther has occasionally glorified Vashti to the detriment of Esther.[2] Vashti is seen as courageous and as standing up for her rights, while Esther is just another 'pretty face'. Although Esther, in contrast to Vashti, does start out as a docile figure (Esth. 2.20),[3] her personality grows in the course of the biblical story, as she moves from obeying to commanding. It is she who commands the fast, develops a plan and implements it. Ultimately, she institutes the festival of Purim. Esther takes charge.[4]

Rabbinic literature did not totally neglect the leadership aspect of Esther's character, although overall it emphasized her other qualities more. One midrash in particular describes the strength of Esther's leadership capacity unequivocally. She is discussed in the context of Jacob's prayer for Benjamin: 'Benjamin is a ravenous wolf; in the morning he consumes the foe, and in the evening he divides the spoil' (Gen. 49.27). There follows a series of suggested figures who might have fulfilled that prediction: Ehud, Saul, the tribe itself, and the sacrificial altar devouring its

1. *Seder 'Olam* 21.
2. M. Gendler, 'The Restoration of Vashti', in Koltun (ed.), *The Jewish Woman*; cf. M.Z. Bankson, 'Nascent Self', in *Braided Streams: Esther and a Woman's Way of Growing* (San Diego: LuraMedia, 1985), pp. 39-53. Cf. pp. 188-89 above.
3. *Midrash Tehillim, mizmor* 22, p. 193; Ginzberg, *Legends of the Jews*, IV, p. 428.
4. Cf. Wyler and Gitay's essays in this volume.

sacrifices. Esther, too, is included in this impressive list. This midrash recognizes Esther as a powerful queen, likening her to a wolf who seizes prey.[1] This is not the meek beauty queen we are accustomed to hearing about.

At the dedication of the Wilderness Tabernacle, the heads of each tribe presented offerings on behalf of their respective tribes (Num. 7.65). Included among the offerings brought by the head of the tribe of Benjamin were two oxen for the peace offering. The midrash finds prophetic symbolism in each of the offerings. Regarding the two oxen brought by Benjamin, it states that these represented the two redeemers ($g\hat{o}$'^{a}$l\hat{i}m$) who would come from the tribe of Benjamin—Esther and Mordecai.[2] This may be the only time that any woman is specifically termed 'redeemer' in rabbinic literature.[3]

In another instance, Esther fights for her place in history. Talmudic sources inform us that Esther sent a letter to the sages requesting that they perpetuate her name, book and festival for all time: 'Write me down for future generations'.[4] This talmudic reference echoes the biblical account of her leadership aspirations (Esth. 9.29-30). At first the sages refused her request, saying that a commemoration of her festival would lead to hatred against the Jews, since it would be celebrating the downfall of non-Jews. Esther, on the other hand, refused to acquiesce, arguing that she was already recorded in the annals of the Persians, and wished to be remembered by her own people. The sages again responded that this would incite the nations against the Jews. Seeking scriptural validation before agreeing, the sages found it by reinterpreting the biblical verses 'inscribe this in a document as a reminder' (Exod. 17.14), which

1. *Gen. R.* 99.3.

2. *Gen. R.* 14.8 (Heb. 14.20).

3. Serah bat Asher, however, was a central figure in the redemption from Egypt, having been given the password for identifying the Redeemer from her father Asher; *Exod. R.* 5.13.

4. *B. Meg.* 7a. The biblical book makes reference to a similar letter sent to all the Jews, in Esth. 9.29-30. Citing Esth. 9.28, Maimonides states (*Mishneh Torah, Hilkhot Megillah* 2, at the end) that while the words of the prophets and hagiographa would become void in the days of the messiah, the scroll of Esther and holiday of Purim would continue forever.

refers to the war against Amalek.[1] (In Jewish tradition Haman is considered to be an Amalekite.[2]) They finally yield and allow her story to be written.

Thus, Esther served as a female authenticator of written tradition. In no other biblical context do we find a woman serving as the catalyst for the writing down of an oral tradition. The book of Esther, telling the story of her deliverance of the Jews from the Persians, reveals that three parties were involved in the establishment of Purim: Esther, Mordecai and the Jews of Persia. The Jews undertook to observe the new festival, relying on what was written in the letter of Mordecai and on the command of Queen Esther (Esth. 9.32).[3] When Esther writes a second letter, issuing a command on her authority alone, the codification of the festival is complete.[4] The biblical scroll (*mᵉgillâ*) about Purim is named for Esther. The actions of Esther, therefore, lead to the writing down of an oral tradition.[5]

It may have been the rabbis themselves who were transformed in their discussion of Esther. Required to confront the model of a woman in an unusual capacity, they came to accept and value her actions. Why they accepted her leadership relatively uncritically, in contrast to how they treated Deborah's, may have something to do with the legal issues of judges and courts that the rabbis were dealing with in their time. Deborah as judge presented more of a threat than did Esther as queen. Esther, after all was said and done, was still a wife, very much under control of her kingly husband. She stood in contrast to

1.   *B. Meg.* 7a.
2.   *B. Meg.* 13a. The slaughter of people occurring at the end of Esther poses a moral difficulty; see for example Moore, 'Book of Esther', pp. 627-38. Rabbinic tradition justified the slaughter by limiting its victims to the evil descendants of Amalek, destined to be wiped out; see the *First Targum* 9.6, 16-18. As the *Second Targum* (9.25) elaborates: 'Then there arose Haman from the lineage of the house of Amalek and devised evil schemes against Israel, but his schemes came back on his own head, and they hanged him and his sons on the gallows'.
3.   Esth. 9.29-31.
4.   See further S. Goldman, 'Esther', in A. Cohen (ed.), *The Five Megilloth* (Hindhead: Soncino, 1946), p. 241; and Paton, *Esther*, pp. 300-302.
5.   C. Camp, *Wisdom and the Feminine in the Book of Proverbs* (Bible and Literature Series, 11; Sheffield: Almond Press, 1985), pp. 143-46.

the so-called 'arrogant' Deborah, who summoned Barak to come to her from afar. Queen Esther waited, with both strength and temerity, to be recognized and summoned into her husband's presence. Perhaps that is why so much is elaborated on her physical beauty: a man influenced by a woman's beauty was something they could understand and accept. This dual role she played, queenly savior of her people and deferential wife, enabled the midrashists to heap glory upon her.

Conclusions

For the rabbis, modesty in women was a cardinal virtue. Dinah was harshly criticized for wantonness on the basis of the phrase 'and Dinah went out'.[1] Boldness at the proper time could sometimes be appropriate, however. The daughters of Zelophehad boldly spoke up for their rights at an appropriate moment, and received rabbinic praise for fidelity to their father.[2] Esther is not usually viewed as a bold figure, but her quiet courage in the face of personal danger is a key element of her character. Like Vashti, she disobeys a royal order (by appearing before the king unsummoned); but her action was the right one to make at the right time and for the right cause.

In the biblical account, Esther's behavior undergoes dramatic change as she comes to fulfill her leadership role. Rabbinic literature, by emphasizing God's constant assistance, in a way diminishes Esther's personal strength and independence of action; but it also increases her spirituality, which was, after all, where rabbinic interest really lay.

The classical rabbis felt that there was a lacuna in the Jewish personality of Esther, so through aggadic methods of interpretation they added the Jewish qualities they wanted her to have. They transformed her into a pious Jewish woman, such a pious woman, in fact, that she is never criticized by them for any flaw or shortcoming. This rabbinic transformation, in turn, may have helped to make the biblical book of Esther more acceptable and to popularize the Jewish festival of Purim in her honor.

1.   *Gen. R.* 80.5 for Gen. 34.1.
2.   *B. B. Bat.* 119a-b; *Sifre Num.* 133. For rabbinic commentary on Dinah and the daughters of Zelophehad, see further my forthcoming book, *From Eve to Esther.* Cf. Num. 27.

ESTHER'S STORY*

Diane Wolkstein

My uncle went to the king's banquet. But he did not eat the food. That's because we are Jewish and eat food prepared in a different way than the Persians. Uncle Mordecai said it was a wonderful banquet. The guests lay on couches in the king's garden and were served on gold and silver plates.

I am only eleven so I am too young to go with Uncle. Uncle Mordecai goes to the palace again tonight. The banquet that the king is giving to celebrate moving the capital of his kingdom from Babylon to Susa goes on for seven nights.

Uncle Mordecai gave me this diary because he knew I'd be alone seven nights in a row. Uncle has taken care of me since I can remember. My mother and father died many years ago in Jerusalem. Uncle said that this was a very special time and even though I could not go with him I could write about what was happening.

I woke up when Uncle came home. I could tell by the way he opened the door that he was troubled. I put on my robe and went to him.

Uncle Mordecai laughed when he saw me and said, 'Here you are, Hadassah—and just at the moment when I am thinking of you. How strange are the workings of heaven and earth.'

Uncle Mordecai took me on his lap and said, 'Your mother gave you a beautiful name, Hadassah, which means sweet-smelling myrtle. But tonight I shall give you a new name, Esther, which means secret or concealed.

'Listen, my child, to the changing ways of those who live on earth and remember our god is constant. Tonight at the

* Used with the permission of the author: to be published by Morrow Junior Books, 1996.

banquet Queen Vashti, the Queen of all Persia, refused to go to the king when he called for her, so she has been banished. She is no longer queen. Tomorrow a search begins throughout Persia for a new queen.'

'Will the new queen be beautiful?', I asked.

'As beautiful as you are.'

'Will she be kind?'

'As kind as you are.'

'And brave?'

'As brave as you are. Can you remember that your new name is Esther?'

'Of course.' I had more questions. But Uncle kissed me good-night, and somehow I knew that the answers, even if I asked for them, were not yet known.

It is not so easy to have a new name. Half of the time when Uncle calls me I forget it's me so I don't answer. Hadassah belongs to my mother and grandparents who lived in Jerusalem. Esther is a new name. It's Jewish and Persian, like me. In Persian Esther means Ishtar, the Goddess of Love and War. She is also the planet Venus who is the first to appear every night in the sky. I often watch for Venus in the evening. It really is very brave of her to appear all alone when it is still dark.

At twelve, I know for certain I am Esther. I have been sent to a new school, a Persian school. I like the school. We are learning to sew and cook, to sing and dance and recite poems.

In our sewing class I'm working on a beautiful dress that I'm making for the contest. It has all the colors I love. Red and pink and purple with a little green and yellow and orange.

I didn't expect it. But I won the contest! My dress won first prize! And then I was sent to wear it in another contest. And now—everything has changed!

I have been sent to the palace. There are a lot of girls here and they told me that we have been chosen so that the king could decide which one he wanted for his queen. They all have wonderful dresses and are much more beautiful than I am. I don't want to be queen. I miss Uncle Mordecai. I want to go home.

Three months have gone by and I am getting used to life in the palace. I have made friends with Hegai who is in charge of all the girls. Uncle Mordecai visits me almost every day. He is a judge at the King's Gate, which is outside the palace, so it is easy for him to visit.

Yesterday, Uncle brought me my favorite food and reminded me of the promise I made to him the night he gave me my new name. I am not to tell anyone that I'm Jewish. I don't know why he worries so much about being Jewish. The king allows everyone in the kingdom to worship whichever gods they wish. I don't want to grow up afraid just because I'm Jewish.

It happened so quickly I hardly had time to prepare. After four years of living in the palace, yesterday afternoon Hegai came to me and told me the king wished to see me last night.

I chose my favorite dress. I made it myself. It has stars and flowers and gold thread. Hegai sprayed me with the king's favorite perfume. The hairdresser wove tiny pink roses into my braids. I was led through the seven gates into the part of the palace where the king lives. No one is ever allowed to walk through the seven gates without permission and an escort. I was eager to see King Ahasuerus who had been looking for a queen for five years.

The king was standing by the window. He looked a little lonely. His arms were folded. I folded mine in the same way. He scratched his head. I scratched mine, and a tiny pink rose fell to the floor. As I bent down to pick it up, the king said, 'How beautiful you are!'

I put the rose in his curly hair and said, 'How beautiful *you* are!'

He laughed. I like his laugh. It is deep and growly and unexpected.

'Laugh again!', I said, and I tickled him.

A big happy laugh came bursting out of him like water from a fountain.

When he stopped laughing, he picked up the crown from the table, and, without asking my name, said, 'You, my shining one, shall be queen.'

Some days I look in the mirror and I see the Queen of Persia.

Other days I see Esther, who was once Hadassah. I have my own rooms and seven servants—my favorite servant is Zuleika.

To celebrate my becoming queen, the king gave many banquets. We had wonderful food and I ate as much as the king. The king often asks me about my relatives and family but each time I find an answer which is not an answer. We laugh a lot and everyone is happy.

No, everyone is not happy. Uncle Mordecai came to see me today and told me that this morning at the King's Gate, he overheard two angry relatives of Queen Vashti plotting to kill the king because he had sent Vashti away. Uncle told me to tell the king as soon as possible. It took three days to get permission to see the king because he was choosing a new prime minister. But, a day after I told the king, the plotters were caught and killed, and Uncle Mordecai's brave deed was written down in *The Book of Records*.

The new prime minister's name is Haman. He speaks very precisely and rarely smiles or laughs. Uncle Mordecai does not trust him because he is an Amalekite, and the Amalekites tried to kill the Jews after they crossed the Red Sea. Uncle Mordecai refuses to bow to Haman which makes Haman very angry. Sometimes I wish that Uncle Mordecai were not so stubborn.

Yesterday when Haman walked out through the King's Gate, and Uncle Mordecai again refused to bow to him, Haman became furious. Zuleika, who is friendly with Haman's servant, told me that Haman spoke to the other judges and when he found out that Uncle Mordecai is a Jew, he decided he would kill all the Jews.

I can hardly believe what Zuleika just told me. It is horrifying. She said that last night Haman threw dice to find out which day would be the best day to destroy the Jews. He and his sons took turns and threw the dice over and over until Haman had his answer. My heart is pounding with fear. I have sent word to Uncle Mordecai to come to the palace.

Uncle Mordecai is wandering through the streets of the city in sackcloth, weeping. Even though I gave Zuleika fine clothes for Uncle so that he would come to speak to me, he refuses to enter the palace. Instead, he sent me a copy of the notice with the king's stamp which Haman has sent to one hundred and twenty-seven countries in the Persian kingdom stating that on the thirteenth day of the month of Adar, the month before spring begins, all the Jews, young and old, men, women and children, are to be killed and their property seized. Uncle Mordecai also wrote a note to me, saying:

> Haman offered the king a great sum of silver for the right to do what he wishes with the Jews. I cannot sit as judge anymore. How can I, if my people are to be killed? My dearest Esther, now is the time for you to go to the king and reveal who you are and beg for his help.

I wrote back at once telling Uncle Mordecai that, as he well knows, no one may see the king without permission. The king has not sent for me for thirty days. If I am to force my way and am killed, what use would I be? I said it is best to wait and plan.

Uncle Mordecai sent a second note, saying:

> Long ago, when Vashti was queen, I was told by an old woman that you would be Queen of Persia. This seemed impossible. But when Vashti was banished, I thought the impossible was coming about for a purpose.
>
> It may be, my dear Esther, that you have been made queen for just this purpose—to save your people. Do not think that because you are queen you are safe. Already, outside Susa in the other lands of the kingdom, they have begun to kill our people. Do not delay!

I am afraid.

In this great palace with the guards and cooks, the messengers and servants—even Zuleika, there is no one I can turn to.

I just got up and, wandering through my rooms, saw the Bible which belonged to my mother. I opened it, and it fell on these words: 'When your hair is white, I will be with you. I made you and will care for you. I will sustain and rescue you.'

There is someone for me to turn to.

I have sent word to Uncle Mordecai telling him to pray for me and asking the Jews in Susa to also fast and pray for me. Then, after three days, I will go to the king, and if I am killed, I will be killed.

I did not eat or drink. I read and wept and prayed. Then, on the third day as I was lying on the floor of my room, I heard a sound which rose up from the bottoms of the earth and was loud enough to pierce the heavens. The sound was coming from thousands of rams' horns. Uncle must have had all the priests in the capital blow the shofar to give me strength!

I stood up. I bathed and put on the dress the king likes best. I started toward the throne room. The guards did not stop me. I walked through the first, the second, the third gates. At the fourth gate, my legs began to tremble. I walked slower, but I kept walking. As I came to the seventh gate and I realized I might not be alive much longer, I stopped. Then, the great sound of the shofar returned to me, and I pushed open the last gate. The king was sitting on his golden throne dressed in his royal purple robes.

For a moment, time stopped. Then, he turned, and lowered his gold scepter, the sign that I am allowed to speak.

'My dear wife. What is your wish?'

I touched the scepter and said, 'My wish, Your Majesty, if it pleases you, is that you and Haman come to a banquet in my room tonight.'

Why didn't I ask him then? I don't know. I just sensed it was not the moment, and tonight when the king and Haman came to my room and drank wine, and the king again asked me, 'My dear wife, what is your wish?', again I said, 'Oh my king, if I have pleased you, my wish is that you and Haman come tomorrow evening to another banquet in my room. And then I will reveal to you what you wish to know.'

I do not know how much longer I can delay before answering the king.

Hammering woke me up. I went to the window and in the early morning light saw Haman and his sons building a great gallows across from the palace. It's still winter, three months until the month of Adar. Why is Haman building a gallows? I hope Uncle Mordecai is safe.

I cannot sleep. There are footsteps in the hall. The king also cannot sleep and has sent for *The Book of Records*. His servant sometimes reads it to him at night. It is so boring, it usually puts him to sleep immediately.

What a day! Today is surely the day of all days! I woke late this morning to the sound of drumming and shouts of laughter. I went out onto the balcony and saw the most extraordinary sight of my life.

A royal parade—with two thousand buglers, five thousand drummers, ten thousand soldiers—and who was at the head of the parade? Who?

Uncle!! Uncle Mordecai was riding on a white horse and dressed in the king's purple robes! And who was leading Uncle Mordecai's white horse by the hand?

The man who hates him the most! Red-faced Haman!!

I shouted with joy and called to Zuleika. She told me that last night when the king was listening to *The Book of Records* he realized that he had not rewarded Uncle Mordecai for saving his life. So this morning at dawn the king summoned his prime minister and asked, 'How shall I reward a man I wish to honor?'

Haman, certain that the king meant himself, answered, 'Let the king hold a great parade and let the man of honor be dressed in His Majesty's clothes, led on His Majesty's white horse by one of His Majesty's highest officials!'

I want to congratulate Uncle Mordecai, but there is no time. I must prepare for the banquet.

After the king and Haman drank and ate, the king asked me, 'Now my dear wife, tell me, what is your wish?'

I answered in one breath, for I did not dare to stop until I had finished. 'Your Majesty, my wish is for my life and my request for the lives of my people. I would not ask you this if we had been sold to be slaves but we have been sold to be slaughtered on the thirteenth day of Adar.'

'Who has made such an order?', the king asked.

I pointed to Haman with tears of anger and answered. 'That man. That evil man used your signet ring to sign a decree ordering that all Jews be killed. I am a Jew, and I, too, will die.'

The king trembled and left the room and went into the garden. Then Haman rushed to the couch on which I was lying and pleaded with me. 'Your Majesty, I beg you, spare my life. I beg you—'

Just then, the king returned, and Haman, in terror, tripped, and fell on top of me. As I pushed him away, King Ahasuerus cried in fury, 'WHAT? Does he dare do this, too? Seize him!'

The guards took hold of Haman and the king said, 'Let Haman hang! Let him hang from his own gallows!'

Although Haman is dead, the decree ordering the people of Persia to kill the Jews has not been stopped. I knew I must speak to the king. But I've waited.

I've waited six weeks until the day I was certain the king would listen kindly to my request. This morning I knew the day had come.

When I entered the throne room, the king lowered his gold scepter.

'What is my dearest wife's wish?', he asked.

I touched the scepter and said, 'It is for my people. The order has been given that my people are to be killed in six weeks.'

'My dear wife,' the king said. 'I have given you Haman's house and wealth. I have made Mordecai prime minister. But once an order has gone out sealed with the king's signet ring, it cannot be changed. That is the law.'

I looked at the king. I did not speak. But I did not take my eyes from his. I waited.

At last, the king shook his head and said, 'But—another letter can be written! What the new prime minister writes can also be sealed with the king's signet ring.' He then took off his ring and gave it to Uncle Mordecai.

Uncle Mordecai sent at once for the king's secretaries who wrote letters in one hundred and twenty-seven languages stating that on the thirteenth day of Adar, Jews may join together to defend themselves against anyone who attacks them. The letters were sealed with the king's signet ring and are being rushed off to the one hundred and twenty-seven countries of the kingdom on the fastest horses.

For six weeks, Uncle Mordecai and I have lived in fear. Two days ago, although all the governors and many of the people knew that it was not the king's wish, in many lands the Jews were attacked. Outside the capital, on the thirteenth day of

Adar, our people defended themselves against their attackers. On the fourteenth day, they rejoiced and held banquets to celebrate their victory and their survival.

Here in Susa, because of the strength of Haman's sons, the fighting went on for one more day. Today, we too celebrated, eating and drinking and dancing with great joy and relief.

Uncle Mordecai has sent letters to the Jews in all the lands asking them to remember these two days—the fourteenth and fifteenth days of Adar—and the miracle in which they played a part.

I, too, am writing to my people to ask them to remember. I want them to remember not only the feasting but the days of fasting. I shall never forget my fear those three days when I was alone in my room. Nor shall I forget being awoken by the sound of the shofar or slowly walking through the seven gates, not knowing what would be.

The Persian word for dice is *pûr*. The people now call this holiday Purim after the dice which Haman threw. Haman threw dice to find out the fate of others and to destroy them. In wishing to destroy his enemy, he destroyed himself.

Many people say I was very brave. I do not remember feeling brave. I remember feeling very afraid yet despite my fear wishing to help my people so they would not be killed.

I am over seventy now and my hair is white. It pleases me greatly to watch my people celebrating, eating and drinking and telling the story of Purim.

When I hear them talk about me, I listen with amazement. Did I do all that? Ah, I think—to be young and to have the chance once again to choose.

Part II
JUDITH: ON POWER, LEADERSHIP AND KNOWLEDGE

SACRIFICE AND SALVATION:
OTHERNESS AND DOMESTICATION IN THE BOOK OF JUDITH*

Amy-Jill Levine

Exegetical studies of the text of Judith have tried to keep pace
with its peripatetic heroine. At first, like Judith on her roof, they
were located in the relatively rarified atmosphere of historical
investigation. Then, just as Judith summoned the Bethulian leaders, so convincing works have called upon predominant forms
of literary analysis. And, like Judith treading that dangerous
path to the foreign camp, recent examinations have made forays
into the alien territories of feminism, psychoanalysis and folklore
studies. Regardless of the approach, however, Judith the character is usually identified as a representation of or a metaphor
for the community of faith. Although her name, widowhood,
chastity, beauty and righteousness suggest the traditional representation of Israel, the text's association of these traits with an
independent woman and with sexuality subverts the metaphoric
connection between character and androcentrically determined
community. This paper explores how Judith the Jew/ess
(*Ioudith*) both sustains and threatens corporate determination as
well as how that threat is averted through her reinscription into
Israelite society.

    *   Reprinted, with permission, from J.C. VanderKam (ed.), 'No One
Spoke Ill of Her': Essays on Judith (Society of Biblical Literature, Early Judaism
and its Literature, 2; Atlanta: Scholars Press, 1992), pp. 17-30. A revised version of 'Character Construction and Community Formation in the Book
of Judith', in D.J. Lull (ed.), Society of Biblical Literature Seminar Papers
(Atlanta: Scholars Press, 1989), pp. 561-69. I am grateful to Laura Lomas,
Laura Augustine, Emily Stevens and, especially, Jay Geller, for their
numerous insightful criticisms and suggestions on earlier drafts, and to
George Nickelsburg, Richard Pervo and David Halperin for their helpful
comments on the seminar paper.

All women are other, as de Beauvoir declares: woman 'is defined and differentiated with reference to man and not he with reference to her...He is the Subject, he is the Absolute— she is the Other.'[1] But this generic otherness itself neither problematizes Judith's potential to represent Israel nor threatens Israelite society. The community is traditionally represented by female figures ranging from the virgin (2 Kgs 19.21//Isa. 37.22; Lam. 1.15; 2.13; Jer. 14.17) to the bride (Jer. 2.2-3; Hos. 2.15b) to the whore (Hos. 1–4; Ezek. 16) to the widow (Lam. 1.1; Isa. 54.5-8). Rather, Judith's being a woman who nonetheless speaks and acts in the world of Israelite patriarchy creates the crisis. At the beginning of the book, when she is apart, ascetic and asocial, Judith is merely a curiosity with metaphoric potential. Present in the public sphere, sexually active and socially involved, she endangers hierarchical oppositions of gender, race and class, muddles conventional gender characteristics and dismantles their claims to universality, and so threatens the status quo.[2] Judith relativizes the normative cultural constructions of the community. Her ultimate return to the private sphere and consequent reinscription into androcentric

1.   S. de Beauvoir, *The Second Sex* (New York: Bantam, 1961), p. xvi.
2.   J.Z. Smith, 'What a Difference a Difference Makes', in J. Neusner and E.S. Frerichs (eds.), *'To See Ourselves as Others See Us': Christians, Jews and 'Others' in Late Antiquity* (Chico, CA: Scholars Press, 1985), p. 36: 'The "other" emerges only as a theoretical issue when it is perceived as challenging a complex and intact world view'. At this point, the different becomes both alien and dangerous. Cf. J.G. Williams, *Women Recounted: Narrative Thinking and the God of Israel* (Sheffield: Almond Press, 1982), p. 78: Judith 'captivates Holofernes and the Assyrians in a fashion reminiscent of the wisdom tradition's warning against...the "alien woman" (Prov. 6.24-25; Sir. 9.8-9; 25.21)'. While Smith notes that 'Difference most frequently entails a hierarchy of prestige and a concomitant political ranking of superordinate and subordinate' ('What a Difference', pp. 4-5) he does not classify women among his proximate others. Feminist criticism, which posits gender as a prime matter of inquiry, suggests that by her very difference, woman challenges traditional methodological and epistemological perspectives. See, among others, E. Showalter, 'The Feminist Critical Revolution', in *idem* (ed.), *The New Feminist Criticism* (New York: Pantheon, 1985), pp. 3-10; G. Greene and C. Kahn, 'Feminist Scholarship and the Social Construction of Woman', in *idem* (eds.), *Making a Difference: Feminist Literary Criticism* (London and New York: Methuen, 1985), pp. 1-36.

Israel both alleviate the crisis precipitated by her actions and discourse and reinforce the norms they reveal. Yet because her return is incomplete, the threat of the other remains.

Judith appears at first to be a classic metaphor both for the nation and for all women. Not only does her name mean 'the Jewess', but also she 'is a widow, for the Jewish nation is living at the time of grave danger and affliction, like a forlorn widow'.[1] Judith is the text's only named woman character and thus the only woman recognized by its male-defined world.[2] Further, because her name is a generic, its applicability can easily be extended beyond the individual. The women of Bethulia are all like Judith in that each is a 'Jewess'. Through her name, Judith is associated with Gentile women as well. Judith the daughter of Merari evokes and rehabilitates Judith the daughter of Beeri, the Hittite wife of Esau who 'made life bitter for Isaac and Rebecca' (Gen. 26.35).[3] But this metaphoric

1.   L. Alonso-Schökel, 'Judith', HBC, p. 810; cf. his 'Narrative Structures in the Book of Judith', *Protocol Series of the Colloquies of the Center for Hermeneutical Studies in Hellenistic and Modern Culture* 11 (ed. W. Wuellner, 1975), pp. 14-15: 'As a widow, [Judith] can represent the Jewish people in her affliction'; 'as a weak woman lacking the support of her husband, she can show and reveal better the force of God (9.10-11; 13.14-15; 16.6)'. Cf. even Luther's comment that 'Judith is the Jewish people, represented as a chaste and holy widow' (cited by, *inter alia*, T. Craven, 'Artistry and Faith in the Book of Judith', *Semeia* 8 [1977], p. 77). On the connection of Israel/the Jewish nation and Judith see also T. Craven, *Artistry and Faith in the Book of Judith* (SBLDS, 70; Chico, CA: Scholars Press, 1983), p. 85; D.R. Dumm, 'Judith', p. 626. On the name's allegorical potential see Williams, *Women*, p. 76, representing literary-critical reading; M.P. Coote, 'Comment on "Narrative Structures in the Book of Judith"', *Colloquies* 11, pp. 21-22, on the significance of the name for the female warrior; and C. Moore, *Judith* (AB, 40; Garden City, NY: Doubleday, 1985), p. 179.

2.   Jdt. 8.1 breaks the pattern of the first seven chapters, in which a plethora of male names and so individual male subjects appear. Alonso-Schökel sees the break caused by the genealogy in terms of plot rather than gender: it interrupts the campaigns of Holofernes and Nebuchadnezzar ('Narrative Structures', p. 4).

3.   Noted by E. Bjorkan, 'Subversion in Judith: A Literary-Critical Analysis' (Senior Thesis, Swarthmore College, 1987), p. 53. One should add to Bjorkan's work the further connection between the two women: neither has children.

identification of Judith with the Jewish community as well as beyond to Gentile women breaks down. Judith the woman can only incompletely represent Israel. The community is historically active; women per se are not. Judith is thus both part of and apart from her people.

Metaphoric connections between the heroine and the community extend beyond Judith's name to gender-determined categories. Yet gender alone does not define their common characteristic. Israel's traditional representations as virgin, continent bride, adulterous whore and celibate widow also share a sexual thematic. Faithful Israel is sexually controlled; her faithless antitype is sexually loose. Consequently, the chaste widow Judith—like the virgin Dinah (Jdt. 9.9-10)—represents the holy community. Yet the connection between widow and virgin is severed as Judith's rhetoric unties the lines identifying her with both Israel and other women. The initial prayer in ch. 9 identifies the rape victim Dinah by a generic term; she is called simply a 'virgin' (*parthenou*, 9.2). But unlike 'Judith', this generic does not function as a proper name. Dinah has been robbed of her personhood. Further, Judith equates Dinah's rape with the siege of Bethulia, and the association is reinforced by the resonance between the name of the town and the Hebrew for 'virgin', *btwlh*.[1] Judith, however, assumes the man's role of protector-avenger associated with her ancestor (cf. 9.2, *tou patros mou symeon*). Indeed, like Simeon she expresses no sympathy for the Shechemite women.[2] That the deity 'gave their wives for a prey and their daughters to captivity' (9.4) Judith interprets as a sign of divine justice. Mention of these victims occurs in the context of social egalitarianism—the deity 'strikes slaves as well as princes' (9.3) and is called the 'god of the lowly, helper of the oppressed, upholder of the weak, protector of the forlorn, savior of those without hope' (9.11)— but Judith herself does not recognize Gentiles as in need of protection. Were Judith fully to embody Israel, then the traditional representation of the deity as the (male) savior of the

1. *Inter alia*, Alonso-Schökel, 'Judith', p. 806, and his less sanguine comments in 'Narrative Structures', pp. 18-19.

2. Cf. the possible contrast to Dinah, who 'went out to visit the women of the land' (Gen. 34.1).

female-figured community would be challenged. Were all women to be like Judith, not only Holofernes would lose his head. Were Judith to represent Gentile women, then the paradigmatic identification of Israel as chosen from among the nations would be compromised. Such separation of Judith from corporate Israel, from Jewish women and from Gentiles preserves the text's patriarchal ethos.

While Judith's widowhood conforms to the traditional representation of Israel as a woman in mourning and while both she and Bethulia are draped in sackcloth, Judith's particular representation—her status, rhetoric, wealth, beauty and even her genealogy—aborts the metaphor.[1] This widow is hardly the forlorn female in need of male protection. Given the negative associations of her husband's name, Manasseh, his absence is almost welcome; he shares the name of the king held responsible for the Babylonian exile (2 Kgs 21.12-15; 23.26-27; 24.3-4). Moreover, the circumstances of his death, heatstroke while watching the binding of barley sheaves, graphically anticipate the decapitation of Holofernes. The phallic imagery of the bound sheaves prefigures the general's dismembered head; both symbolize castration.[2] The psychosexual suggestiveness of this imagery is complemented by barley meal's ritual function: it is the offering required of a man who suspects his wife of infidelity even 'though she has not defiled herself' (Num. 5.15). Linguistic parallels make the ties between Manasseh and Holofernes even more pronounced. While the general is decapitated by Judith, Manasseh is cut down when the burning fever attacks his head (*kai ho kausōn ēlthen epi tēn kephalēn autou*). Each man takes to his bed (*kai epesen epi tēn klinēn auto* [8.3] *kai Olophernēs propeptōkōs epi tēn klinēn auto* [13.2]), and each dies.

---

1. Ironically, the Mishnah's description of widows fits Judith better than the literary metaphor. On the autonomous widow, see the excellent discussion by J.R. Wegner in *Chattel or Person? The Status of Women in the Mishnah* (New York and Oxford: Oxford University Press, 1988), esp. pp. 138-43.

2. On the relationship between decapitation and castration see A. Dundes, 'Comment on "Narrative Structures in the Book of Judith"', *Colloquies* 11, pp. 28-29. The tie between decapitation and genital mutilation adds another dimension to the well-known trope connecting Holofernes with Shechem, and Judith with Dinah/Simeon.

Manasseh's absence is necessitated by the demands of Israelite patriarchy: Judith's actions would have subjected him, had he been alive, to sexual disgrace.[1] Only Holofernes realizes the danger of humiliation: 'It will be a disgrace if we let such a woman go without enjoying her company, for if we do not embrace her she will laugh at us' (Jdt. 12.12). By her sexually charged presence, the widow Judith therefore threatens the masculine ethos of the Assyrian army.

The specified length of Judith's mourning has been claimed 'to heighten the picture of her loyalty and devotion' to her dead husband,[2] but the reference to 'three years and four months' or forty months (8.4) is overdetermined. The length of her mourning and the meaning of her widowhood extend beyond concern for the absent spouse. First, the period recapitulates the forty years Israel spent in the wilderness. From the time of the Passover/the barley harvest, Judith undergoes a period of testing and purification. But this analogy does not require her to mourn for Manasseh any more than the generation in the wilderness needed to mourn for Egypt. Secondly, the three years and four months structurally parallel the thirty-four days of the siege (7.20). Thirdly, the detailed description of Judith's mourning stresses her otherness. Upon her husband's death, Judith removed herself from Bethulian society and specifically, from men.

Judith had to be a widow—that is, sexually experienced but unattached—in order for her to carry out her plan. And she had to stay a widow. Upon completing the festivities in Jerusalem, she 'went to Bethulia, and remained on her estate...Many desired to marry her, but she remained a widow' (16.21-22). Remarriage for levirate purposes would create a new lineage and consequently challenge the power structure of Bethulian society. Further, as a widow safely returned to her proper place, the private sphere, Judith preserves her identification with Israel: no longer active, she no longer subverts the metaphor. A utilitarian reading would even claim that Judith

1. See W. Shumaker, 'Critique of Luis Alonso-Schökel on Judith', *Colloquies* 11, p. 32.

2. M.S. Enslin, *The Book of Judith* (Jewish Apocryphal Literature, 8; Leiden: Brill, 1972), p. 111.

remains a widow both because she had nothing to gain by marriage and because no man was worthy of her. Only the text's
females act in a fully efficacious manner;[1] only Judith displays
well-directed initiative; only her maid competently follows
instructions. The men are weak, stupid, or impaired: Manasseh
dies ignominiously; Holofernes is inept; Bagoas is a eunuch;
Achior faints at the sight of Holofernes' head. Uzziah, who
shares Judith's ethnicity and elevated social status and who,
because he is descended from Simeon, might even be able to
claim levirate privileges, is the biggest disappointment. Judith
must correct his naive theology, and she stands firm while he
wavers in his faith (cf. 7.30-31).[2] The only fit male companion for
Judith is the deity, and it is with him she communes in prayer on
her roof. Yet given the lack of his direct presence in the text,
this relationship is a bit one-sided. Indeed, Coote has argued
that Judith 'represents a kind of reversal of the type of rescue
pattern underlying the exodus story, in which a male hero (the
Lord) rescues a female figure (Israel) from captivity'.[3] Rather
than conform to the traditional image of widow, Judith's representation follows both divine and male paradigms.

Like her name, gender and widowhood, Judith's genealogy
betrays her metaphoric function. This list is not an invention
designed to mock the elaborate pedigrees fabricated by post-
exilic aristocrats (so Bruns), nor is its purpose primarily to indicate Judith's Samaritan origins (so Steinmann).[4] On the one
hand, the genealogy anchors Judith to Israelite history. The
reference in 8.1 to 'Israel' reinforces the symbolic value of
Judith's own name. Further, as the connection to Israel (that is,
Jacob) signals Judith's talents for deception and for crossing

1.   Commenting on 15.11, Craven (*Artistry*, p. 104 n. 73) observes: 'The
text reads *ten hemionon*, "mule" in the singular...Could it be that Judith's
female donkey, like Judith herself, can do what it usually takes a team to
do?'

2.   Cf. T. Craven, 'Redeeming Lies in the Book of Judith' (paper presented to the Pseudepigrapha Section, AAR/SBL Annual Meeting,
Anaheim, 1989).

3.   'Comment', p. 21. Such a reversal endangers both the tradition and
the status quo.

4.   J.E. Bruns, 'The Genealogy of Judith', *CBQ* 18 (1956), pp. 19-22;
M. Steinmann, *Lecture de Judith* (Paris: Gabalda, 1953), p. 72.

boundaries, so names like Gideon, Elijah, Nathaneal, Joseph and
Merari portend her abilities to function in such roles as judge,
prophet, ambassador and priest. She supersedes her genealogy
and so her generation's representative of 'Israel'. On the other
hand, because neither the Israel of 8.1 nor any of the others
listed in her family tree has made his mark in history—they,
unlike Judith, have not lived up to their names—the inscription
of each in history is due entirely to her. She is the one who also
reinscribes the branch of her family that had been written out
(Jdt. 9.2; cf. Gen. 49.7 as well as the silence in Jdt. 8.1-2): the line
of Simeon. Thus, while Judith's genealogy situates her within
the historical community and makes her its representative, it is
Judith herself who confers value, meaning and legitimacy to
those whom she represents. The relationship between the representation (i.e., Judith) and the represented (i.e., her historical
community) which undergirds any metaphoric identification is,
consequently, rendered problematic.

   In terms of her relationship to the present generation of
Bethulians, Judith is marked as other by her wealth, beauty and
religiosity. Rich, gorgeous, pious, as well as independent, Judith
is particularly distinguished from others of her sex. The women
in Bethulia are weak from thirst, robbed of their voice by their
husbands (cf. 4.12), and controlled by the town leaders (7.32b).
Even Judith's maid lacks her freedom. These distinctions are
first established through a geographical notice with attendant
value hierarchies. Judith is defined spatially as superior to the
rest of Bethulia: the 'women and young men' are associated
first with the 'streets of the city and...the passages through the
gate' (7.22); she is on her roof (8.5). They are unsheltered and
in need of protection; she is in a tent and is, additionally, either
unaware of or unconcerned with the danger below: she distributes neither her wealth nor her water. Instead, her wealth
allows her to enhance her beauty and so further distinguish
herself: she has water for bathing while the people are fainting
from thirst (7.22). The text then dwells on the material goods
available for her adornment: 'She bathed her body with water
and anointed herself with precious ointment...and put on a
tiara, and arrayed herself in her gayest apparel...and put on
her anklets and bracelets and rings and her earrings and all her

ornaments...' (10.3b-4). Originally she was 'beautiful in appearance, and had a very lovely face' (8.7); now she rivals Helen of
Troy. Chabris and Charmis notice 'how her face was altered'
(10.7), and to the men in the Assyrian camp she was
'marvelously beautiful' (10.14). Even Judith herself acknowledges the striking 'beauty of her countenance' (16.7). The
enemy soldiers 'marveled at her beauty, and admired the
Israelites, judging them by her...' (10.19). Although they mis-
takenly perceive Judith as representing her contemporaries—
only Judith possesses such striking beauty—the soldier's judgment supports Judith's identification as a traditional metaphor of
Israel.

Judith's piety also supports her metaphoric identification with
Israel even as it severs her connection to the Bethulian population (for example 8.5-6, 28-29, 31; 9.1-14; 10.2, 8). No fanatical
ascetic, the truly observant widow demonstrates her faith both
by fasting and by eating at appropriate occasions (a trait that
will serve her well in Holofernes' camp). This religiosity is distinguished from the bad theology and related practices of the
Bethulian leaders. The men return to their posts (8.36), but
Judith engages in devotional activities 'at the very time when
that evening's incense was being offered in the house of God in
Jerusalem' (9.1). As a woman, she is technically marginal to the
operation of the official cult. But on her roof, she can participate
in devotions without endangering the status quo. Close to the
deity in spirit and in physical location, she is removed from the
people both religiously and spatially. The summary verse of her
introduction (8.7-8) confirms her various unique attributes and
retains the emphasis on her piety. While her beauty plus the
'gold and silver, and men and women slaves, and cattle, and
fields' left to her by her husband would be sufficient to distinguish her from other Bethulians, 'no one spoke ill of her because
(*hoti*) she feared God exceedingly' (8.8).

When the woman of whom the community spoke chooses
herself to speak to them, she unleashes otherness into the public
sphere. By sending her *female* slave out of the female-defined
household into the male-dominated public sphere, Judith weak-
ens the gender divisions defining Israelite society; by conveying
Judith's summons to the town leaders, the female *slave* inverts

social hierarchies. These inversions continue throughout Judith's contact with men in positions of power. By accepting Judith's theological program, the Bethulian leaders both reinforce her metaphoric potential to represent the faithful community and acknowledge her potentially subversive voice. When they endeavor to redirect her discourse toward piety (8.31), she makes public her intent to act; they are reduced to accepting her words (8.33-34; 10.9). And those words subvert the metaphoric understanding of language in the public sphere—the sharing of a common code—just as her actions subvert her metaphoric identification with Israel. For example, Judith promises 'to do a thing which will go down through all generations of our descendants' (8.32), but her 'thing' (*pragma*) is a sign lacking any definitive referent. In the Assyrian camp, Judith continues to transgress linguistic expectations. Her use of *double entendres* (for example, the double referents to 'lord' [*kyrios*] in 11.5, 6, 11; 12.14) furthers her subversive intent.

Exploitation of conventional expectations is indicated by more than Judith's rhetoric. According to Alan Dundes, when Judith removes 'the garments of widowhood and mourning (10.3) to wear attractive alluring garb [she] appears to move metaphorically from death to life'.[1] Yet this is one more metaphor Judith undercuts, for the 'life' into which she moves is of a very peculiar sort. The private widow becomes a public woman; she undergoes a total inversion from ascetic chastity to (the guise of) lavish promiscuity. Nor does she simply enter the life of the community either through association with her neighbors or through levirate marriage; rather, she leaves town. Finally, she moves not directly from death to life but rather from death of one sort, that of the widow separated from her besieged and dying society, to death of another, that of the assassin active among a doomed population. The Assyrian camp is the realm of the dead: characterized by killing and populated by the castrated Bagoas, the beguiled, the besotted and the beheaded. That Holofernes' 'god' is the 'historically dead' Nebuchadnezzar and that the army represents the 'historically conquered' Assyrian empire further denies the Gentiles any

1. 'Comment on "Narrative Structures"', p. 28.

association with life. Only when Judith returns to her people and celebrates with them in Jerusalem does she both create and enter the realm of life. But at that moment, tainted by death as well as confirmed as a dangerous other active in the public sphere, she threatens the structure of the very life she engenders and upholds.

Upon her return, the seeds of Judith's threat begin to flower in Israel. By her actions and by her presence, she offers those previously marginal to or excluded from the power base—Jewish women, Achior the Gentile, the maidservant—roles in society and cult. The conditions under which gender-determined, ethnic and class-based integration occur, however, differ according to the text's treatment of women, proselytes and slaves. Before Judith entered the Israelite public sphere, the Jewish women were separated from their husbands and from the place of action by their leaders' command (7.32). In 15.12-13, 'all the women of Israel' (*pasa gynē Israēl*) gather to see her and bless her; some even dance in her honor. In turn, she distributes branches (*thyrsa*) to her companions.[1] These women, who then 'crowned themselves with olive wreaths', reveal their transformation into active agents. Last, Judith leads 'all the women' (*pasōn tōn gynaikōn*) while 'every man (*pas anēr Israēl*) followed them. Thus the female population of Israel, like the sword-brandishing (13.6-8) and head-bearing (13.15) Judith, become both graphically and by their actions phallic women.[2] Such inversions of male–female leadership patterns are permitted if not necessitated by the extraordinary circumstances of Judith's deed and Israel's rescue. However, they cannot be allowed to continue unchecked. Only by remaining unique and apart can Judith be tolerated, domesticated and even treasured by

1.   The combination of the *thvrsa* with the decapitated head and the women's celebration is strongly reminiscent of the *Bacchae*, another story in which gender roles are muddled and in which an 'other' is both dangerous and desirable.

2.   J. LaPlanche and J.-B. Pontalis, *The Language of Psychoanalysis* (New York: Norton, 1973), define the phallic woman as one 'endowed, in phantasy, with a phallus'. In one such phantasy, she is 'represented...as having an external phallus or phallic attribute' (p. 311). The identification is often applied to threatening women manifesting 'allegedly masculine character-traits' (p. 312).

Israelite society. The women consequently must return to their home and their husbands.

Just as Judith transforms the social roles of the Israelite women, so she transforms the life of the Gentile Achior. Like Rahab before him and like Judith herself, Achior's name and reputation remain alive among the people (14.10). However, because Achior is male, this new social and religious position can be marked on his flesh as well as in his new community. The Gentile man's incorporation into Israel is the inverse of the Jewish woman's position in the Assyrian camp.[1] Achior becomes a Jew first by sharing a meal with the leaders of Bethulia and secondly, primarily, through his circumcision. Judith too is physically altered (10.7) in preparation for incorporation into the alien community, but her mark of difference is not permanent: the makeup is washed off each night. Similarly, Judith refrains from becoming 'like the daughters of the Assyrians' (12.13) by refusing Holofernes' food. Finally, Achior's incorporation into the Jewish community is confirmed by his singular movement. Unlike Judith, who moves back and forth from populated areas to liminal sites, Achior moves only to Israel. While Judith thus is figured as other to both Jew and Gentile, Achior the convert mediates between the two.

Although gender-determined and ethnic integration occur during the course of the narrative, incorporation of Judith's servant does not. On the one hand, she appears to be Judith's double: linguistically, *habra* is related to *habras*—'graceful, beautiful'—which could serve as Judith's other name. Similarly, Judith adopts for herself in 11.5-6 titles of subservience—slave (*doulē*) and handmaiden (*paidiskē* [which can connote 'prostitute'])—used elsewhere for her maid (*paidiskē* in 10.10, *doulē* in 12.15; 13.3). Yet, on the other hand, the patriarchal culture can deal with only one woman who speaks and acts; another such exceptional individual would too severely compromise the status quo. Thus, until Judith's death, her 'favorite slave' must remain silent and in service.

The relationship between Judith and her maid is ironically

1. For a discussion of the parallels between Judith and Achior, see A.D. Roitman, 'Achior in the Book of Judith: His Role and Significance', in VanderKam (ed.), *'No One Spoke Ill of Her'*, pp. 31-45.

paralleled by that of Holofernes and his eunuch. In Jdt. 12.11, Bagoas is described as in charge of Holofernes' personal affairs; we have already been told that the maid oversees Judith's estate. Further, Bagoas summons Judith just as the maid summoned the leaders of Bethulia. In 13.3, both maid and eunuch receive the same instructions. But the parallelism is dramatically incomplete. Bagoas is the only named character in the text who is not somehow brought into Judith's community. Incorporation is accomplished if the act of severing or sacrifice—of the past, of the Gentile community, of one's foreskin—is brought about by the Jews themselves and serves the needs of their community. The form of incorporation in turn supports the text's concern with gender roles. Circumcision and that for which it substitutes, castration, both call attention to sexual difference rather than to undifferentiated integration. This difference is necessary for social organization and so for preservation of the status quo, as the removal of Judith from the public sphere and the return of the Bethulian population to their normative lives indicate. Achior, who as circumcised accepts sexual difference, fits into the community. So does Holofernes, once he is dead, since his (symbolic) castration would otherwise deny that difference. The eunuch, who as castrated but alive problematizes sexual difference, does not fit into the community.

Because she muddles sexual difference through her inversion of gender roles, Judith cannot as easily as Bagoas be erased from the story. She must somehow be domesticated, and this is done in part through representations of the other which evoke Judith yet which lack her subversive force. Achior's conversion, the presence of Holofernes' head, the maid's freedom and, especially, the stories people tell about the pious widow all substitute for Judith.[1] They serve to maintain her presence in the public sphere while concurrently displacing her threat. The future is thereby protected. To preserve the status quo and to restore the sexual difference that determines it, Judith's actions

1.   Cf. Coote, 'Comment', p. 26: 'It is often patriarchal societies, where male and female roles are sharply distinguished and women have a passive role, that in fantasy produce myths of a female savior'. In fantasy, the danger woman poses to the status quo is limited. Woman does in myth what she cannot do in the real world.

must also be rendered kosher. Her concluding psalm reinforces traditional gender roles first by stressing the irregularity of conquest by the 'hand of a female' (*thēleia*)[1] and secondly by giving full glory to the deity. Next, Judith submits to priestly ministrations (16.18); at this time, she also gives up the evidence of her time in the Assyrian camp: 'Judith also dedicated to God all the vessels of Holofernes, which the people had given her; and the canopy which she took for herself from his bedchamber she gave as a votive offering to the Lord' (16.19). This celebration in Jerusalem (16.18-20) reappropriates the sacrifice in 13.6-9. The initial ritualized killing, which included the purification and festive garbing of the celebrant, her sexual abstinence, the painless slitting of the victim's throat (he being 'overcome with wine' [13.2]), the aid of the assistant in disposing of the parts, the retention of a portion of the sacrifice for the community, and the efficacy that such an offering brings to Israel as a whole is given its full value only when the account—and the vessels, the canopy and the general's head—become part of the communal celebration. Moreover, the sacrifice in Judith 16 makes proper the parodic event in ch. 13: Judith's victim is an inappropriate offering; she is not a priest, and the killing required two strokes. The heroine's direct links to the divine, coupled with her temple-oriented piety, suggest she plays the man's role of priest as well as of warrior. But, because such subversion of gender roles threatens Israelite society, her sacrificial and military actions must be constrained and contained.[2] Through the rewriting of her sacrifice as well as the sacrifice of the tokens of her deed, her transgressions are expiated.

Then, Judith herself must leave the public sphere, and life

1. On the use of 'female' rather than 'woman' (*gynē*) cf. 9.10; 13.15; 16.5; Craven, *Artistry*, p. 91 and n. 40; and esp. P.W. Skehan, 'The Hand of Judith', *CBQ* 25 (1963), pp. 94-109.

2. Judith's appropriation of Holofernes' sword is to be equated not only with her assumption of male markers but also with castration. Castration is suggested also by Judith's comparison in 16.7 to figures who castrate their fathers: the young men, the sons of the Titans, and the giants in 16.7. Judith, like Medusa the archetypal phallic woman, castrates with 'the beauty of her countenance' (16.7e). Consequently, she must be disarmed, and her disarming presence must be removed from the public sphere.

must return to normalcy. No longer the united 'people' (cf. *ho laos* in 16.20) comprised of men and women, now 'each man (*hekatos*) returned home to his own inheritance, and Judith went to Bethulia and remained on her estate' (16.21). The women, so prominent during the celebration, are completely erased. The inversion of gender roles is ended, and the status quo is rein-forced. But even in her return, Judith resists complete domesti-cation. Because she is not described as reentering the lifestyle described in 8.4-6[1]—she returns to her estate (16.21), but no mention is made of her earlier ascetic religiosity—she becomes other to her past. Her activities in the public sphere have thus not only changed the fate of the Bethulian population, they have changed Judith herself. On her estate but not on her roof, and in touch with the local population (as one might conclude from the mention of the repeated proposals), Judith is not com-parably closer to the Bethulian society she already once dis-rupted. Like Holofernes, the only way Judith will no longer directly threaten ordered (i.e., gender-determined) Israelite society is through sacrifice, severing and death.

Judith's distribution of property, her death and her burial may be seen as inverse images of Achior's circumcision and Holofernes' decapitation. Complete incorporation requires a sacrifice with attendant communal benefits, and Judith in death conforms to this textual rubric. Because she is not male, she can lose neither her foreskin nor, given the metaphoric connection between decapitation and circumcision, her head. Judith has only two possessions which could be sacrificed: her property and her life. Given the threat even her reputation poses to the community, it is not inappropriate that she surrender every-thing. Consequently, 'she set her maid free. Before she died she distributed her property' (16.23, 24). Then, Judith's only remaining public appearance is her burial; not surprisingly, 16.23 explicitly notes that 'they buried her in the cave of her husband, Manasseh'. In death, she is made to conform to her traditional role as wife.

All that remains of the intrusion of Judith's otherness into the public realm is her 'fame' (16.23). That is, her deed becomes

---

1.   As observed by Roitman, 'Achior in the Book of Judith'.

incorporated into public memory and public discourse, and it is thereby controlled. Yet each time her story is told, this woman who represented the community as well as exceeded that representation will both reinforce and challenge Bethulia's—and the reader's—gender-determined ideology.

JUDITH AS ALTERNATIVE LEADER:
A REREADING OF JUDITH 7–13

Jan Willem van Henten

The story of Judith is often connected to kindred biblical traditions, especially to stories in which a woman brings salvation to
Israel by eliminating the male attacker. Jael and Deborah have
been studied as figures who correspond in many ways to
Judith. Several scholars have suggested that Judges 4–5 functions as a literary model for the story of Judith.[1] In this paper I
do not want to challenge such a reading of the story. It is obvious that Judith contains several allusions to Judges 4–5[2] which
invite the reader to compare Judith with Deborah and Jael. The
book of Judith is, however, a goldmine for readers looking for
possible quotations and allusions, and one does not do justice to
it by focusing on just one perspective of related traditions.
Therefore, I would like to interrelate Judith with biblical traditions which until now have been hardly discussed in connection
with it, and put forward another reading of chs. 7–13 which
does not attempt to contradict other interpretations but to add
to the intricate palette of intertextual relations between Judith
and biblical writings. First, some literary motifs of chs. 7–13 will

1. See with further references S.A. White, 'In the Steps of Jael and
Deborah: Judith as Heroine', in D. Lull (ed.), *Society of Biblical Literature
Seminar Papers 1989* (Atlanta: Scholars Press, 1989), pp. 570-78; reprinted in
J.C. VanderKam (ed.), *'No One Spoke Ill of Her': Essays on Judith* (SBL Early
Judaism and its Literature, 2; Atlanta: Scholars Press, 1992), pp. 5-16; also
F. van Dijk-Hemmes, 'Gezegende onder de vrouwen: een moeder in Israël
en een maagd in de kerk', in *idem* (ed.), *'t Is kwaad gerucht, als zij niet binnen
blijft: Vrouwen in oude culturen* (Tekst en Maatschappij; Utrecht: HES, 1986),
pp. 123-47.
2. For example Jdt. 8.33; 9.9-10; 13.14-15; 15.10; 16.5 (cf. Judg. 4.9, 21;
5.26); Jdt. 13.18; 14.7; 15.10 (cf. Judg. 5.24) and 16.13 (cf. Judg. 5.3).

be discussed which suggest a coherence of these chapters. Secondly, Judith 7–13 will be read with traditions of the Massah and Meribah episode as intertext (Exod. 17.1-7; Num. 20.2-13 and Deut. 33.8-11). These traditions not only correspond quite well to the setting of Judith's performance, but can also explain to a certain extent why Judith is successful. Thirdly, some implications of this reading in connection to Judith's ad hoc leadership are dealt with. Finally, the question whether one can read these chapters satisfactorily as an M or an F voice will be considered briefly.[1]

1. *The Cohesion of Judith 7–13*

The story of Judith is fictitious like the stories of Tobit, Susanna and other pious Jews. But whereas for example the story of Susanna can be imagined without serious difficulties in the setting of the first captives in Babylon and corresponds to data in biblical writings,[2] the author[3] of Judith bluntly contradicts facts

1. The terminology used has been proposed by A. Brenner and F. van Dijk-Hemmes in *On Gendering Texts: Female and Male Voices in the Hebrew Bible* (Biblical Interpretation, 1; Leiden: Brill, 1993).

2. J.W. van Henten, 'The Story of Susanna as a Pre-Rabbinic Midrash to Dan. 1.1-2', in A. Kuyt, E.G.L. Schrijver and N.A. van Uchelen (eds.), *Variety of Forms: Dutch Studies in Midrash* (Publications of the Juda Palache Institute, 5; Amsterdam: Amsterdam University Press, 1990), pp. 1-14; J.W. Wesselius, 'The Literary Genre of the Story of Susanna and its Original Language', in Kuyt, Schrijver and van Uchelen (eds.), *Variety of Forms*, pp. 15-25.

3. There is a reasonable likelihood that the author of (an earlier stage) of the book of Judith was a woman and for this reason I interpret the author as a woman, although a masculine authorship can be defended as well. Cf. R.S. Kraemer, 'Women's Authorship of Jewish and Christian Literature in the Greco-Roman Period', in A.-J. Levine (ed.), *Women Like This: New Perspectives on Jewish Women in the Greco-Roman World* (Atlanta: Scholars Press, 1991), pp. 221-42; the sceptical remarks concerning a possible female or feminist author by E. Schuller, 'The Apocrypha', in C.A. Newsom and S. Ringe (eds.), *The Women's Bible Commentary* (London: SPCK; Louisville, KY: Westminster Press/John Knox, 1992), pp. 235-43, esp. p. 243; T. Craven, *Artistry and Faith in the Book of Judith* (SBLDS, 70; Chico, CA: Scholars Press, 1983), p. 121: 'To put forward the case that the author was an ancient "feminist" would be as groundless as arguing that the author was a Pharisee or a Zealot, or a member of any other sect';

given in biblical sources. Not only is Nebuchadnezzar presented as king of the Assyrians (Jdt. 1.1), but also the historical setting of the book in the reign of Nebuchadnezzar (cf. 1.1, 13; 2.1) is refuted by references to the return from exile (4.3; 5.19). Nevertheless, from a form-critical perspective[1] Judith has much in common with historical writings, especially with histories of rescue of the Jewish people such as Esther and 1, 2 and *3 Maccabees*. This appears for instance from the motif of feasting at the end of the narrative, where we find a feast of rescue including a song of victory and praise (15.8–16.20; see also below).[2] In this part Judith is still the central person. She

van Dijk-Hemmes in Brenner and van Dijk-Hemmes, *On Gendering Texts*, p. 31: 'The fact that a woman appears as the main character in a literary work is by itself no decisive argument for female authorship'. See the last section of this article.

1.   Judith has been characterized as a novella and a wisdom story; see for example P. Weimar, 'Formen frühjüdischer Literatur: Eine Skizze', in J. Maier and J. Schreiner (eds.), *Literatur und Religion des Frühjudentums: Eine Einführung* (Würzburg and Gütersloh: Echter Verlag, 1973), pp. 123-62; H.-P. Müller, 'Die weisheitliche Lehrerzählung im Alten Testament und seiner Umwelt', *Welt des Orients* 9 (1977–1978), pp. 77-98; E. Zenger, 'Judith/Judithbuch', in G. Müller *et al.* (eds.), *Theologische Realenzyklopädie* 17 (Berlin and New York: de Gruyter, 1988), pp. 404-408; G.W.E. Nickelsburg, 'Stories of Biblical and Early Post-Biblical Times', in M.E. Stone (ed.), *Jewish Writings of the Second Temple Period: Apocrypha, Pseudepigrapha, Qumran Sectarian Writings, Philo, Josephus* (CRINT, 2.2; Assen: Van Gorcum; Philadelphia: Fortress Press, 1984), pp. 33-87, esp. pp. 48-49.

2.   Judith shares the following structural elements with these histories:

1.   A decree of a foreign king threatens the existence of the Jewish nation: Jdt. 2.1-3; 3.8; Esth. 3.8-15 MT and the addition of the text of the decree in the Greek text 3.13a-g/B1-7 LXX; 2 Macc. 5.12, 24; 6.1-2, 6-9, 21; *3 Macc.* 2.27-30; 3.11-30.

2.   A prayer by pious Jews precedes a turn for the better: Jdt. 9; Esth. 4.17a-z/C1-30 LXX (cf. 4.1, 8 LXX); 2 Macc. 7.37-38; *3 Macc.* 6.1-15.

3.   Rescue by God or because of his approval of the performance of human saviours: Jdt. 10–13; 14; implicitly in Esth. 5–6 and 8 MT (cf. Esth. 5.1e/D8 LXX); 2 Macc. 8 and 15.1-28; *3 Macc.* 6.16-29.

4.   Revenge on the foreign attacker (not in *3 Macc.*): Jdt. 12.10–13.20 (cf. 14.1, 5-6, 11 with 1 Macc. 7.47 and 2 Macc. 15.32-35); Esth. 7; 2 Macc. 9 and 15.28-35.

5.   The celebration of the rescue during a (national) feast: Jdt. 15.8–16.20; Esth. 9.17-32 and 10.31/F11 LXX; 2 Macc. 10.5-8; 15.36;

appears therefore as the saviour of Israel, like judges in pre-monarchic times or the Maccabees in the period of the composition of the book.[1] In an ironic way Holofernes indicates this role already in 11.3 in his dialogue with Judith. This phrase is one of the famous *double entendres* of Judith[2] and can be translated as 'In any event, you have come to safety [with me, Holofernes]',[3] but also as 'In any event, you have come to rescue [namely, the Jewish people]'. Judith's act of rescue is described basically in chs. 8–13, but there are reasons to connect ch. 7 with these chapters, because ch. 7 seems to function as the point of departure for Judith's performance.

Nevertheless, almost all scholars who study Judith assume a caesura between chs. 1–7 (or 4–7) and 8–16,[4] seduced as they

3 *Macc.* 6.30-40 (cf. 7.15-20 and 6.30: 'hold a festival of deliverance'); cf. 1 Macc. 4.56-59; 7.48-49 and 13.51-52.

On 1 Maccabees as history of liberation see further N. Martola, *Capture and Liberation: A Study in the Composition of the First Book of Maccabees* (Acta Academiae Aboensis Ser. A, 63, 1; Åbo: Åbo Akademi, 1984).

1. The final redaction of Judith probably dates from the Hasmonean period, although scholars disagree over an earlier or later date within this period; see for example E. Zenger, 'Das Buch Judit', in W.G. Kümmel and H. Lichtenberger (eds.), *Jüdische Schriften aus hellenistisch-römischer Zeit* 1.6 (Gütersloh: Gütersloher Verlagshaus/Gerd Mohn, 1981), pp. 427-534, esp. p. 431: after 150 BCE and before 102 BCE; Nickelsburg, 'Stories', p. 51; C.A. Moore, *Judith* (AB, 40; Garden City, NY: Doubleday, 1985), pp. 67-70: most likely during the last years of John Hyrcanus (107–104 BCE).

2. On irony in Judith see L. Alonso-Schökel, 'Narrative Structures in the Book of Judith', in *Protocol Series of the Colloquies of the Center for Hermeneutical Studies in Hellenistic and Modern Culture* 11 (1975), pp. 1-20; Craven, *Artistry and Faith*; Moore, *Judith*, pp. 78-85.

3. Unless indicated otherwise the translations of texts from the Bible and Judith are according to the *New Revised Standard Version with the Apocryphal/Deuterocanonical Books* (The Harper Collins Study Bible; New York: HarperCollins, 1993).

4. According to Craven (*Artistry and Faith*) and several other scholars, the book of Judith consists of two parts (1: chs. 1–7 and 2: chs. 8–16). Weimar ('Formen', pp. 131-32) and Zenger ('Das Buch Judit', pp. 432-33) advocate a composition in three parts (1: chs. 1–3: Nebuchadnezzar appoints himself god; 2: chs. 4–7: who is the real god, Nebuchadnezzar or the Lord? and 3: chs. 8–16: the Lord shows Nebuchadnezzar that he is God). See also Zenger, 'Judith/Judithbuch', p. 405.

are by the attractive figure of Judith, who is introduced only in ch. 8, halfway through the book.[1] Ernst Haag is a dissenter from this common opinion and links ch. 8 with chs. 1–7, advocating a composition in three parts (chs. 1–3; 4–8; 9–16).[2] From a literary point of view, this is hardly more satisfactory than the view that chs. 7 and 8 belong to different parts of the composition. First, there are several significant links between the terminology of chs. 7 and 8. Secondly, motifs introduced in ch. 7 are still important from ch. 8 onwards and up to ch. 13. Thirdly, there is strong evidence for the cohesion of chs. 7 and 8 on the basis of content. This suggests that one is invited to read chs. 8–13 as a continuation of ch. 7, and that this chapter gives the context and starting point for Judith's performance.

Holofernes' malicious attack on the Jews and their deliverance through the hand of Judith involves drinking. Holofernes carries out the plan of the generals of the nations which surround Israel, who have joined his army, and takes possession of the spring near Bethulia (7.6-18), so that the Jews of the city would die of water shortage (7.7, 12, 17, 20-21): 'On the second day [of his campaign against Bethulia] Holofernes... reconnoitred the approaches to their town, and visited the springs that supplied their water; he seized them and set guards of soldiers over them' (7.6-7). He plans that if Bethulia surrenders to him in despair, the whole country of Judah will fall into his hands (8.21). The shameful death of the aggressor is closely connected with his attack through the motif of drinking. Holofernes dies during the aftermath of a drinking bout (12.10, πότος), which he had organized to seduce Judith (12.1–13.2; cf. the drinking motif in Judg. 4.19; 5.25). While the Jews have no

1. Cf. Craven, *Artistry and Faith*, p. 3: 'It has been a perpetuated accident of circumstances that for most scholars the real story of Judith is the story of chs. 8–16 of the book'. See also her n. 10, and pp. 8, 47, 56-57 and 64.

2. E. Haag, *Studien zum Buche Judith: Seine theologische Bedeutung und literarische Eigenart* (Trierer Theologische Studien, 16; Trier: Paulinus-Verlag, 1963), pp. 9-60. Chapter 8 belongs (according to him) to the second part of the book, which he characterizes as 'the people of God in distress'. He proposes that part 1 (chs. 1–3) describes the threat to the people by Nebuchadnezzar, who appears as an enemy of God, and part 3 describes the rescue of the people (chs. 9–16).

water to drink, he drinks too much wine in anticipation of a night with Judith, and is like putty in her hands: 'Holofernes was greatly pleased with her, and drank a great quantity of wine, much more than he had ever drunk in any one day since he was born' (12.20). And after the servants had withdrawn 'Judith was left alone in the tent, with Holofernes stretched out on his bed, for he was dead drunk' (13.2).[1] The water and drinking motif is present from ch. 7 up to 13.2[2] and indicates, alongside other arguments, that chs. 7–13 should be regarded as a unity.[3]

This observation is confirmed by the chronological framework which starts in ch. 7 and ends in ch. 13, when Judith returns to Bethulia with the head of Holofernes in her knapsack. The events in ch. 7 through to ch. 13 take exactly forty days,[4] which cannot be a coincidence. Forty is a meaningful number in the Hebrew Bible, and the author may have hinted at one or more of the biblical passages concerned with this number. One can interpret this chronological datum for example as a realization of Jonah's prophecy that Nineveh shall fall within forty days (Jon. 3.3-4), remembering that in Judith Nebuchadnezzar is king of the Assyrians and that Nineveh is his capital (1.1).[5] Holofernes' threat to the Jewish nation can also be associated with the exodus (cf. Exod. 16.35). The schedule of forty days starts with a chronological marker in 7.1 'on the next day' (τῇ δὲ ἐπαύριον), which is taken up again in 7.2: 'So all their warriors marched off that day'. On this first day Holofernes starts the war on the Israelites. On the second day (τῇ δὲ ἡμέρᾳ τῇ

1. The drinking motif occurs repeatedly in 12.10–13.2; see 12.11, 13, 17-20 and 13.1-2.
2. Cf. also 8.9, 30-31; 11.12; 12.1, 7.
3. Cf. the repetition of the feast motif in Esther; see S.B. Berg, *The Book of Esther: Motifs, Themes and Structure* (SBLDS, 44; Missoula, MT: Scholars Press, 1979), pp. 31-47.
4. Cf. 8.4: Judith has been a widow for three years and four months (that is, 40 months).
5. In Jon. 3.1 the journey across Nineveh is indicated as a three days' journey. This is of course symbolic and indicates the magnitude of the city. Likewise, Holofernes' journey with his enormous army from Nineveh to the plain of Bectileth takes (the symbolic amount of) three days (Jdt. 2.21). I owe this reference to Dr Erik Eynikel.

δευτέρᾳ) he, together with his cavalry, inspects the approaches to Bethulia and its springs, and decides to cut the Jews off from their water supply (7.6-7) as the commanders of the Edomites, Moabites and the people from the coastal region suggest: 'let your servants take possession of the spring of water that flows from the foot of the mountain, for this is where all the people of Bethulia get their water. So thirst will destroy them, and they will surrender their town' (7.12-13). After a siege of thirty-four days (7.20), the inhabitants of the town are in great distress and urge the elders to surrender Bethulia. The elders decide to wait for another five days to see if God will rescue the people and, if his help fails to materialize, to surrender the town to the Assyrians: 'But Uzziah said to them, "Courage, my brothers and sisters! Let us hold out for five days more; by that time the Lord our God will turn his mercy to us again, for he will not forsake us utterly. But if these days pass by, and no help comes for us, I will do as you say"' (7.30-31). If we add up all the days mentioned in ch. 7 we get a total of forty days.[1] Moreover, the decisive last five days of this scenario are described in chs. 8–13, as Judith herself indicates after announcing that she and her maid would leave the city: 'within the days after which you have promised to surrender the town to our enemies, the Lord will deliver Israel by my hand' (8.33).

Judith hears of the people's words and the oath of Uzziah and invites him and the two elders of her town to come to her house in order to explain to them that they have taken a wrong decision. After a prayer in the evening (ch. 9), she makes preparations for her audacious plan and leaves Bethulia on the night before the thirty-sixth day (8.33). 12.7 informs the reader that Judith stays in the camp of Holofernes for three days, that is,

---

1.   The first day, plus thirty-four days plus five days. The 'second day' is the first day of the thirty-four days of the siege of Bethulia mentioned in 7.20. Zenger ('Das Buch Judit', p. 435) also points to a schedule of forty days and includes Jdt. 14.11 in it. He refers to biblical passages where salvation comes after forty days (Gen. 7.4 and 1 Sam. 17.16; cf. also Mk 1.13) or forty years (Num. 14.34; Judg. 13.1). The killings of Goliath and Holofernes are often depicted together in Christian art, for example on a fresco on the ceiling of the San Ignazio church at Rome. See further N. Stone, 'Judith and Holofernes: Some Observations on the Development of the Scene in Art', in VanderKam (ed.), *'No One Spoke Ill of Her'*, pp. 73-93.

days thirty-six to thirty-eight. The *grand finale*, the drinking bout, takes place in the evening on Judith's fourth day in the camp which is, according to the schedule, the thirty-ninth day: 'On the fourth day Holofernes held a drinking bout[1] for his personal attendants only' (12.10). He dies on the night before the fortieth day, and Judith and her maid return to Bethulia on that very night (13.11-20), which means that the promise of 8.33 is fulfilled.

These arguments for the unity of chs. 7–13 contradict the parallel structure of the composition in two parts (chs. 1–7 and 8–16) advocated by Toni Craven and others.[2] Other observations beside the drinking motif and the chronological schedule support the assumption of the cohesion of chs. 7 and 8–13. The repetition of the verb ἀκούω in 8.1, 9, which forms an *inclusio* of the introduction of Judith ('Now in those days Judith heard about these things', 8.1;[3] 'When Judith heard the harsh words spoken by the people against the ruler, because they were faint for lack of water', 8.9) is not necessarily the introduction of a new major part of the composition. There are other phrases with this verb (for example 4.1; 13.12; 14.19–15.1), which do introduce a new scene, but as a reaction to the former scene. Likewise, Judith's acts should be seen as a reaction to the conduct of the people and the leaders in ch. 7. Furthermore, the Achior passages in chs. 5–6 and 14.5-10 supply a beautiful framework for chs. 7–13. The drinking feast for Achior and the elders at Uzziah's house (6.21) forms the transition to the section of chs. 7–13, anticipating the final scene with Holofernes, the drinking bout (cf. ποτός in 6.21 and 12.10).[4] To

---

1. NRSV: 'held a banquet'.

2. Craven, *Artistry and Faith*.

3. NEB: 'News of what was happening reached Judith'.

4. It is impossible to offer a complete structure of the composition of Judith here. But the cohesion of chs. 7 and 8 cannot be denied and appears also from the repetition of similar phrases; see for example ὀλιγοψυχεῖν of the people in 7.19 and 8.9 (which echoes Num. 21.4 and Ps. 76.4 LXX); τὰ ῥήματα (τοῦ λαοῦ) and related phrases in 7.28, 31; 8.9; ἐκδιδόναι with τὴν πόλιν in 7.13, 26 and 8.11; βοηθός, βοηθεῖν or βοήθεια referring to the help of the Lord in 7.25, 31 and 8.11, 15, 17 (cf. also 6.21; 9.4, 11); διαρπαγή and δουλεία (δοῦλος, δουλεύειν) in connection with the people in 7.26-27 and 8.19, 22-23.

summarize: the arguments listed tempt one to consider chs. 7–13 a unity.

2. Judith 7–13 in the Light of Exodus 17, Numbers 20 and Deuteronomy 33.8-11[1]

Because of the forty days framework in chs. 7–13 one is inclined to compare the Assyrian threat to the Jews in Judith with Israel's forty years in the desert after the flight from Egypt. Several details support this association. The situation of the starving Jews of Bethulia, who blame their leaders for not giving in to Holofernes, is similar to that of Israel complaining against Moses and Aaron and hankering after the fleshpots of Egypt. In 7.25 the inhabitants of Bethulia, lacking in faith, say: 'For now we have no one to help us; God has sold us into their hands to be strewn before them in thirst and exhaustion'. Even more reminiscent of the narrative of the exodus is 7.27: 'For it would be better for us to be captured by them. We shall indeed become slaves, but our lives will be spared, and we shall not witness our little ones dying before our eyes, and our wives

---

1. Of course Jdt. 7–13 can be connected to other biblical passages which sometimes appear to be echoed in it; see Haag, *Studien*; P. Skehan, 'The Hand of Judith', *CBQ* 25 (1963), pp. 94-109; Craven, *Artistry and Faith*; Nickelsburg, 'Stories', pp. 48-49; van Dijk-Hemmes, 'Gezegende'; Zenger, 'Das Buch Judit', pp. 440-42; B. Merideth, 'Desire and Danger: The Drama of Betrayal in Judges and Judith', in M. Bal (ed.), *Anti-Covenant: Counter-Reading Women's Lives in the Hebrew Bible* (JSOTSup, 81; Sheffield: JSOT Press, 1989), pp. 63-78; White, 'In the Steps of Jael'. An interesting related story is 1 Sam. 25. The location, description and performance of Abigail correspond to a certain extent to data in Judith's story: the town of Carmel may be associated with Mount Carmel near the plain of Jezreel, where Holofernes' army is located. Abigail is very beautiful, her husband very rich, and she goes on her own initiative to David to prevent him from revenging himself on Nabal. Like Judith Abigail descends the mountain to fulfil her plan, she takes her own food with her, does not inform her husband, kneels down before David and speaks to him as a servant (cf. 1 Sam. 25.23-25 with Jdt. 10.23; 11.5). David praises her wisdom (cf. 1 Sam. 25.32-33 with Jdt. 11.8, 20). When Abigail returns, Nabal is very drunk and he dies ten days later.

and children drawing their last breath.'[1] This thread of the narrative is resumed in Judith's speech to the elders in 8.11-34. Judith challenges the people's and the elders' reaction to the shortage of water and links it to a situation of testing (cf. πειράζειν in 8.12, 25-26). First she says that the elders were wrong to put God to the test, because humans cannot know his decisions: 'Who are you to put God to the test (οἳ ἐπειράσατε τὸν θεόν) today, and to set yourselves up in the place of God in human affairs? You are putting the Lord Almighty to the test, but you will never learn anything!' (8.12-13). In the next part of her speech Judith returns to this testing motif, but in a different way. She represents to the elders the probability that God would try his people by the lack of water:

> In spite of everything let us give thanks to the Lord our God, who is putting *us* [emphasis mine] to the test (ὃς πειράζει ἡμᾶς) as he did our ancestors. Remember what he did with Abraham, and how he tested Isaac (ὅσα ἐπείρασεν τὸν Ισαακ), and what happened to Jacob in Syrian Mesopotamia, while he was tending the sheep of Laban (8.25-26).

If the people remained faithful to the Lord, he would certainly interfere in time (cf. Deut. 8.2; Judg. 2.22 with Jdt. 5.17-21; 8.17-18; 11.11-15). It is clear to Judith that the policy of the leaders is wrong but, since they are bound by their 'oath', she decides to offer help within the five days mentioned by them (7.30-31; 8.30, 33).

The point of departure for Judith's action is therefore the shortage of water in Bethulia. The three motifs that we have observed—the drinking motif, the chronological framework of forty days and the testing motif—can be understood as a reference to the exodus from Egypt or to specific events during this period. There is only one episode in the Hebrew Bible where a situation of lack of water is found together with the testing motif. This is the scene in the desert at Massah and Meribah,[2]

---

1. For more references to this motif see p. 231 n. 4 and Achior's allusions to the exodus in 5.10-14 and 6.5.

2. The name Massah is connected with the root נסה, which occurs in Exod. 17.2, 7 (LXX πειράζειν); the name Meribah with the root ריב, which occurs in Exod. 17.2, 7 (LXX λοιδορεῖν). Cf. the root לון in 17.3 (LXX γογγύζειν).

which is narrated twice in the Torah (Exod. 17.1-7; Num. 20.2-13) and taken up again in the blessing to Levi in Deut. 33.8-11. The episode is referred to several times in other biblical passages and postbiblical literature.[1]

According to Exod. 17.1 Israel travels from the desert of Sin to Rephidim, where it has to cope with a shortage of water (Exod. 17.1-7) and, afterwards, is attacked by Amalek (17.8-16). As before in a situation of distress during the exodus, the people start complaining to Moses that they are afraid of dying and that they should have stayed in Egypt. These themes link up with Exod. 15.22-27 and 16, where the Lord puts Israel to the test. This testing motif occurs during the episode at Marah in 15.25 (נסה/πειράζω), after the bitter water has become sweet: 'There the Lord made for them a statute and an ordinance and there he put them[2] to the test'. In the desert of Sin the Lord gives the heavenly bread of manna to the Israelites, because they have complained to Moses and Aaron that they had plenty of bread in Egypt and wanted to return to the fleshpots (Exod. 16). Exod. 16.4 contains the testing motif: 'Then the Lord said to Moses, "I am going to rain bread from heaven for you, and each day the people shall go out and gather enough for that day. In that way I will test them,[3] whether they will follow my instruction or not."' The testing motif occurs for the third time in the short passage of Exod. 17.1-7 (17.2).

Against this background Judith's remark for the leaders that they must not put the Lord to the test, but that the Lord tested the people of Bethulia through the water shortage (8.25, see above) is fully justified.[4] The question whether or not the Lord would be among the Israelites and would offer help in the situation of water shortage, presented at the conclusion of Exod. 17.1-7, is basically the question which makes the narrative

1.   For instance see Deut. 6.16-17; 8.15-16; Ps. 78.15-20, 40-41, 56; 95.8-9; 106.14, 32-33; Sir. 18.23; Wis. 11.4-10; Mt. 4.7; Lk. 4.12; Mk 1.12-13.
2.   So NRSV. Literally 'there he put him [Moses? see below] to the test'. The LXX confirms the singular.
3.   MT: למען אנסנו; LXX: ὅπως πειράσω αὐτούς.
4.   It is also in line with Deut. 6.16: 'Do not put the Lord your God to the test, as you tested him at Massah'.

of Judith 7–13 so exciting.[1] Judith acts as an instrument of the Lord. Moreover, successive elements of the Massah and Meribah episode match quite well parts of the much larger narrative in Judith 7–13. The successive corresponding elements of the two narratives are:

1.	point of departure, no water	Exod. 17.1	Jdt. 7.1-22
2.	the people complain (complaint to leader [Moses/ Uzziah, elders]: give us water; it is better to be a slave [in Egypt][2] than to die with [women], children [and cattle]	Exod. 17.2-3	Jdt. 7.23-29
		Exod. 17.2-3	Jdt. 7.26-27)
3.	reaction of leader(s) (testing motif: Moses asks the people 'Why do you test the Lord?' Judith criticizes the elders, who put God to the test; it is the Lord who puts them to the test	Exod. 17.2	Jdt. 7.30-32; 8
		Exod. 17.2	Jdt. 8.12, 25-26)
4.	leader [Moses/Judith] calls upon the Lord	Exod. 17.4	Jdt. 9
5.	leader leaves for action to bring salvation (motif of adultery: Moses exclaims 'They are almost ready to stone me'; Judith seduces Holofernes[3]	Exod. 17.4-6	Jdt. 10-13
		Exod. 17.4	Jdt. 10.21–13.2)

---

1. For the motif of God's help see p. 231 n. 4. The question mentioned can be linked to what is considered the central theme of Judith by several scholars, that is, the question, 'Who is God except Nebuchadnezzar?' (formulated by Achior in 6.2) or, put somewhat differently, 'Who is the real God?' See for example Craven, *Artistry and Faith*, pp. 60-62 and 69; Nickelsburg, 'Stories', pp. 46-47; Zenger, 'Das Buch Judit', pp. 432-34.

2. The square brackets indicate details which are given by only one of the two narratives.

3. Although nothing intimate happens between Judith and Holofernes (cf. 13.16), Judith seduces him (cf. the stress on deceiving and seducing in 9.3, 10, 13; 10.4; 11.5; 12.16; 13.16 and 16.8), which may be associated with adultery and stoning, its usual punishment (Deut. 22.22-27). See Merideth, 'Desire and Danger'.

6.	the Lord supports leader at deci-	Exod. 17.6	Jdt. 13.3-10
	sive act		
	(Moses strikes the rock; Judith		
	chops off Holofernes' head	Exod. 17.6	Jdt. 13.4-8)
7.	conclusion 'The Lord is with us'	Exod. 17.7	Jdt. 13.11-20

Although the narrative of Judith 7–13 is certainly much more elaborate than the short story of Exod. 17.1-7, the pattern of actions and the ending of both narratives are strikingly similar. After returning successfully to Bethulia Judith calls to the sentries at the gates: 'Open, open the gate! God, our God, is with us' (13.11).[1] Hence the question of Exod. 17.7, 'Is the Lord in our midst or not?', which dominates Judith 7–13 too, is answered positively at the end.

The basic characters of both texts can also be compared. On the side of the Israelites these are in Exodus (1) the people complaining of thirst, (2) Moses and (3) the Lord; and in Judith (1) the people complaining of thirst, (2) Uzziah and the elders, (3) Judith and (4) the Lord. In Judith, then, the role of the leaders is more complicated: there is a contrast between Uzziah and the elders on the one hand and Judith on the other hand. The elders are mentioned in Exodus 17 too but play a minor role there, like that of Judith's servant. Holofernes, the foreign aggressor, has no equivalent in Exod. 17.1-7, but one can compare his part with the attack by Amalek in Exod. 17.8-16. The elaboration of the leaders' performance in Judith, which is linked to the testing motif, deserves more attention and will be discussed below.

Parallel passages of Exod. 17.1-7 also show correspondences with the story in Judith 7–13. These correspondences, however, have little bearing on the succession of actions. They match several details in Judith 7–13 which are not present in Exodus 17. Some phrases in Judith even echo phrases in Num. 20.2-13 and Deut. 33.8-11, especially in connection to the final scene and the explanation of Judith's conduct. For instance, she strikes the neck of Holofernes twice with all her might (13.8), as Moses strikes the rock twice with his staff according to Num. 20.11.

---

1. μεθ' ἡμῶν ὁ θεὸς ὁ θεὸς ἡμῶν. Cf. Exod. 17.7 LXX: εἰ ἔστιν κύριος ἐν ἡμῖν ἢ οὔ.

The remark about Judith's praying to the Lord at the time when the evening incense offering (τὸ θυμίαμα τῆς ἑσπέρας ἐκείνης) was being offered in the Jerusalem temple (9.1) echoes Deut. 33.10, where Moses indicates that the Levites shall offer the incense offering (LXX: ἐπιθήσουσιν θυμίαμα).[1]

Judith's success is also better understood in the light of Moses' blessing to Levi in Deut. 33.8-11. The blessing seems to indicate a special position within Israel for the Levites, who enjoy the blessing of the Lord: 'Bless, O Lord, his substance, and accept the work of his hands (ברך יהוה חילו ופעל ידיו תרצה; εὐλόγησον, κύριε, τὴν ἰσχὺν αὐτοῦ καὶ τὰ ἔργα τῶν χειρῶν αὐτοῦ δέξαι); crush the loins of his adversaries, of those that hate him, so that they do not rise again' (33.11). Judith seems to refer to this blessing in her prayer in ch. 9 and, during the final scene, in a short prayer for strength to fulfil her plan: 'Give to me, a widow, the strong hand to do what I plan' (δὸς ἐν χειρί μου τῆς χήρας ὃ διενοήθην κράτος, 9.9). In ch. 13 she says, when she has grasped the hair of Holofernes to cut off his head, 'Give me strength today, O Lord God of Israel' (κραταίωσόν με, κύριε..., 13.7). Some verses earlier she asks if God would look in this hour favourably on the work of her hands (ἐπίβλεψον...ἐπὶ τὰ ἔργα τῶν χειρῶν μου) in order to bring glory to Jerusalem (13.4). We find another reference to her strength in the verse in which she chops off the head of Holofernes (ἐν τῇ ἰσχύει αὐτῆς, 13.8).[2] The blessing of Judith by Uzziah in 13.18 (εὐλογητὴ σύ, θύγατερ, τῷ θεῷ τῷ ὑψίστῳ) is probably another echo of the blessing to Levi by Moses in Deut. 33.11.[3] Viewed from this perspective Uzziah's words indicate

1. As the echoes to Deut. 33.8-11 show (see also below), Judith is especially affiliated to the tribe of Levi.
2. Cf. in connection to the Jews 5.3, 23, and concerning Holofernes the ironic verse 11.7.
3. Cf. the blessing motif in 14.7; 15.9-10, 12. There are other possible echoes of Deut. 33.8-11 in Judith; cf. Judith's piety in Jdt. 8.5, 8, 31 with Deut. 33.8 concerning Levi, 'to your loyal one' (לאיש חסידך; LXX: τῷ ἀνδρὶ τῷ ὁσίῳ), and 33.9, 'For they [the Levites] observed your word, and kept your covenant'. Cf. Judith's wisdom (σοφία) and sagacity (σύνεσις) according to 8.29; 11.8, 20-21. Judith announces that she will speak reliable words to Holofernes (ῥήματα ἀληθείας, 10.13; cf. 10.16 and 11.5), which appears to be true and untrue at the same time. Cf. Levi's אורים and תמים in Deut. 33.8

that Judith's success is obvious, because it was the handiwork of a daughter of Levi, blessed by the Lord like Levi himself. By way of analogy, some sayings of Taxo and his seven sons in the *Assumption of Moses* can be similarly understood. They are explicitly presented as Levites (*Ass. Mos.* 9.1); and several phrases in Taxo's admonition to his sons to keep faithful to the Lord and be prepared to die echo Deut. 33.8-11: 'know that neither our parents, nor their ancestors have *tempted* God by transgressing his commandments. Surely you know that here lies our *strength...*' (9.4-5, emphasis mine).[1] After three days of fasting (cf. Jdt. 12.7) Taxo and his sons enter a cave 'on the fourth day' to die (ch. 9). The next passage (10.1-10) indicates the salvation for Israel with the coming of the kingdom of the Lord. One can read this passage in the light of Deut. 33.8-11. This would imply that the deeds of Taxo and his seven sons, like those of Judith, are blessed by the Lord as their ancestor is, because of his faithfulness to the Lord at Massah and Meribah (according to Deut. 33.8 MT).

3. Judith's Leadership

The reading of Judith 7–13 in the light of Exod. 17.1-7 and its parallel passages underlines Judith's role as alternative leader. Moses, the leader of the people at Massah and Meribah, is not blameless (see especially Num. 20). In Judith his role is split into the negatively depicted leadership of Uzziah and the elders and the positive performance of Judith. One aspect of leadership is the testing motif, and the attitude of the elders to testing is part of Judith's criticism of their conduct as leaders in ch. 8. The motif extends beyond the usual context of keeping to the

(rendered by δῆλοι καὶ ἀλήθεια in the LXX). For the striking of Judith's adversaries by the Lord, so that they rise no more, cf. Deut. 33.11 LXX, κάταξον ὀσφὺν ἐχθρῶν ἐπανεστηκότων αὐτῷ καὶ οἱ μισοῦντες αὐτὸν μὴ ἀναστήτωσαν with Jdt. 9.8 (κάταξον τὸ κράτος αὐτῶν) and 13.5 (ποιῆσαι τὸ ἐπιτήδευμά μου εἰς θραῦσμα ἐχθρῶν, οἳ ἐπανέστησαν ἡμῖν). Cf. also Jdt. 13.11, 14, 17-18; 16.17.

1. Translation by J. Tromp, *The Assumption of Moses: A Critical Edition with Commentary* (SVTP, 10; Leiden: Brill, 1993); see also his fine commentary, pp. 223-27.

promises of the covenant[1] by the people, who put the Lord to the test (Exod. 17.2, 7; Ps. 106.14; Jdt. 8.12), or the Lord who tests the people. Although in Numbers 20 an explicit reference to this motif is absent, the acts of Moses imply that Moses himself is somehow put to the test and that the outcome is not completely satisfactory. This contrasts with the MT of Deut. 33.8, which clearly and without any criticism states that God put Levi, that is, Moses, to the test at Massah. A similar reading is possible in the related passage in Exod. 15.25 (see above), where the MT has a singular object: 'There [i.e. at Marah] he put *him* [Moses] to the test'.[2] But the LXX of Deut. 33.8 has it differently, with a plural subject of πειράζειν: the people tested Moses.[3]

In Judith several aspects of the testing motif appear to be combined. Judith criticizes the elders who, together with the people, put the Lord to the test (8.12). She suggests that in fact things are just the other way around: God tests the leaders and the people (8.25-27), as he tested Abraham and Jacob. In addition to this we could also ask whether chs. 9–13 suggest that Judith herself is tested in the camp of Holofernes.[4] We could read these chapters from the point of view of Deut. 33.8, which refers to the testing of Levi/Moses at Massah and Meribah.[5]

1. For a semantic study see B. Gerhardsson, *The Testing of God's Son (Matt 4:1-11 & Par)* (ConBNT Series, 2.1; Lund: Gleerup, 1966), pp. 25-35.

2. Exod. 15.25, וְשָׁם נִסָּהוּ. LXX also sing.: καὶ ἐκεῖ ἐπείρασεν αὐτόν. Cf. also Gen. 22.1 (alluded to in Jdt. 8.26) and 2 Chron. 32.31 concerning Hezekiah.

3. Exod. 17.2, נַסֹּתְכֶם אֶת־יְהוָה; 17.7, נַסֹּתָם אֶת־יְהוָה; וְעַל נַסֹּתָם אֶת־יְהוָה; Deut. 33.8, נִסִּיתוֹ בְּמַסָּה; LXX, ὃν (Λευι) ἐπείρασαν αὐτὸν ἐν πείρα.

4. Cf. Nickelsburg, 'Stories', p. 48, in connection with Jdt. 8.15-17, 25-27: 'The citizens of Bethulia and Judith exemplify respectively those who fail and those who pass the test'.

5. The connection between Levi and Judith is also suggested by Merari, the first name in Judith's genealogy, and the reference to the revenge of the shameful act of Shechem with Dinah by Simeon and Levi (Gen. 34) in Jdt. 9.2-4. Judith's plan is presented as analogous to the performance of Simeon and Levi. The reference to Gen. 34 in Jdt. 9 clearly points forward to the scene with Holofernes; cf. the last part of v. 5 and the emphasis on the bed of Holofernes and his being deceived, which reminds us of the bed of the Shechemites (10.21; 13.2-9) alluded to in Jdt. 9.3. Simeon is mentioned in 9.2-4, but Levi is curiously left out. The possibility that Judith performs the role of Levi may be an explanation for this omission.

Let us recall the motif of drinking, which points to a similar context of lack of water and is present in the book of Judith up to and including the drinking bout in ch. 13.

This reading focuses on the testing of the leader in a situation of an impending catastrophe for the people; and suggests a comparison of the role of Judith, granddaughter of Levi according to Jdt. 8.1, with that of Moses, another descendant of Levi (Exod. 2.1).[1] This comparison is clearly advantageous for Judith, as can be seen from several details. According to Exod. 17.4 Moses is afraid and cries to the Lord: 'What shall I do with this people? They are almost ready to stone me.' Judith accomplishes her mission without complaining and never loses her self-control, neither with the lenient Jewish leaders nor with Holofernes. Moses does not know what to do and turns to the Lord in despair. Judith takes the initiative and realizes her plan, which is supported by the Lord. In Numbers 20 Moses' behaviour gives sound reasons for criticism and, in the context of the book of Numbers, the punishment for this conduct is that Moses is not allowed to enter the promised land (Num. 20.12). Num. 20.7-11 describes how the impatient Moses disobeys the command of the Lord and strikes the rock with his staff: 'he said to them, "Listen, you rebels, shall we bring water for you out of this rock?" Then Moses lifted up his hand and struck the rock twice with his staff.' In comparison to this passage, Judith's obedience to the Lord is striking and consonant with Levi's blessing in Deut. 33.8-11. Moreover, she never gives in to the advances of Holofernes and keeps Jewish dietary laws while in the camp of the enemy.[2] Besides, she attributes all credit for the rescue of the people to the Lord, as appears from the words shouted to the sentries at the gates of Bethulia: 'Open, open the gate! God, our God, is with us, still showing his power in Israel

---

1.   According to Exod. 2.1-10 Miriam saves Moses' life; see J. Siebert-Hommes, *Laat de dochters léven! De literaire architectuur van Exodus 1 en 2 als toegang tot de interpretatie* (Kampen: Kok, 1993). Cf. Num. 12, where Miriam as a prophetess is 'muted'; see van Dijk-Hemmes in Brenner and van Dijk-Hemmes, *On Gendering Texts*, pp. 65-67.

2.   Cf. Dan. 1.3-20; Tob. 1.10-12 and the prayer of Esther in LXX Esth. 4.17k-z/C12-30.

and his strength against our enemies, as he has done today!'
(Jdt. 13.11; cf. 13.14).

In this connection it is important to note a significant difference between Exodus 17 and Numbers 20 on the one hand and
Judith on the other. Judith is not the regular leader of the
people, like Moses in Exodus or Moses and Aaron in Numbers
20, but acts instead of Uzziah and the elders. She decides
independently to intervene and bring the situation to a happy
conclusion within the parameters set by the ordinary leaders.
She develops her strategy on her own and executes the plan
with her servant without even informing the leaders
beforehand. Nevertheless, Uzziah and the elders accept her
authority and let her go with *carte blanche* (8.34-36; 10.6-10). In
this light, the final remark by Judith before leaving the city is a
joke: 'Order the gate of the town to be opened for me so that I
may go out and accomplish the things *you have just said to me*'
(10.9, emphasis mine). Judith dictates the course of things and
acts like a charismatic leader. The reason for the approval of the
leaders is not given explicitly, but can be linked with the wisdom
and prudence of the extremely pious Judith (8.29).[1] She is even
considered by them a woman of God, as indicated by their suggestion that she should pray for rain on behalf of the people
(8.31).[2] Judith acts with the support of the Lord, whom she
beseeches in ch. 9 (9.9, 13-14) and again just before killing
Holofernes (13.4-5). This is also what the leaders indicate in
their words of farewell: 'May the God of our ancestors grant
you favor and fulfill your plans, so that the people of Israel may
glory and Jerusalem may be exalted' (10.8; cf. 8.35; also 13.11
and 15.8, 10).[3]

This sketch of Judith's performance and the phrases

---

1. See p. 237 n. 3. Concerning Judith's piety, see 8.5-6, 8, 31; 10.9; 11.17;
cf. 16.16 (Greek phrases in this connection are εὐσέβεια, φοβεῖσθαι τὸν θεόν
and θεοσεβής).

2. Cf. Samuel in 1 Sam. 12.17; the prayer of Solomon (1 Kgs 8.35-36;
2 Chron. 6.26-27); Elijah (1 Kgs 17.1, 14; 18.1, 41, 44-45); Elisha in 2 Kgs 3.16-
17; Honi the Circledrawer in *m. Ta'an.* 3.8, who is called a Son of God's
household; and the characterization of Deborah as prophetess in Judg. 4.4.

3. This affirms the central importance of the analogous Exod. 17.7; see
above.

associated with it links up with the image of a 'judge'.[1] This appears from phrases which characterize Judith's action. She is sent by the Lord (11.16, 19, 22). Her appearance corresponds to that of so-called judges[2] who come forward for a specific task of rescuing the people from foreign oppressors (cf. Judg. 2.16) and retire from the stage after completing their task, as Othniel, Ehud, Shamgar and Deborah do (Judg. 3.9-11, 15-30, 31; 4–5).[3] The temporary character of Judith's leadership appears from the returning of the usual leaders on the scene after Judith's arrival at Bethulia. And after the triumph over Holofernes' army, even the high priest Joakim and the *gerousia* come over to Bethulia to praise and bless Judith (15.8-10).[4] The Lord brings salvation (indicated by the verb σώζειν or the noun σωτηρία in the LXX, cf. Judg. 2.16, 18; 3.9, 31; 6.36-37; Jdt. 8.17; 11.3) either through the hand of the judge or, in the case of Deborah, Jael and Judith, through the hand of a woman. This is among other things indicated by the phrases 'the Lord will deliver[5] Israel by my hand' (ἐπισκέψεται κύριος τὸν Ἰσραηλ ἐν χειρί μου)[6] in 8.33 and 'may the Lord God go before you' (καὶ κύριος ὁ θεὸς ἔμπροσθέν σου) in 8.35, which echoes Judg. 4.14 concerning Barak ('For this is the day on which the Lord has given Sisera into your hand. The Lord is indeed going out before you'; ὅτι

1.   Zenger ('Das Buch Judit', p. 509) remarks concerning Jdt. 13.11 ('God is with us') that Judith appears as a charismatic saviour in the line of the concept of the war of the Lord (Exod. 3.12; Num. 14.7-10; Deut. 20.4; Judg. 6.12).

2.   See A. Malamat, 'Charismatic Leadership in the Book of Judges', in F.M. Cross, W.E. Lemke and P.D. Miller (eds.), *Magnalia Dei: The Mighty Acts of God: Essays on the Bible and Archaeology in Memory of G.E. Wright* (Garden City, NY: Doubleday, 1976), pp. 152-68, and H. Reviv, 'Types of Leadership in the Period of the Judges', *Beer-Sheva* 1 (1973), pp. 204-21 (Hebrew). For reviews of various opinions cf. H.H. Rösel, 'Die Richter Israels: Rückblick und neuer Ansatz', *BZ* NS 25 (1981), pp. 180-203, and A.D.H. Mayes, *Judges* (OTG; Sheffield: JSOT Press, 1985).

3.   White, 'In the Steps of Jael', pp. 7 and 12. Jael's killing of Sisera is supported by the Lord too; see Judg. 4.23.

4.   Cf. the repetition of 10.8 in 15.9.

5.   Literally, 'look upon'.

6.   Cf. Skehan, 'Hand of Judith', and White, 'In the Steps of Jael', pp. 10-13, with further references.

αὕτη ἡ ἡμέρα, ἐν ᾗ παρέδωκεν κύριος τὸν Σισαρα ἐν τῇ χειρί σου, ὅτι κύριος ἐξελεύσεται ἔμπροσθέν σου). Further, the song of victory in ch. 16 resembles the Song of Deborah and contains several allusions to this song (see above). The concluding verse of the book even contains the formula that concludes an episode of a judge, indicating that Israel enjoyed peace during the rest of his or her life; compare Jdt. 16.25, 'No one ever again spread terror among the Israelites during the lifetime of Judith, or for a long time after her death', with for example Judg. 3.11,[1] 'So the land had rest forty years. Then Othniel son of Kenaz died' (see also Judg. 2.18; 3.30; 5.31; 8.28).

In spite of the fictitious nature of the book of Judith this image of the heroine may well have had a political significance, especially if the socio-historical context of the book is taken into account. It can easily be contrasted with the contemporaneous propaganda of the Hasmoneans, who portrayed themselves as the legitimate successors of kings, high priests and other Israelite leaders (see especially 1 Macc. 2.52-60 and 14.25-49),[2] and tried to support this ideology by—among other things— emphasizing the parallels between the performance of the judges and theirs.[3] 1 Maccabees contains several references to

1. Haag (*Studien*, p. 60) already notes this parallel.
2. See further D. Arenhoevel, *Die Theokratie nach dem 1. und 2. Makkabäerbuch* (Walberberger Studien, Theologische Reihe 3; Mainz: Matthias-Grünewald-Verlag, 1967); E. Janssen, *Das Gottesvolk und seine Geschichte: Geschichtsbild und Selbstverständnis im palästinensischen Schrifttum von Jesus Sirach bis Jehuda ha-Nasi* (Neukirchen–Vluyn: Neukirchener Verlag, 1971), pp. 34-48; J.W. van Henten, 'Das jüdische Selbstverständnis in den ältesten Martyrien', in *idem et al.* (eds.), *Die Entstehung der jüdischen Martyrologie* (SPB, 38; Leiden: Brill, 1989), pp. 127-61, esp. pp. 156-58.
3. Arenhoevel, *Theokratie*, pp. 47-50; J. A. Goldstein, *I Maccabees: A New Translation with Introduction and Commentary* (AB, 41; Garden City, NY: Doubleday, 1976), pp. 7 and 9; K.-D. Schunck, '1. Makkabäerbuch', in W.G. Kümmel and H. Lichtenberger (eds.), *Jüdische Schriften aus hellenistisch-römischer Zeit* 1.4 (Gütersloh: Gütersloher Verlagshaus/Gerd Mohn, 1980), pp. 287-373, esp. p. 292; A. Enermalm-Ogawa, *Un langage de prière juif en grec: Le témoignage des deux premiers livres des Maccabées* (ConBNT, 17; Stockholm: Almqvist & Wiksell, 1987), pp. 11 and 50-51, cf. p. 50: 'Israël est envisagé comme restauré d'après le modèle du temps des Juges'.

the salvation of Israel through Judas the Maccabee and his brothers which echo phrases in Judges passages. These support the construction of the Maccabees as new judges who restore the ideal theocratic state, which automatically affirms the divine support for their leadership. A few examples may suffice. There is a climax in the period of rest for the land of Judah after deliverances by Judas, Jonathan and Simon, running from a few days to two years to all the days of Simon (1 Macc. 7.50; 9.57 and 14.4). The terminology in these verses corresponds to the formula which concludes the era of a judge (Judg. 3.11, 30; 5.31; cf. 8.28).[1] After Samson's victory upon a thousand Philistines he says to the Lord: 'You have granted this great victory by the hand of your servant' (Judg. 15.18).[2] A similar phrase, stating that the Lord brings rescue by the hand of his servant the judge, occurs in connection with Judas the Maccabee. In the song of praise for him (1 Macc. 3.1-9), which precedes the narrative of the wars of liberation, it is said 'and deliverance prospered by his hand' (1 Macc. 3.6; cf. 4.25 and 5.62).[3]

Thus with regard to the issue of the legitimate leader who delivers the people from a perilous attack by a foreign aggressor, the books of Judith and 1 Maccabees share important concepts and vocabulary. Against the backdrop of a roughly contemporaneous origin, and the fact that the Maccabees were presented as the leaders exclusively supported by the Lord (1 Macc. 5.62), the figure of Judith may have functioned as a way of releasing criticism against the new Hasmonean dynasty, firmly in control at the time.[4] That Judith is also depicted as a model for the people, which appears from her name and a genealogy ending with 'Israel',[5] seems to support this assumption. The name could even have been chosen in contrast to the

---

1. Janssen, *Gottesvolk*, p. 44; Enermalm-Ogawa, *Un langage de prière*, p. 21.
2. Similar phrases can be found in Judg. 6.36-37; 2 Sam. 3.18 (David); 2 Kgs 14.27 (Jeroboam).
3. Cf. Judg. 15.18 LXX, σὺ ἔδωκας ἐν χειρὶ τοῦ δούλου σου τὴν σωτηρίαν, with 1 Macc. 3.6, καὶ εὐοδώθη σωτηρία ἐν χειρὶ αὐτοῦ.
4. 2 Maccabees may have had a similar function; cf. van Henten, 'Das jüdische Selbstverständnis', pp. 158-61.
5. Haag, *Studien*, pp. 38-39.

name 'Judas' the Maccabee: 'If one accepts a Hasmonaean date...the name "Judith" naturally suggests a comparison with Judas Maccabaeus'.[1] However, one can only guess which group might have uttered these views.[2]

4. M or F Voice?

What are the implications of our reading so far if we try to gender the Judith story?[3] Which readerly interests are being served by the book? The possibility that the model of Judith appeals especially to men in the context of entertainment—often stimulated by an erotic dimension and the figure of a predatory female[4] or, more seriously, as a correction of male leadership, is obvious. The basic frame of reference is androcentric, and military conflict dominates the chapters before the appearance of Judith. All main actors except Judith are male too; the leaders of the Jewish people, except Judith, are male again (the great priest Joakim, Uzziah and the elders Chabris and Charmis). Yet the possibility that an F voice is speaking (too) in Judith cannot be ruled out entirely.[5] The supreme commander of the enemy, Holofernes, second only to the lord of the whole earth (2.4-5), is humiliated in an unbelievable way through the hand of a

1. Nickelsburg ('Stories', p. 49 n. 86), indicates some striking similarities between Judith and 1 Maccabees (cf. Jdt. 4.3 with 1 Macc. 4.36-51 and Jdt. 14.1 with 1 Macc. 8.33-50 [read 7.33-50 and cf. 2 Macc. 15.32-35]); see also p. 51.
2. Some data point to a priestly group; perhaps the Levites, given the associations with Levi (see above) and the symbolic name Bethulia (בית אלוה or בית האלהים) which may refer to the temple. Cf. also Jdt. 8.24: 'Therefore, my brothers, let us set an example for our kindred, for their lives depend upon us, and the sanctuary—both the temple and the altar—rests upon us'.
3. See Brenner and van Dijk-Hemmes, *On Gendering Texts*.
4. Cf. Schuller, 'The Apocrypha', p. 240: 'feminists criticize her blatant use of physical beauty and sexual wiles'. See also pp. 241-43, and van Dijk-Hemmes in Brenner and van Dijk-Hemmes, *On Gendering Texts*, p. 31: 'Heroines like Esther and Judith fit perfectly into a man-made gallery of ideal femininity'.
5. Van Dijk-Hemmes rightly emphasizes the possibility that in texts two voices might be speaking, an M voice as well as an F voice; or to put it differently, that a text may be read as an M or F text. Cf. Brenner and van Dijk-Hemmes, *On Gendering Texts*, p. 109.

woman. This makes men uneasy, as appears from Abimelech's last words to his armour-bearer: 'Draw your sword and kill me, so people will not say about me, "A woman killed him"' (Judg. 9.54). The phrase 'by the hand of a woman' appears three times in the text of Judith and is a marker of gender roles (9.10; 13.15 and 16.5).[1] Judith's acts are superior to all the male acts in the story.[2] Therefore, it seems worthwhile to investigate the gender aspect of a few passages in the book and see whether we can hear an F voice in them beside the M voice.[3]

An ancient reader who certainly supports the M reading of the story is Clement of Rome, who refers to Judith in his *First Letter* and seems to adapt the picture of women in the book to his masculine norms. Interestingly, this affects especially the issue of leadership. In ch. 55 of his *Letter to the Corinthians* Clement points to pagan and Jewish examples of men and women who saved their country by an act of self-denial or self-sacrifice.[4] He mentions Judith and Esther in this context of praise of the Christian 'nation', where pagan and Jewish examples serve as forerunners for Christian heroines. Clement's reference to Judith in 55.3-5 begins as follows: '*Many women* who were empowered by the grace of God accomplished *many manly deeds.* Judith, the blessed, *asked from the elders of the city permission* to go to the camp of the foreigners when the city was besieged' (55.3-4). This detail, that Judith had to ask for permission to leave Bethulia, runs contrary to the story, where

1. Schuller, 'The Apocrypha', p. 242.
2. Cf. Nickelsburg, 'Stories', p. 49: 'As the narrative unfolds, Judith is consistently depicted as superior to the men with whom she is associated'.
3. In doing so I will take as guidelines the criteria developed by Brenner and van Dijk-Hemmes in *On Gendering Texts*, as well as van Dijk-Hemmes's discussion of the forms of 'women's texts' in the Hebrew Bible; cf. pp. 25-109. The criteria for attributing texts to female voices are summarized on p. 106 as: '1) Does the text contain traces of a less androcentric intent? 2) Is there in it talk of a (re)definition of reality from a female perspective, so that the story contains defineable differences between the views of the male as against the female figures?'
4. The risking of Judith's life for the benefit of the people is mentioned in her praise by Uzziah (Jdt. 13.18-20). This again fits in with the picture of the sons of Mattathias in 1 Maccabees; see van Henten, 'Das jüdische Selbstverständnis', pp. 151-52.

Judith simply informs the leaders that she will leave to carry out her plan and does not even tell them what she has in mind (Jdt. 8.32-34; 10.9-10).

This process of domesticating women is also assumed for the book of Judith itself by Fokkelien van Dijk-Hemmes, in a discussion of three biblical women who are called 'blessed among women': Deborah, Judith and Mary.[1] She considers the story of Judith a productive reception of Judges 4 and 5 and stresses the tendency to depict the woman who brings life for Israel by killing a man in more agreeable terms for men. She points to the fact that in Jdt. 13.18 *men* are blessing Judith: 'Then Uzziah said to her, "O daughter, you are blessed by the Most High God above all other women on earth..."'. According to her the 'blessed among women' was transformed into an idealized picture attractive to men. The dangerous mother of Israel who gives life by killing someone was rendered harmless.[2] The androcentric frame of reference in Judith cannot be denied, but our reading of Judith as an alternative leader, an alternative to men and even to the great Moses, may be seen as a redefinition of reality from a female perspective.

This assumption is supported by some indications that the book of Judith is an unconventional Jewish writing from the perspective of gender relations. The introduction of Judith begins, for instance, with a very extensive and extraordinary genealogy, which vastly surpasses the genealogical references concerning the male leaders in Judith (6.15). The genealogy is clearly fictitious (8.1).[3] It starts with the name Merari and ends with the name Israel. All the names are biblical and probably echo biblical figures. In the Hebrew Bible there is only one Merari, the third son of Levi (Exod. 6.16). Thus the genealogy

1. Cf. Lk. 1.42; van Dijk-Hemmes, 'Gezegende'.
2. Van Dijk-Hemmes, 'Gezegende', p. 141.
3. Craven, *Artistry and Faith*, pp. 84-85. See also J.E. Bruns, 'The Genealogy of Judith', *CBQ* 18 (1956), pp. 19-22. In general, see J. Liver and I.M. Ta-Shma, 'Genealogy', *EncJud*, VII (Jerusalem, 1971), pp. 377-84; W. Speyer, 'Genealogie', *Reallexikon für Antike und Christentum*, IX (Stuttgart: Anton Hiersemann, 1976), pp. 1145-268, and M.D. Johnson, *The Purpose of the Biblical Genealogies with Special Reference to the Setting of the Genealogies of Jesus* (SNTSMS, 8; Cambridge: Cambridge University Press, 1969).

probably begins with a reference to the tribe of Levi and ends with the father of the twelve tribes. This affirms my earlier observation that Levi and his descendants play a prominent role in the book and that Judith can also be considered as a model for the people (Israel) as a whole.[1] One other tribe besides Levi seems to be highlighted in the genealogy by the fourteenth and fifteenth names.[2] Salamiel and Sarasadai are a well-known combination in the Bible (Num. 1.6; 2.12);[3] they belong to the tribe of Simeon, which can be read as an anticipation of Judith's prayer with the allusion to the revenge on the Shechemites by Levi and Simeon (Jdt. 9.2-4; Gen. 34, see above).[4] Somehow, the author depicts Judith in this genealogy as the ideal Israelite woman, who represents more than one tribe. The names point to the tribes of Ephraim and Manasseh (Joseph; Gideon),[5] Issachar (Nathanael/Nethanel),[6] Zebulon (Eliab?)[7] and especially to Simeon (Salamiel; Sarasadai)[8] and Levi (Oziel/Uzziel; Elkiah/Hilkiah; Gideon?; Ahitub; Eliab).[9]

1.   Haag, *Studien*, pp. 38-39.

2.   According to Bruns ('Genealogy') the genealogy connects Judith with Jael, which cannot be deduced from the names in the genealogy.

3.   Num. 1.6 'From Simeon, Shelumiel son of Zurishaddai'. Likewise Num. 2.12; 7.36, 41; 10.19.

4.   Uzziah is also of the tribe of Simeon (6.15), which may enhance the contrast between Judith and him.

5.   Cf. Deut. 33.13-17. The judge Gideon is of the tribe of Manasseh (Judg. 6.11, 15). See, however, n. 9.

6.   The most prominent Nathanael in the Hebrew Bible is the son of Zuar; Num. 1.8; 2.5; 7.18, 23; 10.15.

7.   Num. 1.9; but see below, n. 9.

8.   Following J. Jeremias, Johnson (*Purpose*, p. 102), traces the 'tribe' of Judith back to Simeon only.

9.   Cf. Uzziel the son of Kohath according to Exod. 6.18 and other passages. Hilkiah is a priestly name which may refer to the high priest during the reign of Josiah (2 Kgs 22.8 and elsewhere); cf. 1 Chron. 6.45 and Neh. 8.4; 12.7, 21. The name Gideon (Γεδεων) in LXX manuscripts is sometimes the translation of the Hebrew Gershon (one of the sons of Levi, Gen. 46.11; Exod. 6.16; Num. 3.17); see for example Josh. 21.6 and 1 Chron. 6.1 according to the Codex Alexandrinus. Ahitub is again a priestly name, used for example for the son of Pinehas (1 Sam. 14.3; 22.9) and the father of Zadok (2 Sam. 8.17). Eliab may be associated with Levi—cf. 1 Chron. 6.27;

These data become even more significant when we compare
them to the reference to Judith's husband in 8.2, which almost
seems to be a joke: 'Her husband Manasseh, who belonged to
her tribe and family, had died during the barley harvest'. Which
tribe is meant? Simeon or Levi, or one of the others? That is
very difficult to determine. Moreover, the husband derives his
identity from his wife, not the other way around. Judith is given
an extensive genealogy, but her husband is only introduced by
a reference to Judith's family. This is very unconventional in the
Bible and also differs from the introduction of other heroines in
Hellenistic Jewish literature. Esther, for example, is called the
cousin of Mordecai who adopted her (Esth. 2.7). Esth. 2.15
identifies her as 'the daughter of Abihail the uncle of Mordecai'.
Esther has no genealogy of her own, unlike Mordecai in Esth.
2.5: 'Mordecai son of Jair son of Shimei son of Kish, a
Benjaminite'. Esther's family is indicated through Mordecai.
According to the LXX Esther is the daughter of Aminadab. This
name may well be a symbolic reference to Mordecai, meaning
'the brother of my father is generous'.[1] Thus Esther derives her
identity from Mordecai, which fits in with the unfolding of the
story. It is Mordecai who persuades Esther in the end to go to
the Persian king in order to rescue her people (ch. 4). Likewise,
Susanna, the daughter of Hilkia, is introduced as the wife of
Joakim in Susanna 1 (Theodotion). If we compare Jdt. 8.1-2 with
the introduction of women who are considered models for
Judith, the atypical introduction of Judith stands out again.
Miriam is introduced anonymously in Exodus 2 as Moses' sister
(2.4) and later as Aaron's sister in Exod. 15.20.[2] As is well
known, Deborah is characterized as a prophetess and further
identified as 'wife of Lappidoth' (Judg. 4.4). Similarly, Jael is
introduced as 'wife of Heber the Kenite' (Judg. 4.17).[3] In the
light of these parallels, Jdt. 8.1-2 is a significant deviation from

15.18, 20; 16.5—but also with other tribes. The names Ox/Uz
(cf. Gen. 22.21), Ananias, Raphain and Elijah cannot convincingly be
associated with a specific Israelite tribe.
    1. *KB*, III, p. 799.
    2. Cf. Num. 12.1 and 26.59.
    3. Cf. also 1 Sam. 25.2-3.

established patterns of introductions of women in biblical narratives.[1]

The relation between Esther and Mordecai draws our attention, by contrast, to another characteristic of Judith's story. Judith does not act on the advice of a man, but takes the initiative in an independent manner. After the decision of the leaders to turn over the city to the Assyrians if after five days God has not intervened, Judith invites them into the shelter on the roof of her house (probably a *sukkâ*)[2] and teaches them a lesson (8.9-36): 'Listen to me, rulers of the people of Bethulia! What you have said to the people today is not right; you have even sworn and pronounced this oath between God and you, promising to surrender the town to our enemies' (8.11). The leaders do not protest against the sharp reproaches of Judith, but suggest that she pray for rain (8.31). Judith ignores the request of the elders: 'Listen to me. I am about to do something that will go down through all generations of our descendants...Only, do not try to find out what I am doing; for I will not tell you until I have finished what I am about to do' (8.32-34). The visit ends with the magistrates' blessing of Judith and their return to their posts (8.35-36). Thus, Judith manages to get *carte blanche* from them.[3]

A third indication of a possible F voice seems to be the departure from the traditional pattern of men who act as warriors and liberators, and women who sing the song of victory. The Hebrew Bible contains several specimens of such a victory song or references to it (Exod. 15.20-21; Judg. 11.34; 1 Sam. 18.6-7).[4] Judith 15–16 corresponds to them, but again it is the deviation from the usual pattern which gives reason to assume a narrative F voice. 1 Sam. 18.6-7 reads, for instance, 'As they were coming home, when David returned from killing the Philistine, the women came out of all the towns of Israel, singing and dancing,

---

1.   This is also observed by White, 'In the Steps of Jael', p. 7.

2.   Cf. Neh. 8.14-17.

3.   See above, p. 241.

4.   S.D. Goitein, 'Women as Creators of Biblical Genres', *Prooftexts* 8 (1988), pp. 1-33; Brenner and van Dijk-Hemmes, *On Gendering Texts*, pp. 32-43. Cf. Haag, *Studien*, p. 56, concerning Jdt. 15.12-14: 'Judith wiederholt hier die Rolle der Mirjam als Chorführerin der israelitischen Frauen, die Jahwes Sieg über den Pharao feiern (Ex. 15, 20f.)'.

to meet King Saul, with tambourines, with songs of joy, and with musical instruments'. In the book of Judith a similar event is being described. All the women from Israel come together, start dancing and singing with timbrels, praising the victor (Jdt. 15.12-14; 16.1).[1] However, if one focuses on the role of the leaders and on gender patterns, a different picture emerges. In fact, not men but Judith and her maidservant rescue the Jews from the siege of the Assyrians, and they are supported by the Lord. After the killing of Holofernes the battle of the Jews and the Assyrians is a simple matter, and the author takes less than a chapter to describe it (14.11–15.7). Moreover, it is Judith who gives the orders for the counter-attack of the Jews (14.1-5). In 16.1-17 we find an extensive song of triumph, started by Judith and joined by the rest of the people (15.14). The overture to this song in 15.8-13 is very interesting, compared to the songs of victory just mentioned. It looks like a reversal of gender roles. First Joakim the high priest and the senate come from Jerusalem to Bethulia 'to witness the good things that the Lord had done for Israel, and to see Judith and to wish her well' (15.8). They acknowledge that it was Judith who rescued Israel (cf. 15.10: 'You have done all this with your own hand; you have done great good to Israel, and God is well pleased with it'). Jdt. 15.12-13 refers to the dancing and singing of all women from Israel, gathered to see Judith. The men join the party (15.13). It is very clear that a woman is the hero here:[2] 'They [the women] blessed *her*, and some of them performed a dance in *her* honour' (emphasis mine). In contradistinction to the other references to songs of victory in the book of Judith, female (and male) singers and dancers are found together with female liberators.

One can only speculate about the original context of the passages of Judith discussed in this final section. There is a possibility that they were originally composed as a parody of male leadership for a female audience. But it is impossible to

1. As in Exod. 15.20-21 the Lord is praised in the song in Jdt. 16 as victor (16.1-2, 12-17; cf. 16.19).

2. A significant detail is that Judith and the other women crown themselves with olive wreaths (15.13). This confirms the image of Judith as victor.

demonstrate this convincingly. However, the significant adaptations of the androcentric patterns which can be observed in these passages seem to justify reading parts of the narrative of Judith as F voices within a dominant male framework.[1]

1. A fourth indication of an F voice may be that Judith is a heroic widow, like the Mother of the Maccabean 'martyrs', but that does not mean that she should be associated with the weak and marginal members of the society, contrary to what one would expect in the context of literature from the Second Temple period (cf. 2 Macc. 8.28, 30). She is a rich and independent woman with a female servant as caretaker of her property (Jdt. 8.7, 10).

I thank my colleagues Dr Jonneke Bekkenkamp and Dr Caroline Vander Stichele and also Dr Francis Watson (London) and Professor Athalya Brenner (Haifa) for their helpful comments on the draft of this paper.

HEAD HUNTING:
'JUDITH' ON THE CUTTING EDGE OF KNOWLEDGE*

Mieke Bal

Introduction

How does one approach, analyse and study a text so strange
and so familiar, stemming from a culture different from our
own, yet so integrated in even the most common, everyday
fantasies of today's western society that it seems too well
understood even to notice that it isn't? Reconstructing the
original ideology, literary genre, formal background and
intertexts has been done before me by people much better
equipped to do so. I also foster doubts about the relevance, for
my own project, of such endeavours. For my goal is not
archaeological reconstruction but analysis of today's culture as
the messy, by no means straightforward product of the past.
Yet 'Judith' is with us in that culture, although, clearly, a
historical object. How can we grasp what 'it', or 'she', means?
Asking myself these questions, suddenly I made one of those
minor discoveries we tend to attribute to chance.

Looking over my initial notes for this lecture I opened my
Carey Moore edition, and, completely at random, stumbled on
the words: 'Look! Holofernes is lying on the ground! And his
head is missing!' The phrase is a direct representation of
character speech,[1] yelled by Bagoas to Judith (14.18). As an

*   This paper was presented as the 11th annual *JSOT* lecture, delivered
at the University of Sheffield on 10 March 1994, and was first published in
JSOT 63 (Sept. 1994), pp. 3-34.
    1.   The term 'character speech' as well as other narratological terms are
from my book, *Narratology: Introduction to the Theory of Narrative* (trans.
C. van Boheemen; Toronto: University of Toronto Press, 1985).

eager reader of thrillers, this seemed to me quite thrilling indeed. And suddenly it occurred to me that my notion that I read thrillers as a distraction from my academic work is totally wrong. 'Losing my head' is what such reading is about. When you lose your head, there is, in addition to other aggravation, a problem of rationality and knowledge. So 'Judith' set me thinking about thought. And I went in search of the missing head, through the history of western culture. And I found this (see Figure 1).

Figure 1. Michelangelo da Caravaggio, *Medusa's Head*, 1600–1601 (Museo Uffizi, Florence; by permission).

Confusionism and Caravaggio

Fear not. This woman cannot kill. She is only an image. Caravaggio's *Medusa's Head* shows us the essence of the *femme fatale*. The *femme fatale* is not only a representative of the killing powers attributed to women by men. It is crucial that the killing happen by visual means. So the figure is also bound up with vision. Medusa is the monster who is able to 'visually' kill men, just by looking, and being looked at. Jacques Lacan understood the creepy, spooky quality of this being-looked-at-ness, and made it an important element in his reconsideration of the gaze.[1]

But let's not forget that, although Medusa allegedly killed by means of looking, she ended up dead by being looked at. Was that a killing turned inward, an introjection of a death drive, a suicide perhaps? Or, is being-looked-at the same as looking? That would entail a confusion of subject and object. The separation between subject and object is the most central dogma, not only of modern epistemology, but also including, or perhaps, given its object of study, in particular, of art history.[2]

Look at Medusa. No, she won't kill. But not simply because she is 'just' an image. Even within the game we play, the game of 'reading fiction', of 'willing suspension of disbelief', she won't kill. Like most Medusas in the history of art, this head, allegedly able to petrify the spectator, is without power because without look. She averts her eyes. Medusa looks away, and she looks terrified herself. What could possibly frighten her who cannot even see the frightening snakes on her own head?[3]

1. J. Lacan, *The Four Fundamental Concepts of Psycho-Analysis* (ed. J.-A. Miller and trans. A. Sheridan; Harmondsworth: Penguin Press, 1979). For a detailed understanding of Lacan's concept of the gaze in connection to feminism, see Silverman, 'Fassbinder and Lacan' in *Male Subjectivity at the Margin* (New York: Routledge: 1992).

2. On modern epistemology, see L. Code, *What Can She Know? Feminist Epistemology and the Construction of Knowledge* (Ithaca: Cornell University Press, 1991). On the contradictions of art history in terms of repressing its interpretive moments, see M.A. Holly, *Panofsky and the Foundations of Art History* (Ithaca: Cornell University Press, 1984). For an alternative, cf. M. Bal, *Reading 'Rembrandt': Beyond the Word–Image Opposition* (New York: Cambridge University Press, 1991).

3. On the meanings of the Medusa myth, see J.-P. Vernant, *La mort dans*

There is a story attached to this vision, a story we can read. But that's only a pre-text. According to that pre-text, Perseus has petrified Medusa by means of the mirroring effect of his own shield, thus being able to behead her. And who would not be terrified at being beheaded? This story is dissolved, however, by the confrontation with the image, because the painting is a self-portrait. And the self-portrait presupposes a mirror, too, and makes the figure, the monster, change sex. There is still a mirror in this visual story, but a mirror that failed as a shield. Is Perseus merged into Medusa? Is the painter the model? The starting point for a reading could be: the insistent look is not mirrored. Yet the portrait remains an event of *facing*, strangely reassuring, because Medusa loses her otherness in the partial exchange with him who sees her. As the late Louis Marin pointed out in an interpretation of this painting, 'the frontal portrait doubles and visually animates, figuratively, the correlation of subjectivity...the model is "I" and "you" and the spectator is "you" and "I"'.[1]

The mythical pre-text is not irrelevant, but it becomes an intertext, 'brought in for questioning', if you allow me to continue to use mystery novels as an epistemic lead. The viewer is implicated in the gendered myth of assigning lethal power and monstrosity by some sort of identification stimulated by the transsexual movement between model and figure. This confusion allows a sensitization to the fright, not provoked but *undergone* by Medusa. The look that looks away instores narrativity by turning the figure into the character of a narrative, not the ancient one about Perseus, but the visual one in which things happen between a canvas and a viewer. Medusa looks away in order to get you to look away with her, to escape the myth that binds her into an evasion from that frightening role. Medusa 'speaks', visually, in an exhortative mode, enticing 'you' to look,

les yeux (Paris: Hachette, 1985), and J. Clair, *Méduse: Contribution à une anthropologie des arts du visuel* (Paris: Gallimard, 1989). In particular, N. Hertz, *The End of the Line: Essays on Psychoanalysis and the Sublime* (New York: Columbia University Press, 1985).

1. L. Marin, 'Le trompe-l'oeil', un comble de la peinture', in R. Court (ed.), *L'effet trompe-l'oeil dans l'art et la psychanalyse* (Paris: Bordas/Dunod, 1988), pp. 75-92.

with her, for the true source of the fright, located in the ideology that turns women into monsters.[1]

Beheading is a symbol of castration, Freud contended, and he used Medusa's story as an example. The recurrence of the story in the history of western culture seems to confirm this interpretation. That is allegedly why, in psychoanalytically oriented discussions, Medusa is so often juxtaposed to, and even confused with, Judith. But the question is, Who's who, in beheading and in castration—and whodunnit. According to Mary Garrard, whose book on Artemisia Gentileschi is a classic art historical study on that painter, this print by Golzius (Figure 2) after Spranger, for example, presents a Judith with the head

Figure 2. Hendrik Goltzius, after Barthelomeus Spranger, *Judith*, c. 1585.

1.   The use of linguistic terminology for the analysis of visual art is not an empty metaphor. Speech act theory in particular has specific relevance in this area. See M. Bal and N. Bryson, 'Semiotics and Art History', *Art Bulletin* 73.2 (1991), pp. 174-208. On speech act theory, see J.L. Austin, *How to Do Things with Words* (Cambridge, MA: Harvard University Press, 1975), and S. Felman, *Literary Speech Acts* (Ithaca: Cornell University Press, 1987).

of Holofernes which resembles Cellini's *Perseus*, itself inspired by Donatello's *Judith*.[1] Which gender kills becomes totally confused.

Garrard is a bit too quick, I think, in estimating, with standard views, that in this print 'Judith displays the head in a triumphant gesture'. I think astonishment is perhaps a better word, more specific in its characterization of a confrontational, dramatic expression so oddly in contrast with her body's set pose of sexual display. Her face stands in marked contrast to that of her victim who, oddly enough, seems to smile. It is almost as if he played a trick on her, rather than the other way around. The facial expression needs to be taken as a relatively autonomous visual sign, beheading the figure so to speak, in order to counter the tendency to coherent reading and allow, instead, more complexity.

But if beheading signifies castration, and the obsessive representation of it reflects the fear of castration, it seems, again, relevant that Medusa is a woman figure, her hatchman a male one, while Holofernes is a man killed by a woman. Confusion of gender, or of subject and object, seems at stake. Caravaggio's *Judith* contains an emphatic sign of such a confusion (see Figure 3).

The image is clearly unequal in its treatment of the protagonists. Between the women, the contrast in age is emphasized. Between Judith and Holofernes the contrast is more complicated. Garrard mentions the tendency, at the time, to turn Holofernes into a tragic hero,[2] as well as the incapacity on the part of the painter to identify strongly enough with a woman character to flesh her out with the same level of human interest; as a result, she alleges, Judith is not dramatically involved in the scene:

> Caravaggio's rendering of such aesthetically imbalanced types— the female conventional, the male real—is less likely to be explained by Renaissance art theory or Jesuit theology than by the influence of gender on the practice of an artist who happened to be male.[3]

1. M. Garrard, *Artemesia Gentileschi: The Image of the Female Hero in Italian Baroque Art* (Princeton: Princeton University Press, 1988), p. 287 (Figure 2, above, appears there).
2. Garrard, *Artemesia*, p. 291.
3. Garrard, *Artemesia*, p. 291.

Figure 3. Michelangelo da Caravaggio, *Judith Beheading Holofernes*, 1598–99 (Galleria Nazionale d'Arte Antica, Palazzo Barberini, Rome; by permission).

Figure 4. Michelangelo da Caravaggio, *Boy with a Basket of Fruit*, 1593–94
(Borghese Gallery, Rome; by permission).

This seems an implausible dualism between male and female, verging on essentialism, especially in the case of an artist who represented male figures as explicitly androgynous (Figure 4) or inscribed them with the signs of femininity. It is hard to maintain, without further exploration of nuances, that Caravaggio as an artist just 'happened to be male', as if there were just one kind of masculine identity, and to ignore the possibility of artistic results of homosexual subjectivity.[1] It is, moreover, essentialist

1.   Gay studies have provided ample evidence to the contrary. The most spectacular analyses of homosexual subjectivity in visual art (e.g. Fassbinder's films) to my mind are those carried out by K. Silverman, *Male Subjectivity at the Margin* (New York: Routledge, 1992).

Figure 5. Michelangelo da Caravaggio, *David with the Head of Goliath*, c. 1605–1606 (?) (Borghese Gallery, Rome; by permission)

and simplistic to explain his representations of men and women figures through his biological sex. He even did a painting that is as close to a Judith as they come (see Figure 5), and here also one could allege that the young David is less dramatically involved in the scene than one could expect. No revelling in his glory, no triumphant look, no ecstasy of power. Perhaps decapitation is not enough, by far, to change power relations.

Nonetheless, I propose we make more of a pictorial detail that the Judith image insists on in several ways. Then, another interpretation becomes possible; one that is not the result of looking with a set assumption attributed to artistic intention; one that is not the result of looking for what we already know. Instead, one can take the image as a device to gain knowledge. The sign I am alluding to consists of the blood spurting out of the victim's neck. This blood draws, in realistic terms, implausibly straight stripes of red, set off emphatically on the flesh of the body, then on the white pillow and sheet. The blood is so emphatically detached from the body it could be expected to soil that the spurts leave a shadow on the neck. Whereas this shiny white rhymes with the immaculate bodice of the heroine, the red gush that crosses out his whiteness echoes the curtain behind him. But most importantly, the red spurts alliterate with the sword which is slightly behind them. And this order of things matters.

'Logically', realistically that is, the blood *follows* the sword as its consequence; this is so obvious that one tends to take it as the natural and inevitable meaning. Visually, however, according to the eye's itinerary into the representation, being closer to the picture plane, the blood precedes the sword, as its visual 'cause': *because* we see the blood, we subsequently see the sword. This seems an irresistible reminder of the deconstruction of pin and pain, rendered classical by Jonathan Culler's use of it as primary example.[1] In both cases, the relation between violence and suffering is questioned.

The difference between Judith's statuesque quality and Holofernes' dramatic one, striking indeed, is not caused by stereotypical gender positions, but questions these. Each character is objectified, but which objectification precedes, or causes, the other is now an open, disturbing question. The difference matters, but it seems wise to resist the double temptation of hierarchization and coherence.

If Caravaggio's *Medusa* (Figure 1, above) confused the gender of the beheaded/castrated victim as well as the positions of subject and object of looking, his Judith painting adds to that confusion the one between cause and consequence, adding, that is, confusion about another logic that is at the core of our standard epistemology. Challenging causality, it thus questions the stories of origin through which we culturally construct responsibility and guilt.

The two confusions that Caravaggio's two representations of two 'dangerous women' submit to the viewer are, of course, related. Subject and object confusion in terms of gender, and

1.   J. Culler, *On Deconstruction: Theory and Criticism after Structuralism* (Ithaca: Cornell University Press, 1983), pp. 86-87.

confusion of causality in terms of origin, responsibility and guilt, are together constitutive of a thematic field that is profoundly crucial for an understanding of our culture, where both gender inequity and epistemic authority seem almost impossible to challenge. This specifies epistemology itself as an inquiry into gender relations.

Instead of taking Judith as a female figure whose heroism is opposed to her wickedly seductive act in a binary struggle for gendered allegiances, therefore, I would like to take her as a figure who stands at the cutting edge of knowledge; who represents a challenge, not so much to faith and chastity, nationality and group solidarity, but to our assumptions, the certainties that reign in our academic work, about what it is and how it is we can *know*. Of course, I am not suggesting that the traditional 'Judith' themes are irrelevant or misplaced; but if these were crucial at one time in history, the very attempt to base our current dealings with 'Judith' on this archaeology is caught up in the very confusion of causality that the painting sets out to demonstrate. Using ancient readings of 'Judith', then, is a way of denying Caravaggio the use of his art, a way of refusing to look, a way of ignoring what strikes the eye. Wasn't blindness about castration, after all?

As feminist philosophers of science have repeatedly argued, the identification of knowledge with objectivity is itself a confusion.[1] Now, before I carry on I ask you not to misunderstand me; I am not saying that rules to organize the game of knowledge acquisition are by definition pointless. If there is a problem inherent in the notion of objectivity, and such a problem has been pointed out many times, the major problem is that it is taken, precisely, to be the only, central, most important rule, thus confusing many issues which thus become invisible, in favour of privileging separation and simplification, antagonistic reasoning and immobility. So, if 'Judith' stands for confusion, there may be a lot of things we can learn from the topos. But as far as I am concerned, 'anything goes' is not one of them.

1.   See Code, *What Can She Know?*, and E.F. Keller, *Reflections on Gender and Science* (New Haven: Yale University Press, 1985); and, specifically about the potentially lethal aspects of the obsession with objectivity, Keller's *Secrets of Death* (New York: Routledge & Kegan Paul, 1992).

Misconstruing my argument in that direction is, precisely, evidence of an attempt to stay within the kind of binary opposition this confusionism tries to undermine.

Epistemic Risks and Gentileschi

What 'Judith' represents is 'danger' in terms of knowledgeability, and 'knowledgeability' in terms of danger. Hence, 'Judith' is a clear case of what I have termed elsewhere an *ideo-story*.[1] By that term I mean a narrative whose structure lends itself to be the receptacle, or projection screen, of different, often opposing ideologies which the narrative appears to emblematize. Such stories display a representational makeup that promotes concreteness and visualization. In particular, they exemplify group interests in individual characters. Their characters are strongly opposed so that dichotomies are established as if 'naturally'. Their fabulas are open enough for opposing ideologies to be housed in them with ease. Ideo-stories are not closed but extremely open; yet, they appear to be closed, and this appearance of closure encourages the illusion of stability of meaning. But their openness makes it 'naturally' necessary to fill them up, so as to suggest closure. Hence the recurrence of such stories in cultural history. For in their openness they pose a threat to ideological certainties, including cognitive ones; they put knowledge at risk. They challenge cultural agents to endorse, substantiate and 'work through' André Gide's maxim, so influential for Roland Barthes among others, that 'incoherence is preferable to a distorting order'.[2] Well-known examples are the stories of Eve, Delilah, Jael, Judith, Mary. Guess what they have in common.

Freud, let's never forget it, foregrounds 'confusion' in his treatment of Judith more than anywhere in his work, and perhaps more than anybody else did apropos of Judith. Writing about virginity, he is irresistibly drawn to consider not the young woman's position but that of the man about to deflower her,

---

1. M. Bal (ed.), *Anti-Covenant: Counter-Reading Women's Lives in the Hebrew Bible* (Sheffield: Almond Press, 1989), pp. 11-24.
2. S. Burke, *The Death and the Return of the Author* (Edinburgh: Edinburgh University Press, 1992).

and who dreads the encounter. As I have argued in my book on women in the book of Judges, *Death and Dissymmetry*, Freud constantly shifts positions, between his scientific endeavour to explain a phenomenon and the desire to justify it, between a male and a female view, between a cultural value and a taboo. The value attached to virginity is phrased in a discourse of scientific logic and subjective justification, of which I cannot resist quoting the opening passage:

> The demand that a girl shall not bring to her marriage with a particular man any memory of sexual relations with another is, indeed, nothing other than the logical continuation of the right to exclusive possession of a woman, which forms the essence of monogamy, the extension of the monopoly over the past.[1]

The logic presents a mixture of legal (monopoly, right) and cognitive concerns (memory). The crux of Freud's essay is a circular argument that moves from the woman's feeling via the male act to the male feeling that inspires his guilt, its projection onto the woman, and thus, ultimately, her hostility. From lasting bondage, defloration leads to lasting hostility; from a value, virginity becomes a danger. And by the time we reach the second half of the essay, the prototypical virgin is called Judith. Judith the heroine, or the dreaded castrating female—the chaste widow who might almost be assumed to have 'lost the memory' of sexual intercourse. Or the lewd provocative whore that Rubens depicted; for, if his Delilahs and Judiths are any indication, Rubens was quite fond of lewd, provocative whores.

These stereotypical views of women that catch Judith between two impossible roles have been sufficiently criticized since the advent of feminism. But what has perhaps been less systematically rehearsed is just how profoundly these views affect issues seemingly far removed from views of women, indeed, from women, period—since these issues touch, precisely, upon the participation of women in the adventure of knowledge.

---

1. S. Freud, 'The Taboo of Virginity' *The Standard Edition of the Complete Psychological Works* (trans. and ed. J. Strachey *et al.*; London: Hogarth Press, 1918), XI , p. 193; see my analysis of the essay in connection with the story of the sacrifice of Jephthah's daughter in Judg. 11, M. Bal, *Death and Dissymmetry: The Politics of Coherence in the Book of Judges* (Chicago: University of Chicago Press, 1988), pp. 52-59.

For Freud, Judith represents a figure that enables him to develop a thought that is immensely rich and confused, cognitively invaluable and affectively loaded. This, I contend, is Judith's primary cultural function. A locus of confusion, 'Judith' as a topos of thought and representation challenges so many of our most dearly held certainties that she/it scares many of us out of our wits. It is much easier to defend a figure, or character, on humanistic grounds as 'good', heroic, loyal, strong, against the implausible yet persistent representations of the figure as depraved, mean, deceitful and misandristic, than to face the undermining ideas that she/it imposes. In order to avoid excessive personification of thoughts, I refer to 'Judith' as a topos, of which any narrative or depiction is a concretization.

And confusion and indeterminacy are at the core of those ideas. Mary Jacobus, author of another classic on Judith, hits the nail on the head, to use an overdetermined metaphor,[1] when she claims that Donatello's sculpture *Judith and Holofernes* of 1455 should not be read as the representation of an androgynous subjected male and a phallic female figure. Such a reading would be as reductive as it would be to take it as a political allegory of the Florentine Republic, or as a Renaissance Christianizing of pagan forms and motives, like in the standard interpretations. Instead, she sees in it

> a narrative of representation itself—that is, as an instance of the power of representation to structure, and hence allay, the anxieties attending indeterminacy.[2]

Her view of the statue makes it more than 'Janus-like', as it has been called. Circular rather than double, it deprives the viewer of any fixed ground. Jacobus writes, 'The dynamic movement is not that of the figures themselves, but that of the gaze that

---

1.   This metaphor is literalized in the story of Judith's colleague Jael, who drove a tent peg through the temple of the enemy leader Sisera in Judg. 4 and 5. See my study on that story (M. Bal, *Murder and Difference: Gender, Genre and Scholarship in Sisera's Death* (trans. M. Gumpert; Bloomington: Indiana University Press, 1988).

2.   See M. Jacobus, 'Judith, Holophernes, and the Phallic Woman'. The quoted passage is from p. 128.

circles them, looking for a point on which to fix'.[1] If that point, then, turns out to be the upraised sword, we can estimate the meagre consolation that cognitive anxiety is able to muster.

Cognitive anxiety, or rather, the anxiety over cognitive certainties, is not only effectively demonstrated by the Judith story as it comes to us in the biblical book, which poses the anxiety-ridden question of authorship, or, more interestingly, to use Fokkelien van Dijk and Athalya Brenner's terminology, of status as F or M text.[2] This anxiety shows up in scholarship, as well as in other forms of reception of that story, most notably in visual representations. Jacobus connects this unconscious invest-ment of indeterminacy as displayed by the Donatello's thema-tization of the 'natural' lack of fixity in sculptural form, with Freud's theory of penis envy. This is in turn connected to fetishism, and she alleges as an example the standard interpreta-tions of Artemisia Gentileschi's *Judith* (Figure 6) as a case of such envy, so masterfully refuted by Elena Ciletti.[3] The horror this image inspires has led to biographical and psychoanalytical reductionistic interpretations which I won't rehearse.

More relevant for my purpose is the visual difficulty the image poses, discussed by Germaine Greer.[4] Changing the direction of Caravaggio's spurts of blood, Gentileschi makes the image confusing, not in the detail that works as a sign, but in its over-all structure, as if to insist on what was too easily overlooked in the Caravaggio. The spouting blood turns in the other direction, threatening to stain Judith, but this contamination is only a pointer, synecdochically signifying the confusion of arms and of jobs being done. Needless to insist on the resemblance of Holofernes' arms to *thighs*, even stronger in the earlier version

---

1. M. Jacobus, *Reading Woman: Essays in Feminist Criticism* (New York: Columbia University Press, 1986), p. 128. The absence of such a point makes it rather pointless, of course, to reproduce a photograph of the sculpture here.

2. See A. Brenner and F. van Dijk-Hemmes, *On Gendering Texts: Female and Male Voices in the Hebrew Bible* (Leiden: Brill, 1993).

3. E. Ciletti, 'Patriarchal Ideology, in the Renaissance Iconography of Judith', in her 'Prefiguring Woman: Gender Studies and the Italian Renaissance' (lecture, University of Rochester, 1988).

4. G. Greer, *The Obstacle Race: The Fortunes of Women Painters and their Works* (London: Secker & Warburg, 1979).

Figure 6. Artemisia Gentileschi, *Judith Slaying Holofernes*, 1620
(Museo Uffizi [Bardazzi], Florence; by permission).

(see Figure 7) where the end of the thigh has been omitted or cropped. The confusion emphasizes the resemblance between the three major jobs in women's lives according to the tradition to which 'Judith' belongs: life-giving, life-taking, and, in between, hard work. The fact that the baroque whirling of arms circles around the man's head as the still center only emphasizes that the confusion is a meaningful organizational principle, not a compositional flaw or baroque *folie*.[1]

The head is central, static in the middle of movement, and thereby doubly detached, from the body and from the surrounding drama. And the confused arms radiating out of the central head signify that confusion with something like concentration; they relate, after all, to a center. The arms express strength and determination, the faces commitment to the task at hand. There is something passionate about the figures that has nothing in common with the traditionally applied qualifications like triumph, cruelty or horror, something passionate that Caravaggio's Judith completely lacks. There, all passion is concentrated in the victim's face—Garrard was right about that. Gentileschi's work radiates a contained and serious, almost organized passion that enhances the sense of efficacy of the work being done. This is the feature that for me underlies the confusion, which can then be spelled out as: a serious and passionate commitment to confusion, to a complexity over clarity, to mobility over fixity, to collusion over collision, to intersubjectivity over objectivity. This gives the struggle an epistemological slant. It puts knowledge, as it is traditionally construed, at risk.

Vision and Narrative as Epistemologies

The epistemological proposition implied here involves two modes of representation that both have a controversial epistemological status. There are aspects in the Judith topos that make it particularly suitable for *visual* representation, and those aspects also address specific problems of the possibility to know.

1. Buci-Glucksmann, *La folie du voir: De l'esthétique baroque* (Paris: Galilée, 1986).

Figure 7. Artemisia Gentileschi, *Judith Slaying Holofernes*, 1612–13
(Museo di Capodimonte, Naples; by permission of the Italian
Ministry of Culture).

Vision is connected to such issues as 'the mind's eye', empirical evidence, the possibilities and limits of observation, the separation of object from subject which the sense of sight alone appears to guarantee, and the like. There are also aspects that encourage the use of narrative, aspects that are partly obvious, like the centrality of suspense and action, but these, too, can be connected with problems of knowledge production. One only needs to think of the place of narrative in the historical disciplines, and of the reflections, in the wake of Hayden White, on the fits and misfits between the actual historical narratives and the events they purport to describe, but also, *construct*.[1] In her critique of physics as the paradigm of knowledge construction, feminist philosopher Lorraine Code suggests that there are narrative reasons why epistemology values simplicity. Narratives are by definition messy; but so is the world knowers wish to understand:

> Clean, uncluttered analyses are valued more highly than rich, multifaceted, but messy and ambiguous narratives.[2]

This remark strongly suggests that there is a relation between narrative form and epistemological competence, between the ability to handle complex knowledge and the ability to tell and read complex stories, as much as between cleanliness and simplicity. In other words, if Code is right here, as I think she is, then narrative theory and analysis have a lot to offer in the important area of reflection on what it is and how it is we can know. And in particular, narrative analysis of such ideo-stories as 'Judith' with their epistemic potential and their cultural position might be of crucial importance to the understanding of contemporary culture.[3]

In the first place, some stories, and our culture's most powerful ideo-stories are among these, tend to be both rewritten over

---

1.   H. White, *Meta-History: The Historical Imagination in Nineteenth-Century Europe* (Baltimore: Johns Hopkins University Press, 1973); *idem*, *Tropics of Discourse* (Baltimore: Johns Hopkins University Press, 1978); M.A. Holly, 'Past Looking', *Critical Inquiry* 16.2 (1990), pp. 371-96.

2.   Code, *What Can She Know?*

3.   Which is why, I think, the department of Biblical Studies at Sheffield is in a good position to put itself forward as a 'Department of Biblical and Cultural Studies'.

and over again and to be represented visually. 'Judith', of course, is a very strong case. Now, while we keep looking at these two Judiths, let us consider a meeting place between narrative and visuality in a different cultural practice, namely theory. Freud's story of fetishism may shed some light on, as well as being a case of, what I want to point out.[1]

This Freudian theory, exposed in 'Female Sexuality', makes a characteristic shift again, connecting (female) penis envy with (male) fetishism. Fetishism is commonly defined as a strong, mostly eroticized attachment to a single object or category. As is invariably the case in psychoanalysis, that attachment is explained through a story of origin—of which the central event is the perception, crucially visual, of women's lack. It is a story of semiotic behaviour.

The story has been told and retold.[2] Here, I am interested in its visual rhetoric, in the way in which that rhetoric knots together the actantial function of vision and the narrative mode needed to make that vision appear as an epistemic instrument instead. The child 'seeing in a flash' that the mother has no penis, identifies with this shocking sight in a first metaphorical transfer of 'absence of penis' to 'fundamental, existential lack', and acts upon it. This negative presence in the mother, because of its negativity, can only be the product of symbolization; visual as the experience is, it demonstrates that there is nothing object-ive nor primal about vision. 'Lack' is not the object seen but the supplement provided by the seeing subject. If this negative vision is as crucial in the formation of subjectivity as it appears to be in Freudian theory, I wish to emphasize the crucial negativity of vision that it implies. Vision, then, is both bound up with gender formation and with semiotic behaviour; it is an act of interpretation, of constructing meaning out of nothingness. In

1.   The following analysis is based on my article 'A Narrative Perspective on Collecting'.

2.   S. Freud, 'Some Psychological Consequences of the Anatomical Distinction between the Sexes', in *The Standard Edition of the Complete Psychological Works* (ed. J. Strachey, and trans. J. Strachey *et al.*; London, Hogarth Press, 1963 [1925]), XXI, pp. 149-57; and O. Fenichel, 'Fetishism', in *The Psychoanalytic Theory of Neurosis* (London: Routledge & Kegan Paul, 1936), pp. 341-51.

Freud's construction, absence lays the foundation of vision as an epistemic tool, as a basically negative, gendered, act of fictionalization.

The child denies the absence in a second act of symbolization. This time, he denies the negativity. Superposing fiction upon fiction, the absence becomes presence. Later on, the fixation of this denial results in the displacement of the absent penis onto some other element of the body, which must then be eroticized for the grown-up child to become fetishistic. This constitutes the third act of symbolization. This other element of the body—this object that must become the paradigm of object-ivity: semiotically invested objecthood—is subjected to a complex rhetorical strategy. In this strategy three tropes contribute to the perversion of meaning: synecdoche, the figure where a part comes to stand for the whole from which it was taken; metonymy, where one things stands for another adjacent to it in place, time or logic, and metaphor, where one thing stands for another on the basis of similarity, that is, something they have in common.

These rhetorical strategies work as follows in the structure of fetishism. First, the substitute for the penis is synecdochically taken to stand for the whole body of which it is a part, through synecdoche: a foot can become eroticized in this way, for example, or 'a shine on the nose' in Freud's story of the English nurse. Or the substitute can be valued as contiguous to the body, through metonymy: for example, a fur coat, stockings, a golden chain. But second, the whole is defined, in its wholeness, by the presence of a single part that is in turn a synecdoche for wholeness, the penis whose absence is denied. In another world this body part might not have the meaning of wholeness, and therefore of lack, that 'we' assign to it. However, if taken synecdochically, the penis can only represent masculinity, whereas the object of fetishism in this story is the woman's body, essentially the mother's. Hence, metaphor intervenes at this other end of the process, in other words, the representation of one thing through another with which it has something in common. The wholeness of the female body can only be synecdochically represented by the stand-in penis that is the fetish, if that body is simultaneously to be metaphorically represented by the male body.[1] Now, here is a cluttered, messy narrative for you; invaluable, nonetheless, for it teaches us more about how theory is constructed, and hence, how knowledge comes to circulate, than any neat articulation could do.

Now, it matters that this entire rhetorical machine, which puts the female subject safely at several removes, is set in motion by a *visual* experience.[2] This multiple removal allows us to get a first glimpse of the violence involved in this story, which might well become a classical horror story, as harrowing as the story of Judith. It is a narrative, a story of origin which replaces the articulation of a problem. The story of origin becomes part of the articulation.[3] It is a story of an original visual experience, perhaps even the first visual act that counts in the formation of the subject, and it is an act of miss-seeing, of the same order as miss-taking arms for thighs, women for men, man for baby, murder for birthgiving. A miss-seeing that is plausible enough to draw attention to the difficulty of seeing.

Yes, we were talking about 'Judith'. Mustered for and against either side of this opposition, 'Judith' as an ideo-story betokens the event that underlies Freud's story of fetishism: castration. But the confusion of loyalties, which failed to benefit a figure like Delilah, for example, as she came to us through the book of Judges at least, opens the story up to the figuration of an alternative. Could she/it be the representation of an alternative story of origin, not one where the one gender's wholeness must be safeguarded by the other's fragmentation, but one where fragmentation is endorsed to prevent 'wholeness' from being pressed into service as an excuse for the fierce safeguarding of

1. For a feminist critique of fetishism, see N. Schor, 'Salammbo Bound', in *Breaking the Chain: Women, Theory, and French Realist Fiction* (New York, 1985), pp. 111-26; and for a feminist reflection on female fetishism, her article, 'Female Fetishism', in S.R. Suleiman (ed.), *The Female Body in Western Culture: Contemporary Perspectives* (Cambridge, MA: Harvard University Press, 1986).

2. For a more extensive analysis of the intimate—and narrative— connections between psychoanalysis and visuality, see the chapter, 'Blindness or Insight? Psychoanalysis and Visual Art', in my book, *Reading 'Rembrandt'*, pp. 286-325.

3. Pavel, 'Origin and Articulation', in *Style* (1813), Special Issue: *Psychopoetics at Work*.

separation? Gentileschi's various *Judith* paintings each contribute an element to the topos of 'knowledge on the cutting edge' at the intersection of visuality and narrative, a place where Gide's maxim takes hold: 'incoherence is preferable to a distorting order'.

'Judith' as Epistemology, Gentileschi as Philosopher

Here is Gentileschi's second *Judith* (Figure 8), according to the chronology established by Garrard. The concentration on the act, the work as work, that characterized the decapitation scenes becomes here sheer attention, as the isolated, autonomous theme. The two women, each carrying the instrument of her work, are easily integrated in the narrative pre-text, as they

Figure 8. Artemisia Gentileschi, *Judith and her Maid Servant Leaving the Enemy Camp*, 1613–14 (Galleria Palatina, Palazzo Pitti, Florence; by permission).

seem watchful, perhaps responding to a sound or threat. Narratively speaking, they are clearly positioned in time: one is aware of the precise moment of the greatest danger: they must now leave the enemy camp unseen. But their attentive pose is first of all a pose of attention, a sign, that is, of the importance of listening and looking elsewhere. It links observation with narrative.

Figure 9. Rembrandt, *Judith and Holofernes*, c. 1652
(Museo di Capodimonte, Naples; by permission).

One of Rembrandt's rare representations of Judith (see Figure 9) provides a nice counterpart to this painting. As in the Gentileschi, things happen here. One of the things that happen is that a woman is cutting a man's throat. Again, one might speculate about the care her facial expression seems to convey. But I want to draw attention to the small signs the syntactic structure includes in the image: the two soldiers outside who, epistemically speaking, are losing their heads.

As narrative elements, the soldiers function on different levels. In the fabula, they fail their duty to stand guard. In the story, they represent focalization, the narrative equivalent of perspectival centring. The event happening in the foreground is not being *seen*. In the text, they serve as rhetorical figures. Synecdochically, as part representing the whole, soldiers representing the army, they signal the military frame in which the event happens, and from which it derives its meaning. Thus, the figures of the soldiers drive home the important point that Judith is being heroic, not lurid. Metonymically, as signs of what comes next, they signify that she is in danger of being caught in the act. As a metaphor, the soldiers represent distraction, a statement on vision and its difficulty; a narrative form of blindness. They fail to heed the biblical indicator of knowledge: 'Behold!'; they invert the words, 'Look! Holofernes is lying on the ground! And his head is missing!'

Against this blindness, the Gentileschi women display concentrated attention; an attention that makes the story go on, that enables them to bring the heroic narrative to a satisfying closure. An attention, also, that turns the story into a story of vision. Where soldiers and victim misinterpret Judith's attractive appearance as harmless, just because, blinded by lust, they could only see what they already knew—about women—these two working women stand still in order to observe; they don't jump to conclusions, hence, don't lose their head.

Attention to what happens outside the pre-established frame is also the theme in a later *Judith* (see Figure 10, below). As Garrard noticed, the element of seduction in the story is here not at all signified iconically, but only through a symbolic reference to the Venus Pudica pose, the sword replacing Venus' hand that covers her genitals. Garrard makes much of the telling detail of Judith's exposed, heavy shoe, which signals her involvement in heavy duty work, of a military nature. An anti-fetish, so to speak. She also cleverly sees an allusion to the painter's name in the half-moonlike shape of the section of Judith's face that is illuminated, which she alleges to be an allusion to Diana, hence, to Artemis. Thus it functions as a veiled signature. But the Caravaggesque lighting emphasizes another element as well. The new addition to what I am construing as a

Gentileschian epistemology is the hand. This hand does many things at once. It warns and directs, signals the leader as it signals attention. Attention becomes the equivalent of action; to see is to do; just as miss-seeing is helping along undoing.

But whereas the previous painting could be taken to emphasize hearing as the major sense of perception, here visuality is foregrounded. And thus the cognitive link between narrative and visuality is the epistemological theme of this work. It is signified as such in many different ways. First of all, the candle, instrument of caravaggesque chiaroscuro but also the bearer of the light that enables one to see. It enables Judith to see, within the story that is implied, and it enables us to see Judith, to see her face and her active way of looking, her looking as an act. Her being-looked-at-ness becomes a lesson in looking.

The flame also illuminates her hand, emphatically so, and stressing that emphasis once more by form, by the rhyming shapes of flame and hand. Like a hand offered to a fortuneteller, this hand foretells the cautious actions to follow, which will bring complete success to Judith's self-assigned mission. But in a visual image, there is more to a hand than meets the eye.

Hands are often important signs in visual art, and this is not surprising. In Rembrandt, they replace eyes sometimes, but also, they shield eyes when the sight is too painful, inducing blindness. They can also directly be related to techniques of vision as connected to ideological abuse, as the sketch of *Susanna* shows to be the case in Rembrandt's painting of *Susanna surprised by the Elders* in Berlin.[1] Finally, in his *Danae*, the well-lit woman's hand *directs*.[2] It directs the gaze of the viewer outside the bedroom, as if it were dismissed as indiscreet. Here, too, visual accessibility of what there is to see is organized by the female figure whose power it is to turn events around. She turns events around within the story about her, as well as the event her story yields: a story of visual access.

1.   For a detailed analysis of this painting in terms similar to my argument here, see Bal, *Reading 'Rembrandt'*, ch. 4.
2.   With my apologies for all these self-references, in order to abridge and to avoid repetition I have to refer the reader to my paper, 'His Master's Eye', in D.M. Levin (ed.), *Modernity and the Hegemony of Vision* (Berkley: University of California Press, 1993), pp. 379-404, for a philosophical discussion of the *Danae*.

Figure 10. Artemisia Gentileschi, *Judith and her Maid Servant with the Head of Holophernes*, c. 1625 (©Detroit Institute of Arts; gift of Mr Leslie H. Green).

Against this background, Gentileschi's hand functions as a similar pointer. It directs our gaze outside, to the source of light; it illuminates the directing function of illumination, suggesting the importance of a mode of looking that is not obvious. The clarity so desired must be sacrificed, or delayed, in favour of something more messy, that takes more time, more effort and more complexity. A new, more effective kind of clarity is the result. Not surprisingly, Gentileschi depicted herself, in her work, in her status as a visual artist, in a pose that echoes this Judith's hand (see Figure 11, below). The hand that signalled fine-tuned attention yielding autonomy over fate here signals cultural productivity. The connection matters; it implies a proposition to the effect that representing, making images, is always also a form of responding to the world, of looking, listening, *reading*.

This self-portrait does nothing to prettify the depicted woman. Slightly falling forward to the picture plane, she looks plumper than strictly necessary; the pose and position almost dwarf her. What is clearly the major focus of this portrait is the arm. A rather fleshy arm, full of muscle. A raised arm—or should we say, elevated? This woman is physically strong, has to be, for the job she is doing is hard work. We recognize the arm, if not the face, because of the tension 'work' necessitates. From confinement to the transgression of the picture frame, from confusion to a different kind of clarity—such is the epistemological itinerary that Gentileschi's *Judiths* propose. Instead of the immediate clarity of binary opposition that the tradition of Judith is so often taken to embody in its dichotomy between heroism and sexual depravity, loyalty to the nation versus betrayal of an entire gender, these works offer a theory of knowledge that is more congenial to what feminist philosophy today is trying to elaborate. But they do so in connection to other cultural expressions, for alternatives, too, come about as a form of reading.

Where does that leave Freud's story of origin, as in penis envy, as in fetishism? Mary Jacobus has established the connection between the original visual experience as narrated by Freud's fiction of the little boy and the little girl seeing the mother's body, and modes of theorizing. She writes,

> for Freud the boy, seeing nothing, arrives at a theory, the girl, seeing something, is confronted by so-called fact. Perception follows from theory in his case, but in hers perception makes *her* jump to conclusions. Her refusal to accept them leads to penis envy.[1]

---

1.   Jacobus, *Reading Woman*, p. 130 (emphasis mine).

Figure 11. Artemisia Gentileschi, *Self-Portrait as the Allegory of Painting*, 1630
(Kensington Palace, London; The Royal Collection ©1994
Her Majesty the Queen).

At first sight—an expression that has lost its innocence now—
the boy practices deduction as a mode of reasoning, the girl
induction. Theory over fact; either the story favours theory
over against empiricism, or else it favours girls over boys in

terms of cognitive skills. But here again a cultural dichotomy confuses the issues rather than clarifying them, in spite of the simplification that is its prize tag. For, as Jacobus point out, Freud skips one step in the account, namely, 'the girl's adoption of the boy's fiction as a matter of fact'.[1]

That is to say, there is no 'first sight'; there is no innocent, objective, isolated fact. The story of origin, of original sight, covers up the embarrassing situation that the girl had no other mode of seeing available than the boy's fiction, taken over from those who looked before him. This, precisely, is the nature of the gaze as Lacan has theorized it. Like a discourse, it is ready for you to step in and work with, but whatever you make of it, whatever you see, is structured and, to a certain extent, semantically filled *for* you. The to-be-looked-at-ness around which Caravaggio's *Medusa* turned is part of your looking. Around the corner, or outside the picture frame, stands a mirror; so beware of what you claim to see.

If this aspect of Lacanian theory turns out to be represented in these *Judiths*, then it is doubtlessly not a coincidence that another flash of insight is enabled by these paintings. Seeing, in a glance, thighs in Holofernes' arms, imposes a choice of two fictions: either the head is a head, but of a baby, or the head is a penis, and being cut off. These arms/thighs work like the skull in Holbein's *Ambassadors* as discussed by Lacan: invisible yet highly visible, they draw attention to what Freud's story declares unseeable, and thus they offer a theory of seeing as insight.

Revisiting the Nude

That the gaze always precedes an act of looking, hence, that original visual experience is not what shapes identity, but, on the contrary, that 'original', culturally imposed blindness does so, is obvious enough in the history of visual representation as we know it. But perhaps, although this may be true, we don't know it well enough. The long line of representations of the female nude body, castrated by desperate attempts to make it less frightening because frightening it had been positioned to be, continues to pose a challenge to cultural historians, so much

1. Jacobus, *Reading Woman*, p. 132.

so that they continue their efforts to miss-see it.

From Giorgione's *Sleeping Venus* via Titian's awakening one to Manet's unsettling version of the attempt to keep women in their place in *Olympia*, contemporary artists like Frida Kahlo and Francis Bacon demonstrate the consequences of this obsession to impose cognitive restrictions. If women cannot get access to full subjectivity, they die as a consequence of their objectification, says Kahlo. Bacon (see Figure 13, below) denies the very possibility of such a confinement. He places the female figure in a pose of sexual desire, inscribes the tabooed body hair in the figure, and positions her like a Holofernes without Judith, as if giving birth to him/herself.

Autogenesis—is that the meaning of Caravaggio's self-portrait as Medusa? But if so, the genesis of self is only possible by means of the wilful endorsement of the confusions 'Judith' embodies. In their identical actantial function, Medusa and Judith's product, Holofernes, represent the mutuality between subject and object. Of castration, of the look, connected in the story of origin. Subject and object of the look, this painting tells

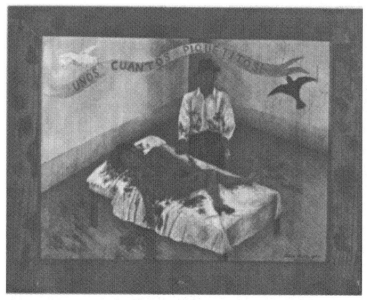

Figure 12. Frida Kahlo, *'Unos cuantos piquetitos'* (1935).

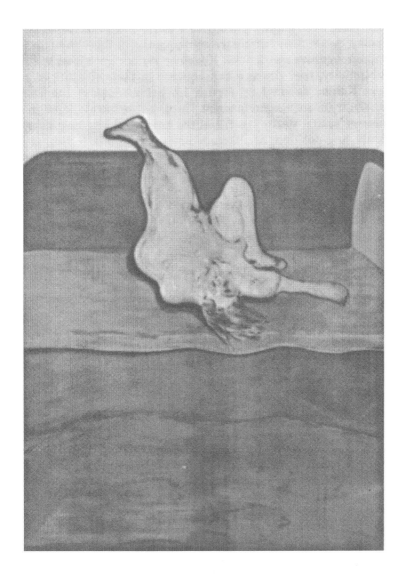

Figure 13. Francis Bacon, *Reclining Woman* (1961) (The Tate Gallery, London; by permission of the Estate of Francis Bacon).

us, cannot be disentangled. Neither can one make a watertight distinction between male and female subjects, much more 'in touch', so to speak, than conventional separations attempt to suggest. Most importantly, Caravaggio's painting projects a confusion between cause and consequence, for if Medusa looks away from the horror she is supposed to embody, who knows which side of the mirror is inhabited by horror. All these messy mixes return in Gentileschi's works, demonstrating that she knew the productive, creative, careful looking that can be.

Where does that leave us, today, as western intellectuals, in relation to 'Judith'? Instead of, or, I should say, in addition to, trying to reconstruct the irretrievably lost origin of this ideo-story's M or F subjectivity, I suggest we give it at least its epistemological due, acknowledge its status as a 'theory', and look around to see what we can still learn from it. And although I will have to refrain from any attempt to simplify in order to 'clarify' what that lesson is, it has to do with the ambiguity that lies at the heart of vision: the deceptive illusion of wholeness that the separation involved in looking so blatantly falsely suggests. Rather than imposing yet more words on a topos that militates for vision, I will wind up by repeating my earlier question: Could she/it be the representation of an alternative story of origin, not one where the one gender's wholeness must be safeguarded by the other's fragmentation, but one where fragmentation is endorsed to prevent 'wholeness' from being pressed into service as an excuse for the fierce safeguarding of separation? This question, then, sheds some light on the paradox this paper has been mapping: how a topos that has invariably been connected with severing and cutting can serve to relate, to link. But this paradox is dissolved as soon as one realizes that in Gentileschi's cutting scene the head is not missing but absolutely central. And although it is narratively in the process of being cut off, it is visually a knot, firmly attaching arms, legs and other members to itself. It is all in the mind, after all.

Part III
SUSANNA: THE READER'S POWER/KNOWLEDGE—
ON VIEWING A JEWISH WOMAN/COMMUNITY

THE ACCUSED: SUSANNA AND HER READERS*

Jennifer A. Glancy

What do readers find when they read Susanna?[1] According to many critics, Susanna is a tale about a virtuous woman who resists seduction. But is it? I am interested in examining the mechanisms of gender representation in this narrative and in rereading the story to ask why an attempted rape resists classification as such. These two endeavors may be related; the text represents femininity in terms of passivity and 'to-be-looked-at-ness',[2] thus according a privileged view of Susanna to the

---

* This article first appeared in *JSOT* 58 (1993), pp. 103-16.

1. I rely exclusively on the more familiar Theodotion version rather than the briefer account found in the LXX.

2. 'In a world ordered by sexual imbalance, pleasure in looking has been split between active/male and passive/female. The determining male gaze projects its phantasy onto the female figure which is styled accordingly. In their traditional exhibitionist role women are simultaneously looked at and displayed, with their appearance coded for strong visual and erotic impact so that they can be said to connote *to-be-looked-at-ness'* (L. Mulvey, 'Visual Pleasure and Narrative Cinema', *Screen* 16.3 [Autumn 1975], pp. 6-18, here p. 11). Feminist film theory has been instrumental in underscoring the importance of the masculine gaze, and I shall rely on many of its findings in my analysis of Susanna. Obviously, there are differences between a written text and a film; notably, in a written text one does not actually 'see'; a reader is not a spectator. Nonetheless, with its insistence on the importance of the elders' gaze, Susanna raises theoretical questions about the relation between the representation of gender and 'looking' as a gendered activity. According to Mulvey, 'film reflects, reveals and even plays on the straight, socially established interpretation of sexual difference which controls images, erotic ways of looking and spectacle' ('Visual Pleasure', p. 6). I shall argue that Susanna similarly reflects and reveals the socially established interpretation of sexual difference both in ancient Israel and among critics today.

elders, a view readers are invited to share. The elders tell each other they have been seduced by Susanna's beauty; are readers similarly 'seduced' by the narrative conventions of the text? Because the preponderance of scholarly discussion suggests an affirmative answer I will discuss the ways the text encodes this response. I will also try to account for the complexity of women's responses to a story that offers a 'positive image' of woman,[1] but only at the cost of representing a woman as the object of others' stories and not the subject of her own.[2]

Rape occurs when one person forces another to engage in sexual intercourse. Seduction occurs when one person persuades another to engage in sexual intercourse. When the elders confront Susanna and announce that she will either submit sexually to them or face execution on the capital charge of adultery, their very real threat of force defines their action as attempted rape, not attempted seduction. Nonetheless, scholarly literature consistently describes the elders' actions as seduction. For example, the notes on Susanna in the Oxford Annotated Edition of the RSV (and now the NRSV) refer to the incident simply as an 'attempted seduction'.[3] For many readers, these notes provide an authoritative guide for interpretation of the text. As the reader reads, she or he is being instructed

---

1. 'Any positive view of a female character has to be reevaluated for its recuperation within male interests (M. Bal, *Lethal Love: Feminist Literary Readings of Biblical Love Stories* [Bloomington: Indiana University Press, 1987], p. 2). In this article, I am only marginally interested in the question of whether Susanna is represented positively (she is); I am rather concerned to shift 'the critical focus from the issue of the positive or negative representations or images of women to the question of the very organization of vision and its effects' (M.A. Doane, *The Desire to Desire: The Women's Film of the 1940s* [Bloomington: Indiana University Press, 1987], p. 176).

2. See A. Bach, 'Breaking out of the Biblical Framework (Gen. 39)', in A. Brenner (ed.), *A Feminist Companion to Genesis* (The Feminist Companion to the Bible, 2; Sheffield: Sheffield Academic Press, 1983), pp. 318-42, for an extended treatment of this phenomenon.

3. H.G. May and B.M. Metzger (eds.), *The New Oxford Annotated Bible with the Apocrypha: Revised Standard Version* (New York: Oxford University Press, 1977), p. 214 of the Apocrypha; B.M. Metzger and R.E. Murphy, *The New Oxford Annotated Bible with the Apocrypha/Deuterocanonical Books: New Revised Standard Version* (New York: Oxford University Press, 1991), p. 180.

to think of the events narrated in terms of seduction and not rape. I argue that standard codes for representing gender are the major factor in the classification of this tale as attempted seduction.

In the course of this discussion I interrogate ideological pre-suppositions of both the text and its interpreters. Whether to designate the story an attempted rape or failed seduction is a modern question. My understanding of the central narrative event as attempted rape arises out of contemporary concerns, just as the general perception that the tale involves seduction relies on persistent and unexamined contemporary assumptions about gender. The text itself does not label the elders' action seduction or rape. However, after carefully delineating the cir-cumstances of a coercive sexual assault the narrative approves Susanna's assessment that a woman's experience of forced sex renders her guilty. I question the implicit narrative promotion of the idea that a virtuous woman prefers death to the dishonor a rape brings to a man's household.

A few preliminary remarks on theoretical perspective and methodology will clarify my procedure for analysis of the text. Feminist scholars widely concur that gender is typically con-figured both in written texts and now in film in terms of subject–object relations, in which masculinity is associated with subjectivity and femininity with objectivity. In particular, man is conventionally represented as the subject of the gaze, and woman as the object of the gaze. To see is to control; to have one's vision represented is to have one's perception of the world ratified. To be seen is to be subject to control; to represent women solely as objects of others' vision denies women their subjectivity. A danger inherent in the definition of femininity as 'to-be-looked-at-ness' is that while female characters are thereby denied subjectivity, they are simultaneously held responsible for exciting the desire of male viewers.[1] This observation is crucial as we analyze Susanna,

---

1.   A partial list of relevant scholarship includes: Mulvey, 'Visual Pleasure'; Doane, *Desire*; T. de Lauretis, *Alice Doesn't: Feminism, Semiotics, Cinema* (Bloomington: Indiana University Press, 1984); *idem, Technologies of Gender: Essays on Theory, Film and Fiction* (Bloomington: Indiana University Press, 1987).

which represents men (particularly the elders) as those who see, and Susanna as the one who is seen. Susanna both reflects and contributes to the conventional representation of gender.

In her writings on narratology, Mieke Bal proposes three methodological questions to guide investigation of texts: Who acts? Who sees? Who speaks?[1] Each question involves us in a different level of textual analysis; it will be helpful to keep this in mind as analysis of the text proceeds. The answers to the second two questions give clues to the ideology of the text: whose vision of events do we share? Who tells the story? To say that the story of Susanna centers on a female character is insufficient. We must also note that she is typically the object, not the subject, of verbs of perception; the story does not allow us to share her vision. Nor does Susanna have an opportunity to narrate her own version of what has happened. Instead, the elders' vision literally dictates the parameters of the story.[2]

We may also consider Bal's first question: Who acts? Susanna acts decisively twice, but only in reaction to others' initiatives. The elders are the subject of the first half of the action, and Daniel the subject of the latter half. While in the first half of the plot Susanna primarily figures as object of the elders' desire and action, in the latter half she barely figures at all. Daniel's vindication of Susanna rests on the elders' conflicting testimony; Susanna herself drops out of the plot as an actor. One of the effects of a plausible narrative is to make its ideology seem natural or inevitable;[3] Susanna is effective as a story largely because

1.   Bal, *Lethal Love*, p. 21; see *idem, Narratology: Introduction to the Theory of Narrative* (Toronto: University of Toronto Press, 1985) for a detailed presentation of her approach.

2.   The framework of the narrative describes the elders as evil (v. 5); this 'external' view of the elders suggests a limit to the validity of their vision. However, as the story progresses, what they see shapes what the reader 'sees'. See Bal, *Narratology*, pp. 110-14 for a discussion of 'levels of focalization'. In Susanna, the narrator and reader 'look over the shoulders' of the elders as they gaze at Susanna.

3.   'The critical reaction to any given text is hermeneutically bound to another and preexistent text: the *doxa* of socialities: Plausibility then is an effect of reading through a grid of concordance' (N.K. Miller, 'Emphasis Added: Plots and Plausibilities in Women's Fiction', *Publications of the Modern Language Association* 96 [1981], pp. 36-48).

its codes for gender accord with wider societal expectations
about femininity in the ancient Mediterranean world and among
readers today. I begin with an analysis of the text that highlights the ways in which the story invites readers to look at
Susanna and so unveil certain problematic assumptions of the
ideology it expresses.

Joachim is the first character introduced to the reader; in the
initial verses we learn that he has taken a wife, is very wealthy,
and has a garden bordering his house (vv. 1-4). His wife
Susanna is very beautiful and fears the Lord, since her parents
have raised her according to the law of Moses (vv. 2-3). This
description enhances Joachim's prestige; his wealth and power
are epitomized by his possession of such a wife and such a
garden. As the account progresses, wife and garden function as
interchangeable metonyms for Joachim's household. What is at
stake in the story is not Susanna's physical well-being as she is
threatened with rape and death but the honor of Joachim's
household. When garden and wife are closed against intruders,
Joachim's honor is secure. When the garden is open to intruders, or if the wife is open to a young lover, the entire household
is ashamed, its honor lost.[1] Even the household slaves are terribly ashamed when they hear the elders' accusations against
Susanna (v. 27). The tale suitably closes with Susanna's parents
and husband rejoicing, not because Susanna is going to live, but
because she is innocent of disgracing the household (v. 63). This
ending also vindicates Susanna's father Hilkiah and his wife.
Because the ancient economy of gender views a daughter as a
unit of exchange between father and husband, Hilkiah's reputation as a purveyor of pure goods is preserved.

Each midday Susanna enters her husband's garden and walks
in it (v. 7). The story reports this daily event, and then we
learn: 'The two elders used to look at her each day entering
and walking and they desired her' (v. 8). The habitual event

---

1.   M.J. Giovanni ('Woman: A Dominant Symbol within the Cultural
System of a Sicilian Town', *Man* 16 [1981], pp. 408-26) analyzes six types of
women, for example virgins and wives, as symbols of the health and well-
being of households in a contemporary Mediterranean culture. A household's prestige is inextricably linked with its ability to protect its women
from the sexual advances of outsiders.

only becomes relevant for the story when Susanna has become an object of perception; she is not important as the subject of an action but as the object of others' gaze. From this point, the story is focused on the mechanics of the gaze: who sees whom, who controls the gaze, determines the outcome of the story. The consistent and exclusive object of the gaze is Susanna, thus presenting femininity as 'to-be-looked-at-ness'.[1] Together, the elders are the subject of the gaze, because the activity of looking is a privilege of masculinity. M. Miles writes about the tradition depicting Susanna in Western religious art:

> These paintings attempt to reproduce, in the eyes of an assumed male viewer, the Elders' intense erotic attraction, projected and displayed on Susanna's flesh. The Elders, placed in crepuscular shadows, do not bear the weight of communicating the urgency of their active desire; rather, her body represents that desire. Viewers are directed—trained—by the management of lights and shadows and by the central position of Susanna's body to see Susanna as object, even as cause, of male desire. In the paintings Susanna's innocence becomes guilt as her body communicates and explains the Elders' lust.[2]

This process has already begun in the story itself as it emphasizes the elders' ongoing surveillance of Susanna.

The elders' desire causes them to abandon righteousness. Although Susanna is virtuous, she is implicated in their guilt; as

---

1. The representation of femininity rests on this assumption in the narrative of Susanna. Woman as spectacle functions in an analogous fashion in film. 'The apparatus of looks converging on the female figure integrates voyeurism into the conventions of storytelling, combining a direct solicitation of the scopic drive with the demands of plot, conflict, climax and resolution. The woman is framed by the look of the camera as an icon, an image, the object of the gaze, and thus, precisely, spectacle...It is the male protagonist, the "bearer" of the spectator's look, who also controls the events of the narrative, moving the plot forward...In this manner, both visually and narratively, cinema defines woman as image: as spectacle to be looked at and object to be desired, investigated, pursued, controlled, and ultimately possessed by a subject who is masculine, that is symbolically male' (de Lauretis, *Technologies*, p. 99).

2. M. Miles, *Carnal Knowing: Female Nakedness and Religious Meaning in the Christian West* (Boston: Beacon Press, 1989), p. 123. Miles's brief analysis of the narrative of Susanna is one of the most insightful commentaries on this work that I have read.

Daniel charges, her beauty beguiles and cheats them (v. 56). To see a beautiful woman is to desire her. The woman is reduced to object, and a guilty object at that. When the elders see, they metaphorically avert their eyes from heaven (v. 9). Does looking at a beautiful woman render a man unfit to look at heaven? At first the elders keep their desire to themselves and do not confide even in each other. Independently of one another, they substitute for seeking after the things of God a sensual seeking of Susanna: 'And they zealously watched every day to catch sight of her'. The reiteration of verbs of perception (*paratereo* and *horao*) suggests the centrality of the gaze to the progress of the story. When the elders catch each other in the act of spying on Susanna, they confess their desire to each other and begin to conspire against her. That is, they zealously keep watch on her together.

The conspiracy succeeds; one day, when the elders are hidden in the garden zealously watching (v. 16), Susanna enters the garden with her female servants. The day is hot, and she wants to bathe, so she sends the servants to bring her oil and cosmetics for a bath. She instructs them to close the doors to the garden (v. 17). Susanna protects the garden, her husband's property, as carefully as she protects herself—also her husband's property. The servants leave; the reader is assured that they have indeed shut the doors, exiting by a side door. The wife in the garden seems secure. However, the servants fail to see the elders, because they are hidden (v. 18). Who sees whom? The elders see but cannot be seen; hiding guarantees their invisibility and ensures that they will continue to be the subject of the controlling gaze.

> When the servants have departed the elders run to Susanna and say, 'See! The doors of the garden are shut, and no one sees us, and we desire you. Therefore submit to us and be with us. If not, we will testify against you that a young man was with you and because of this you sent your girls away' (vv. 19-21).

Susanna's efforts to close the garden against intruders backfire; she has tried to protect herself and thus Joachim's household by securing the garden doors. The sealed garden instead exacerbates Susanna's vulnerability. The elders recognize that their power in the situation derives from the absence of any third party looking in. No one can challenge their view of events.

Susanna interprets the situation as a choice between two dire alternatives: to submit to the elders, which she believes is a sin against the Lord, or to resist, which will cause the elders to accuse her of the capital crime of adultery (v. 22-23). Susanna chooses what seems to her the virtuous path and cries loudly, halting the rape but almost certainly condemning herself to death. Readers can recognize Susanna's courage and still reject her moral code, which implies that the preservation of women as intact property is more important than the preservation of women's lives. According to this ideology Susanna's choice preserves the real (though not the perceived) integrity of Joachim's household; she will remain unpenetrated by any other men. As the slaves run to the garden, one of the elders throws open the garden door so that he can claim that Susanna's lover has just escaped (v. 25). Susanna has secured herself, but the open garden door causes Joachim's household and the Jewish community to see things in a different light. The gendered polarity of the gaze—in which looking represents masculinity and 'to-be-looked-at-ness' represents femininity—continues to shape the final scene, the trial first of Susanna and then of the elders. The court convenes at Joachim's house. The elders send for Susanna who enters surrounded by her parents, children, and all her kinfolk. The narrator informs the readers that Susanna was extremely delicate and beautiful in form, and then says that the lawless ones demand that Susanna be unveiled so that they might again be filled by her beauty (vv. 31-32). The elders thus continue their voyeurism with impunity. Through her tears, Susanna looks up at heaven (v. 35). The elders ceased looking to heaven when they began to look at Susanna; Susanna now turns her eyes to heaven, which precludes the possibility that she might return their gaze or challenge their vision.

The false testimony of the elders rests on what they claim to have seen. Since there are two witnesses, their testimony is sufficient to convict Susanna. The elders claim to have seen lawlessness; they claim to have seen Susanna fornicating with a young lover who then escaped through the garden door, leaving it open (vv. 38-39). When no one contests their vision the court sentences Susanna to death. Daniel's cross-examination, however, challenges the verisimilitude of their vision. When he separates the two and questions them individually on what they have seen, each locates the events they claim to have seen under a different tree. The court understands that their disagreement about the geography of the garden indicates a lie about the character of Susanna. They have not truly seen the garden; the vision they report concerning Susanna is equally deceptive. The narrator never reports that Daniel looks at Susanna. Daniel restores Susanna's reputation as an upright matron, but looking at Susanna has known dangers; although the elders are consistently depicted as wicked, the story has also suggested that Susanna's beauty ensnared them (v. 56). Daniel controls the gaze of the story by proving the elders' vision false, but he resists the temptation of looking at the lovely Susanna himself. The gendered gaze thus propels the narrative of Susanna; it also reinforces readers' expectations concerning masculinity and femininity. Men and their concerns dominate Susanna's story. After all, it is Joachim's household which is disrupted and restored, the elders who see Susanna and 'naturally' try to have her (i.e. rape her), Daniel who takes control of the situation, challenges the elders' vision, and finally vindicates the reputation of Joachim's household. As a technique of storytelling, the emphasis on the gaze is successful because it engages readers' experiences of seeing, and being seen. Let us focus for a moment on what it means for the story of Susanna to invite readers to share the elders' voyeuristic gaze. Scholars have noted the success of this storytelling technique. C.A. Moore notes:

> The bathing scene not only excited the elders, thereby enabling them to attempt their dastardly deed, but it can also fire the imagination of some readers. Of such considerations are good stories made![1]

In a similar vein, R. Dunn suggests:

> The statement of the judges [to Daniel], 'Come, sit down among us, and show it us...' invites the reader to consider whether his own responses to the descriptions of Susanna's beauty have been

---

1.   C.A. Moore, *Daniel, Esther and Jeremiah: The Additions* (AB; Garden City, NY: Doubleday, 1977), p. 97.

purely moral and disinterested. Or perhaps he has also felt something of the elders' desire in the detailed description of their voyeurism.[1]

Because the elders' gaze consistently shapes the story's perspective, the reader may participate in their voyeurism.[2] Indeed, scholars explicitly note the sharing of visual pleasure via readers' fantasy as a component of the pleasure derived from reading this text. The story's emphasis on masculine perception of feminine beauty as a device to explain motivation and plot remains a successful storytelling convention because modern readers still recognize the codes that posit looking and being looked at as gendered activities. However, whether the invited voyeurism is pleasurable for the reader may hinge at least partially on whether the reader is male or female.

Susanna's brave opposition to the elders continues to earn her the epithet 'virtuous' from modern critics. What is at stake in focusing on Susanna's virtue? If she had submitted to the elders in order to preserve her life, would modern readers consider her less virtuous? The elders are not seducing Susanna; they are not coaxing her to act on her own desire. They use coercion, backed by the threat of execution on a disgraceful capital offense, to try to force her to submit. Despite this, scholars regularly refer to the incident as an attempted seduction. The elders are not rapists but would-be 'suitors'.[3] The escapade is likened to a 'mid-life crisis'.[4] The so-called seduction fails when 'Susanna refuses the offer'.[5]

1. R. Dunn, 'Discriminations in the Comic Spirit in the Story of Susanna', *Christianity and Literature* 31 (1981–81), pp. 19-31.

2. 'Traditionally, the woman displayed has functioned on two levels: as erotic object for the characters within the screen story, and as erotic object for the spectator within the auditorium, with a shifting tension between the looks on either side of the screen. For instance, the device of the show-girl allows the two looks to be unified technically' (Mulvey, 'Visual Pleasure', pp. 11-12).

3. A. Lacocque, *The Feminine Unconventional: Four Subversive Figures in Israel's Tradition* (Minneapolis: Fortress Press, 1990), p. 22.

4. Dunn, 'Discriminations', p. 24.

5. M.P. Carroll, 'Myth, Methodology and Transformation in the Old Testament: The Stories of Esther, Judith, and Susanna', *SR* 12 (1983), pp. 301-12, esp. p. 307.

Why do critics rely on the category of seduction rather than rape when they refer to the elders' actions? The most important factor is that, as we have seen, the narrative of Susanna relies on a code that represents femininity in terms of 'to-be-looked-at-ness'; this code is often used to excuse men from responsibility for their actions since woman's beauty is considered the cause of men's lust. When we turn to the secondary literature on Susanna we find this hypothesis confirmed. One critic notes, 'What these details [about Susanna bathing in the garden] suggest is that the old judges have a reason for responding to Susanna the way they do, for she is shown as especially lovely'.[1] According to this view, when the elders gaze on Susanna, her beauty seduces them. Thus, when scholars refer to the bathing scene as culminating in a seduction rather than a rape, we may wonder who is seducing whom: are the elders trying to seduce Susanna or has she already seduced them? Critics who willingly adopt the elders' voyeuristic gaze are likely to consider the scene as one of courtship and seduction rather than one of force and rape. Although the code that defines looking as masculine and being looked at as feminine has been largely responsible for leading critics to read this as a story of seduction, a few other factors are also relevant. To avoid repeating the text's treatment of Susanna as passive object we must take seriously her words as the elders assault her: 'If I do this, it is my death. If I do not do this, I will not escape your hands. It is better for me not to do this and so fall into your hands than to sin before the Lord' (vv. 22-23). Susanna does not suggest that she expects God to rescue her. Her stance is courageous; she risks death to remain morally pure. My recognition of Susanna's bravery does not imply that I agree with her moral judgment. I question Susanna's assertion—and thus the ideological stance of the text—that acting to preserve her life would be a sin against the Lord, since an implicit premise of her statement is that any rape victim is by definition guilty. I also question other readers' responses to her words; even in Susanna's exposition of her choices the event is not presented as a seduction. Whatever decision Susanna makes leaves her in the hands of the elders.

---

1.   Dunn, 'Discriminations', p. 25.

The terms in which she frames her alternatives indicate that she perceives herself to have no real choice; the elders' power over her is presented as an inescapable fact of the situation.

Israelite law on perjury stated that whoever registered a false accusation was to receive the punishment he or she had attempted to inflict on another. Thus, the court sentences the elders to death because they had tried to guarantee Susanna's execution (vv. 61-62). For some readers this seems to be a final contributing factor in the designation of the incident as a seduction. While the text indicates that the punishment intended for Susanna is parallel to the punishment the elders receive, some readers infer that the crime of which Susanna is accused—adultery—is therefore parallel to the crime of which the elders are guilty: 'Two Jewish elders attempt to force her [Susanna] to commit adultery. Unsuccessful, they accuse her of their own crime'.[1] In fact, the elders are guilty of attempted rape against Susanna whom they charge with adultery. The crimes are different; only from the perspective of a husband whose primary concern is whether his property (i.e. his wife) has been damaged could they be considered even equivalent.

To conclude our discussion of the difference between seduction and rape, let us briefly consider Daniel's address to the elders. He says, 'Thus you [pl.] used to do to the daughters of Israel, and they, who were afraid, had sexual relations with you, but a daughter of Judah resisted your lawlessness' (v. 57). An allusion to another story is embedded in Susanna's narrative, a fiction within a fiction. What story can we imagine to make sense of Daniel's accusation? The shadowy women who previously submitted to the elders did so out of fear. Again, this untold story embedded in a fuller narrative limns the elders as men who achieve their sexual ends not by playing on women's desire, which is seduction, but by exploiting their fear, which we must learn to recognize as rape.

Representation of gender in the story of Susanna rests on the gendered polarity of the gaze; actively looking defines masculinity and 'to-be-looked-at-ness' defines femininity. Modern readers still share this ancient code; I suggest that identification with

---

1. Lacocque, *Feminine Unconventional*, p. 21.

the masculine gaze has been a factor in seducing most critics into classifying the elders' crime as adultery rather than rape. Do all readers identify with the masculine gaze? More specifically, are women readers likely to share the pleasure of the elders' voyeurism?[1] Women readers respond to the same textual codes that elicit men's responses, and so women readers also share the elders' gaze as they attempt to possess Susanna. If women readers did not participate in this code, the story would simply not make sense to us. At the same time, though, most women have had the experience of being the unwilling object of a man's gaze;[2] for many women, being the object of such a gaze is an experience linked to sexual harassment, coercion and rape. Still more women experience incidents in which a casual stroll turns unpleasant or threatening because of the unwanted leers of men encountered. I propose that many modern women readers of Susanna find themselves in the complex and uncomfortable position of identifying at least as much with the object of the controlling gaze as with the voyeuristic elders.[3] The complexity of such response calls into question any monolithic reading of the narrative of Susanna. In its contradictory assumptions, such a response also reveals the limitations of an understanding of gender that relies on an equation of masculinity with activity and femininity with passivity.[4]

1.   I would like to avoid the reductionist idea that men read one way and women another way. Some women may permit the masculine gaze to shape their perceptions entirely, while some men may resist having their perceptions controlled by the masculine gaze. My purpose in considering the responses of women readers to this narrative is to open up the question of the multiplicity of readings and the intersection of readers' codes with the text's codes.

2.   Naturally, a man can be the object of a woman's gaze; a woman can be the object of another woman's gaze, or a man of another man's gaze. What I am emphasizing here is the case that has come to be an important part of the gender code: man as voyeur, woman as object of voyeurism.

3.   See the discussion of Mulvey and de Lauretis in Doane, *Desire*, pp. 6-8. How does one account for women's pleasure as spectators of film, or readers of such literature as Susanna? Simultaneous or oscillating identification with both the masculine gaze and the feminine as image is a major component of such pleasure.

4.   'The analogy that links identification-with-the-look to masculinity

Ultimately, identification with a character depicted solely as an object is difficult to sustain.[1] When I began to read the narrative of Susanna, I wanted to agree with C.A. Moore, who proclaims 'Daniel is not the hero of the Susanna story: Susanna is!'[2] However, the mechanisms of gender representation render the character of Susanna almost entirely as object. Susanna's vision never shapes the story; the reader is never invited to share her perspective (although, as I have suggested, many women will inevitably imagine what it is like to be in her predicament). Perhaps more frustrating, Susanna never recounts her own version of events. She speaks, but does not tell her story: not to her husband, her parents, her children, her slaves or the court. The court convicts the elders of perjury, and the extent of their transgression is implied, but the court never hears an account of what actually transpired. The narrator thus minimizes the subjective role of Susanna who finally disappears from the action. Susanna is the symbol of the integrity of Joachim's household, the object of the elders' desire, and the vehicle of Daniel's rise to prominence, but she does not emerge as a subject in her own right.

On the level of the plot, however, Susanna does act decisively twice. Her loud cry in the garden thwarts the elders' attempt to rape her. As the story has been unfolding, the reader follows the elders' gaze as they try to trap Susanna; hence, Susanna's brave resistance to their attack is unanticipated. When Susanna explains her reasons for withstanding the elders' coercive advances, the icon speaks. While readers may disagree with her assessment of the situation (yielding to force does not impute guilt to the victim), Susanna demonstrates an ability to analyze her situation and to act accordingly. At the trial Susanna's cry to

and identification-with-the-image to femininity breaks down precisely when we think of a spectator alternating between the two, as is inevitable' (de Lauretis, *Alice*, pp. 142-43).

1.   'How can the female spectator be entertained as subject of the very movement that places her as object, that makes her the figure of its own closure...No one can really *see* oneself as an inert object or a sightless body; neither can one see oneself *altogether* as other. One has an ego, after all, even when one is a woman' (de Lauretis, *Alice*, p. 141).

2.   Moore, *Daniel*, pp. 90-91.

302 A Feminist Companion to Esther, Judith and Susanna

heaven prompts God to stir Daniel to her defense. Susanna is at least indirectly the agent of her own deliverance. Her prayer, on one level an illustrative manifestation of piety, shapes the direction of the plot. Only at this point, and seemingly for this reason, does God rouse Daniel. Thus, at two crucial points in the plot Susanna's enunciative action shifts the direction of events. She is not only the object of others' actions but also, momentarily, an actor in her own right. However, once Susanna calls out for God's help she drops as an actor from the text. She becomes the pretext for Daniel's ascendancy.

I have primarily been interested in exposing the mechanisms of gender representation at work in the narrative of Susanna and considering how these mechanisms affect the reception of the text. I have argued that the gendered polarity which characterizes 'looking' is a code still familiar to modern readers. Complicity with this code is the major factor that has led contemporary scholars to describe the incident in the garden as a seduction rather than a rape. While the narrative invites readers to assume the elders' position of spectatorship, some readers may find that they also identify with Susanna as she becomes the unwilling object of the gaze. The reactions of women readers are likely to be complex; we identify both with the subject of the gaze and the object of the gaze as we struggle with the question of the (im)possible representation of female characters as subjects. A function of narrative is to make ideology seem inevitable. I hope that by focusing on the mechanisms of gender representation I have shown that texts construct our understanding of gender; as we learn to write other kinds of texts, perhaps we can liberate our understandings of gender as well.[1]

1. Readers may also be interested in the treatment of Susanna in M. Bal, *Reading Rembrandt: Beyond the Word–Image Opposition* (Cambridge: Cambridge University Press, 1991), pp. 138-76, which appeared after I completed work on this article.

'HEMMED IN ON EVERY SIDE':
JEWS AND WOMEN IN THE BOOK OF SUSANNA*

Amy-Jill Levine

I am a Jew. My interest in the origins of Christianity began
when a neighbor accused me of 'killing her Lord'. As far as I
knew, I hadn't killed anyone, so I told her she was wrong. 'My
priest said so', she replied. I knew priests didn't lie: if they did
their special collars would choke them. I was seven years old,
and I was very confused.

I am a woman. My awakening to what was only later labeled
feminist consciousness occurred when my father died. I accompanied my mother to say Kaddish, and the men of my synagogue would not (initially) count either of us for the *minyan*. I
was thirteen, and I was furious.

I am a student of religion. When I entered college, I naively
believed that if I could understand the scriptural origins of anti-
Semitism, I might help eliminate its modern recrudescence.
Moreover, if I could understand how the canon marginalizes
women and how women's history might be reconstructed, I
could aid in countering sexism. I was eighteen, and I was
optimistic.

I am a professor of religion. Twice as old now as when I
began my formal studies of Scripture, I am still angry, still confused, but much less optimistic. I have seen how many of my
teachers and colleagues in ostensibly secular settings interpreted
the psalms and the prophets through ecclesiastical lenses; how
the rabbis read these same texts was not often noted, and how
the texts might be interpreted in light of their own time period
alone was seen as insufficient. The TaNaK had become the Old

* Reprinted, by permission, from F. Segovia and M.A. Tolbert (eds.),
Reading from this Place (Fortress Press, forthcoming).

Testament. And I have encountered many feminist Christians who found the assertion that Jesus liberated women 'to' their full potential insufficient for both lectern and pulpit. They then claimed—either explicitly or implicitly—that Jesus liberated women 'from' something, and that something was inevitably the repressive, patriarchal Jewish system. The perspective of the academy, although beginning to change, remains male and Christian, as well as white, Western and heterosexual.

Subtle forms of disenfranchisement continue to afflict all those outside the dominant group. For example, the Vanderbilt proposal,[1] although it speaks of 'Jews and Christians', suggests that:

> by using interpretations of the Bible as the basis for reflection on social location, a common text, read and studied by many diverse groups in many diverse ways, can be employed as the center of discourse, for while we may say many different things about the Bible, we are at least speaking about the same, publicly recognized text. All of these different voices, in one way or another, continue to look to the Bible for support and authority (p. 3).

Nowhere does the proposal define 'Bible', but the underlying presupposition is that the reference is to the Bible of the church, not the Bible of the synagogue. The talk of pluralism is a pluralism on Christian terms, and the public is the Christian one.

Yet Jews today often find that their own perceptions of marginalization are disregarded, attributed to paranoia, or seen as special pleading. 'You are part of the establishment', we are told. 'You are the oppressor, not the oppressed.' Worse, we hear, 'You are the occasion for your own oppression'. Anti-Semitism remains, in many circles, a political bonus rather than a liability. I am writing these words while, in Philadelphia, signs from the 'Lost-Found Nation of Islam' line the streets; they ask: 'Are the Jews Hiding the Truth?' The stereotypes continue: of Jewish-American princesses, of wealthy, lustful, (im)potent businessmen, of covert political machinations, of clannishness, of Zionist racist conspirators...Worse still, many within the Jewish community internalize these concerns and so fulfill the

---

1. The grant that sponsored the collection of essays from which this essay is reprinted.

expectations of their Gentile associates. Jewish men tell JAP[1] jokes and so attempt to integrate into Gentile society by distancing themselves from Jewish women, and Jewish women (and men) submit to rhinoplasty to conform to a WASP ideal. While Jewish identification remains strong, Jewish identity has been compromised by acculturation, assimilation and ignorance of our own history and literature.

Thus I come to my project, which concerns the depiction of Jewish women in Hellenistic narratives. At first, my interest was in the reclamation of that which had been neglected on the *bima* and at the lectern. I desired both to remedy this lack and to contribute to a rethinking of the history of Jews, both male and female, and of the history of women, both Christian and Jewish. That these texts have been ignored is no surprise. One might claim that Pseudepigrapha such as *The Marriage and Conversion of Aseneth (Joseph and Aseneth)* or the *Testament of Job* have been under-represented because of their absence from modern religious canons and the (resulting) lack of manuscript availability. For the Apocrypha, however, the problem is more complex. In part, the relevant texts fail to address the academy's disciplinary desiderata. In biblical studies, theology has been privileged over narrative, canon over deuterocanonical texts (and so, consequently, Protestant concerns over Catholic), history over fiction. The narrative portions of the Apocrypha—Judith, Tobit, the Additions to Esther, the story of the Maccabean widow and her seven sons, the tale of Susanna—were rarely adduced in general, let alone for a study of women's history.

Here in the Greek texts, I thought, I could find female protagonists, worthy men, righteous behavior, and models of uncompromised diaspora existence. 'Susanna and the Elders' seemed a gem in miniature: 64 verses depicting a righteous Jewish woman, the wisdom of Jewish youth, and an autonomous community unaffected by its Babylonian setting. But the Jewish men and Jewish women of Hellenistic narratives, like their biblical predecessors, are rarely ideal figures: they are morally ambiguous; not always clearly motivated; torn between divine and secular interests. As individual characters,

---

1. 'Jewish American Princess'.

metonymies of the community, or representatives for the deity, they continue to thwart the optimistic hopes of those seeking access to the history of Jewish women and their communities.

The reading of the character of Susanna in the modern academy and ecclesia is unequivocally positive: she 'is cast in the role of the righteous one, condemned to death because of her obedience to God'.[1] Descriptions of her social setting, however, while generally positivisitic are less positive. Some offer theological correctives to perceived social inequities: 'In societies where a woman's word isn't worth much, the story says that God pays attention to the powerless, so the community should also'.[2] Others address the extent of Jewish patriarchy: 'Susanna also reflects the isolation of upper-class Jewish women in post-biblical times through virtual confinement to the home and the use of the veil in public'.[3]

This distinction between Susanna, constructed as admirable, and her setting, constructed as repressive, dates to early Christian exegesis. Patristic writers viewed the lecherous elders as the twin threats of Judaism and paganism against Susanna the Mother Church. More recent commentaries parallel Susanna with the Christ of Mt. 27.24;[4] the connection of the elders to the rabid Jerusalem crowd of the Matthean passion is unstated, but undeniable. Origen and Hippolytus even accused the Jews of

---

1.   G.W.E. Nickelsburg (*Jewish Literature between the Bible and the Mishnah* [Philadelphia: Fortress Press, 1981], p. 25; *idem*, 'Stories of Biblical and Early Post-Biblical Times', in M.E. Stone [ed.], *Jewish Writings of the Second Temple Period* [CRINT, 11; Assen: Van Gorcum, 1984], p. 38) equates her story with the persecution and vindication of the righteous in, for example, Gen. 34, Esther, Ahikar and Wis. 2–5. See also C.A. Moore, *Daniel, Esther and Jeremiah: The Additions* (AB, 44; Garden City, NY: Doubleday, 1977), pp. 8-9; J.C. Dancey, *Shorter Books of the Apocrypha* (Cambridge Bible Commentary; Cambridge: Cambridge University Press, 1972), p. 224.

2.   C.A. Moore, 'Susanna', *Bible Review* 8.3 (June 1992), p. 52.

3.   D.W. Suter, 'Susanna', *Harper's Bible Dictionary* (San Francisco: Harper & Row, 1985), p. 1001. The Apocryphon indicates neither isolation nor restriction. Rather, Susanna has a substantial entourage (Sus. 30, Θ). She is also, unlike Tobit's Sarah, apparently on good terms with her servants (Sus. 27).

4.   W.H. Daubney, *The Three Additions to Daniel* (Cambridge: Deighton, Bell, 1906), p. 161.

deliberately removing Susanna from their Scriptures because of its negative portrayal of the community's leaders.[1] Continuing in this tradition, D.M. Kay concludes that 'the story would not be popular with elders, and it was elders who fixed the canon. Susanna was useless for the polemical purposes of Judaism.'[2]

But Susanna's sex and class impede any unambiguous reading of her character as a paradigm of righteousness or her setting as the epitome of patriarchy. Susanna, as character and as text, carries possibilities for condemnation as well as praise, for the

1.   Susanna is absent from the Dead Sea Scrolls, the works of Josephus and, except perhaps in vastly different formulation, the rabbinic texts. See R. Pfeiffer, *History of New Testament Times with an Introduction to the Apocrypha* (New York: Harper & Brothers, 1949), p. 443; E.J. Bickermann, *The Jews in the Greek Age* (Cambridge, MA: Harvard University Press, 1988), p. 95; A. LaCocque, *The Feminine Unconventional: Four Subversive Figures in Israel's Tradition* (Minneapolis: Fortress Press, 1990), p. 28. Origen also mentions a Jewish informant who added the following charming detail about the elders: they were in the habit of approaching respectable women and telling them that God had given them the power of fathering the messiah, and by this means they were able to seduce. See N. DeLange, *Apocrypha: Jewish Literature of the Hellenistic Age* (New York: Viking, 1978), p. 129; for further discussion of this motif see Bickermann, *Jews in the Greek Age*, p. 94.

2.   'Susanna', in R.H. Charles (ed.), *Apocrypha and Pseudepigrapha of the Old Testament* (Oxford: Clarendon Press, 1913), I, p. 642; also cited by LaCocque, *Feminine Unconventional*, p. 28. Kay does not consider the 'elders' who fixed the canon of the church. Moore (*Additions*, p. 80 [cf. p. 109]) suggests, conversely, that 'the story of Susanna was ultimately, and rightly, regarded by the Jews as a very unsuitable introduction to the materials in the canonical Daniel. Not only is the background of the Susanna story basically different from that of Daniel 1–6, but in "Susanna" Daniel himself is poorly presented.' By applauding the good taste of the Jews, Moore implies that the church, which canonized this text, lacked aesthetic sensibility. Consideration of canonical status thus descends into ironic triumphalism. While the canonical placement of the narrative varies—the LXX and Old Latin have Susanna as the preface to the book of Daniel; the Vulgate makes it ch. 13; in the Jacobite Syriac it is placed with Judith, Ruth and Esther—the book itself complements the Daniel tradition and therefore is not inappropriately included within the canon. Debates on canonicity might be better placed in the context of language and date rather than content, as Julius Africanus recognized in his letter on Susanna to Origen and as Porphyry (quoted by Jerome) also noted. See Pfeiffer, *History*, pp. 442 and 443 n. 10.

recognition of women's social and religious freedom as well as
their confinement, for the discovery of how Judaism survived
challenges to its self-definition as well as the compromises it
made in this process.

Nor is the reader in an unambiguous position. As Mieke Bal
comments: 'Although the unveiling is condemned, the visual
feast is promised by the same token. Perniciously, the moral
dimension of the tale absorbs the pornographic one and provides the innocent reader with an excuse to anticipate the pleasure sanctioned rather than countered by the moral
indignation.'[1] The text situates its readers as both accomplice
and victim; the narrative renders us voyeurs, looking on with
the elders at the naked Susanna at her bath and at her trial.
Like Susanna, we cannot leave the garden without shame. Our
task is to read without having the interpretation of social setting
bleed over into anti-Semitism, the critique of the title character
succumb to sexism, or the analysis of the narrative descend into
pornography.

My own social location raises the questions of Jewish history
and women's history, and it sensitizes me to the dangers of
viewing either as less than ideal. At the same time, it gives me a
privilege less readily available to my Gentile and male colleagues:
committed to both feminism and Judaism, I am less likely to be
charged with sexism or anti-Semitism should I point out less-
than-ideal aspects of the subject matter. The death of objective
history brings with it an inevitable but no less problematic privileging of some perspectives over others: those previously on the
margins now appear to inhabit the moral high ground. A criticism of a liberation-theological reading, for example, is apt to be
viewed as a sign of the troglodyte. To be unconvinced is to be
unsympathetic. But the true task of global interpretation means
to me not merely the recognition of other perspectives, interests
and readings; it seeks a critical awareness of the problems as
well as the benefits of such exercises.

Awareness of my own marginalized setting and the means by
which I negotiate the twin tasks of self-affirmation and intercul-
tural contact leads directly to my appreciation of Hellenistic

1. M. Bal, *Reading Rembrandt: Beyond the Word–Image Opposition*
(Cambridge: Cambridge University Press, 1991), p. 155.

Judaism. Like any product of a community facing the threats occasioned by diaspora and colonialism, the ancient texts indicate the mechanisms by which such groups achieve self-identity. Specifically, they address ethnic pride, personal piety and class structure. And they locate their discussions, subtly but inexorably, on the bodies of women.

The conquest of the Near East by Alexander the Great in the fourth century BCE created a crisis for the Jewish population: Greek began to replace Hebrew as the language of Scripture and Aramaic as the language of trade. Biblical motifs, especially gender-coded ones, were then adapted to respond to such challenges to ethos and ethnos. The covenant community had traditionally represented itself as a woman: virgins (2 Kgs 19.12//Isa. 37.22; Lam. 1.15; 2.13; Jer. 14.17); brides (Jer. 2.2-3; Hos. 2.15b); whores (Hos. 1–4; Ezek. 16); and widows (Lam. 1.1; Isa. 54.4-8). The fracturing of the political unity is embodied by accounts of rape (Gen. 34; 2 Sam. 13).[1] In the so-called deuterocanonical materials, women continue to represent the covenant community, but Susanna, Judith, the various women of Tobit, and their sisters, have more completely drawn personalities. This change is more than a formalistic move from metaphor to character or prophecy to narrative; the shift in representation appears to be the means by which the Jews, suddenly finding themselves part of an alien empire, worked through their disorientation and the threat to cultural cohesion.

Both to represent and to counter the challenge to communal self-identity, the Hellenistic texts employ three dominant motifs. First, women's bodies, like the community itself, become the surface upon which are inscribed the struggles between the adorned and the stripped, the safe and the endangered, the inviolate and the penetrated. As Susan R. Suleiman observes: 'The cultural significance of the female body is not only (not even first and foremost) that of a flesh-and-blood entity, but of a symbolic construct'.[2] Next, the women's husbands are depicted as inept, impaired, or simply stupid. Finally, the

---

1. I thank Alice Keefe for calling my attention to this implication of the rape narratives.

2. S.R. Suleiman, 'Introduction', in *idem* (ed.), *The Female Body in Western Culture* (Cambridge, MA: Harvard University Press, 1986), p. 2.

muddying of borders, both of body and society, is expressed through an emphasis on boundary-transgressive events: a focus on eating, defecating, burial and sexual intercourse as well as a confusion between public and private, privileged and marginalized. The women characters in particular are, consequently, not primarily (if at all) windows into an anterior social world; rather, they are literary tropes. They tell us less about the lives of real women than about the social construction of 'woman' by a particular community at a particular time. The women of the Apocrypha and Pseudepigrapha are the screen on which the fears of the (male) community—of impotence, assimilation, loss of structure—can be both displayed and, at least temporarily, allayed.

That women's bodies are threatened in ancient literature is hardly news to students of the TaNaK. However, unlike their counterparts in Genesis and the Deuteronomic history, the women of the Apocrypha and Pseudepigrapha retain both physical and moral integrity in the face of foreign or domestic foes. Esther makes clear only in the Additions her rejection of her doltish husband's culture: 'I abhor the bed of the uncircumcised and of any alien...I have not honored the king's feast or drunk the wine of any libation' (14.16). The Maccabean widow 'threw herself on the fire so that no one would touch her body' (4 *Macc.* 17.1). Judith's transformation from pious widow to forward seductress is only illusory; Holofernes, not Judith, loses his head and so his integrity. For Susanna, the enemies are domestic: she is threatened first with rape and then, for refusing to submit, with death by the elders of her own community.[1] Her husband and father fail to protect her or even to come to her defense. Unlike Esther, the widow and Judith, Susanna requires male intervention to resolve the threat; Daniel functions as the deity's proxy. Apparently, when the threat is external, women/the community can act; when the threat is internal—that is, when it threatens the very core of the community—a

---

1.   For very helpful observations on why the attempted rape resists classification as such, see J.A. Glancy, 'The Accused: Susanna and her Readers', in this volume. While Glancy's article and my essay were written independently and reflect different methodological interests, they reach similar conclusions.

man, or, more precisely, the deity whom the man represents, must preserve the existence of the male-defined community and must reinstate its honor. Although she speaks, Susanna is not (first and foremost) subject, she is object. And she is abject.

Susanna is a projection of the threatened covenant community. Part of the diaspora whose (b)orders have been shattered, she faces the temptation to lose self-integrity, self-respect and self: to submit is to be raped; to refuse will likely lead to a death sentence. Not only is she threatened, she is also threatening, as her iconographic reception (with the notable exception of the work of Artemisia Gentileschi[1]) has suggested. No inexperienced child, she is a married woman with children of her own and with a husband occupied by affairs of state. Like Judith, her potential for illicit sex is clear. And this potential, this threat, is underscored by her story's setting, its intertextual references, and its forcing the reader into the voyeuristic role.

Although set in the Babylonian diaspora, the book of Susanna does not depict a lamenting community. The Jews possess wealth, autonomous governance, even the power of capital punishment.[2] They are comfortable, and the most comfortable of all is the wife of the wealthy Joachim. His home is the locus of communal administration, and thus he is, by implication, the wealthiest and most socially prominent Jew in Babylon. But this economic situation is one less admired than critiqued. And the critique comes in the form of a woman.

Initially, Susanna's description is entirely admirable: she is well married, very beautiful, pious and educated: 'Her parents were righteous, and had taught their daughter according to the Law of Moses' (Sus. 3). And she participates in the lifestyle that accompanies such a social situation: free from domestic, juridical and religious responsibilities, her one independent daily action is to walk in her husband's garden. However, the setting is redolent with negative or at best ambivalent references. First, Susanna represents unencumbered luxury: her walks occur in counterpoint to the lawsuits argued in her husband's house.

1. Cf. Mieke Bal's article in this volume.
2. Bickermann, *Jews in the Greek Age*, pp. 49-50, offers historical parallels but appropriately questions 'how far the author was describing the institutions of his time and how much he was simply inventing' (p. 96).

Secondly, although her Babylonian setting is emphasized in the first verse, neither she nor her family is suffering in exile. Rather than lamenting by the waters of Babylon, she bathes in them. Few could identify with her in terms of status.[1] Representing the threatened covenant community, she is already a warning to those who would enjoy social privileges in foreign settings: no garden is safe.

For the Apocrypha and Pseudepigrapha, communal integrity is located genealogically rather than geographically; the endogamous family, even if displaced, is the principal source of cultural cohesion.[2] Yet the family is continually at risk. And women, who define the borders of families and communities, are the source of that instability. According to Theodotion's version (Θ), Susanna's parents, children and relatives are at the trial; the LXX mentions her parents and four children.[3] But her husband is absent.[4] Susanna's public shame is his shame,[5] and his shame is

---

1.   Later versions of the story reinforce the status differential. The Samaritan text makes her the daughter of the high priest Amran. According to the Chronicles of Jerahmeel, she is the daughter of Shealtiel (cf. Ezra 3, 8) and the sister of Zerubbabel. Her husband becomes identified with the Judean King Jehoiachin, which then makes Susanna the bride of her grandfather (but cf. Lev. 18.10). See M. Wurmbrand, 'A Falasha Version of the Story of Susanna', *Bib* 44 (1963), pp. 34-36.

2.   A.-J. Levine, 'Diaspora as Metaphor: Bodies and Boundaries in the Book of Tobit', in J.A. Overman and R.S. MacLennan (eds.), *Diaspora Jews and Judaism* (Atlanta: Scholars Press, 1992), pp. 105-17.

3.   Theodotion (Θ) underlies the church's canon and hence modern English translations. The LXX survives in three manuscript traditions: the ninth-century papyrus codex Chisianus 88 rediscovered in 1783; the Ambrosian Syro-Hexaplar from Origen's edition; and the Kölner Papyrus 967 (c. 150 CE). See Moore, *Additions*, p. 33.

4.   Also absent from the trial, and from the text, are other spouses: the wives of the elders; Daniel's wife. Comparable are the absent (dead) husbands of Judith and the Maccabean martyr; the deaths of Sarah's earlier husbands in Tobit; the fractious relationship between Tobit and Anna and between Job and his first wife in the *Testament of Job*; Esther's repulsion of her husband as well as her orphaned status; the war among the sons of Jacob in *Aseneth*, and so on.

5.   M.D. Garrard ('Artemisia and Susanna', in N. Braude and M.D. Garrard [eds.], *Feminism and Art History: Questioning the Litany* [New York: Harper & Row, 1982], p. 152) notes that 'Susanna herself is a

magnified by his failure to act. While the LXX locates the trial at the community synagogue, Theodotion places it at Joachim's house and so magnifies his silence. The flaws in the community leadership extend beyond the elders to Joachim himself. Only upon Susanna's exoneration do 'Hilkiah and his wife praise God for their daughter Susanna, *as did her husband Joachim* and all her relatives, because she was found innocent of any impropriety' (Sus. 63). Failing, however, to acknowledge either Susanna's brave resistance or her religiosity, they appear simply to be thankful that she was not guilty.

Evoking the phenomenon contemporary feminists have labeled 'blaming the victim' is one reading of Susanna 7-8: 'When the people left at noon, Susanna would go into her husband's garden to walk. Every day the two elders used to see her, entering and walking around, and they began to lust after her.' According to Bal, 'the sequence of the two sentences suggests...that it was because Susanna exposed herself unknowingly that they became inflamed'.[1] Victims are not always innocent. While the repeated notices of Susanna's piety and fidelity reinforce her innocence, the references and the character are both compromised by the elders' desires. For the story to function, their desire must be comprehensible to the reader, and thus Susanna must be a figure of desire to us as well. And once we see her as desirable, we are trapped: either we are guilty of lust, or she is guilty of seduction.[2]

---

personification of the good Israelite wife, whose sexuality was her husband's exclusive property, and Susanna's total fidelity to Joachim is demonstrated in her willingness to accept death rather than dishonor him by yielding to the Elders'. Similarly, Glancy: 'I question the implicit narrative promotion of the idea that a virtuous woman prefers death to the dishonor a rape brings to a man's household' (p. 288 above). Yet Susanna's total fidelity is to the law of Israel, not to her husband. Her cry in the garden concerns 'sin' (Sus. 23), not marital honor. Further, his honor is in any case compromised: either his wife is an adulterer, or she is a victim of rape (which he does not stop), or she is brought to trial and humiliated.

1. *Rembrandt*, p. 149.

2. On the question of her 'guilt', see now Glancy, 'The Accused'. Readings informed by lesbian and gay critiques would complicate even more the status of the reader. For example, Susanna must be desirable to women as well as to men. And Daniel, who prefigures and replaces

Multiple intertextual resonances of both the scene of bathing naked in the garden and the trial help to shift the onus from reader to Susanna. The bath, for example, is a known locus of seduction, and its association with Bathsheba is a likely antecedent to Susanna's story. Both women are married, and both have husbands occupied with political responsibilities; both are spied at their baths and then propositioned by the local authority (2 Sam. 11). Whereas Bathsheba submits to David's coercive courting, Susanna opts to take her chances in the divine court. Yet the intertextual connection alerts the reader to the possibility that Susanna, too, might have consented.

Jub. 33.2-9 and *T. Reub.* 3.10–4.1 both employ the trope of the seductive naked bather in their depiction of Bilhah.[1] The former text reads:

> And Reuben saw Bilhah, the attendant of Rachel (and) his father's concubine, washing in the water privately, and he desired her. And hiding at night, he entered Bilhah's house…and he lay with her…And she lamented greatly concerning this matter. And she did not tell anyone at all.

The *Testament* extends the parallel by including a condemnation of the woman herself:

> Do not devote your attention to a woman's looks, nor live with a woman who is already married, nor become involved in affairs with women. For if I had not seen Bilhah bathing in a sheltered place, I would not have fallen into this great lawless act. For so absorbed were my senses by her naked femininity that I was not able to sleep until I had performed this revolting act…Bilhah became drunk and was sound asleep, naked in her bedchamber.

Reuben blames the victim: even before he condemns Bilhah for drunkenness, he has already assigned her the burden of guilt: had she not bathed, had she not been so alluring, he would not have sinned. From this textual perspective, Susanna's ignorance of the elders does not excuse her: as a beautiful woman and

Susanna as the object of desire, must be desirable to men as well as to women.

1.   Noted by R. Doran, 'The Additions to Daniel', *Harper's Bible Commentary* (San Francisco: Harper & Row, 1988), p. 866. *Jubilees* predates Susanna; the date of the *Testaments of the Twelve Patriarchs* remains uncertain.

therefore necessarily an object of desire, she is the occasion for sin.

Finally, the bath as well as Susanna's call for oil and cosmetics may be both compared and contrasted to parallel scenes in Esther and Judith. The former is 'provided with her cosmetic treatments...and with seven chosen maids' (Esth. 2.9) in order to 'go into King Ahasuerus' (Esth. 2.12); the latter bathes and adorns herself in order to conquer Holofernes and so protect her community (Jdt. 10.3). Esther is forced into sexual action; Judith is compelled by her sense of justice; Susanna simply pampers herself. Placed in juxtaposition to the juridical proceedings of the community, her luxuriating is a form of self-delusion: the problems of law and behavior cannot be washed away.

Beyond the bath is a second negative implication of the setting: the garden (παραδέισος). In both classical[1] and biblical writings the garden symbolizes sensuality and seduction. The immediate comparison of Susanna to Eve uncovers much. Both are given impossible choices by cunning, explicitly or implicitly sexual figures. Both naked women come to recognize shame, both are humiliated before the male gaze, both are taken from the garden, both have husbands who fail to display loyalty. Like Eve, Susanna too is forced from her Edenic existence. Once accused of adultery, once displayed to the community, her innocence is lost. So too for women and for diaspora Jews: even when innocent of any crime, the accusations remain and thus do sexism and anti-Semitism prevail. As Susan Kappeler states: 'We also need to challenge the literalism of the argument of fiction experts that the victimization in pornographic representations is only make-believe, and that in fact the women model (usually) gets up unharmed after the photographic session, or does not really exist in the case of literature'.[2]

The intertextual references then move from Eden to the patriarchal sagas, and again, the traditional representation of

1. For example, Achilles Tatius 1.15.1; see R. Pervo, 'Aseneth and her Sisters: Women in Jewish Narrative and in the Greek Novel', in A.-J. Levine (ed.), *'Women Like This': New Perspectives on Jewish Women in the Greco-Roman World* (EJL, 1; Atlanta: Scholars Press, 1991), p. 148 and n. 21.
2. S. Kappeler, *The Pornography of Representation* (Minneapolis: University of Minnesota Press, 1986), pp. 14-15.

Susanna's innocence is compromised. Susanna's antecedents also include the story of Joseph and Potiphar's wife. Both Susanna and Joseph are chaste, beautiful, naked individuals displaced from their homeland. Both are propositioned by people in positions of authority, and both fail to confront their accusers. Both stories depict impotent husbands and leaders, and both require supernaturally inspired knowledge for redemption. Indeed, the story of Susanna deliberately draws from the Genesis text: 'day by day' (Sus. 12//Gen. 39.10); 'sin against the Lord' (Sus. 23//Gen. 39.9); mention of the household (Sus. 26//Gen. 39.14-15); and of a fleeing lover (Sus. 39//Gen. 39.18).[1] However, because Joseph may be assigned some responsibility for his unfortunate position, Susanna suffers guilt by association. A pampered son, a spy, and perhaps even a narcissist, the young man is sold by his jealous brothers into slavery. For those readers who sympathize with the less-loved brothers, Joseph's fate may be met with *Schadenfreude*. Conversely, the lack of closure to Mrs Potiphar's story coupled with her husband's willingness to cede his authority to Joseph serves to mitigate the wife's negative reception.[2]

Joseph, the man, can parlay his connection to heaven for social advancement: he becomes master of Potiphar's house, of the prison and of Egypt; he exacts retribution from his brothers. Susanna, unaccompanied by notices of divine favor, does not become a master by refusing to become a mistress. She is

1.   Nickelsburg, *Jewish Literature*, pp. 26 and 39 n. 19; *idem*, 'Stories', ii, p. 38; and, following Nickelsburg, LaCocque, *Feminine Unconventional*, p. 23. The parallel was noted as early as John Chrysostom, whose Sermon on Susanna asserted that she 'endured a severe fight, more severe than that of Joseph. He, a man, contended with one woman, but Susanna, a woman, had to contend with two men, and was a spectacle to men and to angels' (cited by LaCocque, *Feminine Unconventional*, p. 23).

2.   See discussion in LaCocque, *Feminine Unconventional*, pp. 22-23; Pfeiffer, *History*, p. 453; Stith-Thompson, IV, 480-82 (the Genoveva motif). Pfeiffer suggests that the earliest occurrence of the motif is the story of Tamar and Judah (Gen. 38), yet here actual impropriety does take place: Tamar has sexual intercourse with someone other than her husband or betrothed. Judah exonerates her, and thus his word takes precedence over any external legal system. More comparable is the rabbinic tradition of Beruriah.

dependent on Daniel, who assumes Joseph's positive roles for her: Daniel, like Joseph, is the Jew in the foreign court, the interpreter of dreams, the dispenser of justice.

Susanna may also be compared to the sexually engaged woman of the Song of Songs.[1] Not only are both placed in the context of the fertile lushness of nature, Susanna's name evokes the Song's natural setting: šôšānâ, the lily, is in full bloom (cf. Song 2.1b); she entices us and our response is to deflower her. Her name also creates a later parallel to *Leviticus Rabbah* 19: the account of Nebuchadnezzar's permitting the wife of Joachim to have intercourse with her husband in prison and therefore to continue the Davidic line.[2] But she tells Joachim, כשושנה אדומה ראיתי, 'I have seen something like a red lily' (i.e., I am menstruating), and therefore he does not sleep with her.

Moving to the Ketuvim and beyond to the Apocrypha, one finds Susanna in the company of other sexually problematic women. LaCocque expresses the point as follows:

> Ruth allures Boaz…Esther is wife to a pagan king, Susanna is accused of fornication and adultery, and Judith plays the harlot with Holofernes. The intent of such stories is clear. They want to drive home the idea that women can indeed become God's instruments, even when they use the most controversial resources of their femininity'[3]

But Susanna has no resources, and she does not use her 'femininity' to solve the problem. Conversely, one could argue that LaCocque's comparison of Susanna with the other three explicitly sexually active women, and women involved somehow with Gentiles at that, shows the perceived and received underlying sensuality as well as otherness of her character. Like Judith, Ruth and Esther of the Additions, Susanna of Babylon

---

1. LaCocque, *Feminine Unconventional*, p. 24. The name appears in masculine form in 1 Chron. 2.31, 34, 35; feminine form in 2 Chron. 4.5; Hos. 14.5. In Christian tradition, it is the name of one of the followers of Jesus (Lk. 8.3)—who is apparently unencumbered by domestic ties or responsibilities.

2. N. Bruell, 'Das apokryphische Susannabuch', *Jahrbücher für Jüdische Geschichte und Literatur* 3 (1877), pp. 1-69, followed *inter alia* by Wurmbrand, 'Falasha', p. 35, and LaCocque, *Feminine Unconventional*, p. 25.

3. LaCocque, *Feminine Unconventional*, p. 2.

needs to be reintegrated into the covenant community on both religious and ethnic levels. Further, her sexuality needs to be controlled. Judith returns to the isolation of her home; Esther emphasizes her distaste for the marriage bed; Ruth is domesticated through marriage and childbearing. And Susanna is, only at the conclusion of the trial, directly associated with her husband.

Among the sexually charged intertextual references of the trial are two long-recognized associations: the first with Solomon's judgment in 1 Kgs 3.16-27; the second with the 'suspected woman' of Num. 5.11-31 and *m. Soṭ.* 1.5.[1] Origen had already compared Daniel's wisdom to that of King Solomon, and the connection is acknowledged as well in relatively recent commentaries.[2] Yet these interpreters, by concentrating on the relationship of Daniel to Solomon, do not comment directly on the further implications of the parallel: Solomon is judging a case between two prostitutes; Daniel is concerned with the charge of adultery. Male wisdom is required to harness the chaotic power of woman's sexuality. Although the 'good prostitute' is proclaimed innocent and regains her child, she remains a prostitute. Although Susanna is exonerated, she is still shamed through her public humiliation.

According to the Mishnah, the accused woman who denies her guilt is to have her clothes torn by the priest 'until he exposed her bosom', and to have her hair disheveled at her trial. 'R. Judah says, "if her bosom be beautiful, he does not expose it"'. The intent of the action is to present the woman in the state of just having left her adultery. While Theodotion has only Susanna's veil lifted (v. 32), the earlier LXX does not limit the accusers' voyeuristic intent to her face. Indeed, the treatment she is accorded at the trial is not just that of the dishonored wife, but also that of the adulterer or prostitute, as

1.   See, for example, F. Zimmerman, 'The Story of Susanna and its Original Language', *JQR* 48 (1957–58), pp. 236-37 n. 2; Doran, 'Additions', p. 867.

2.   LaCocque, *Feminine Unconventional*, p. 22; cf. Pfeiffer, *History*, p. 449 and Daubney, *Three Additions*, p. 3, who also draws connections to the Johannine accounts of the woman caught in the act of adultery and to the sexually active Samaritan woman (pp. 124, 133).

Hos. 2.3, 10 and Ezek. 16.37-39 display.[1] Although the book ends with the reincorporation of Susanna into her family by her parents and husband, since she has been treated like the *sôṭâ*, her life will always be suspect.

To avoid any such suggestions, later versions of the tale eliminate any possibility of Susanna's sexual complicity. The Samaritan account depicts her as a Nazirite on Mt Gerizim. In the Falasha rendition, she is another Judith: 'Her father, the king, said to his daughter, "Come, get married". But she refused and said to her father, "I shall not marry after the death of my husband. I have devoted myself to the Lord, my Creator."'[2] This revised Susanna returns to the deity, not to her husband; the silent, doubting figure of the earlier texts here fulfills his role: he is dead. And Susanna herself returns rewarded: already a queen in the Falasha version, she earns 'a double reward for her faithfulness: queenship on earth and bliss in heaven'.[3]

But the deuterocanonical Susanna can at best go back to her status quo. As metaphor for the community, she is ultimately an example of the protection fidelity to the Law of Moses provides: she is unpenetrated and unpenetrable. But her humiliation—as a character, before the elders and the entire community; as a nation, before the world—remains. The Jewish community, particularly that of the diaspora, is vulnerable: apart from its traditional religious leaders in court and Temple, it can survive only with divine help. Charismatic figures, inspired by the holy spirit, can arouse the community and return them to the righteous path.

While women serve as metonymies for the covenant community, they remain on the margins of human–divine interaction. The situation is similar in the text's Apocryphal counterparts: women pray to the deity, and the deity responds with either silence or a male voice. Judith offers an impassioned prayer, but there is no direct mention of the deity's aiding her. The Maccabean mother dies a martyr. Tobit's Sarah prays for either

1. See Doran, 'Additions', p. 867; and Moore, *Additions*, p. 103.
2. Wurmbrand, 'Falasha', p. 32. On her widowhood, see also H. Engel, *Die Susanna-Erzählung* (Göttingen: Vandenhoeck & Ruprecht, 1985).
3. Wurmbrand, 'Falasha', p. 34.

death or salvation, but the angel Raphael, who does solve her problem, deliberately avoids her company. Predestined to be Tobias's bride, Sarah—like the married Susanna—cannot save herself.

Susanna's relationship to heaven is established in her garden speech: 'I am completely trapped. For if I do this, it will mean death for me; if I do not, I cannot escape your hands. I choose not to do it; I will fall into your hands, rather than sin in the sight of the Lord' (Sus. 22-23). Her mention of divine sight, however, is ironic: unlike the elders, unlike the reader, the deity is *not* looking at her nudity. Heavenly recognition comes only when she cries out at her trial (Sus. 44); the deity is not a voyeur. Yet because her comment may be read as indicating that heaven will take notice of her *only* when she sins, the divine sight at first looks as wayward as that of the elders, who 'turned away their eyes from looking to heaven...' (Sus. 9).

At her trial, Susanna confirms both her faith and her impotence.

> Then Susanna cried out with a loud voice and said, 'O Eternal God, you know what is secret and are aware of all things before they come to be; you know that these men have given false evidence against me. And now I am to die, though I have done none of the wicked things that they have charged against me!' And the Lord heard her cry (Sus. 42-44).[1]

The people at the trial, however, are looking rather than listening: no one had sought Susanna's testimony; nor did she offer it.

Redemption comes therefore in the form of someone who can both speak to the importance of geographically based identity and speak against the Babylonian community's internal governance. Daniel represents the hope of the future: the pious (male) who can rescue fair, exiled Israel from her distress. Ethnic pride, not women's liberation, is at the heart of Daniel's speech. He 'does not come to the rescue of the woman, but of the righteous (here identified with Judah)'.[2] Indeed, no voyeur he,

---

1.   In the LXX, she prays when she is charged; in Θ, she prays at her condemnation; the Syriac inserts the prayer at both points. See Moore, *Additions*, p. 103.
2.   LaCocque, *Feminine Unconventional*, p. 26.

Daniel is never seen as looking at Susanna.[1]

The nationalistic concern is voiced by the narrator as early as v. 5 (Θ); in reference to the elders 'the Lord has said, "Wickedness came forth from Babylon..."'[2] It is reinforced when Susanna first speaks: the LXX identifies her not by name but as 'the Jewess' (ἡ Ἰουδαία). Daniel confirms the connection between exile and evil, ethnic pride and ethical behavior: 'And he said to them, "Why was your progeny corrupted like Sidon and not like Judah?"' (Sus. [LXX] 56). Sidon, home to Jezebel (1 Kgs 16.31) and Athaliah (2 Chron. 21.6; 22.10-12),[3] suggests that the elders have been corrupted by descent from promiscuous Gentile women. Theodotion speaks of them as 'offspring of Canaan' (cf. Gen. 10.15, where the connection of Canaan to Sidon is explicit). Daniel confirms the narrator's racial interests by distinguishing 'this daughter of Judah' from the 'daughters of Israel'. 'This is how you have been treating the daughters of Israel; and they were intimate with you through fear; but a daughter of Judah would not tolerate your wickedness' (Sus. 57).[4] The distinction in this verse also explains the assignment of the title 'daughter of Israel' to Susanna in v. 48: there, Daniel is referring to the judgment passed by the misguided people. They did not hesitate to 'condemn a daughter of Israel without examination and without learning the facts'. For the people, the woman is already other, already alien, and so already guilty. Only through Daniel's reclamation of her

1. Pointed out by Glancy, 'The Accused'.
2. The citation is Jer. 29.21-23. Bruell ('Das apokryphische Susannabuch') proposes that the elders in Susanna are Ahab and Zedekiah, the two prophets condemned in Jer. 29.22-23 for committing adultery with their neighbors' wives.
3. See Moore, *Additions*, pp. 111-12; Zimmerman ('Story of Susanna', p. 237) points to examples of Phoenician bastardy in *Gen. R.* 37.
4. See Moore, *Additions*, p. 112, on anti-Samaritanism. Bickerman (*Jews in the Greek Age*, p. 95) finds the contrast 'curious'. LaCocque, more sensitive to the political implications of the phrase, states that 'such a characterization smacks of the ideology of the conservative party. Here, in the mouth of Daniel, it is unexpected' (*Feminine Unconventional*, p. 26). Read in the context of the Apocrypha, of Susanna as metaphor for the community, and in light of the tendency of threatened communities to circumscribe women's bodies, however, the line is neither curious nor unexpected.

does Susanna regain her righteousness and her true ethnic identity.

How Daniel could know of the elders' past actions, just as he could know what transpired in the garden, is explicable only by the divine 'spirit of understanding' that overtakes him. His transformation confirms the impression that diaspora existence is unstable: the private sphere becomes public; the chaste Susanna is accused of adultery; judges commit crimes; and youth supplants the elders of the community. Even the plot hinges on instability: the young man in the garden is the pivot on which the story turns, but he does not exist. And this non-existent figment is himself unable to consummate his tryst. Nothing is as it seems, or as it should be. Daniel resolves this instability by displacing, embodying and redeeming the absent lover: this 'young man' (νεώτερος; LXX 44, 52, 55, 60; Θ only 45), the disguised voice of heaven, substitutes for the 'young man (νεανίσκος) [who] fled in disguise' (Sus. [LXX] 39). The youth becomes the wise elder; the mother becomes his dependent. And thus the woman and the *ethnos* both enter safely into Daniel's charge. In turn, Daniel's case rests not on Susanna's protestation but on the elders' testimony.[1] Then the woman and the book are incorporated into the canonical version of Daniel and so safely tucked away into a story revolving around men's concerns.

But Susanna cannot be left to rest easily there. Susanna's exile from the peace and privacy of her own garden, the diaspora setting of the text, its problematic canonical history, and the marginalization of the modern Jewish woman engaged in analysis interweave around shifting borders. What may be celebrated from one perspective may be condemned from another. Susanna's freedom from domestic responsibilities may indicate to some the economic success of the diaspora community; to others it signals complacency and indolence. For some, she is a heroine whose righteousness is recognized by heaven; for others she is a weak figure unable or unwilling to protest her own innocence in the public sphere until seemingly too late. Recognition of class differences provokes an entry into the

---

1. See Glancy, 'The Accused'.

critique of Susanna-as-character and thereby allows exploration of intertextually negative associations. Recognition of her marginalized position as a woman leads to the discovery of the relationship between the constructs of gender and ethnicity in Hellenistic Jewish narratives. Recognition of the value of her education, her piety and her prayer reinstates a more positive social role for Jewish women, which is often overlooked by those wedded to Christian or select rabbinic constructions. I have asked questions that arise from my own various, marginalized situations. The explorations they generate and the tentative answers those explorations provide incorporate all fellow travelers across religious and sexual borders into the ongoing re-creation of Jewish history, of women's history, of human history.[1]

1.   Grants from National Endowment for the Humanities and from the American Council of Learned Societies have enabled me to continue my analysis of the representations of Jewish women in Hellenistic literature. I also thank Jay Geller for his contributions to the substance and style of this article.

BIBLIOGRAPHY

Aarne, A., *Verzeichnis der Märchentypen* (Helsinki: Suomalainen tiedeakatemia, 1910).

Abu-Lughod, L., *Veiled Sentiments: Honor and Poetry in a Bedouin Society* (Berkeley: University of California Press, 1986).

Aejmelaeus, A., *On the Trail of the Septuagint Translators: Collected Essays* (Kampen: Kok Pharos, 1993).

Albright, W.F., 'The Lachish Cosmetic Burner and Esther 2.12', in H.N. Bream, R.D. Heim and C.A. Moore (eds.), *A Light unto My Path: Old Testament Studies in Honor of Jacob M. Myers* (Philadelphia: Temple University Press, 1974), pp. 25-32.

Alonso-Schökel, L., 'Judith', HBC.

—'Narrative Structures in the Book of Judith', in W. Wuellner (ed.), *Protocol Series of the Colloquies of the Center for Hermeneutical Studies in Hellenistic and Modern Culture*, 11 (1975), pp. 1-20.

Althusser, L., *Lenin and Philosophy* (trans. B. Brewster; London: Monthly Review, 1971).

Anderson, B.W., 'Esther', IB, III (1954), pp. 823-74.

Arenhoevel, D., *Die Theokratie nach dem 1. und 2. Makkabäerbuch* (Walberberger Studien, Theologische Reihe, 3; Mainz: Matthias-Grünewald-Verlag, 1967).

Asbjørnsen, P.C., and J. Moe, *Norwegian Folktales* (trans. P.S. Iversen and C. Norman; New York: Viking, 1960).

Austin, J.L., *How to Do Things with Words* (Cambridge, MA: Harvard University Press, 1975)

Avi-Yonah, M., 'Goodenough's Evaluation of the Dura Paintings: A Critique', in J. Gutman (ed.), *The Dura Europos Synagogue* (Missoula, MT: Scholars Press, 1973), pp. 117-35.

Bach, A., ' "So the Witch Won't Eat Me..." ', paper delivered at the AAR/SBL Annual Meeting (Washington, DC, November 1993; forthcoming in *Semeia*).

—'Breaking out of the Biblical Framework (Gen. 39)', in A. Brenner (ed.), *A Feminist Companion to Genesis* (The Feminist Companion to the Bible, 2; Sheffield: Sheffield Academic Press, 1993), pp. 318-42.

Bakhtin, M., *Problems of Dostoevsky's Poetics* (trans. R.W. Rose; Ann Arbor, MI: Ardis Books, 1973).

Bal, M., *Death and Dissymmetry: The Politics of Coherence in the Book of Judges* (Chicago: University of Chicago Press, 1988), pp. 52-59.

—'His Master's Eye', in D.M. Levin (ed.), *Modernity and the Hegemony of Vision* (Berkley: University of California Press, 1993), pp. 379-404.

—*Lethal Love: Feminist Literary Readings of Biblical Love Stories* (Bloomington: Indiana University Press, 1987).

—*Murder and Difference: Gender, Genre and Scholarship in Sisera's Death* (trans. M. Gumpert; Bloomington: Indiana University Press, 1988).

—*Narratology: Introduction to the Theory of Narrative* (trans. C. van Boheemen; Toronto: University of Toronto Press, 1985).

—*Reading Rembrandt: Beyond the Word–Image Opposition* (Cambridge: Cambridge University Press, 1991).

Bal, M. (ed.), *Anti-Covenant: Counter-Reading Women's Lives in the Hebrew Bible* (Sheffield: Almond Press, 1989), pp. 11-24.

Bal, M., and N. Bryson, 'Semiotics and Art History', *Art Bulletin* 73.2 (1991), pp. 174-208.

Bankson, M.Z., 'Nascent Self', in *Braided Streams: Esther and a Woman's Way of Growing* (San Diego: LuraMedia, 1985), pp. 39-53.

Bardtke, H., *Das Buch Esther* (KAT, 17.5; Gütersloh: Gerd Mohn, 1963).

Beal, T.K., 'Ideology and Intertextuality: Surplus of Meaning and Controlling the Means of Production', in D.N. Fewell (ed.), *Reading between Texts: Intertextuality and the Hebrew Bible* (Louisville, KY: Westminster Press/John Knox, 1992), pp. 27-39.

—'The System and the Speaking Subject in the Hebrew Bible: Reading for Divine Abjection', *Biblical Interpretation* 1994 (forthcoming).

Beauvoir, S. de, *The Second Sex* (trans. H.M. Parshley; New York: Bantam, 1961; Vintage, 1989).

Bechtel, L.M., 'Shame as a Sanction of Social Control in Biblical Israel: Judicial, Political, and Social Shaming', *JSOT* 40 (1991), pp. 47-76.

Ben-Amos, D. (ed.), *Folklore Genres* (Publications of the American Folklore Society, Bibliographical and Special Series, 26; Austin: University of Texas Press, 1976).

Berg, S.B., *The Book of Esther: Motifs, Themes and Structure* (SBLDS, 44; Missoula, MT: Scholars Press, 1979).

Berquist, J.L., *Reclaiming her Story: The Witness of Women in the Old Testament* (St Louis, MO: Chalice Press, 1992).

Bettan, I., *The Five Scrolls: A Commentary on the Song of Songs, Ruth, Lamentations, Ecclesiastes, Esther* (The Jewish Commentary for Bible Readers; Cincinnati: Union of American Hebrew Congregations, 1950).

Bickerman, E.J., 'The Colphon of the Greek Book of Esther', *JBL* 63 (1944) pp. 339-362.

—*Four Strange Books of the Bible* (New York: Schocken Books, 1967).

—*The Jews in the Greek Age* (Cambridge, MA: Harvard University Press, 1988).

Bjorkan, E., 'Subversion in Judith: A Literary-Critical Analysis' (Senior thesis, Swarthmore College, 1987).

Brenner, A., 'Esther in the Land of Mirrors', *Beth Miqra* 3.76 (1981), pp. 267-78.

—*The Israelite Woman: Social Role and Literary Type in Biblical Narrative* (The Biblical Seminar, 2; Sheffield: JSOT Press, 2nd edn, 1989).

Brenner, A., and F. van Dijk-Hemmes, *On Gendering Texts: Female and Male Voices in the Hebrew Bible* (Biblical Interpretation Series, 1; Leiden: Brill, 1993).

Brenton, L.C.L., *The Septuagint Version of the Old Testament, with an English Translation* (London: Samuel Bagster, 1844; Grand Rapids: Zondervan, 1970).

Bronner, L.L., From Eve to Esther: Rabbinic Reconstructions of Biblical Women (Gender and the Biblical Tradition; Louisville, KY: Westminster Press/John Knox, forthcoming).

Bruell, N., 'Das apokryphische Susannabuch', Jahrbücher für Judische Geschichte und Literatur 3 (1877), pp. 1-69.

Bruns, J.E., 'The Genealogy of Judith', CBQ 18 (1956), pp. 19-22.

Buber, S., Midrasch Aggadat Esther (Cracow, 1897); repr. in Midrash Leqaḥ Tov (Jerusalem: Wagshall, 1989).

—Midrash Tehillim (Vilna, 1891).

—Sammlung Agadischer Kommentare zum Buche Ester, enthält Midrasch Abba Gorion; Midrasch Ponim Acherim; Midrasch Lekach Tob (Vilna: 1886).

Burke, S., The Death and the Return of the Author (Edinburgh: Edinburgh University Press, 1992).

Butler, J., Troubling Gender: Feminism and the Subversion of Identity (Thinking Gender; New York and London: Routledge, 1990).

Camp, C.V., Wisdom and the Feminine in the Book of Proverbs (Bible and Literature Series, 11; Sheffield: Almond Press, 1985).

Carroll, L., Alice's Adventures in Wonderland and through the Looking Glass (New York: Bantam Books, 1981; originally published in 1865 and 1871 respectively).

—The Annotated Alice (with Introduction and notes by M. Gardner and the original illustrations of J. Tenniel; London: Penguin, 1970; original text published by Macmillan).

Carroll, M.P., 'Myth, Methodology and Transformation in the Old Testament: The Stories of Esther, Judith, and Susanna', SR 12 (1983), pp. 301-12.

Cazelles, H., 'Notes sur la composition du rouleau d'Esther', in H. Gross and F. Mussner (eds.), Lex tua veritas: Festschrift für Hubert Junker (Trier: Paulinas, 1961), pp. 17-29.

Ciletti, E., 'Patriarchal Ideology, in the Renaissance Iconography of Judith', in 'Prefiguring Woman: Gender Studies and the Italian Renaissance' (lecture, University of Rochester, 1988).

Cixous, H., 'We Who Are Free, Are We Free?', Critical Inquiry 19 (1993), pp. 201-19.

Clair, J., Méduse: Contribution à une anthropologie des arts du visuel (Paris: Gallimard, 1989).

Clines, D.J.A., The Esther Scroll: The Story of the Story (JSOTSup, 30; Sheffield: JSOT Press, 1984).

Code, L., What Can She Know? Feminist Epistemology and the Construction of Knowledge (Ithaca: Cornell University Press, 1991).

Cook, H.J., 'The A-Text of the Greek Versions of the Book of Esther', ZAW 81 (1969), pp. 369-76.

Coote, M.P., 'Comments on "Narrative Structures in the Book of Judith"', in W. Wuellner (ed.), Protocol Series of the Colloquies of the Center for Hermeneutical Studies in Hellenistic and Modern Culture 11 (1975).

Craven, T., 'Artistry and Faith in the Book of Judith', Semeia 8 (1977), pp. 49-61.

—'Redeeming Lies in the Book of Judith' (paper presented to the Pseudepigrapha section, AAR/SBL Annual Meeting, Anaheim, 1989).

—Artistry and Faith in the Book of Judith (SBLDS, 70; Chico, CA: Scholars Press, 1983).

Culler, J., *On Deconstruction: Theory and Criticism after Structuralism* (Ithaca: Cornell University Press, 1983), pp. 86-87.

Dancey, J.C., *Shorter Books of the Apocrypha* (Cambridge Bible Commentary; Cambridge: Cambridge University Press, 1972).

Daube, D., *Collaboration with Tyranny in Rabbinic Law* (The Riddell Memorial Lectures, 1965; London: Oxford University Press, 1965).

Daubney, W.H., *The Three Additions to Daniel* (Cambridge: Deighton, Bell, 1906).

Davis, J., *People of the Mediterranean: An Essay in Comparative Social Anthropology* (London: Routledge & Kegan Paul, 1977).

Delaney, C., 'Seeds of Honor, Fields of Shame', in D.D. Gilmore (ed.), *Honor and Shame and the Unity of the Mediterranean* (American Anthropological Association Special Publication, 22; Washington, DC: American Anthropological Association, 1987), pp. 35-48.

DeLange, N., *Apocrypha: Jewish Literature of the Hellenistic Age* (New York: Viking, 1978).

Derrida, J., *Dissemination* (trans. B. Johnson; Chicago: University of Chicago Press, 1981).

Dijk-Hemmes, F. van, 'Gezegende onder de vrouwen: een moeder in Israël en een maagd in de kerk', in *idem* (ed.), *'t Is kwaad gerucht, als zij niet binnen blijft: Vrouwen in oude culturen* (Tekst en Maatschappij; Utrecht: HES, 1986), pp. 123-47.

Doane, M.A., *The Desire to Desire: The Women's Film of the 1940s* (Bloomington: Indiana University Press, 1987).

Dommershausen, W., *Die Estherrolle: Stil und Ziel einer alttestamentlischen Schrift* (Stuttgart: Katholisches Bibelwerk, 1968).

Doran, R., 'The Additions to Daniel', *Harper's Bible Commentary* (San Francisco: Harper & Row, 1988), pp. 863-71.

Dundes, A., *The Morphology of North American Indian Tales* (Helsinki: Suomalainen tiedeakatemia, 1965).

—'Comment on "Narrative Structures in the Book of Judith"', in W. Wuellner (ed.), *Protocol Series of the Colloquies of the Center for Hermeneutical Studies in Hellenistic and Modern Culture*, 11 (1975).

Dundes, A. (ed.), *The Study of Folklore* (Englewood Cliffs, NJ: Prentice–Hall, 1965).

Dunn, R., 'Discriminations in the Comic Spirit in the Story of Susanna', *Christianity and Literature* 31 (1980–81), pp. 19-31.

Enermalm-Ogawa, A., *Un langage de prière juif en grec: Le témoignage des deux premiers livres des Maccabées* (ConBNT, 17; Stockholm: Almqvist & Wiksell, 1987).

Engel, H., *Die Susanna-Erzählung* (Göttingen: Vandenhoeck & Ruprecht, 1985).

Enslin, M.S., *The Book of Judith* (Jewish Apocryphal Literature, 8; Leiden: Brill, 1972).

Feldman, L.H., 'Hellenizations in Josephus' Version of Esther', *Transactions and Proceedings of the American Philological Association* 101 (1970), pp. 143-70.

Felman, S., *Literary Speech Acts* (Ithaca: Cornell University Press, 1987).

Fenichel, O., 'Fetishism', in *The Psychoanalytic Theory of Neurosis* (London: Routledge & Kegan Paul, 1936), pp. 341-51.

Foucault, M., *The History of Sexuality Volume 1: An Introduction* (trans. R. Hurley; New York: Vintage, 1978).

Fox, M.V., *Character and Ideology in the Book of Esther* (Studies on Personalities of the Old Testament; Columbia: University of South Carolina Press, 1991).

—*The Redaction of the Books of Esther: On Reading Composite Texts* (ṢBLMS, 40; Atlanta: Scholars Press, 1991).

Freud, S., 'The Taboo of Virginity' and 'Some Psychological Consequences of the Anatomical Distinction between the Sexes', in *The Standard Edition of the Complete Psychological Works* (trans. and ed. J. Strachey *et al.*; London: Hogarth Press, 1918), XI , p. 193.

Fuerst, W.J., *The Books of Ruth, Esther, Ecclesiastes, The Song of Songs, Lamentations: The Five Scrolls* (Cambridge: Cambridge University Press, 1975).

Gan, M., 'The Book of Esther in the Light of Joseph's Fate in Egypt', *Tarbiz* 31 (1962), pp. 144-49 (Hebrew).

Gantner, J., *Konrad Witz* (Vienna: Anton Schroll, 1943).

Garrard, M.D., 'Artemisia and Susanna', in N. Braude and M.D. Garrard (eds.), *Feminism and Art History: Questioning the Litany* (New York: Harper & Row, 1982), pp. 147-71.

—*Artemesia Gentileschi: The Image of the Female Hero in Italian Baroque Art* (Princeton: Princeton University Press, 1988), p. 287

Gaster, T.H., *Purim and Hanukkah in Custom and Tradition* (New York: Schuman, 1950).

Gendler, M., 'The Restoration of Vashti', in E. Koltun (ed.), *The Jewish Woman* (New York: Schocken Books, 1976), pp. 241-47.

Gerhardsson, B., *The Testing of God's Son (Matt 4:1-11 & Par)* (ConBNT, 2.1; Lund: Gleerup, 1966).

Gerleman, G., *Studien zu Esther: Stoff-Structure-Stil-Sinn* (Neukirchen–Vluyn: Neukirchener Verlag, 1966).

—*Esther* (BKAT, 21; Neukirchen–Vluyn: Neukirchener Verlag, 1973).

Gilmore, D.D., 'Introduction: The Shame of Dishonor', in *idem* (ed.), *Honor and Shame and the Unity of the Mediterranean* (American Anthropological Association Special Publication, 22; Washington, DC: American Anthropological Association, 1987), pp. 2-21.

Ginzberg, L., *The Legends of the Jews*, IV (Philadelphia: Jewish Publication Society, 1941).

Giovanni, M.J., 'Woman: A Dominant Symbol within the Cultural System of a Sicilian Town', *Man* 16 (1981), pp. 408-26.

Goitein, S.D., 'Women as Creators of Biblical Genres', *Prooftexts* 8 (1988), pp. 1-33.

Goldman, S., 'Esther', in A. Cohen (ed.), *The Five Megilloth* (Hindhead: Soncino, 1946).

—'Narrative and Ethical Ironies in Esther', *JSOT* 47 (1990), pp. 15-31.

Goldstein, J.A., *I Maccabees: A New Translation with Introduction and Commentary* (AB, 41; Garden City, NY: Doubleday, 1976).

Goodenough, E.R., *Jewish Symbols in the Greco-Roman Period* (New York: Pantheon, 1964), IX.

Gordis, R., 'Studies in the Esther Narrative', in C.A. Moore (ed.), *Studies in the Book of Esther* (New York: Ktav, 1982); also in *JBL* 95 (1976), pp. 49-53.

—*Megillat Esther with Introduction, New Translation and Commentary* (New York: The Rabbinical Assembly, 1974).

Gottwald, N., *The Tribes of Yahweh: A Sociology of the Religion of Liberated Israel 1250–1050 BC* (Maryknoll, NY: Orbis Books, 1979).

Greenberg, M., 'Rabbinic Reflections on Defying Illegal Orders: Amasa, Abner, and Joab', in M.M. Kellner (ed.), *Contemporary Jewish Ethics* (New York: Sanhedrin, 1978), pp. 211-20.

Greene, G., and C. Kahn, 'Feminist Scholarship and the Social Construction of Woman', in *idem* (eds.), *Making a Difference: Feminist Literary Criticism* (London and New York: Methuen, 1985), pp. 1-36.

Greenberg, I., *The Jewish Way: Living the Holidays* (New York: Summit Books, 1988).

Greer, G., *The Obstacle Race: The Fortunes of Women Painters and their Works* (London: Secker & Warburg, 1979).

Griffith, W. (ed.), *Great Painters and their Famous Bible Pictures* (New York: Wise, 1925).

Grossfeld, B. (trans. and ed.), *The Two Targums of Esther, Translated, with Apparatus and Notes* (Aramaic Bible, 18; Collegeville, MN: Liturgical Press/Michael Glazier, 1991).

Gunkel, H., *Das Märchen im alten Testament* (Religionsgeschichtliche Volksbucher, II, Reihe 23.26; Tübingen: Mohr, 1917, 1921).

—*Esther* (Religionsgeschichtliche Volksbucher, II, Reihe, 19.20; Tübingen: Mohr, 1916).

Gunn, D.M., and D.N. Fewell, *Gender, Power and Promise: The Subject of the Bible's First Story* (Nashville: Abingdon Press, 1993).

Haag, E., *Studien zum Buche Judith: Seine theologische Bedeutung und literarische Eigenart* (Trierer Theologische Studien, 16; Trier: Paulinus-Verlag, 1963).

Hanhart, R., *Septuaginta Vetus Testamentum Graecum, VIII,3: Esther* (Göttingen: Vandenhoeck & Ruprecht, 2nd edn, 1983).

Harris, M., *Cannibals and Kings: The Origins of Cultures* (New York: Random House, 1978).

Heath, P (ed.), *The Philosopher's Alice* (London, 1974).

Henten, J.W. van, 'Das jüdische Selbstverständnis in den ältesten Martyrien', in *idem et al.* (eds.), *Die Entstehung der jüdischen Martyrologie* (SPB, 38; Leiden: Brill, 1989), pp. 127-61.

—'The Story of Susanna as a Pre-Rabbinic Midrash to Dan. 1:1-2', in A. Kuyt, E.G.L. Schrijver and N.A. van Uchelen (eds.), *Variety of Forms: Dutch Studies in Midrash* (Publications of the Juda Palache Institute, 5; Amsterdam: Amsterdam University Press, 1990), pp. 1-14.

Herr, M., 'Esther Rabbah', *EncJud*, VI, p. 915.

Hertz, N., *The End of the Line: Essays on Psychoanalysis and the Sublime* (New York: Columbia University Press, 1985).

Holly, M.A., *Panofsky and the Foundations of Art History* (Ithaca: Cornell University Press, 1984).

—'Past Looking', *Critical Inquiry* 16.2 (1990), pp. 371-96.

Horn, S., 'Mordecai, A Historical Problem', *BR* 9 (1964), pp. 14-25.

Humphreys, W.L., 'A Life-Style for Diaspora: A Study of the Tales of Esther and Daniel', *JBL* 93 (1973), pp. 211-23.

—'The Story of Esther and Mordecai: An Early Jewish Novella', in G.W. Coats (ed.), *Saga, Legend, Tale, Novella, Fable: Narrative Forms in Old Testament Literature* (JSOTSup, 35; Sheffield: JSOT Press, 1985), pp. 97-113, 149-50.

Irigaray, L., *This Sex Which Is Not One* (trans. C. Porter with C. Burke; Ithaca, NY: Cornell University Press, 1985).

—*Speculum of the Other Woman* (trans. G.C. Gill; Ithaca, NY: Cornell University Press, 1985).

—*Je, Tu, Nous: Toward a Culture of Difference* (trans. A. Martin; New York: Routledge, 1993).

Jacobus, M., 'Judith, Holophernes, and the Phallic Woman', in *Reading Woman: Essays in Feminist Criticism* (New York: Columbia University Press, 1986), p. 128.

Jameson, F., 'Magical Narratives: Romance as Genre', *New Literary History* 7.1 (Autumn, 1975), pp. 133-36.

—*The Political Unconscious: Narrative as a Socially Symbolic Act* (Ithaca, NY: Cornell University Press, 1981).

Janssen, E., *Das Gottesvolk und seine Geschichte: Geschichtsbild und Selbstverständnis im palästinensischen Schrifttum von Jesus Sirach bis Jehuda ha-Nasi* (Neukirchen-Vluyn: Neukirchener Verlag, 1971).

Jellinek, A., *Bet ha-Midrasch* (Jerusalem: Wahrmann, 1967).

Johnson, M.D., *The Purpose of the Biblical Genealogies with Special Reference to the Setting of the Genealogies of Jesus* (SNTSMS, 8; Cambridge: Cambridge University Press, 1969).

Jones, B.W., 'Two Misconceptions about the Book of Esther', *CBQ* 39 (1977), pp. 171-81; repr. in C.A. Moore (ed.), *Studies in the Book of Esther* (New York: Ktav, 1982).

Joüon, P., *Grammaire de l'hebreu biblique* (Rome: Pontifical Biblical Institute, 3rd edn, 1965).

Kappeler, S., *The Pornography of Representation* (Minneapolis: University of Minnesota Press, 1986).

Kay, M.D., 'Susanna', in R.H. Charles (ed.), *Apocrypha and Pseudepigrapha of the Old Testament* (Oxford: Clarendon Press, 1913), I, pp. 638-51.

Keller, E.F., *Reflections on Gender and Science* (New Haven: Yale University Press, 1985).

—*Secrets of Death* (New York: Routledge & Kegan Paul, 1992).

Knowles, J.H., *Folk-Tales of Kashmir* (London: Kegan, Paul, Trench, Trubner, 1893).

Kraemer, R.S., 'Women's Authorship of Jewish and Christian Literature in the Greco-Roman Period', in A.-J. Levine (ed.), *Women Like This: New Perspectives on Jewish Women in the Greco-Roman World* (Atlanta: Scholars Press, 1991), pp. 221-42.

Kristeva, J., *Desire in Language: A Semiotic Approach to Literature and Art* (trans. T. Gora, A. Jardine and L. Roudiez; New York: Columbia University Press, 1980).

—*The Powers of Horror: An Essay on Abjection* (trans. L. Roudiez; New York: Columbia University Press, 1982).

—*Revolution in Poetic Language* (trans. M. Waller; New York: Columbia University Press, 1984).

Kropat, A., *Die Syntax des Autors der Chronik verglichen mit seinen Quellen: Ein*

Beitrag zur historischen Syntax des Hebräischen (BZAW, 16; Giessen: Töpelmann, 1909).

Lacan, J., *The Four Fundamental Concepts of Psycho-Analysis* (ed. J.-A. Miller and trans. A. Sheridan; Harmondsworth: Penguin Press, 1979).

LaCocque, A., *The Feminine Unconventional: Four Subversive Figures in Israel's Tradition* (Minneapolis: Fortress Press, 1990).

Lamsa, G.M., *Old Testament Light: The Indispensable Guide to the Customs, Manners and Idioms of Biblical Times* (San Francisco: Harper & Row, 1964).

LaPlanche, J., and J.-B. Pontalis, *The Language of Psychoanalysis* (New York: Norton, 1973).

Lauretis, T. de, *Alice Doesn't: Feminism, Semiotics, Cinema* (Bloomington: Indiana University Press, 1984).

—*Technologies of Gender: Essays on Theory, Film, and Fiction* (Bloomington: Indiana University Press, 1987).

Leach, M., *A Guide to the Gods* (London, Detroit and Washington: Gale Research International, 1992).

Lebram, J.C.H., 'Purimfest und Estherbuch', *VT* 22 (1972), pp. 208-22.

Lettinga, J.P., *Grammatica van het Bijbels Hebreeuws* (Leiden: Brill, 8th edn, 1976).

Levine, A.-J., 'Diaspora as Metaphor: Bodies and Boundaries in the Book of Tobit', in J.A. Overman and R.S. MacLennan (eds.), *Diaspora Jews and Judaism* (Atlanta: Scholars Press), pp. 105-17.

Lightbown, R., *Sandro Botticelli* (London: Paul Elek, 1978), II.

Linafelt, T., 'Taking Women in Samuel: Readers/Responses/Responsibility', in D.N. Fewell (ed.), *Reading between Texts: Intertextuality and the Hebrew Bible* (Louisville, KY: Westminster Press/John Knox, 1992).

Liver, J., and I.M. Ta-Shma, 'Genealogy', *EncJud*, VII, pp. 377-84.

Lubitch, R., 'A Feminist's Look at Esther', *Judaism* 42.4 (1993), pp. 438-46.

Lüthi, M., *The European Folktale: Form and Nature* (Philadelphia: ISHI, 1982).

Magonet, J., 'The Liberal and the Lady: Esther Revisited', *Judaism* 29 (1980), pp. 167-76.

Malamat, A., 'Charismatic Leadership in the Book of Judges', in F.M. Cross, W.E. Lemke and P.D. Miller (eds.), *Magnalia Dei: The Mighty Acts of God: Essays on the Bible and Archaeology in Memory of G.E. Wright* (Garden City, NY: Doubleday, 1976), pp. 152-68.

Malina, B.J., *The New Testament World: Insights from Cultural Anthropology* (Louisville, KY: Westminster Press/John Knox, rev. edn, 1993).

Marin, L., 'Le trompe-l'oeil', un comble de la peinture', in R. Court (ed.), *L'effet trompe-l'oeil dans l'art et la psychanalyse* (Paris: Bordas/Dunod, 1988)

Martola, N., *Capture and Liberation: A Study in the Composition of the First Book of Maccabees* (Acta Academiae Aboensis Ser. A, 63.1; Åbo: Åbo Akademi, 1984).

May, H.G., and B.M. Metzger (eds.), *The New Oxford Annotated Bible with the Apocrypha: Revised Standard Version* (New York: Oxford University Press, 1977).

Mayes, A.D.H., *Judges* (OTG; Sheffield: JSOT Press, 1985).

Meinhold, A., 'Die Gattung der Josephsgeschichte und des Esterbuches: Diasporanovelle, I', *ZAW* 87 (1975), pp. 306-24.

—'Die Gattung der Josephsgeschichte und des Esterbuches: Diasporanovelle, II', *ZAW* 88 (1976), pp. 72-93.

Mendenhall, G., *The Tenth Generation* (Baltimore: Johns Hopkins University Press, 1973).

Merideth, B., 'Desire and Danger: The Drama of Betrayal in Judges and Judith', in M. Bal (ed.), *Anti-Covenant: Counter-Reading Women's Lives in the Hebrew Bible* (JSOTSup, 81; Sheffield: JSOT Press, 1989), pp. 63-78.

Metzger, B.M., and R.E. Murphy (eds.), *The New Oxford Annotated Bible with the Apocrypha: New Revised Standard Version* (New York: Oxford University Press, 1991).

Meyers, C.L., *Discovering Eve: Ancient Israelite Women in Context* (Oxford: Oxford University Press, 1988).

—'Everyday Life: Women in the Period of the Hebrew Bible', in C.A. Newsom and S.H. Ringe (eds.), *The Women's Bible Commentary* (Louisville, KY: Westminster Press/John Knox, 1992), pp. 244-51.

Miles, M., *Carnal Knowing: Female Nakedness and Religious Meaning in the Christian West* (Boston: Beacon Press, 1989).

Miller, N.K., 'Emphasis Added: Plots and Plausibilities in Women's Fiction', *Publications of the Modern Language Association* 96 (1981), pp. 36-48.

Moore, C.A., *Esther* (AB, 7b; Garden City, NY: Doubleday, 1971).

—*Daniel, Esther and Jeremiah: The Additions* (AB, 44; Garden City, NY: Doubleday, 1977).

—'On the Origins of the LXX Additions to the Book of Esther', in *idem* (ed.), *Studies in the Book of Esther*.

—'A Greek Witness to a Different Hebrew Text of Esther', in *idem* (ed.), *Studies in the Book of Esther*.

—*Judith* (AB, 40; Garden City, NY: Doubleday, 1985).

—'Book of Esther', *ABD*, II, p. 641.

—'Susanna', *Bible Review* 8.3 (1992).

Moore, C.A., (ed.), *Studies in the Book of Esther* (New York: Ktav, 1982).

Müller, H.-P., 'Die weisheitliche Lehrerzählung im Alten Testament und seiner Umwelt', *Welt des Orients* 9 (1977–78), pp. 77-98.

Mulvey, L., 'Visual Pleasure and Narrative Cinema', *Screen* 16.3 (1975), pp. 6-18.

Newsom, C.A., 'Women and the Discourse of Patriarchal Wisdom: A Study of Proverbs 1–9', in P.L. Day (ed.), *Gender and Difference in Ancient Israel* (Minneapolis: Fortress Press, 1989), pp. 142-60.

Nickelsburg, G.W.E., 'Stories of Biblical and Early Post-Biblical Times', in M.E. Stone (ed.), *Jewish Writings of the Second Temple Period: Apocrypha, Pseudepigrapha, Qumran Sectarian Writings, Philo, Josephus* (CRINT, 2.2; Assen: Van Gorcum; Philadelphia: Fortress Press, 1984), pp. 33-87.

—*Jewish Literature between the Bible and the Mishnah* (Philadelphia: Fortress Press, 1981).

Niditch, S., 'Legends of Wise Heroes and Heroines', in D. Knight and G. Tucker (eds.), *The Hebrew Bible and its Modern Interpreters* (Chico, CA: Scholars Press, 1985), pp. 445-63.

—*Underdogs and Tricksters: A Prelude to Folklore* (San Francisco: Harper & Row, 1987).

Niditch, S., and R. Doran, 'The Success Story of the Wise Courtier', *JBL* 96 (1977), pp. 179-93.

Olrik, A., 'Epic Laws of Folk Narrative', in Dundes (ed.), *The Study of Folklore*, pp. 131-41.

Panofsky, E., *Meaning in the Visual Arts* (Garden City, NY: Doubleday, 1955).

Parsons, M.C., 'Reading a Beginning/Beginning a Reading: Tracing Literary Theory on Narrative Openings', *Semeia* 52 (1991), pp. 11-31.

Paton, L.B., *The Book of Esther* (ICC; Edinburgh: T. & T. Clark, 1976 [1908]).

Paul, S.M., 'Jerusalem of Gold—A Song and an Ancient Crown', *BAR* 3 (1977), pp. 38-41.

—'Jerusalem—A City of Gold', *IEJ* 17.4 (1967), pp. 259-63.

Pavel, 'Origin and Articulation', in *Style* (1813, Special Issue: *Psychopoetics at Work*.

Peristiany, J.G., and J. Pitt-Rivers (eds.), *Honor and Grace in Anthropology* (Cambridge: Cambridge University Press, 1992).

Pervo, R., 'Asenath and her Sisters: Women in Jewish Narrative and in the Greek Novel', in A.-J. Levine (ed.), *'Women Like This': New Perspectives on Jewish Women in the Greco-Roman World* (EJL, 1; Atlanta: Scholars Press, 1991), pp. 145-60.

Pfeiffer, R., *History of New Testament Times with an Introduction to the Apocrypha* (New York: Harper & Brothers, 1949).

Phipps, W.E., *Assertive Biblical Women* (Westport, CT, and London: Greenwood Press, 1992).

Pitt-Rivers, J., *The Fate of Shechem or the Politics of Sex: Essays in the Anthropology of the Mediterranean* (Cambridge: Cambridge University Press, 1977).

Pudney, J., *Lewis Carroll and his World* (London: Thames & Hudson, 1976).

Radday, Y.T., 'Chiasm in Joshua, Judges and Others', *Linguistica Biblica* 3 (1973), pp. 6-13.

—'Esther with Humour', in *idem* and A. Brenner (eds.), *On Humour and the Comic in the Hebrew Bible* (JSOTSup, 92; Bible and Literature Series, 23; Sheffield: Almond Press, 1990).

Rahlfs, A., (ed.), *Septuaginta: Id est Vetus Testamentum graece iuxta LXX interpretes* (Stuttgart: Deutsche Bibelgesellschaft, 2nd edn, 1982).

Reviv, H., 'Types of Leadership in the Period of the Judges', *Beer-Sheva* 1 (1973), pp. 204-21 (Hebrew).

Roitman, A.D., 'Achior in the Book of Judith: His Role and Significance', in J. VanderKam (ed.), *'No One Spoke Ill of Her': Essays on Judith* (Atlanta: Scholars Press, 1992), pp. 31-45.

Romney-Wegner, J., *Chattel or Person? The Status of Women in the Mishnah* (New York and Oxford: Oxford University Press, 1988).

Rösel, H.H., 'Die Richter Israels: Rückblick und neuer Ansatz', *BZ* NS 25 (1981), pp. 180-203.

Rosenthal, L.A., 'Die Josephsgeschichte mit den Buchem Ester und Daniel verglichen', *ZAW* 15 (1895), pp. 278-84.

—'Nochmals der Vergleich Ester-Joseph', *ZAW* 17 (1897), pp. 126-28.

Rosenzweig, R., *Solidarität mit den Leidenden im Judentum* (Berlin and New York: de Gruyter, 1978).

Sandmel, S., *The Hebrew Scriptures: An Introduction to their Literature and Religious Ideas* (New York: Oxford University Press, 1978).

Sasson, J.M., 'Esther', in R. Alter and F. Kermode (eds.), *The Literary Guide to the Bible* (Cambridge, MA: Harvard University Press, 1987).

Schedl, C., 'Das Buch Esther', *Theologie und Gegenwart* (1964), pp. 85-93.

Schneider, J., 'Of Vigilance and Virgins', *Ethnology* 9 (1971), pp. 1-24.

Schor, N., 'Female Fetishism', in S.R. Suleiman (ed.), *The Female Body in Western Culture: Contemporary Perspectives* (Cambridge, MA: Harvard University Press, 1986).

—'Salammbo Bound', in *Breaking the Chain: Women, Theory, and French Realist Fiction* (New York, 1985).

Schuller, E.M., 'The Apocrypha', in C.A. Newsom and S.H. Ringe (eds.), *The Women's Bible Commentary* (Louisville, KY: Westminster Press/John Knox, 1992), pp. 235-43.

Schunck, K.-D., '1. Makkabäerbuch', in W.G. Kümmel and H. Lichtenberger (eds.), *Jüdische Schriften aus hellenistisch-römischer Zeit* 1.4 (Gütersloh: Gütersloher Verlagshaus/Gerd Mohn, 1980), pp. 287-373.

Sedgwick, E.K., *Between Men: English Literature and Male Homosocial Desire* (New York: Columbia University Press, 1985).

—*Epistemology of the Closet* (Berkeley: University of California Press, 1990).

Showalter, E., 'The Feminist Critical Revolution', in *idem* (ed.), *The New Feminist Criticism* (New York: Pantheon, 1985), pp. 3-10.

Shumaker, W., 'Critique of Luis Alonson-Schökel on Judith', in W. Wuellner (ed.), *Protocol Series of the Colloquies of the Center for Hermeneutical Studies in Hellenistic and Modern Culture* 11 (1975).

Siebert-Hommes, J., *Laat de dochters léven! De literaire architectuur van Exodus 1 en 2 als toegang tot de interpretatie* (Kampen: Kok, 1993).

Silverman, K., 'Fassbinder and Lacan', in *Male Subjectivity at the Margin* (New York: Routledge, 1992).

Simon, M. (trans.), *Midrash Rabbah, Esther* (London: Soncino, 1951).

Skehan, P.W., 'The Hand of Judith', *CBQ* 25 (1963), pp. 94-109.

Smith, J.Z., 'What a Difference Difference Makes', in J. Neusner and E.S. Frerichs (eds.), *'To See Ourselves and to See Others': Christians, Jews and 'Others' in Late Antiquity* (Chico, CA: Scholars Press, 1985).

Speyer, W. , 'Genealogie', *Reallexikon für Antike und Christentum*, IX (Stuttgart: Anton Hiersemann, 1976), pp. 1145-268.

Steinmann, M., *Lecture de Judith* (Paris: Gabalda, 1953).

Sternberg, M., 'Gaps, Ambiguity and the Reading Process', in *The Poetics of Biblical Narrative* (Bloomington: Indiana University Press, 1985), pp. 186-229.

Stone, N., 'Judith and Holofernes: Some Observations on the Development of the Scene in Art', in J.C. VanderKam, *'No One Spoke Ill of Her': Essays on Judith* (SBL Early Judaism and its Literature, 2; Atlanta: Scholars Press, 1992), pp. 73-93.

Striedl, H., 'Untersuchung zur Syntax und Stilistik des hebräischen Buches Esther', *ZAW* 55 (1937), pp. 73-108.

Suggit, J.N., 'Fasting', in B.M. Metzger and M.D. Coogan (eds.), *The Oxford Companion to the Bible* (New York: Oxford University Press, 1993), p. 225.

Suleiman, S.R., 'Introduction', in *idem* (ed.), *The Female Body in Western Culture:Contemporary Perspectives* (Cambridge, MA: Harvard University Press, 1986), pp. 1-4.

Suter, D.W., 'Susanna', *Harper's Bible Dictionary* (San Francisco: Harper & Row, 1985), p. 1001.

Talmon, S., ' "Wisdom" in the Book of Esther', *VT* 13 (1963), pp. 419-55.

Thompson, S., *The Folktale* (New York: Holt, Rinehart & Winston, 1946).

—*The Motif-Index of Folk-Literature* (Bloomington: Indiana University Press, 1955–58).

Thompson, S. (ed. and trans.), *The Types of the Folktale* (Helsinki: Suomalainen tiedeakatemia, 1973 [an expanded edition of A. Aarne's *Verzeichnis der Märchentypen*]).

Toorn, K. van der, *Van haar wieg to haar graf: De rol van de godsdienst in het leven van de Israëlitische en Babylonische vrouw* (Baarn: Ten Have, 1987); ET *From her Cradle to her Grave: The Role of Religion in the Life of the Israelite and the Babylonian Woman* (trans. S.J. Denning-Bolle; Biblical Seminar, 23; Sheffield: JSOT Press, 1994).

Torrey, C.C., 'The Older Book of Esther', repr. in C.A. Moore (ed.), *Studies in the Book of Esther* (New York: Ktav, 1982).

Tromp, J., *The Assumption of Moses: A Critical Edition with Commentary* (SVTP, 10; Leiden: Brill, 1993).

Ungnad, A., 'Keilinschriftliche Beiträge zum Buch Ezra und Esther', *ZAW* 58 (1964), pp. 20-24.

Uspensky, B., *A Poetics of Composition: The Structure of the Artistic Text and Typology of a Compositional Form* (trans. V. Zavarin and S. Wittig; Berkeley: University of California Press, 1973).

Vernant, J.-P., *La mort dans les yeux* (Paris: Hachette, 1985).

Walker, W.S., and A.E. Uysal, *Tales Alive in Turkey* (Cambridge, MA: Harvard University Press, 1966).

Waskow, A., *The Season of our Joy: A Celebration of Modern Jewish Renewal* (New York: Bantam Books, 1982).

Weems, R.J., *Just a Sister Away: A Womanist Vision of Women's Relationships in the Bible* (San Diego: LuraMedia, 1988).

Weimar, P., 'Formen frühjüdischer Literatur: Eine Skizze', in J. Maier and J. Schreiner (eds.), *Literatur und Religion des Frühjudentums: Eine Einführung* (Würzburg and Gütersloh: Echter Verlag, 1973), pp. 123-62.

Weiss, R., 'The Language and Style of the Esther Scroll', *Mahanayim* 104 (1966), pp. 56-63 (Hebrew).

Wesselius, J.W., 'The Literary Genre of the Story of Susanna and its Original Language', in A. Kuyt, E.G.L. Schrijver and N.A. van Uchelen (eds.), *Variety of Forms: Dutch Studies in Midrash* (Publications of the Juda Palache Institute, 5; Amsterdam: Amsterdam University Press, 1990), pp. 15-25.

White, H., *Meta-History: The Historical Imagination in Nineteenth-Century Europe* (Baltimore: Johns Hopkins University Press, 1973).

—*Tropics of Discourse* (Baltimore: Johns Hopkins University Press, 1978).

White, S.A., 'Esther', in C.A. Newsom and S.H. Ringe (eds.), *The Women's Bible Commentary* (Louisville, KY: John Knox, 1992), pp. 124-29.

—'Esther: A Feminine Model for Jewish Diaspora', in P.L. Day (ed.), *Gender and Difference in Ancient Israel* (Minneapolis: Fortress Press, 1989), pp. 161-77.

—'In the Steps of Jael and Deborah: Judith as Heroine', in D. Lull (ed.), *Society of Biblical Literature Seminar Papers 1989* (Atlanta: Scholars Press, 1989), pp. 570-78; reprinted in J.C. VanderKam (ed.), *'No One Spoke Ill of Her':*

Essays on Judith (SBL Early Judaism and its Literature, 2, Atlanta: Scholars Press, 1992), pp. 5-16.

Williams, J.G., *Women Recounted: Narrative Thinking and the God of Israel* (Sheffield: Almond Press, 1982).

Wischnitzer, R., 'From My Archives', *Journal of Jewish Art* 6 (1979), p. 15.

Wurmbrand, M., 'A Falasha Version of the Story of Susanna', *Bib* 44 (1963).

Wynn, K.H., *The Sociohistorical Contexts of the Recensions of Esther* (dissertation, Southern Baptist Theological Seminary, 1990).

Zenger, E., 'Judith/Judithbuch', in G. Müller *et al.* (eds.), *Theologische Realenzyklopädie*, 17 (Berlin and New York: de Gruyter, 1988), pp. 404-408.

Zenger, E.,'Das Buch Judit', in W.G. Kümmel and H. Lichtenberger (eds.), *Jüdische Schriften aus hellenistisch-römischer Zeit*, 1.6 (Gütersloh: Gütersloher Verlagshaus/Gerd Mohn, 1981), pp. 427-534.

Zimmerman, F., 'The Story of Susanna and its Original Language', *JQR* 48 (1957-58), pp. 236-41.